BROKE

Broke

THE RACIAL CONSEQUENCES
OF UNDERFUNDING
PUBLIC UNIVERSITIES

+ + + + + + + + + + + + + + + + + +

LAURA T. HAMILTON
AND KELLY NIELSEN

THE UNIVERSITY OF CHICAGO PRESS
CHICAGO AND LONDON

The University of Chicago Press, Chicago 60637
The University of Chicago Press, Ltd., London
© 2021 by The University of Chicago
Published 2021
Printed in the United States of America

29 28 27 26 25 24 23 22 21   1 2 3 4 5

ISBN-13: 978-0-226-60540-1 (cloth)
ISBN-13: 978-0-226-74745-3 (paper)
ISBN-13: 978-0-226-74759-0 (e-book)
DOI: https://doi.org/10.7208/chicago/9780226747590.001
.0001

Library of Congress Cataloging-in-Publication Data

Names: Hamilton, Laura T. (Laura Teresa), author. | Nielsen,
    Kelly, author.
Title: Broke : the racial consequences of underfunding public
    universities / Laura T. Hamilton and Kelly Nielsen.
Description: Chicago ; London : The University of Chicago
    Press, 2021. | Includes bibliographical references and index.
Identifiers: LCCN 2020030515 | ISBN 9780226605401 (cloth) |
    ISBN 9780226747453 (paperback) | ISBN 9780226747590
    (e-book)
Subjects: LCSH: University of California, Merced. | University
    of California, Riverside. | Public universities and colleges—
    California. | Public universities and colleges—United States. |
    Racism in higher education—California. | Discrimination in
    higher education—California. | Educational equalization—
    California. | Government aid to higher education—
    California. | Minority college students—California—Social
    conditions.
Classification: LCC LC212.422.C2 H36 2020 | DDC
    378/.0509794—dc23
LC record available at https://lccn.loc.gov/2020030515

♾ This paper meets the requirements of ANSI/NISO
Z39.48-1992 (Permanence of Paper).

To the brilliant, resilient, and spirited students of UC-Merced and UC-Riverside, who inspired us to write this book.

Contents

Preface ix

Introduction 1

THE CHANGING FACE OF THE UC

1 Battle with the Rankings *29*

2 P3 Paradise *50*

3 Running Political Cover *73*

RESPONSES TO UNDERFUNDING

4 Austerity Administration *95*

5 Tolerable Suboptimization *119*

DEALING IN DIVERSITY

6 Student Labor and Centers of Support
(*with Veronica Lerma*) *145*

7 Marketing Diversity *173*

Breaking the Cycle *190*

Acknowledgments 205

*Methodological Appendix: On Being White
and Studying Race 209*

Notes 221

References 251

Index 279

Preface

The production of *Broke* was done from home during the global pandemic of 2020. Copyediting, revising, blurbing, and proofing were carried out by people confined to their homes under shelter-in-place orders from their respective governors. Fortunately for us, everyone involved in the process *could* work from home. The deadlines remained the same even as everything else changed. Many millions of Americans have filed for unemployment; this country has not seen this level of job loss since the Great Depression and never in such a short span of time. These figures are unprecedented and catastrophic.

The world in which *Broke* was researched and written is altered in ways that we will try to understand for years to come. A shock like COVID-19, the disease that overwhelmed public health systems around the world and brought the global economy to a near standstill, can create conditions for changes—both negative and positive—that were once unthinkable. The failures of public systems weakened by decades of austerity, privatization, and market ideology are glaring. In the unfolding crisis, greater investment in public services like health care and education seems not only desirable, but essential.

Although we cannot know precisely how this will play out, it is likely that a fiscal catastrophe is coming to higher education. *Broke* provides a rich picture of the racial and class dynamics at play in higher education before COVID-19. As states tighten their belts, there is potential for the inequalities documented in this book to be dramatically compounded. Affluent, predominately white research universities—both private and public—have historically had the greatest resources to weather any storm. In contrast, public universities serving disadvantaged populations tend to struggle under austerity, as these organizations have limited access to private funding. We need to remain vigilant to ensure that COVID-19 does not deepen already existing disparities in postsecondary education.

Alternatively, this crisis—especially with the momentum of a thriving Black Lives Matter movement—could be a chance to reimagine public higher education in a way that offers more, not less, support to our least advantaged students. A fall in the number of students able and willing to pay full tuition, along with the possibility that students will attend college closer to home out of an abundance of caution, may shift even research universities' focus to regional student populations and low-income students for the foreseeable future. The universities at the center of *Broke* are models for how to do this successfully. But they also serve as a warning. Without substantial public support, public universities will struggle to remain afloat.

The last time there was a societal disruption of this magnitude was in the context of World War II and the subsequent Cold War. The US responded by embarking upon a massive expansion of postsecondary education, which created more space for marginalized groups to demand access and equity from public higher education. But militarization is neither a necessary nor desirable precursor for postsecondary investment. Instead we can imagine supporting public universities on the basis of social welfare rather than military or scientific dominance. With more extensive, rather than exhausted, governmental support, we can seize opportunity from crisis and work toward a more equitable and just public higher education system.

The ground beneath our feet has shifted dramatically. *Broke* exposes the promises and perils for public higher education in the days, months, and years ahead.

Laura T. Hamilton and Kelly Nielsen
April 17, 2020

Introduction

Vesta would arrive on campus with a faded and beat-up black skateboard, until it finally lost a wheel. Like the majority of students on her campus, she was Latinx, the first in her family to attend college, and low-income. Vesta was also whip-smart and driven to make her campus a better place for the many students who shared similar life and educational experiences. She was full of observations about how her university worked compared to whiter and wealthier universities in California and punctuated her insights with warm smiles and obscenities—sometimes in the same sentence.

Vesta's background was not unique among the students we studied. Her parents emigrated from Mexico before she was born. In the US, her father worked at a "sweatshop," cutting fabric into patterns. Her mother sold "anything from thread to clothes" at outdoor swap meets. Vesta grew up in South Central Los Angeles during the mid-1990s and early 2000s. LA is one of the most racially and economically divided cities in the US, and South Central encapsulates this dynamic. It is home to the University of Southern California (USC), a majority-white elite private university, so desired by affluent families that they have resorted to illegal means to gain admission. Outside of the university, the area is almost entirely non-white and marked by unemployment, poverty, and racial unrest. A few years before Vesta was born, riots broke out on a South Central street corner, in response to Rodney King's brutal beating at the hands of police.

Vesta's parents had high hopes for their daughter, and encouraged her academically, emphasizing, "Education's the only way we can really move up." Unfortunately, the K–12 schools in South Central were less than ideal. The charter school Vesta attended did not offer classes necessary for four-year college admission. When Vesta transferred to a public high school, she was placed in remedial classes because her family spoke Spanish—even though she was fluent in English.[1] School officials were perplexed when she performed exceptionally well in math on a standardized state test. As Vesta noted, "That was the only thing that seemed off to [the school]. They were like, 'Maybe she's just really smart in math and pretty stupid in everything else.'"

Although USC was "right there," Vesta never felt comfortable setting foot on campus. USC has been described as an "isolated fortress" that has neglected the local neighborhood, at best, and displaced residents through development and gentrification, at worst.[2] With its fortress-like security separating the university from the surrounding neighborhood, USC can be a forbidding place for local residents. Vesta instead dreamed of attending the University of California-Los Angeles, a world-renowned public university northwest of where she lived. As a teenager, she had accompanied her father, whom she described as having a "critical way of thinking," to open lectures at the university. "I have no idea how he [found out about the talks], but he'd be like, 'I'm going to UCLA. There's a talk.' And then, he'd take me. I have high expectations for what the university is supposed to be because of UCLA." She applied to UCLA—but also to UC-Merced and UC-Riverside, two majority-student-of-color universities in the same system, as backup options. When she was wait-listed at UCLA, she selected Merced over Riverside, sight unseen, as she could not afford to visit. Merced came out on top because the scholarship was largest by a thousand dollars.

Vesta managed to navigate a primary and secondary educational system that consistently denied her opportunities. Gaining admission to the University of California was a major feat, and UC-Merced offered a campus filled with other motivated and racially underrepresented students just like Vesta. Had she been born ten miles away, in affluent and white Beverly Hills, Vesta likely would have ended up at UCLA or USC. In one sense, there is no reason to believe that either school would have provided her a better educational experience. Elite, historically white universities are often particularly toxic for racially marginalized students.[3] US higher education, however, is increasingly characterized by sharp inequalities in organizational wealth and resources. This would matter for Vesta.

When Vesta was a college senior in 2016, each student on USC's campus corresponded to $117,551 in endowment assets. At UCLA this number was $39,479. At cash-strapped Merced, it was only $1,370. Thus, the per-student endowment amount at Merced corresponded to roughly 1/86 of that at USC and 1/29 of the amount at UCLA. Endowment assets can be saved, reinvested to create even more wealth, used for business and operational purposes, and spent in ways that enhance student experiences. Resource gaps were obvious to Vesta and many of her UCM peers, who understood that race and money intersected in ways that directly shaped their college educations and future possibilities.

These gaps were manifest at UCM in the limited number of advisory and student support staff, severe space constraints, and lack of cultural programming, among other things. Vesta would thus devote her college years to fighting for a cultural center. Research shows that cultural centers matter for the experiences and outcomes of racially marginalized students.[4] At the time, UC-Merced was the only University of California campus without at least one such space. As Vesta noted, "This school knows who the students are, they acknowledge that [fact] to get more of us [from racially marginalized backgrounds to come to UCM in order] to get more money, but … where are the resources?" Her anger was often directed at the university, but these inequalities were rooted in the underfunding of public universities that would most directly impact Merced and Riverside—the two schools with the largest Latinx and low-income student populations in the UC system.

Broke: The Racial Consequences of Underfunding Public Universities tells an organizational story about the growing number of "new universities" like UC-Riverside and UC-Merced—schools that pair high research ambitions with predominately disadvantaged student populations. New universities are not all "new" in the temporal sense. To the contrary, with the exception of UC-Merced, these are existing public universities, some quite old, that have begun shifting their organizational practices and priorities, often in response to postsecondary defunding. They are remaking old universities into something new. One major shift, necessary for survival, is enrolling greater numbers of racially and economically marginalized youth. These students become the lifeblood of the new university, supporting its research mission but also keeping the doors open for future students who are seeking social mobility.

The term "broke" in our title has a triple meaning. We refer to the "broken" postsecondary system that continues to segregate students by both race and social class, the extent to which new universities—far more than predominately white research universities—are fiscally "broke" in a country that has withdrawn support for public higher education, and the promise of new universities to "break" the mold for a research university by challenging status hierarchies based on student background. We delve into the organizational details of these universities in ways that are not typical for books on higher education, but always with the goal of understanding what it means that the research university experience looks different for Vesta, and students like her, than for white college students of both the past and present.

What Is the New University?

New universities are a result of demands for access to research universities by groups barred from the top rungs of the higher education system. They typically enroll racially marginalized students from low-income families—part of the "new majority" of US postsecondary seekers. The new majority is not affluent, white, or from households with college-educated parents. These students primarily attend community colleges, open-access schools, and for-profit universities.[5] When they gain access to research universities, small numbers are admitted to predominately white schools, but many more are concentrated in reinvented organizations that just twenty to thirty years ago served very different populations or, in the unique case of UC-Merced, did not exist.[6] New universities organize around inclusion, rather than exclusion, and focus on offering social mobility to historically marginalized students.

We see public research universities serving racially and economically disadvantaged students as a dynamically emerging organizational form. Whether or not a particular school fits the description of a new university should be considered relative to the state's demographic composition and higher education policies, which dramatically shape the race and class composition of public universities. In the University of California system, for instance, the bar for a new university is higher, given a racially diverse state population and generous state subsidies for students from low-income families.[7]

Typically, however, at least a quarter of the new university student population identifies as historically underrepresented racially marginalized students (URS); this includes Black and Latinx students, as well as students from some Southeast Asian groups, Native Americans and Alaskan Natives, and Native Hawaiian and other Pacific Islanders.[8] In the US, URS have experienced systematic economic and educational barriers. These students are more likely to be from low-income families and the first in their immediate families to attend a four-year college.[9] New universities enroll economically disadvantaged URS, as well as other low-income students. Students receiving federally funded Pell Grants—a proxy for low-income—frequently constitute a third of the student body, often far more.[10]

Research is central to the mission of the new university, and not by accident. Around the world, prestige is tightly linked to university research and is central to a global economy of knowledge.[11] New universities are aspirational organizations that compete on the basis of research in order to secure status and financial resources, such as grants and donations. They are typically ranked among the top 200 national universities according to the *U.S. News and World Report* and are designated as either Research 1 (R1) or Research 2 (R2) by the Carnegie Classification system. Evidence of striving is patently visible: University web pages advertise cutting-edge science, noteworthy faculty, and a proliferation of research institutes. Less visibly, new university faculty may experience growing pressure to increase research and grant production.

In this way, new universities are different from open-access and regional public universities, which are hit even harder by disinvestment in public higher education. As inequality between universities increases, investments in research have become necessary to surge ahead, as well as to prevent falling behind. Competition is stiff. New universities, for instance, are not nearly as wealthy as other top-ranked universities and struggle to build and maintain research infrastructure. They are not (yet) included in the country's top fifty universities.

The new university has at least two historical analogues. The first is the Historically Black College and University (or HBCU), which produced virtually all Black college graduates in the US before World War II.[12] HBCUs developed in response to the racially exclusionary practices of historically white universities.[13] More than half a century after the landmark *Brown v. Board of Education* Supreme Court case, which required schools to racially integrate, higher education is still sharply racially segregated. New universities provide access for disadvantaged groups; many carry designations such as Hispanic Serving Institution (HSI) or Asian American and Native American Pacific Islander Serving Institution (AANAPISI). Unlike HBCUs, however, new universities frequently lack an explicit mission of service for the students they enroll.[14]

The second analogue is the predominately white land grant university, which was founded starting in the late nineteenth century.[15] By the post-WWII era, these universities had opened their doors to new populations and brought research to underserved areas of the country.[16] Now that most flagship public universities are exclusive, quasi-private organizations (not enrolling URS or low-income students in large numbers), new universities have taken up the charge, but they are doing so in a profoundly different context. While the predominately white land grant university was an act of the federal government, instantiated in legislation, the new university has evolved as the state's role in postsecondary education has devolved.[17]

There are new universities all over the country. Arizona State University is, in some ways, the prototype. ASU president Michael Crow even coined the term "new university" in his manifesto *Designing the New American University*.[18] Other examples include but are not limited to: University of

Central Florida, Georgia State University, University of Illinois-Chicago, University of Maryland-Baltimore County, University of Massachusetts-Boston, Rutgers University-Newark (New Jersey), University at Albany-SUNY (New York), University of Houston (Texas), and George Mason University (Virginia). New universities will increase in numbers as the racial demography of the US continues to change, the wealth gap between the richest and poorest Americans grows, and declining fertility rates shrink the size of the college-going population.[19] Simply put, there will be fewer affluent domestic white or international students to enroll. Many predominately white universities will look to the new majority for organizational survival, and many regional universities already serving URS will intensify research in order to maintain (or hopefully gain) ground.

Unlike prior waves of public university students, the racially and economically marginalized students that fuel new universities have not been backed by governmental support. The schools that serve them have developed as calls for fiscal austerity have grown—coalescing in the 1970s and reaching a fever pitch in the Great Recession of 2008.[20] We have seen reductions in public commitments to higher education, often as funds are reallocated elsewhere. In California, for instance, postsecondary budget cuts occurred alongside massive growth in the prison industry.[21]

These changes are indicative of what social scientists have referred to as neoliberalism. Neoliberalism is a moral and economic ideology, a set of policies and practices, and a broader social imaginary that supports the deflation of public spending on social welfare and the intensification of private market competition.[22] Educational scholars have been fascinated by transformations wrought by neoliberalism—including funding cuts to public higher education and increased reliance on families, corporations, granting agencies, and wealthy donors.[23] They have focused on the impact of neoliberalism on socioeconomically disadvantaged students.[24] But race rarely enters into the picture.[25] In *Broke*, we bring this scholarship in conversation with race theory and emerging thought on the racialized nature of neoliberalism to argue that postsecondary neoliberalism is not only a classed phenomenon but also, especially in the US, "at its core a racial project."[26]

The Political-Economic Context

As early as 1898, W. E. B. Du Bois recognized that the micro-level educational realities confronting Black students in the US—such as the limited availability and condition of K–12 schools, lower levels of literacy, and exclusion from attending colleges with whites—had to be situated in the macro-level political economy.[27] We take a page from Du Bois and argue that the new university origin story, and the unequal distribution of resources to schools serving racially marginalized students, can only be understood in the context of neoliberal policies shaping the postsecondary system. While neoliberalism has taken different forms across time and place, below we focus on consistent features of neoliberal thought and policymaking.

The end of the imperial era in Europe set the neoliberal project in motion. As democracy spread around the globe, it produced new forms of political intervention in the economy—from fascism and communism to the economic self-determination of newly independent nations and the mobilization of the working classes, all of which appeared to an emerging group of neoliberal thinkers as threats to the flow of capital and even freedom itself.[28] Neoliberals responded by designing and building institutions, such as the World Trade Organization, that would move the global economy out of the reach of individual nation-states and insulate markets from political actors. According to historian Quinn Slobodian, who documented these developments, "The normative neoliberal world is a ... world kept safe from mass demands for social justice and redistributive equality by the guardians of the economic constitution."[29]

There were racial underpinnings to this thinking. Prominent neoliberals like Friedrich Hayek rejected race as a category of analysis. However, the end of empire meant the transformation of the global racial order, and the commitment of some neoliberals to constraints on mass democracy was "reinforced by deep-seated anti-black racism" and belief in "a world of races."[30] For example, the economist William H. Hutt advocated for nondiscrimination in labor markets at the same time that he warned of "black imperialism."[31] Hutt "promoted a color-blind market" but only alongside a ballot box that "saw first in black and white" in order to "lessen the likelihood of economic protectionism and redistribution."[32]

The intellectual center of neoliberalism had moved to the US by the 1970s.[33] Particular forms of governmental involvement in economic markets—from generous welfare policies to support for unions and public ownership of industry—were framed by neoliberals as market constraints and the source of economic problems. Demands for racial justice in the economy, from civil rights and student movements, made race central to debates over the welfare state.[34] Prominent thinkers and figures across the political spectrum shared hostility to governmental economic redistribution as a response to racial inequality.

For example, Gary Becker and Milton Friedman, who claimed to reject racism, nonetheless argued that free markets would take care of racial inequality, while antidiscrimination legislation would only make things worse.[35] In Virginia, James Buchanan responded to the *Brown v. Board of Education* ruling by creating a new center at the University of Virginia with funding from the governor that would develop arguments against federal encroachment in Virginian economic and social life.[36] Murray Rothbard, who would help spawn the US "alt-right," embraced biological ideas about racial difference to argue against a robust welfare state.[37]

Backlash against redistribution came to a head during the 1970s, which were characterized by low economic growth and high inflation, or stagflation. In 1979, Federal Reserve chairman Paul Volcker restricted the money supply and pushed up interest rates. This came to be known as the "Volcker Shock." It curbed inflation but also produced a deep recession, increased unemployment, and undermined organized labor. The Volcker Shock signaled that public spending would henceforth be disciplined through the interest rate system and ushered in neoliberal governments led by Ronald Reagan, in the US, and Margaret Thatcher, in the UK.[38] The "solution" to any economic ill became austerity, which has been referred to as the voluntary deflation of public spending precisely because it was (and remains) a choice.[39] In the place of government spending, the state was called on to create, maintain, and spread so-called "free markets," all while protecting the economy from labor unions, welfare advocates, civil rights activists, and militant students.[40]

But what would ultimately drive the populace to embrace austerity, abandoning a governmental "social safety net" in favor of an "individual responsibility ethos"?[41] Inflation was not especially harmful to many Americans.[42] Furthermore, only the US investor class stood to unambiguously benefit from mid- to late twentieth-century policies that restored returns on private investment eroded by inflation, reinscribed the significance of family wealth for economic well-being, and decreased the role of the government in managing welfare.[43] The racially marginalized were among the hardest hit, but the vast majority of Americans were hurt by stagnant wages, rising debt, precarious work, and growing inequality.

Racial divisions are a blunt tool for whipping up public dissatisfaction with left-leaning tax and industrial policies.[44] For example, neoliberal policies developed on the heels of demands from Black people for access to the "Fordist family wage"—the income, credit, and other benefits derived from inclusion in unions, pensions, and homeownership.[45] A national tax revolt started in California when residents of wealthier, white school districts refused civil rights–based court decisions requiring the state to distribute public funding equitably to schools across the state. Tax revolt was a "delicious dish" for Republicans to feed white suburbanites, who soon categorically rejected governmental social expenditures that benefited racially and economically marginalized groups.[46] Indeed, research indicates that funding for K–12 education declines when older white voters are asked to support school-aged populations from other racial groups.[47] As we suggest below, the defunding of higher education is part of this story.

Scholars argue that the reduction of public support for social welfare, including spending on education, has historically been fueled by a "politics of resentment" against people of color, who are demonized as unfairly draining societal resources.[48] Ronald Reagan's deployment of the mythical "welfare queen," a racialized image of Black women fraudulently collecting exorbitant welfare benefits, is frequently cited as an example of this phenomenon, as it preceded legislation to cut means-tested programs.[49] Some scholars contest the causal relationship between racial animus and specific austerity policies.[50] However, the use of coded language around race, known as dog-whistle politics, often obscures the racial character of calls for austerity and can lead a reluctant public to accept these conditions.[51]

Arguments for austerity posit that individuals get what they earn in the competitive marketplace through hard work and should not have to share their rewards with "undeserving" others.[52] This belief rests on colorblind racism; it indicates that everyone should be treated "equally," without regard to race.[53] Colorblind racism helps perpetuate the notion that those who struggle have earned their hardships. It does not acknowledge the structural advantages and disadvantages produced by race.[54] At the same time, dog-whistle politics imply that if white people are struggling, it is because the government has disadvantaged them in favor of supporting non-whites. In either case, austerity is the answer.[55]

There is no need to prove racial intent, though, for these policies to have a racialized impact. The spread of market logics and austerity in a social system organized by racial hierarchies reproduces race-based inequalities. The retraction of social safety nets that offer some relief for historically marginalized groups forces individuals to rely on family-based systems of support and material advantages, which are vastly uneven and shaped by a long history of racial domination and exclusion.[56] The lasting legacy of slavery and the Jim Crow era in the US, as well as the continuing centrality of race to educational, legal, economic, political, and other societal systems, ensures unequal access to wealth.[57] Indeed, the median wealth of white households is twenty times that of Black households and eighteen times that of Latinx households—and these gaps are larger than they were in the early 1980s.[58] Neoliberalism thus helps generate a "massive, disenfranchised ... largely [but not entirely] black and brown ... U.S. subaltern stratum."[59]

The Origins of the New University

How did austerity come to higher education? Low-cost public higher education existed in the US during much of the Cold War period, from the late 1940s up until about 1980. We argue that the new university—a competitive research university serving racially underrepresented and low-income youth—is predicated on the demise of the government-supported Cold War University in the wake of increasing demand for access. That is to say, the new university would not exist, at least not in the same way, if the kind of governmental support that characterized the Cold War period in the US had been extended to recent waves of marginalized students.

The Cold War University was the result of an unprecedented partnership between universities and state and federal governments, whereby higher education produced educated workers and scientific knowledge in exchange for public investment.[60] Talent was recruited from all race and class groups, and higher education expanded—first to veterans through the Servicemen's Readjustment Act of 1944 (or GI Bill), then to women, those with low incomes, and finally to people of color.[61] The Higher Education Act (HEA) of 1965 was intended to "strengthen the educational resources of our colleges and universities and to provide financial assistance for students."[62] Recognizable features of US postsecondary funding programs, such as direct grants for infrastructure, need-based financial aid, and work-study, were established.[63] In California this project was perhaps most fully realized, as the state imagined and pursued universal public higher education infrastructure on an unparalleled scale.[64,65]

The de-whitening of US postsecondary universities accelerated with the affirmative action movement—a product of the civil rights era that offered remedial action for structural inequalities in access to educational and employment opportunities.[66] The federal government issued racial representation benchmarks for students, faculty, staff, and governing boards.[67,68] Universities responded not by examining how criteria for admission advantaged whites, but by admitting some students of color as "exceptions."[69] The University of California-Davis School of Medicine, for instance, set aside sixteen out of every hundred spaces for students from underrepresented racial groups.[70] There was potential for change on the horizon—although it was predicated on a fragile mechanism.

As scholars of race and education point out, advantaged groups adjust to equalization efforts by developing new "opportunity hoarding" strategies.[71] That is, they adapt by finding different ways to maintain existing advantages. Despite the *Brown* ruling and the affirmative action movement, today's postsecondary system is still highly segregated by both race and social class.[72] In addition, organizational wealth is now more sharply stratified and maps tightly onto student advantage, whereby the most marginalized students attend the least-resourced schools.[73]

How did historically underrepresented racially marginalized students or (URS) end up concentrated in new universities heavily impacted by austerity, rather than in better-resourced research universities with their affluent white peers? As racially marginalized youth, often from low-income households, began to enter higher education in significant numbers, sentiment around government financing soured. Although causation is difficult to prove, the timing is striking. For most of the twentieth century, families of color, as part of the tax base, were paying for wealthy white students to attend universities where their own offspring were not welcome. Everything changed as marginalized populations gained more access to historically white organizations. Affluent whites would need to help pay for the postsecondary education of Black and Brown youth, as well as the white working class. This did not happen. Instead, over the next thirty years, the dismantling of affirmative action and the end of "the state-university partnership" would occur in lockstep.[74]

Affirmative action was dealt a heavy blow in the 1978 *Regents of the University of California v. Bakke* case. Allan Bakke, a white man, sued the UC-Davis School of Medicine, arguing that the practice of ensuring spots for people of color constituted "reverse discrimination." The Court ruled that quotas or set-aside spots were unconstitutional. The only "compelling government interest" that allowed a public university to explicitly consider race was "diversity."[75] This shift was deeply consequential. The US moved from recognizing URS as deserving of "educational compensation" for structural racism, to seeing student race as but one of many individual identities that comprise a diverse college campus.[76] Several other Supreme Court cases have also upheld and elaborated an anti–affirmative action stance.[77]

The backlash against affirmative action was fueled by Reagan's portrayal of the affirmative action student as the postsecondary welfare queen—another racialized figure depicted as unfairly draining governmental coffers to the detriment of whites.[78] This is despite the fact that white women were primary beneficiaries of affirmative action policies and the fact that research universities in the US remained predominately white spaces.[79] The Reagan administration directly upheld segregation by accepting state postsecondary desegregation plans that did not meet the representation benchmarks laid out by the Federal Office of Civil Rights.[80] Reagan also pledged to overturn policies mandating what he perceived as "federal guidelines or quotas, which require race, ethnicity, or sex ... to be the principal factor in hiring or education."[81] Only a turn to the invisible hand of the "free market," Reagan argued, could protect against what he saw as abuses of government welfare, including in higher education.[82]

In the following decades, the states that would adopt bans on affirmative action were those with a decline in the percentage of white students at flagship universities.[83] That is to say, when a mechanism for the racial dominance of whites was threatened, states responded aggressively. In California, one of Reagan's many anti–affirmative action appointees to the Department of Justice would later found the Center for Equal Opportunity, which collaborated with University of California regent Ward Connerly on California's Proposition 209 referendum.[84] Approved in 1996, Prop. 209 prohibited state employees from considering race, sex, or ethnicity in university admissions, with the intent of blocking affirmative action. Prop. 209 filtered students of color away from the UC's most prestigious campuses.[85] At both the federal and state levels, other affirmative action policies, such as legacy and athletics admissions that sorted wealthy white students into higher-status universities, were left uncontested.[86]

Defunding started in the late 1960s and early 1970s and ran parallel to the destruction of affirmative action. During this time in California, then-Governor Reagan targeted university social activism around the civil rights movement and Vietnam War, evoking racial fears about liberal, often non-white students, who were portrayed as out of control, ungrateful for their education, and tainting a supposedly apolitical space.[87] As governor, he ruled over the system with an iron fist, simultaneously orchestrating the firing of Clark Kerr, a central architect of California's statewide plan for postsecondary access, and proposing the introduction of tuition to California's public higher education system.[88] Reagan promised that, as president, he would tackle "big education" by dismantling the Department of Education and unleashing the free market on the postsecondary sector.[89]

Reagan's doomsday failed to materialize, but the 1972 reauthorization of the Higher Education Act (HEA) facilitated a gradual drain on public resources for higher education. The original HEA included an institutional aid measure that was never funded. Instead of directly funding schools—which would have been harder to cut—reauthorization linked postsecondary funding to individual students.[90] Economists saw the change as encouraging "freer play of market forces and challeng[ing] prevailing public subsidy patterns."[91] States could more readily withdraw support for higher education and offload financing to students and families. A competitive market for student dollars was created, and universities were incentivized to fill funding gaps by raising tuition. Thorny issues of university "quality" were left up to the market—as

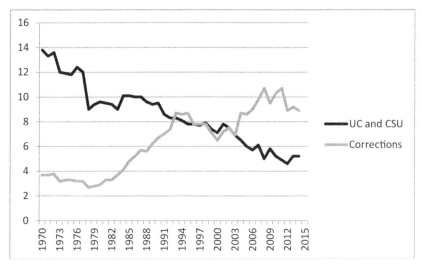

Figure 0.1. Share of state funding for University of California (UC) and California State University (CSU) versus corrections, 1970 to 2014.

Note: Data are drawn from the University of California Info Center, State Spending on Corrections and Education.

student aid was expected to allow higher-quality students (as measured by standardized tests) to attend, and higher-quality universities were expected to survive. In the 1992 HEA reauthorization, Congress took steps to subsidize and incentivize federal loan provision through private lenders—fueling a student loan crisis.[92]

Declines in state funding for higher education over the last four decades have paralleled a shift in spending for other priorities, such as health care and prisons.[93] For example, figure 0.1 displays the relationship between the share of state funding for the four-year postsecondary systems in the state of California and corrections between 1970 and 2014. The share of funding for universities dips precipitously while, after 1980, corrections spending spikes. In other words, state support was channeled away from public welfare to punitive functions that target marginalized populations.[94]

The financial crisis that began at the end of 2007 also contributed to defunding. State and local tax revenues, which are a major source of support for public higher education, declined significantly. A decade after the crisis began, state funding for two- and four-year colleges around the country was nearly $9 billion below 2008 levels.[95] But funding never returned to pre–Great Recession levels. On average, four-year public universities have experienced more than a 30 percent per-student state and local funding cut over the past thirty years.[96]

The impact of defunding has not been even. Elite private universities have amassed vast organizational wealth over time and have pulled away from public competitors.[97] These schools exist in a different stratosphere. Yet, flagship state universities have been protected relative to other public colleges and universities.[98] In order to compensate for defunding, the most prestigious state universities have increased enrollment of international and out-of-state students, who typically pay two to three times state tuition to attend—shrinking the number of seats available to URS and low-income residents.[99] Among publics, predominately white flagships also tend to have the greatest capacities to attract philanthropic donations, seek support from alumni, draw on endowment funds, and land large grants.

As the death of affirmative action and the end of the Cold War University became realities, college attendance among URS grew exponentially. Between 1996 and 2012, enrollment among Latinx students ages eighteen to twenty-four increased by 240 percent, the result of prior waves of immigration. Increases among Black students (at 72 percent) also outpaced whites (at 12 percent).[100] Without redistributive mechanisms, new forms of segregation accompanied this groundswell.[101] Today, elite research universities, both private and public, only enroll a tiny fraction of the college-going student-of-color population—primarily affluent, high-achieving students of color.[102] URS from low-income families remain vastly underrepresented at these schools, with the majority attending increasingly low-resource community colleges or predatory for-profit universities that tend to graduate students at lower rates.[103]

The new university is born from demands for access to research universities in a racially segregated system. Without affirmative action, students like Vesta lack the accumulated privilege that would dramatically increase the odds of entry to the most prestigious schools, like USC or UCLA. As predominately white public research universities scramble for tuition dollars from non-resident students (many of whom are wealthy and white), new universities have expanded reach within their states, in part to survive under conditions of defunding. By capturing an underserved student population, they ensure their own existence.[104]

In the context of a competitive environment reliant on family and corporate resources, universities that enroll large numbers of URS, especially from low-income families, are penalized. Schools generate organizational prestige and attract resources in large part by recruiting "selective" or "meritorious" students, who are more likely to be white and affluent. As we argue throughout the book, the racialized construction of "merit"—and, relatedly, university "quality"—creates an imaginary wedge between racial inclusion and excellence in ways that sustain white dominance. New universities make visible the political nature of this construction and the damage that it does to talented and motivated URS.

A Tale of Two Schools

Broke: The Racial Consequences of Underfunding Public Universities asks: How does the defunding of public higher education shape the organizational practices of research universities serving racially marginalized students? What strategies must new universities employ to survive, even thrive? And how does defunding affect URS from low-income families, whose access to a research university is likely to come via a new university?

The book is set in the University of California system. The UC is a monument to the spectacular postsecondary expansion that occurred in the middle of the twentieth century and has emerged as one of the leading university systems in the world.[105] The system produces scientifically innovative and cutting-edge research while also providing high-quality and relatively affordable education to state residents from a variety of class and racial backgrounds.[106] UC campuses tend to serve far greater numbers of marginalized students than similarly ranked peers in other states. Thus, if there is an ideal home for the new university, the UC is it.

The system is also more equitable than others. There is no "flagship" UC campus. System leadership maintains that there are nine "equal" undergraduate-serving campuses in the system.[107] The even distribution of state funds on a per-student basis, as we detail later in the book, reflects this commitment to a unified system. And while California's higher education systems have not been spared funding cuts, the UC is far from the worst off. The current California state legislature also values racially and economically marginalized state residents and expects its research universities to do the same. Therefore, the dynamics introduced in this book are likely worse in most other state systems.

Even in the UC, however, there is a hierarchy. Schools' reputations and rankings correspond to student race and class. At the top, Berkeley has the lowest percentage of Latinx and Black students, and Berkeley and UCLA have the lowest percentage of Pell Grant recipients in the system. These two schools also enroll significant out-of-state and international populations. Neither fits the new university mold. At the bottom, Riverside and Merced have, by far, the highest percentages of Pell and Latinx students and enroll greater percentages of Black students. Like other UCs, both schools enroll substantial Asian populations, but UCR and UCM have higher proportions of Southeast Asian subgroups (e.g., Cambodian, Filipino, Hmong, and Laotian) that are historically underrepresented, economically marginalized, and thus share some common experiences with Black and Latinx students on their campuses.[108,109] Notably, both UCM and UCR are composed of almost entirely in-state populations.

Our two focal schools, UC-Riverside and UC-Merced, are new universities. They are the least resourced in the system and the most reliant on dwindling state contributions. This book is, in many ways, a testament to the great successes that UCR and UCM achieve under difficult conditions. For all that they share, however, the two schools also provide a contrast. They represent the ends of a spectrum of new universities—from the relatively better-positioned UC-Riverside to the more structurally and fiscally challenged UC-Merced. These differences arise from the historical origins of the two universities.

Originally considered the "Swarthmore of the West," Riverside opened as a predominately white liberal arts college in 1954. The campus was built alongside the UC Citrus Experiment Station in a once wealthier agricultural region east of Los Angeles known today as the Inland Empire. Almost as soon as it opened, UCR shed its liberal arts character. In 1959, it was designated a "general" campus with the aim of becoming a large research university. This required growing the campus rapidly—a task that was handily accomplished in the context of Cold War postsecondary expansion projects.

Designs for another world-class university were impeded, however, by a changing regional economy and environmental crisis. As the Inland Empire developed a largely industrial and low-wage service sector economy, air quality worsened dramatically. In 1971, Riverside mayor Randall Lewis requested that the region be declared a disaster area. By 1979, UCR had 25 percent fewer students than eight years earlier. Former chancellor Ivan Hinderaker (1964–1979) recalled that the campus nearly closed as negative press drove both students and faculty away.[110]

The crisis marked a turning point for UCR. As the mayor sought an emergency declaration from the state, African Student Programs and Chicano Student Programs opened their doors on the UCR campus. UCR began developing a national reputation for racial and ethnic cultural centers. The school capitalized on this fact: It became the perfect recipient for the new surge of enrollment, known as Tidal Wave II, which included historically underrepresented populations. The regents of the University of California, in consultation with the university, slated UCR for massive expansion. The passage of

Prop. 209 further cemented the school as the research destination for California's URS; more prestigious schools could no longer pursue racial affirmative action.

As a new university converted from a predominately white university, UCR benefited from established structural features—buildings, faculty and staff positions, cultural centers, and whole schools—that would persist under less favorable conditions. Conversion was at least initially instrumental, offering a way to solve the problem of an underpopulated campus. The shift was helped along by campus leaders such as Tomás Rivera, the first Latino chancellor in the UC, and Ray Orbach, who embraced the culture of inclusion that had its roots in the cultural centers. Eventually Riverside would become the first UC to meet criteria for a Hispanic Serving Institution (HSI), opening up access to special Title V grants.[111] Now one of the most established new universities in the country, UCR is well positioned to push back against disadvantageous postsecondary hierarchies.

In contrast, Merced was only founded in 2005—a new university from inception. It enrolled more students of color than white students (a pattern that would quickly intensify), and in less than five years included more Pell Grant recipients than non-recipients. As a twenty-first-century university, UCM does not enjoy inherited resources. This fact has fundamentally shaped the campus's identity and development.

UC-Merced is located in the Central Valley of California, a neglected region of the state stretching around 450 miles from Bakersfield at the southern point, through Fresno and Sacramento, up to Redding. The Central Valley is characterized by some of the highest levels of air pollution in the US, has been dubbed "Prison Alley" given the density of correctional facilities, and is referred to as the "Appalachia of the West" and "Calibama" (a derogatory reference to Alabama)—terms that reflect high levels of non-urban poverty.[112] The school is more isolated than UC-Riverside. Cow-filled pastures and fields of solar panels surround the concrete and metal buildings.

By 2016 and the start of the study, UC-Merced had miraculously weathered the Great Recession. However, space and staffing needs were at a crisis point, and the school was nearing the end of extra UC system support, which was necessary to get the campus off the ground. In order to achieve fiscal stability, it needed to bring in more tuition dollars. But getting more students required more buildings, and the channels by which virtually every other public university had built their campuses had gone dry. The school would embark on the largest public-private partnership (or P3) in the history of US higher education—highlighting the university's difficult financial position.

The Study

Broke is grounded in parallel yearlong ethnographic and in-depth interview studies at UCM and UCR. Laura is a tenured faculty member in sociology at Merced and had the unique opportunity to study the campus and the students about which she cares deeply. She is also an expert in postsecondary organization and inequality.[113] Kelly grew up in Southern California, not far from Riverside, and received his PhD in sociology at the University of California-San Diego. This project brought him back to the Riverside area, where he had previously spent four years studying community college students.[114] Both of us are white. We discuss the ways that this shaped our research questions, methods, data analysis, and writing in a methodological appendix at the end of the book.

The book is intentionally focused on the organizational cogs of new universities. We wanted to understand how everything worked in the face of resource shortages, and how Latinx and Black students on campus were impacted. Our focus was broad and wide reaching: We examined academic programs, advising, career counseling, housing, mental and physical health support, philanthropic efforts, social clubs and activities, cultural programming, financial aid, facilities operation and maintenance, budgeting and financial planning, and programs for historically underrepresented groups. Historical and regional analyses helped us make sense of current conditions, as well as past and future trends.

Ethnographic observations were conducted by the authors and, at UCM, a team of undergraduate and graduate student researchers, whose knowledge and perspectives were vital to the research. We observed student orientations in English and Spanish, numerous protests, social events and cultural programming open to the public, diversity programming, classes of interest, faculty information sessions and town halls, and group-specific graduations. With the generous support of staff in the School of Social Sciences, Humanities, and Arts at Merced, Laura was able to shadow academic advisors during sessions with students. Video footage and media coverage of relevant events were also analyzed.

The experiences of all constituents involved in undergraduate education, not just students, were relevant to our research.[115] Thus, we conducted ninety-three interviews with university employees, almost evenly split between the two schools. These interviews included chancellors, vice provosts, deans, faculty at all ranks (identified by students as allies), student-facing staff in a variety of units, and staff dealing primarily with other university employees. As we moved higher up the ladder, interviewees were more likely to be white.

Participants were told that we were interested in understanding how universities support or fail to support students of color and were asked a series of questions about their background, job duties, interactions with students, race relations on campus, and perspectives on the campus in general.

We chose to focus our student portion of the project on Latinx and Black students, who were among the most and least represented groups on our campuses. They shared experiences as students of color—for example, feeling racially targeted during the Trump campaign and presidency. However, their positionality on campus, and in the larger state, was very different. Black students reported more racial microaggressions and, particularly at UCM, were highly likely to engage in unpaid labor to make the campus livable for racially marginalized students. California also has a relatively small Black population (6.5 percent in 2015); in certain areas, Black students were very visible and targets of policing.

We intentionally sampled student leaders involved in clubs, organizations, and protest activities—particularly at UCM where student unrest was more pronounced. These participants were primarily Black and Latinx, but also included a few Asian and white students. At both campuses, we also drew random samples of full-time Black and Latinx students in their first and fourth years.[116,117] We completed eighty-four student interviews in total (thirty-one targeted and fifty-three random), with just over 60 percent of student interviews at UC-Merced.[118] Students were asked about family life, academic and social experiences, career goals, race relations on campus, interactions with campus employees, involvement in student organizations, and protest activities.[119]

Occasionally we found it essential to follow our trail of inquiry off campus. For example, because we chose to analytically embed Merced and Riverside in the larger UC system, interviews with two officials in the UC Office of the President, as well as analysis of system-wide documents and data, were necessary. We also conducted interviews with three corporate actors and former UCR students connected to career placement but not officially employed by the University of California. An interview with a former legendary leader of UC-Riverside, Ray Orbach, required travel to another state.

Throughout the book, we have made intentional language choices. We focus on race, a system of oppression based on the placement of people into hierarchically ranked categories believed to correspond to biological differences.[120] Racial groups are often associated with multiple ethnic traditions. However, when we refer to Black, Latinx, Asian, or white, we are referring to ascribed racial categories. Readers will also notice that while we capitalize most racial categories, we have chosen not to capitalize "white." Capitalization is a political decision.[121] We elect to capitalize Black and Latinx, in particular, to emphasize the political agency, collective identity, and solidarity of these communities in a racist society.[122] Although there is ongoing debate about this terminology, we use Latinx when gender is unspecified, nonbinary, or to refer to a community, and Latina/Latino when discussing respondents who use these terms to describe themselves.[123]

Postsecondary Racial Neoliberalism

We use the term "postsecondary racial neoliberalism" to describe the particular way that race and class, as systems of oppression, have recently intertwined in higher education—blocking access to postsecondary resources for URS and disadvantaging universities serving these students. As intersectional scholars of color remind us, race frequently relies on other systems of oppression, making racial inequalities durable and difficult to combat.[124] Our goal is to help readers recognize that postsecondary neoliberalism is not just about class oppression; it is also a racialized phenomenon that operates, in part, through class.

Like neoliberalism more generally, postsecondary racial neoliberalism relies on colorblind austerity, reproducing racial hierarchies in part by intensifying the role of class resources in individual and organizational success. Neoliberal racial projects also sweep up poor whites, along with others who do not have sufficient privilege on other dimensions to protect themselves from being on the receiving end of structural inequalities. The white students served by new universities are, for example, often almost entirely working class. These students are also subject to the consequences of defunding, but they are small in number relative to racially underrepresented students. Furthermore, a long tradition of scholarship, from W. E. B. Du Bois to Amanda Lewis and John Diamond, has demonstrated that whiteness carries privileges even for economically disadvantaged white people.[125] Being white at a school like UCR or UCM, as we will show, can be protective.

Below, we illustrate a racial neoliberal cycle set in motion in higher education under conditions of broad access and public defunding. The cycle supports the opportunity hoarding of affluent whites, channeling organizational resources toward their youth. We show how the social construction of "merit," rooted in beliefs about racial differences in ability, produces racial segregation—even absent a legal system of exclusion. Racial segregation contributes to the development of an organizational hierarchy that establishes a seemingly inevitable link between race and university "quality," all while not appearing to be about race at all. The hierarchy justifies and generates

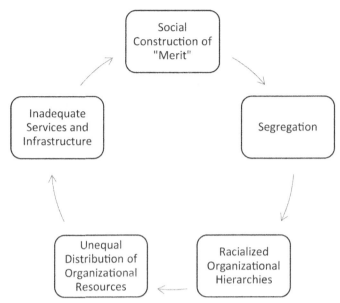

Figure 0.2. The racial neoliberal cycle in higher education.

vast differences in organizational wealth, with consequences for student access to valuable resources.[126] These differences between public schools serving racially marginalized students and historically white universities seem to "prove" initial assumptions about merit.[127] Figure 0.2 provides a visual of the argument.

Dominant groups have long used racial privilege to shape criteria for college admission in the US.[128] Today, classification techniques used to draw distinctions between students cannot appear to be about race.[129] They are instead supposed to be colorblind predictions of future academic performance and thus require systematic "prospecting for potential."[130] "Merit"—a combination of SAT scores, high school performance, and extracurricular accomplishments—is the current metric. But merit often bears little relationship to college performance. We know, for instance, that SAT and ACT scores do an exceptionally poor job of forecasting future grades.[131]

What does merit achieve, then? It redraws racial boundaries. We now have solid evidence that at least some past university leadership intentionally adopted test scores to block the admission of Black students. University of Texas–Austin archives show that just two weeks after the *Brown* ruling, administrators were passing notes about "how to exclude as many Negro undergraduates as possible." Eventually, the university's Committee on Selective Admissions realized that white incoming students had higher aptitude test scores than Black students. They noted that a cutoff "point of 72 would eliminate about … 74% of Negroes…. [which] would tend to result in a maximum of 70 Negroes in a class of 2,700" and recommended that the university president work with other state schools to establish similar test-based protocols.[132]

The SAT, the current testing regime, is a racially biased instrument based in research by a psychology professor and member of the Eugenics Society (a white supremacist group focused on maintaining racial "purity").[133] He wrote *A Study of American Intelligence* about the inferiority of immigrants and Black people and concluded that the intelligence tests he developed for the US Army confirmed these beliefs.[134] This test served as the basis for the SAT. Research has concluded that the SAT continues to function differently for Black and white students. The SAT has preserved white advantage by weighing questions in favor of white students and discarding items on which Black students have scored higher.[135]

Merit is also assessed via a record of strong academic performance, enrollment in Advanced Placement (AP) classes, enrichment in music and the arts, and commitment to sports valued by elite colleges (e.g., rowing, lacrosse, and tennis). White families are more likely to have resources to devote to tutors, coaches, test preparation, cultural activities, sports equipment and memberships, and other performance enhancements; their children are also more likely to attend better-resourced schools that enable demonstration of "excellence." Mitchell Stevens refers to the transformation of familial advantage into individual merit as the "laundering" of privilege.[136] This process is often talked about in terms of class advantages. But these advantages are as raced as they are classed. For example, the ability to pay exorbitant tuition rates for exclusive primary and secondary schools often comes from homeownership and other forms of credit historically more available to whites.[137] Similarly, racial segregation ensures that disparities in neighborhood school resources also map onto racial hierarchies.[138]

Merit offers a seemingly colorblind sorting mechanism that shunts URS and white students to different schools, helping shore up arguments against racial equity. Since 1995, 82 percent of new white postsecondary enrollees have attended the 468 most selective colleges in the US, while 72 percent of new Latinx enrollees and 68 percent of new Black enrollees have attended far less prestigious two-year and open-access schools.[139] Prestigious research universities continue to enroll limited numbers of Black and Brown students. Most of these students are from affluent families or are part of what Anthony Jack refers to as the "privileged poor"—small numbers of disadvantaged students who, despite the odds, managed to gain admission to the nation's most elite high schools, setting them on new educational trajectories.[140] New universities are the exception that proves the rule for URS; when they attend research universities, the majority do so with other students like themselves.

The classifications attached to students are transposed onto the universities that serve them. There are "selective" and "less selective" universities—with the proportion of URS declining sharply as selectivity increases.[141] This relationship is codified in the *U.S. News and World Report* rankings, which, even in their most recent formulations, systematically reward universities that enroll wealthy white students. These rankings, not coincidently, were created in the early 1980s, as schools began to compete more aggressively for private resources. As detailed in the next chapter, the *U.S. News* has historically included factors that are a better indicator of the privilege and resources with which students arrive than of what universities offer their students. Because of how merit is constructed, schools serving low-income URS populations typically hold the bottom, while predominately white organizations serving affluent students rest comfortably at the top.

Organizational hierarchies serve as effective mechanisms for racialized resource distribution. In many state systems, prestige is linked to the share of state resources available to a given organization. Under conditions of defunding, however, disparities are often most pronounced in access to private sources of funding. For example, the most elite research universities can attract well-heeled donors and charge higher tuition rates. New universities, by contrast, are heavily reliant on shrinking public appropriations. Universities with greater prestige can use their acclaim to produce more wealth, which can be utilized to enhance prestige, in cyclical fashion.[142] What might start as smaller gaps in organizational resources and wealth can therefore be magnified over time.[143]

These differences matter for how students experience higher education.[144] Wealthier schools can provide supportive infrastructure that makes it easier to navigate college comfortably and successfully. For example, they can spend more on student services, offer comprehensive advising support, and provide smaller classes. Evidence suggests that these types of structural supports boost completion—but such supports are least available to the students who need them most.[145] The result is a "separate and unequal system of higher education," in which URS from low-income households are the most disadvantaged.[146] Not surprisingly, students who do not have racial privilege and attend universities that are systematically underfunded may struggle to graduate, compete with their white peers from more elite universities, and become wealthy alumni who can advance the university's standing. Thus, the racialized consequences of the postsecondary neoliberal cycle feed back into the construction of merit.

Why are people not up in arms about this? Merit, as a colorblind narrative, is deeply persuasive. Like arguments for austerity, merit suggests that people get what they deserve as a result of hard work. The racially and economically advantaged are loath to recognize the "leg up" that they receive in postsecondary competitions. At the same time, it is depressing for less advantaged students to acknowledge the ways in which the deck is stacked against them. If they do call out racial inequities, they may be blamed for "introducing race" to the conversation. Those who manage to succeed may not understand why others fail to do the same. High-achieving marginalized students in elite universities are also used by the public as evidence that the system is "fair"; however, stark patterns of segregation tell us that this is an illusion.

Although counterintuitive, "diversity" has also played a role in papering over real differences in the presence of URS across the postsecondary hierarchy. As detailed above, diversity is a colorblind ideology introduced in the anti–affirmative action *Bakke* case. It does not require (and may not even allow) remediation of educational racial inequalities. Instead, diversity draws attention away from racial disparities, celebrating a wide array of individual "differences."[147] Most universities have institutionalized a highly visible and "benign commitment" to diversity, characterized by new forms of infrastructure and personnel, such as chief diversity officers, mandatory multicultural education, and multicultural centers. Research suggests that diversity initiatives, despite the intentions of the individuals involved, often fail to create substantive change in racial representation.[148] As a result, scholars often conclude that diversity discourse and infrastructure may be new tools to maintain the status quo.[149]

The racial neoliberal cycle occurring in higher education seems deterministic. Readers may wonder if it is possible to break the cycle, given the current political-economic context. We argue that the legitimacy of a separate and unequal system is beginning to crumble. New universities, although hampered by sharp resource disparities, offer a different model for higher education, in which research universities are judged in part by their abilities to offer access and social mobility. We also address the challenges and costs of making racial inclusion a source of revenue and prestige in a postsecondary system no longer grounded in public support.

Book Roadmap

The empirical heart of *Broke* is divided into three major sections. The first section, *The Changing Face of the UC*, introduces readers to our focal campuses and the University of California system. The section leverages cross-campus contrasts in this large and venerated system to explore the impact of post-secondary racial neoliberalism on new universities and their larger state systems.

Chapter 1, "Battle with the Rankings," describes the reinvention of UC-Riverside in the early 1990s. We detail the racialized organizational hierarchies encountered by the school, but also highlight organizational efforts to promote "inclusive excellence" as a new status criterion. UCR is in a unique position to launch this challenge, given its Cold War infrastructure and early conversion to a new university. By contrast, chapter 2, "P3 Paradise," focuses on UC-Merced—a campus founded after over twenty-five years of post-secondary defunding. This chapter delves into the organizational vulnerabilities that can plague the least-resourced new universities, introducing the potentially risky public-private partnership (or P3) as a strategy for building and maintaining large portions of a campus.

The final chapter in this section, "Running Political Cover," places both new universities within the larger ecology of the UC system. We argue that public systems often utilize particular campuses to do a disproportional share of "institutional diversity work." As systems are defunded and come to depend more on private revenue, resources may be concentrated at campuses with advantaged student populations and sparse at schools serving disadvantaged populations.

The second section of the book, *Responses to Underfunding*, examines how new universities manage in the face of limited public financial support. We argue that choices for administrators and staff are not ideal and are often further limited by a culture of austerity that helps produce an environment of scarcity. This section also highlights the unintended racial consequences of organizational responses to underfunding.

In chapter 4, "Austerity Administration," we show that new university administrators, motivated by the idea that public disinvestment is inevitable, engage in austerity practices. They aim to grow big, cut costs, be market-smart, and think (inter)nationally. These practices, however, are often counterproductive—entrenching austerity and generating racial inequalities. The following chapter explores the on-the-ground consequences of "Tolerable Suboptimization," an official austerity policy at UCM. The chapter is told from the perspectives of frontline staff and racially marginalized students. We describe the negative consequences for academic advising, mental health services, and cultural programming.

The final third of the book, *Dealing in Diversity*, highlights the limits of "diversity" as the primary framework for attending to race in the new university. We argue that diversity creates organizational pressure to avoid the appearance of racial remediation and encourages the exchange of racially marginal-ized students as commodities for university benefit.

Chapter 6, "Student Labor and Centers of Support," shows how a multi-cultural approach to cultural programming, rooted in colorblind diversity logics, can reinscribe racial inequalities. We instead emphasize the impor-tance of cultural centers rooted in collective identity for reducing the burden placed on URS to create a positive campus environment.[150] Our final empiri-cal chapter considers the complexities that arise when new universities trade on racial marginalization to gain resources or status. We primarily consider university partnerships with corporations seeking to improve workforce di-versity. Finally, we explain that "Marketing Diversity" is a predictable out-come of the shift to market-based funding—but one with potentially ex-ploitative elements.

In "Breaking the Cycle," we conclude by exploring possibilities for posi-tive social change. Change will require disrupting the racial hierarchies that sort students and organizations, as well as the resource flows legitimated by those hierarchies. We acknowledge that higher education is not, and never has been, a primary driver of racial equality. However, we offer five recom-mendations that may provide greater support for racially marginalized stu-dents and the new universities that serve them.

Part 1

THE CHANGING FACE OF THE UC

1 *Battle with the Rankings*

New universities, or research universities serving substantial numbers of racially and economically marginalized students, are a relatively new phenomenon in the US. Why do existing universities transition to new universities? How do these universities evolve? Where do they come from? And, given the racialized nature of university rankings, as exemplified by the *U.S. News & World Report*, what are the status challenges they face? Is it possible for new universities to hold reputational ground or even beat other research universities at the same game—potentially reshaping the way that status is determined? What conditions would need to be in place for that to happen?

In this chapter we use one of our focal schools, UC-Riverside, to answer these questions. The school illustrates a typical path to a new university— conversion from a predominately white university (PWU). Conversion occurs when PWUs face threats to survival that require them to dramatically reshape the student populations they enroll. Specifically, when the pool of affluent, white students willing to attend a university shrinks or is too small to meet the demand for growth, leadership begins to think differently about historically underrepresented racially marginalized students (URS) from low-income households. Eventually, cultural changes may or may not follow, as campuses vary in how they respond to their new student population. The success or failure of a new university can depend as much on changing culture as changing demographics; challenging a deeply entrenched status system requires whole new ways of thinking about what it means to be an elite university.

UCR is an early converter, as the shock to the student body—the result of a local environmental disaster—happened before many other PWUs would face their own pressures for transformation. It is also an example of a campus that underwent a radical cultural conversion, adopting an identity and claims for status that center its URS population. UCR allows us to see how a process of conversion unfolds over a twenty-five-year period.

Conversion is risky, and Riverside is unique in the magnitude of its success. The university has won numerous awards for improving student outcomes, received plaudits from political leaders across the country, and even climbed the academic rankings. But this success was not immediate. In prior decades, Riverside experienced a gradual slide in the *U.S. News* rankings, as it encountered racialized organizational hierarchies that devalued the converting campus. The story of how it managed to leap back up—to a better rank than before the slide began—is a function of unique conditions not in place for most new universities. UCR is perhaps the highest-ranked new university in the country. Its success as a new university may mark it as the exception that proves the rule. At the same time, the fact that the school eventually won a small but meaningful victory in the battle with the rankings suggests the potential to challenge the penalties faced by new universities more broadly.

Becoming Diverse

UC-Riverside opened in 1954 as an elite liberal arts campus that university leaders hoped would grow into the "Swarthmore of the West" in "the prosperous heart of Southern California's citrus agriculture." The sense of promise was unbound. At UCR's dedication ceremony, UC president Robert Gordon Sproul acknowledged the "brilliant" faculty and high-quality students that the university attracted. The heady promise of UCR in the "worried days of the mid-century" was to teach "the art of living together, of how to harness primeval instincts into lives of harmonious emotional stability.... as governments of man across the globe seek the formula for peace and friendship."[1] It was a vision of collective purpose and political will.[2]

The university's time as a liberal arts campus was short-lived. It transitioned to a research university in the early 1960s. As former chancellor Ivan Hinderaker (1964–1979) recalled in a 1998 interview, this decision was essential to "keep the campus alive" and to access available funding opportunities from the Cold War science machine. The state provided ample infrastructure for research and graduate education. Hinderaker recalled, "The buildings were all in line before I got here [in 1964].... In other words, that was a stated commitment, and obviously the campus needed this to get to graduate work ... So they were ready, and the groundwork had been all set, certainly before me."[3]

Like most colleges and universities of the mid-twentieth century, UCR was a PWU. As Victor Ray argues, the whiteness of an organization is important because resources tend to consolidate among dominant groups, and PWUs have more resources than organizations with large proportions of URS.⁴ Resources can include material objects like buildings or private money donated to build an iconic clock tower. But they can also be cultural, like the meanings attached to labels like the Swarthmore of the West or the University of California. As a PWU during the height of state support for public higher education, UCR was on the same material and cultural development path as its UC peers.

Why did UCR transition to a new university? In all likelihood, Riverside would have continued to grow as a PWU and increase its stature like nearby UC-Irvine or the one other inland campus of the time, UC-Davis, if not for the air. The smog crisis of the 1970s captured the national imagination and depopulated the campus. Major media outlets published photos of Riverside joggers wearing gas masks. Students were described as feeling their way to class because the smog was so dense. In 1975, the school abandoned its football program due to lack of attendance at games. With the student population down by a quarter in less than a decade, the situation was looking dire. As Hinderaker noted, "You can imagine the gloom that is produced in a period like that."

Everything changed, however, as UCR headed into the 1990s. The school entered a period of rapid growth. Figure 1.1 highlights the process of conversion. In 1980, white students made up 74 percent of undergraduates and Asian students made up 10 percent. By 1995, Asian students, many of whom were URS, comprised the largest group.⁵ But in the early 1990s, the percentage of Latinx students on campus began to grow rapidly, setting on a course to overtake that of Asian students. The Black student population also gradually increased for decades. By 2016, white students comprised only 12 percent of the student population. The school became a new university, and this cemented its existence.

How did conversion occur? Leadership at UCR reliably gave the same answer—Ray Orbach, chancellor from 1992 to 2002. Orbach's status on campus is still larger than life, despite having left the university over a decade prior to our study. After working in the Department of Energy and as the first undersecretary for science during George W. Bush's presidency, Orbach settled at the University of Texas-Austin, in a distinguished professor appointment. He generously agreed to an interview, so Kelly flew to Texas. The conversation unfolded across many hours that included coffee in his humble office, a long lunch at the imposing Texas Longhorns' football stadium, and a walking tour of the enormous campus.

As Orbach recalled, "[When I became chancellor], my job was to ensure that [the UCR] campus developed. At that point, the system-wide office was

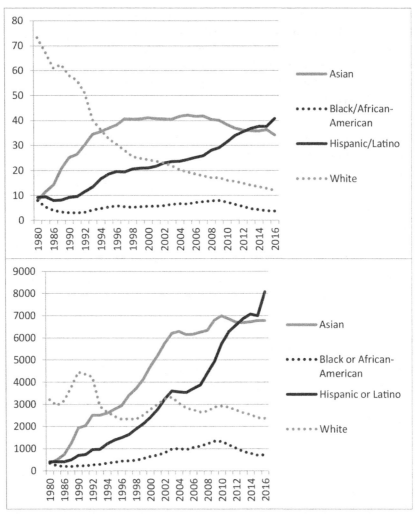

Figure 1.1. Racial distribution of UCR enrollment, fall 1980 to fall 2016.

Panel 1: By percent; Panel 2: By count.

Note: Data are drawn from the National Center for Education Statistics (NCES) until 1992, and from University of California-Riverside Institutional Research Fall Enrollment Headcounts thereafter.

very skeptical about Riverside.... They just didn't believe in the campus, if I could say that. That's probably unfair, but it's not inaccurate." Orbach understood that it would be harder to finance campus expansion than in the past. But students could still be leveraged to gain more state and system resources. Thus, when asked why enrollment growth was so important, he explained,

"Simple.... You were given resources on the basis of your student numbers, and without resources, we couldn't grow."

The smog crisis had subsided, but the damage to the school's ability to recruit was done. Orbach would need to look for a new student population to fill the campus. He found students in the surrounding areas. Riverside was no longer the white, wealthy desert getaway that it had been nearly forty years earlier. The area had grown tremendously during the 1980s, when air quality was poor, becoming much Blacker and Browner in the process.[6] This population change is consistent with research on environmental racism; racially marginalized groups are disproportionally exposed to environmental hazards.[7]

The demographic shift represented an opportunity for UCR to repopulate. And enrolling more URS may have saved the university. Treating students as organizational resources in this way is hardly unusual.[8] For example, many colleges and universities adopted coeducation in the 1960s and 1970s out of strategic self-interest, as women had become a resource in the competition for male students.[9] In this case, Orbach sought out a new population—poor and working-class communities of color in the Inland Empire—to keep UC-Riverside's doors open.

Orbach's outreach efforts, if strategic, were still unique, especially for the time period.[10] So unique, in fact, that he caught the attention of the *New York Times*.[11] During the 1990s, California passed a number of racialized propositions: Prop. 209 against affirmative action, but also anti-immigrant and tough-on-crime propositions that disproportionately harmed the racially marginalized.[12] It was in this context that, as the *NYT* piece noted, "Almost every week the chancellor rides the circuit of the region's high schools." Orbach personally spoke to everyone from Black students and parents in South Central LA, sixty miles west of UCR, to Latinx farmworkers and their families in Indio, an agricultural town seventy miles to the east. As he explained to Kelly, "There was never an issue about whether the chancellor was involved. The chancellor gave the address. So it was a lot of work."

Orbach labored to produce the students UCR needed. He produced booklets in English and Spanish, "passed out by the thousands," that helped families of middle and high school students understand the requirements necessary for UC admission. Staying on track to complete the math sequence was a sticking point. As he explained, "My mantra was algebra. I would say, if your child is not taking algebra in the eighth grade, tomorrow I want you to go to the principal's office and ask him or her why your child is being robbed of a college preparatory education." The booklets also contained information about how to obtain a full financial aid package. He noted, "These are families ... who've been taken to the cleaners by loan sharks and others. They do not want to go into debt."

His efforts paid off. As Orbach recounted, "With that, the campus grew, and it grew in a wonderful way. We were able to bring students who not only had no one in the family who had gone to college, but they hadn't even thought about it. These were first-generation students, and they were marvelous. They were hungry. They worked as hard as they could. They did, I thought, beautifully."

It is tempting to narrate a story solely about Orbach, as went the legend on Riverside's campus; however, he did not operate in a vacuum. Demographic and structural factors aligned to push UCR into a new university. For instance, the population of California was becoming increasingly Latinx. The surge in applications known as "Tidal Wave II" included the children of Baby Boomers (referred to as the Baby Boom echo), but also first-, second-, and third-generation immigrant youth. High school graduation rates were improving, and more racially marginalized youth were meeting the requirements for acceptance to the UC.[13]

Around the same time, the UC's move to a "multiple filing system" allowed applicants to apply to as many campuses as they wished, dramatically increasing UC applications. The UC referral pool then redirected applicants who did not get into their top choices to UCR—even if they did not apply to UCR. UC-Riverside suddenly had access to a much larger number of students, although the referral system simultaneously marked the school as the "least desirable" UC.[14] Many of these students were Black and Latinx, due to racialized inequities in K–12 education that left them less formally qualified in competition for admission.[15]

Following the approval of Proposition 209, which effectively ended affirmative action in the system, enrollment of URS at more selective schools also fell precipitously (by more than 50 percent between 1995 and 2002 at Berkeley and UCLA), while numbers of Black and Latinx students swelled at UCR.[16] Orbach worked in tandem with the system to absorb an untapped pool of underserved students in the state, setting annual growth targets of 6.3 percent for UCR—the highest in the system.

Orbach also benefited from cultural centers put in place decades in advance by staff, faculty, and students of color. Chicano Student Programs (CSP) and African Student Programs (ASP) were established in 1972. They were housed in Costo Hall, named after local Native American scholars and activists who were close friends of Chancellor Tomás Rivera (1979–1984). Rivera was the first Latino leader of a major research university in the US, and played a mentorship role for the few Latinx students on campus at the time.[17,18] As one of our interviewees reported, from personal experience, many of Rivera's mentees stuck around to "help our people" as UCR staff members. These centers and mentees were connected to racially marginalized communities outside of UCR—connections that facilitated Orbach's efforts.

The students that arrived at UCR during Orbach's term offered a way for the campus to lay claim to state resources during a tight period. During the mid-1990s, California faced a budget shortfall of $8 billion.[19] Orbach worked with a group of local leaders he called the "Monday morning group" to lobby the governor on behalf of UCR:

> About two years in, we went to Sacramento, and the head of the Monday morning group stood up, with the governor present, and said, "You've got to help us. We're not getting funding for the students. We are growing…." And I am told that he [Governor Wilson] made a motion that his staff understood to fix it, and so suddenly we got the funding…. The combination of the growth and the governor's actions paid off. I suddenly was able to fund the campus and hire more faculty to deal with the large increase in student enrollment.

The pleas for more support worked in part because Orbach skillfully evoked the notion of a unified system, in which Riverside should grow "according to the University of California model, which was Berkeley."

The resources that came with more students helped support UCR's research mission. As one faculty member recalled, "We ended up with a much better infrastructure for research…. Orbach repaired all the roofs, he got high-powered electricity on campus, he changed the air-conditioning system, and he built huge lab buildings and made all the difference…. He improved it big time. The science library, it's amazing what he did." Under Orbach's tenure, Riverside grew its entomology program into a world-class operation, became a leader in nanotechnology, developed an elite engineering school, and laid the groundwork for a medical school. These achievements would not have been possible without state support, which was acquired because of the turn to URS.

In short, UC-Riverside's successful conversion relied on the unique convergence of people, places, and historical events.[20] Most PWUs undergoing conversion in more recent years are not in the same position. The rapid depopulation of a research university is rare. The UC system with its formal equality between campuses is highly unusual. Most states lack the racial diversity of California. Nevertheless, in the next decade, many universities will see a dearth of potential applicants—the result, in part, of declining fertility rates during the Great Recession.[21] With the turn to austerity, overall state funding for higher education has been decimated, and requesting more state resources may be a riskier gamble.[22] Conversions are happening as former PWUs turn to more disadvantaged populations to stay afloat, but they are unlikely to experience the fortuitous circumstances that smoothed the way for UCR.

Racial Status and Penalty

While wildly successful at bringing students and infrastructure to UC-Riverside, Orbach's solution had a major downfall: In a racially stratified system, expanding the pipeline undermined the school's mandate, as a UC campus, to gain prestige. In fact, a question at the center of the *NYT* piece featuring Orbach was "How bad is it to go to Riverside?" UCR, as an early and emerging new university, was developing a reputation as a second-choice school in the system—referred to derisively as "UC Reject." The article offered backhanded compliments and outright snubs, observing that "Riverside has almost all the trappings of a serious university" and describing it as "the kind of technocratic, friendly, bland and utilitarian institution summed up by the words 'second-tier.'" While the piece praised UCR's "active sense of social mission," it implied that a school filled with Black and Latinx students from poor communities had to be anything but a desirable option.[23]

How did a high concentration of racially marginalized students come to be defined in opposition to organizational status? For much of their existence, predominately white universities, especially elite schools, gained status from their ability to exclude most of the population; students of color were barred from admission.[24] As new populations were forced to engage with the postsecondary enterprise, due to growing dependence on college degrees for economic success during the mid-twentieth century, the excluded challenged the legitimacy of prestige derived from their categorical exclusion.[25] "Merit," rooted in presumed academic ability, was fronted as a supposedly neutral way to determine student, and thus university, status. As noted in the introduction, however, merit is anything but race neutral.[26]

What merit as a system of exclusion does allow, however, is the elevation of *some* students of color into previously exclusionary universities, which has shored up organizational legitimacy to a great extent in the post–civil rights era. The ability to compete for and enroll this select group of students, who have strong records despite structural barriers to success, is now itself a form of prestige.[27] As sociologist Ellen Berrey explains, elite organizations seek to achieve "selective inclusion" by including high-performing students of color.[28] Most of these students are affluent domestic students of color, Asian students who are not URS, international students coded as non-white in the US, or exceptional low-income students of color who matriculate from private high schools like Exeter and Andover.[29] These students are expected to slide smoothly into the existing organizational infrastructure. They must be a small but visible portion of the overall student body, available to grace brochures, but not disruptive to the overall whiteness of the space.[30] In fact, their visible presence, in a sea of white faces, can actually confirm a university's whiteness.

Enrolling too many URS, especially in an organization not already established as exclusive, still poses a status threat.[31] The implicit assumption is that, in such great numbers, these must be the "wrong kind" of racially marginalized students. At play here are persistent racist beliefs about typical academic abilities of Black and Brown youth.[32] The result is a substantial status penalty for postsecondary organizations, like UCR, that become coded as "for" students of color from low-income households. This is a key feature of the postsecondary racial neoliberal cycle, as detailed in the previous chapter.

The disadvantage experienced by new universities that enroll substantial numbers of URS has also been instantiated in postsecondary rankings. The *U.S. News & World Report*, in particular, has held a decades-long monopoly over the assignment of university prestige. Until fall 2018 (when 2019 rankings were released), *U.S. News* rankings unilaterally hurt schools serving racially and economically marginalized students. A penalty was built into all aspects of the formula.

Nearly a quarter (22.5 percent) of *U.S. News* rank was based on first-year retention rates and overall six-year graduation rates. This disadvantaged schools enrolling URS from lower-income households, as these students, on average, have lower college completion rates than their more privileged white peers. Another 22.5 percent was devoted to undergraduate academic reputation—a survey of presidents, provosts, and deans of admission, who are overwhelmingly at predominately white research universities. "Exclusionary impulses" are intense among leaders of these organizations, who may be inclined to highly rate other organizations that share similar characteristics.[33] Selectivity accounted for 12.5 percent, and was most centrally determined by student SAT and ACT test scores (which tend to be higher among affluent white applicants) and school acceptance rates (which are more favorable among schools already viewed as prestigious).[34]

Other factors included faculty resources (at 20 percent), which were measured by indicators such as class size and faculty pay, as well as per-student spending on instruction, research, and student services (at 10 percent). Both are typically higher at better-resourced universities that are more likely to be predominately white. Five percent was devoted to the alumni-giving rate; schools with more affluent alumni typically find it much easier to convince their alumni to "give back" at little personal cost. Only graduation rate performance (at 7.5 percent) took into account features that typically disadvantage new universities; this measure was intended to show the effect of the college's programs and policies on student graduation rates after controlling for spending and student characteristics, such as test scores and the proportion receiving Pell Grants.[35]

This way of calculating university prestige places status in direct opposition to the percentage of URS on campus. As one goes up, the other typically goes down.[36] New universities thus start with a handicap—regardless of how well they serve their student populations.[37] Indeed, the formula does a poor job of actually measuring school quality. *U.S. News* rank says more about student characteristics (from a biased perspective) than about what a school offers to students.[38] The "value added" to the lives of students is not assessed. Enrolling students who enjoy multiple forms of privilege, and who are likely to succeed in any context, is strongly rewarded. In contrast, universities have little incentive to enroll large numbers of racially and economically marginalized students, who bring strengths little recognized in the current ranking system, unless it is absolutely necessary to survive.

Creating and Marketing "Inclusive Excellence"

Orbach refused to accept the notion that youth in surrounding communities could not fuel a University of California campus. The university needed these students to stay open and pursue a research mission. But Orbach also realized that continuing to draw them to UC-Riverside, and keeping them there, would require shifting commitments. The university needed to undergo a transformation. As an administrator involved with Orbach's outreach noted, "When Chancellor Orbach started this we, in fact, were changing culture."

The efforts of earlier figures to create cultural centers started the work necessary to welcome URS. The school would become a national model for cultural programming and infrastructure, as detailed in chapter 6.[39] But at the time that Orbach took office, UCR was also known as "UC Racism."[40] Only weeks after Orbach arrived, a large protest event called "Rally against Racism" drew hundreds of students and resulted in a confrontation with the police.[41] To make the transition more difficult, many faculty members were not immediately onboard with the changing student population. There was a lot of work to do.

A major part of this task was getting everyone on the same page with the changes happening on campus. Orbach worked to create connections with the student body. After the protest, he went "from one group [of students] to another trying to ... let them know that they were important ... that [he] wanted to work with them to make the campus attractive and vital to them. That it was their campus." Each morning, he would walk across campus with his wife, Eva, and pick up trash because the campus "was a godawful mess." It was a "question of pride" on a campus with strong feelings of "inferiority." Once a month, he held a public Q&A called "Rapping with the Chancellor," where he "would stand up in front of the [campus's famous] bell tower with a microphone and students could say whatever they wanted"—despite the insistence of advisors that this might make him a target. Orbach recalled that one time a student complained about how long it took her to get from the parking lot to the campus, so he said he would park in the same lot for the rest of the semester and they would walk together.

The growing student body also "created a lot of tension and friction with the faculty," said one senior administrator, because of the perception that "these students were not prepared to be here." A faculty member who arrived at Riverside the same year as Orbach remembered the chancellor's insistence that "We have these students now, we have to educate them. Now we have to do right by them." Faculty needed to recalibrate their teaching around the strengths and needs of this student population, which required additional work for faculty members who were used to teaching different students. Orbach led by example. As he explained, "They knew that I was ... teaching freshman physics. I wasn't separated from them. I had the same problems they had in the classroom. I would have office hours in the chancellor's office." Orbach also got faculty to embrace UCR's new role by including them in outreach. An administrator who had been there at the time explained, "We had faculty fully engaged [and] that was a way to get them to own it. They were out there meeting with the families, they were meeting with students. It wasn't large numbers or a large percentage of our faculty, but it was enough that they were out there sharing the stories."

Orbach believed UCR "could carry out a [UC research] mission at the highest quality level and in a community that was poor. A community that needed help." As a senior administrator who had been a doctoral student at UCR in the late 1980s suggested, "I'm not sure that anybody was articulating that vision [yet].... I don't think that we achieved this because we looked at anybody. I have to go back to Chancellor Orbach because of his commitment to providing access." Thus, under Orbach what has come to be known as "inclusive excellence" was happening, without being articulated as such.

According to an Association of American Colleges & Universities (AACU) initiative in 2005 (three years after Orbach stepped down as chancellor), inclusive excellence occurs when "diversity is a key component of a comprehensive strategy for achieving institutional excellence." The AACU model involves more than student body representation. Organizational change has to occur in terms of access and equity, campus climate, diversity in both the informal and formal curriculum of the campus, and in how student learning and development is approached. Orbach's UCR hit many, but not all, of these points.

Chancellors after Orbach would see inclusive excellence as central to UC-Riverside's identity. For instance, as Chancellor Timothy White's (2008–2012) "Pathway to Preeminence" Strategic Plan for 2020 states at the outset, "Diversity is both a measure of excellence and a means of achieving it."[42] Similarly, a contemporary top-level administrator explained: "I aspire for us to become a place that becomes at least 'a' if not 'the' pipeline for future faculty [of color] in America. We're transforming ourselves by raising in stature. Most universities that have gone through that transformation become whiter and richer.... [But] we've increased diversity at the same time; that is a reflection of deliberateness." This administrator would continue to suggest that UCR's investments in student diversity created a virtuous cycle contributing to academic quality: "You go to great universities with great professors and that's what a great university is—all the great scholars are there. But to a certain extent faculty come here because of the students who are here, and the ethos, so it becomes self-fulfilling at a point."

Over time, UCR has built a cohesive culture around the central elements of inclusive excellence. An almost religious fervor around the idea of serving marginalized students and their communities came through in almost every interview that we conducted with university employees of all racial backgrounds. As one high-ranking official, and a person of color, noted, "Part of the satisfaction that comes from here—the term I use is that we have a righteous mission.... People don't necessarily use that language, [but] I think they feel that." This is not to say that everyone on campus felt this way, but the shared sense of purpose was palpable even in public events, including a faculty town hall that involved faculty from around the campus. Statements like "We have the students we want, and we need to step up to protect those students" were frequent and met with loud agreement.

One of the limits of inclusive excellence, however, is its grounding in the notion of "diversity." As we discussed in the previous chapter, racial diversity may require the presence of some URS; however, it is explicitly not about racial justice. In fact, diversity is discussed first and foremost as a feature of an *organization*. The AACU initiative, for instance, described diversity as "a lever for, and measurement of, institutional vitality."[43] The primary goal is not to reduce racial disparities in educational access, resources, or opportunities, or to engage in reparations for past harms, but to produce organizational "vitality." Striving for inclusive excellence can have many positive effects for URS—Riverside's story makes that clear. But the primary beneficiary of inclusive excellence is the organization.[44]

As new universities struggle to stay afloat under conditions of public defunding, inclusive excellence also becomes an organizational resource to market. It has commercial appeal in a society concerned about diversity. UCR has seized on the opportunity to sell a public image of inclusive excellence. The marketing web page in 2019 reflects this approach. "The UCR Brand" emphasizes that Riverside is a UC of:

- Strategic Results: Pioneering research with economic, scientific, and social impact on the real-world challenges faced in California and beyond.
- Accessible Excellence: Putting a superb education within every student's reach.
- Inland Southern California: Catalyzing and guiding the positive growth of our region.
- The Future: [Imagined as] a diverse, inclusive, globally focused community that reflects California's many cultures and perspectives [and] a university on the rise.

"The brand" is a sophisticated pairing of research excellence with diversity and inclusion. It can be read as a genuine celebration of serving California's students from a wide variety of racial and class backgrounds *and* an attempt to commodify these students to garner more attention and money. Both reads are, in fact, accurate.

In some recent marketing materials, UC-Riverside has pivoted to using the term "accessible excellence." This helps the school beat out competitors—more elite schools that have adopted the term "inclusive excellence" as an AACU buzzword, without even enrolling substantial numbers of URS. The shift also serves the purpose of being clear about what UC-Riverside is seeking to celebrate. The university's emphasis on accessibility in its brand points to the fact that it not only includes some URS, but is also broadly accessible to marginalized populations in the region and state, even as it remains a top research university.[45]

UCR vs. U.S. News

UC-Riverside has sought to translate the image of inclusive excellence into measurable status gains. For many years it seemed that this was not going to happen. For instance, in 2010 when the UCR 2020 Path to Preeminence plan was released, UCR was ranked ninety-fourth in the *U.S. News & World Report*. Between 2010 and 2018, as the public image of inclusive excellence was being honed, UCR's ranking fell thirty places to 124th. Clearly, the rankings did not reflect UCR's rising self-image. That would change.

No one has leaned harder into inclusive excellence and sought to capitalize more on the groundwork laid by Orbach than the current chancellor, Kim Wilcox, who started at UCR in 2013. As a longtime faculty member remarked, "[UCR] was the secret jewel in the UC system that nobody really knew about, and Chancellor Wilcox has made it his mission to get the word out." As the Wilcox administration explained to us, UCR was not going to be known for football. And even though it has a number of exceptional research programs, any "president or chancellor—name your state—could tell you they have the number-one this and the number-one that." Rather, inclusive excellence, as one leader noted—"that's our hook."

During Wilcox's tenure, leadership has made the decision to openly challenge the legitimacy of *U.S. News* rankings. Thus, in a *Washington Post* article aptly titled "UC-Riverside vs. *U.S. News*: A University Leader Scoffs at the Rankings," Chancellor Wilcox argued, "Whatever this system [of rankings] values is inconsistent with what public universities provide." Instead, what UCR is doing is "the kinds of things America wants." He deemed it "most unfortunate" that *U.S. News* rankings are "the benchmark."[46] The battle with the *U.S. News* was on, but it would be a few years before UCR could hope for a win.

In 2013, Governor Jerry Brown called out UC-Riverside in a University of California Regents meeting for low graduation rates relative to other established UC campuses. This was somewhat of an unfair target, given that other schools have more advantaged populations and, as we discuss in chapter 3, greater resources. Chancellor Wilcox responded by forming a Graduation Rate Task Force that would recommend policies and practices to support improvements. Riverside increased graduation rates—and in dramatic fashion. Between 2012 and 2017, four-year graduation rates increased by 12 percentage points and six-year graduation rates by 9 percentage points, with large gains visible even in just two years.

Organizational actors offered no single account of how the numbers skyrocketed. They noted that UCR developed a "Finish-in-Four" campaign, improved data analytics available to advisors, increased efforts to engage undergraduate students in research, assessed its myriad support and engagement programs and invested in those that were working, and centralized business and operational services in a single building (named the "Highlander One-Stop Shop," after the campus mascot) in order to increase accessibility. Other efforts extended longtime commitments to inclusivity, including adding a Middle Eastern Center (the seventh cultural center on campus), creating one of the first administrative positions in the country focused on fostering diversity and inclusion, and working with surrounding communities to increase the educational preparedness of youth who could matriculate to UCR.

The accolades were suddenly flowing. In 2015, Robert Reich, former secretary of labor under President Clinton, visited Riverside and heaped praise on the university: "I don't think there is any institution of higher education of this degree of prestige and excellence that has this large a percentage of undergraduates who are Pell Grant eligible. So you have here what I would hope will be cloned across the country; an institution that really does provide opportunities."

A year later, in 2016, Ted Mitchell, former undersecretary of education under President Obama, visited UCR. As Chancellor Wilcox looked on with pride, Mitchell praised the parity in graduation rates across groups. At UCR, there were none of the usual race and class gaps. He effusively remarked, "You are showing … the kinds of commitments that need to be made if we are going to … have the kind of higher education system that supports a diverse democracy…. The future is always invented in California, and to me that future looks pretty bright." Mitchell's visit corresponded with the school's $300 million "Living the Promise" fund-raising campaign. The artfully produced and moving promotional video for the campaign highlighted the "grit, courage, [and] determination" of UCR's student body, showcased science and knowledge production, and asserted that "we each rise faster when we all rise together." It ended with a promise to extend "our hand to the next generation," and the image of a Latina student gazing at the iconic bell tower on campus.

By 2017, the Education Trust had identified UCR as one of the top eighteen colleges and universities in the country (and the only California-based university) for closing graduation gaps between Black and white students.[47] The *Los Angeles Times* did an exceptionally positive write-up of this report, with none of the snide remarks that marred the *New York Times* coverage during Orbach's era.[48]

The positive press likely helped UCR attract resources for student success efforts. In particular, its School of Natural Sciences (officially named the College of Natural and Agricultural Sciences) has won substantial grant monies for learning communities, undergraduate research, and other programs aimed at improving student outcomes. As one administrator—a key figure in turning inclusion into funding—explained, "I've … gotten to the point where I don't go after funding unless it's pretty big money. I don't waste my time on proposals that aren't gonna generate at least a million dollars because to do the things I want to do, at the scale I want to do them, takes millions of dollars." At the time of the interview, he was waiting on a decision for a $6 million Department of Education grant to expand learning communities to transfer students.

One of the most notable things about UC-Riverside's positive coverage is that the school got credit not only for what it did after 2012–2013 (i.e., sharply increase graduation rates) but for what it was *already doing*, starting many years prior—that is, enrolling large numbers of historically marginalized students and graduating students across sociodemographic and racial groups at remarkably similar rates, with some marginalized groups even slightly outperforming advantaged groups.[49] As one faculty member put it, "Whatever new accolades and recognitions are coming to UCR now began and matured many years ago."

Why has UCR finally been able to translate Orbach's vision into positive attention, even status? The public perception of higher education has changed. Calls for accountability to state taxpayer interests are increasing. That is, the public wants to see universities use taxpayer contributions in ways they deem desirable. Some state legislatures are pushing for evidence that universities offer demonstrable social goods—while failing to offer sufficient funding. Universities, unlike in the past, are not shielded from unfavorable press, litigation, or public pressure.[50] Attention has been drawn to race and class dynamics on college campuses. Students of color, in particular, have not remained silent.

There is no better illustration of change in how universities are evaluated than in the research of economist Raj Chetty and colleagues. In 2017, they produced a widely publicized method of assessing universities—the "mobility report card." This report card uses analyses of federal income tax and student loan data to reveal substantial variation in the amount of intergenerational social mobility produced by postsecondary schools in the US.[51] Chetty's metrics are sensitive to the percentage of low-income students enrolled at universities and, indirectly, to graduation rates, which strongly shape earnings outcomes. His findings highlight public university workhorses that serve as "engines of upward mobility." Riverside makes a favorable appearance in the report.

Contemporary UCR leadership has, for several years now, hoped to ride the sea of change to a higher-status position in the academic hierarchy. Paraphrasing the hockey player Wayne Gretsky, a top administrator explained:

> You don't skate to where the puck is, you skate to where the puck is going to be, and that's something I've always thought about in American higher education. We tend to chase a few leaders. We chase Harvard or UNC. And we all talk about Berkeley, which, as far as I'm concerned, was kind of the standard for American public higher education in 1968, which is awesome, but the focus is somewhere else [now].

UCR has therefore latched on to, promoted, and embodied a movement in higher education to determine university quality a different way than in the past. The choice to unabashedly promote inclusive excellence is strategic, as well as ethical—about organizational positioning and image as much as doing right by the students that UCR enrolls. As a staff member explained, "UC Riverside puts the language out to the nation that diversity is of importance when we think about prestige." Leadership readily admitted that the long-term goal was to break into the highly prestigious American Association of Universities (or AAU)—a group that currently does not include a single new university.

In this movement, UCR leadership has intentionally acquired allies. The university is a central member of the University Innovation Alliance (UIA), which defines itself as:

> The leading national coalition of public research universities committed to increasing the number and diversity of college graduates in the United States. We share an urgency about this work because we are public universities with a public mission. Higher education needs to do a better job of graduating students across the socioeconomic spectrum, particularly low-income students, first-generation students, and students of color. Raising graduation rates is imperative for social mobility and U.S. global competitiveness.[52]

The UIA, like UCR, promotes inclusive excellence: This group defines their diverse body of students as a resource unavailable to other schools. Value is added via high-quality and cutting-edge university programming, bringing economic opportunity and mobility to the states these schools serve.

Even among this group, however, UCR stands out for its racial and class composition. Just four of the eleven UIA schools are new universities in their states—UC-Riverside, but also Arizona State University, Georgia State University, and the University of Central Florida. Only Georgia State has a student body as historically underrepresented as UCR. The fact that the UIA has been able to draw heavy hitters (six universities are already members of the prestigious AAU, such as The University of Texas-Austin and The Ohio State University) suggests the extent to which it is desirable to at least effect a posture of commitment to inclusive excellence.

In recent years, a number of alternative ranking systems have emerged that take into account the extent to which universities offer social mobility to historically marginalized groups. For example, in 2014, UC-Riverside was ranked second in the nation in the *Washington Monthly* ratings. As the magazine noted:

> The UC campus in Riverside, ranked number two this year, stands out as a model for other public universities to follow. Riverside falls below most of its system peers by conventional measures. It's not part of the ultra-exclusive Association of American Universities. It doesn't enroll students with SAT scores so high that their graduation is all but guaranteed. Instead, Riverside is unusually focused on social mobility. Since 2006, its enrollment has grown by 25 percent. Half of all freshmen are first-generation college students, and the campus is the most racially and ethnically diverse within the UC system. Riverside's focus on public service exceeds that of almost every other national university.[53]

UCR has also ranked highly in the *Social Mobility Index* (or SMI)—fifteenth in 2017. Notably, that same year Harvard University was ranked 969th and Stanford University 1004th.

The ultimate mark of UC-Riverside's success occurred in 2019, when it gained ground in the battle with the *U.S. News*. UCR enjoyed the biggest boost of any university in the US, jumping thirty-nine places from 124th to eighty-fifth in just one year—surpassing the 2010 rank by nine spots; it also became the thirty-fifth-ranked public university in the country. This massive change in rank resulted from the *U.S. News's* first real concession to issues of inclusion and accessibility: The 2019 rankings took 2.5 percent of rating criteria from the reputational category and another 2.5 percent from selectivity in order to include a set of social mobility indicators focused on Pell Grant graduation rates. These measures included both absolute rates of graduation for Pell Grant recipients and comparisons to non-Pell students—measures on which UC-Riverside excelled.

Changing the Game?

Is UC-Riverside's win against the *U.S. News* indicative of the changing position of new universities in the larger postsecondary hierarchy? Will new measures of university value, quality, and even prestige reformulate what it means to be a high-status university? Can other new universities effectively mimic UCR and shed some measure of the stigma associated with serving URS?

It is important not to underestimate shifts in university rank. Universities are under enormous pressures to improve their *U.S. News* position, as it shapes the size of the applicant pool, donations from alumni, and employer interest. Schools will thus model policies and practices in ways that optimize their standings.[54] If the criteria for success reflect the degree to which universities offer mobility to marginalized populations, then universities will be compelled to address these populations. Some new universities, like UCR, will be able to capitalize on this attention. This will matter for Riverside's racially marginalized students, who will leave with a degree that has greater "market value" than just a decade ago.[55] In addition, efforts to push back against criteria penalizing schools that enroll and graduate disadvantaged students will help pave the way for many other new universities to move up in rank.

We remain skeptical, however, about the scope of the change. As organizational researchers have noted, "Once a status hierarchy is established, it tends to remain and be self-sustaining."[56] Universities confer social status and legitimate economic position for individuals, families, markets, governments, and other social institutions that are often deeply invested in maintaining the status quo.[57] Because universities are themselves racialized organizations, they are unlikely to succeed in dramatically shifting larger racial dynamics.[58] We can see this inertia by looking even more closely at the university rankings arena.

For example, what the *U.S. News* did in 2019 did not fundamentally reconfigure university status. The shake-up was confined to the middle and bottom of the top-200 field. The top fifty schools were hardly touched. Ironically, if the top were to dramatically shift, the *U.S. News* might lose some of its monopoly over university ranking. This is because rankings are determined to be more or less valid based, in part, on how they square up with established notions of prestige. The fact that the same elite Ivy League universities consistently land at the top of the *U.S. News* year after year helps make this ranking system legitimate in the eyes of the public.

Well-resourced PWUs also have ample resources to game the rankings, especially when social mobility is only one small portion of the overall score. For example, when elite privates did not hold the highest slots in the *Washington Monthly* rankings, they wrested away the top positions. In 2015, when UCR was ranked second by *Washington Monthly*, UC campuses occupied the top four spots, including UC-San Diego at number one. All but two of the top ten were public universities; Stanford and Harvard were fifth and eighth, respectively. But by 2018, Harvard, Stanford, MIT, Princeton, Yale, and Duke University were the top six, and Georgetown was in the eighth spot. Only three publics remained—UC-San Diego, UCLA, and UC-Davis. UCR fell from the penultimate position to twenty-eighth in just three years.

This is not a function of changes in how the rankings were calculated. Rather, as the *Washington Monthly* rankings continued to get more press, elite private universities figured out how to maximize criteria that counted. Researchers have pointed out that universities often find ways to work around status criteria without making substantive changes.[59] For instance, some universities ranked highly on social mobility measures may, in fact, serve disproportionately few low-income students; it is much easier to produce a high Pell student graduation rate if low-income students form only a tiny fraction of the population.[60] With racial affirmative action effectively a "third-rail" issue in higher education, it is also unlikely that status criteria will evolve to include direct measures of student racial background—or measures of students who are multiply marginalized, on both race and class indicators.

Other new universities may also be unable to emulate UCR's path. The university's conversion to a new university capable of challenging existing status hierarchies was contingent upon particular institutional structures, unique historical events, exceptional organizational resources, and charismatic figures at key junctures, not to mention fortuitous timing. The shared standards of the UC system and the ability to extract funds from the state meant that UCR could enroll large numbers of students of color without losing its claim to elite status, even as it fell in stature relative to its peers. The environmental crisis that depopulated the campus, and the incredible racial diversity of California, created the conditions for UCR to establish a new model of growth that placed historically underrepresented students at the center. UCR also took the unusual step of creating cultural organizations that could support a growing population of Black and Latinx students, enabling leaders like Chancellor Orbach to develop a culture of inclusive excellence that others would consolidate, promote, and market. By the time a postsecondary culture of inclusive excellence had become widely valued, UCR was well positioned to stake a claim as a university of the future.

Riverside is not alone, however. A few new universities, most notably Arizona State University, have managed to capture public attention, under some similar conditions. But Riverside and its allies' abilities to continue changing the game will require resources. It will be tricky to keep up with the tactics of universities far better positioned to shift prestige hierarchies in their favor. Getting those resources is difficult in a racially stratified postsecondary system. Indeed, as we explore in the rest of the book, the siphoning of resources from new universities in the contemporary era constrains their potential to break the mold for the twenty-first-century research university.

2 *P3 Paradise*

On the same day that Ted Mitchell visited UC-Riverside and lavished praise upon the school, 350 miles to the northwest, the University of California–Merced was breaking ground on the biggest public-private partnership (or P3) in the history of US higher education. In the postsecondary sector, the P3 is an educational delivery strategy in which public universities contract private-sector entities to provide infrastructure no longer offered by the state. UCM had entered into a thirty-nine-year deal with Plenary Properties Merced, a consortium of private engineering, design, construction, maintenance, operations, and financial partners, in order to grow the campus. The deal was a consequence of the young university's efforts to meet the needs of its disadvantaged student population with exceptionally limited resources.

Let's set the scene. The groundbreaking ceremony for the Merced 2020 Project, named for the year in which the buildings were to be completed, took place in the campus's "South Bowl," a large indentation in the ground, with steps descending into a flat space of brittle grass and dirt. Golden shovels spiked in the soil demarcated one area as a dig spot, where photo ops would occur after officials spoke. A stage had been constructed nearby for this purpose. Rufus the Bobcat, the campus mascot, was working the crowd and dressed for the occasion in a suit and Chuck Taylor sneakers.

A line of students snaked around a tent offering 2020 "swag." Also popular were booths that produced keepsake pictures with a mock-up of the future campus in the background. Another tent, removed from the throngs of students, housed the officials—or "suits," as a student ethnographer referred to them. These middle-aged white men, in business attire, had arrived earlier in the day by helicopter. They seemed surprised when an ethnographer approached to inquire how they were affiliated with the event. "We're the contractors," one explained. "These guys are the architects" (pointing at three other men). The suits soon moved toward rows of white chairs set in front of the stage. It was clear that no students were allowed. As one crowd member remarked, "Oh, the important people are coming down now."

Chancellor Dorothy Leland was the first on stage. She asked the students to "Give me a shout-out," and, as they cheered, remarked that "our students represent the very best of California. They are the energy and diversity of the future." "Thanks" were offered to students, faculty, and the community. The chancellor continued with commentary about the expansion, which would nearly double the physical size of the campus. She claimed the ambitious project would allow "generations of young people all over California, most just like our students today," to be the "first of their families to attend a university." At this point, the yelling of protestors became impossible to ignore.

A group of nearly thirty students, all but a few of whom were of color, marched toward the stage chanting: "Power to the students," "2020 or bust, we choose bust," "Stop privatization of our education," and "We demand dignity and respect." Their signs read "Diversity ≠ Numbers," "We need adequate resources," and "Minorities are not profit." They were part of a student-led campus organization that had issued demands to the administration, including that "UC-Merced halt enrollment until basic needs are met." They wanted to "center conversations and vision on students — not economic interests, not physical capital, not projected growth, not exploitation, but student experiences in the institution."

Chancellor Leland was visibly flustered. She asked the two women on stage with her — including UC system president Janet Napolitano — "What do I do?" and was told to "Keep going!" She thanked the protestors and continued, explaining that Merced's largely Latinx schoolchildren had strongly advocated for a UC in their hometown: They sent "not just one, not two, not three, but 6,000 postcards [that] flooded the mailboxes of regents … with honest and straightforward and sincere statements of what a University of California campus in Merced would [mean] for … their community." President Napolitano suggested the 2020 P3 was a brilliant example of "how we could expand access to public research universities," particularly in an era of limited state support. During these comments the protestors weaved their way out of the crowd and moved to a nearby hill where they were just audible.

As mementos of that day, two sets of official groundbreaking photos stand out. The first set included the all-woman group of UC leaders who spoke at the ceremony, as well as several students of color. Another round of pictures depicted the chancellor and six white men — local government leaders and representatives of Plenary Properties Merced. The contrast is notable. The UC system has grown and flourished in part by supporting women, people of color, and low-income students. Without adequate state support, the system's newest university has become deeply reliant on a private partner that has no such imperative.[1]

UCM's 2020 Project underscores the challenges faced by the most resource-poor organizations serving a large percentage of historically under-represented racially marginalized students (URS), especially in a system with dwindling public investments. As student protestors correctly intuited, the race and class composition of the student body was related to the limited availability of funding and space, and the need to pursue an unconventional building strategy. In other words, the situation perfectly encapsulated elements of the postsecondary racial neoliberal cycle outlined in the introduction. Merced may not have had any other viable options. But, as we emphasize below, public-private partnerships are typically imperfect "solutions" for meeting the needs of disadvantaged populations. They are rarely employed when clear alternatives exist.

New universities are not alone in using P3s to build. As public universities try to stay viable in states that are not sufficiently contributing to higher education, funding infrastructure (new buildings, but also basic maintenance and retrofitting for climate-related events) has become exceptionally difficult. P3s already exist on many other campuses—but they are typically focused on student housing. If trends outside of higher education are any indicator, we suspect that new universities will be among the first and most aggressive adopters of public-private partnerships as a *modal* means of growth and maintenance, far beyond student housing. It is thus important to understand why some campuses might choose to adopt a large-scale P3, document how the process works, and identify potential downfalls.

Merced's Challenges

What are the challenges that led UC-Merced to pursue such a large P3 project? We highlight three important factors: 1) limited access to financial resources; 2) lack of intentionality in recruiting URS; and 3) absence of a coherent organizational identity around serving historically disadvantaged students.

A TWENTY-FIRST-CENTURY UNIVERSITY

UC-Merced should have been built half a century earlier. In fact, the 1960 California Master Plan for Higher Education called for the planning and development of additional university facilities in the San Joaquin Valley (a subset of the larger Central Valley and the eventual location of UCM), as well as in Los Angeles.[2] UC-Riverside's growth into a research university helped fulfill this promise for the LA area. Yet, UCM only opened many decades later. Why the delay?

The San Joaquin Valley is home to a large population of first-generation Mexican immigrants and well-established Mexican American families—many of whom are connected to farm work. Asian immigrants (specifically, Hmong, Thai, Cambodian, Laotian, and Vietnamese), who arrived following the Vietnam War, have also settled here. The Valley, often referred to as the "food basket of the world," is the most productive agricultural area in the country. Yet, these communities of color have little political voice, relative to coastal white communities. The San Joaquin Valley is also one of the most-impoverished areas in the nation, with a high percentage of residents living below the federal poverty line.[3] It suffers from limited access to clean air and water, employment opportunities, and health care. In short, communities in the San Joaquin Valley are subject to intense systemic racism. The withholding of research investment in the area is simply another manifestation of the same problem.[4]

UC regents who govern the system did not authorize a University of California for the San Joaquin Valley until 1989—nearly thirty years after the Master Plan. But in the early 1990s, an economic downturn shrank the state budget and slowed UC enrollment. Drastic cuts resulted, leading to staff layoffs, frozen wages, unfilled positions, and deferred maintenance.[5] During this time, the UC president and regents proposed discontinuing planning for the new campus, citing the need to preserve funding for existing campuses, including UC-Riverside. The project was at an impasse until 1997, when two state assemblymen proposed a compromise: UC-Merced would be funded outside of the UC system budget until 2010. Including UCM as a separate line item, however, made it vulnerable in future downturns. Indeed, in a major blow during the early 2000s, state legislators cut $162 million from the campus's capital budget in favor of preserving funds for an energy crisis.[6]

Site selection was another political football. Most visitors to the San Joaquin Valley bypass Merced, unless headed to Yosemite National Park. Many Valley residents were thus shocked when Fresno, a more central and larger urban area, was not selected. However, as an editorial articulated in 2002, "MERCED was chosen for the campus primarily because of the offer of free land, because of pressure from [white] politicians who wanted to position themselves as saviors of the valley, a politically important region, and because developers wanted to make a killing on adjacent land—not as a result of any rational needs or efficiency studies."[7] While the land was an incredible gift, it was also undeveloped—not near existing electrical lines, plumbing for water, or sewers—thus increasing costs.

Outside of the supportive Latinx community of Merced, the campus also faced many local detractors. White conservatives voiced concerns about the encroachment of "liberal" students and professors. Others argued that a research university in the Valley would only serve a relatively small number of students, while large community colleges in the area desperately needed more funding. Environmental activists opposing campus construction were buoyed by the discovery of endangered fairy shrimp on the land.[8] These and other hurdles delayed the campus's opening, and every delay fed negative public sentiment. California Senate president pro tem John Burton even referred to UC-Merced as "the biggest boondoggle ever."[9]

The accumulation of delays meant that the ninth undergraduate-serving UC campus would be built in a much less supportive era than virtually all other public research universities in the country.[10,11] Merced did not benefit from Cold War prosperity. Shifting funding strategies in the state instead helped prisons to spring up in the Valley.[12] Once the initial and reduced contributions from the state were gone—used to launch the small campus—the school was on its own. As one UC Office of the President representative noted to us, by the time Democratic governor Jerry Brown took office in 2011, California "just basically stopped issuing debt on behalf of anyone, [except for] specialized projects like high-speed rail or water." A lack of built infrastructure, and no way to pay for new development, presented an almost insurmountable problem for the campus.

In addition, UC-Merced would enter the postsecondary field with the process of "financialization" well underway, meaning that the practice of financing a university looked dramatically different than in past decades. Financialization is the spread of financial markets and market logics that encourage the pursuit of profit through financial channels, rather than trade and commodity production.[13] If state defunding is one prong of the neoliberal project outlined in the introduction, financialization is another. Concretely, financialization means that universities are increasingly reliant on financial instruments and investment returns to operate and incur large debts to acquire the necessary capital to meet basic needs.

The impact of financialization is uneven. As Charlie Eaton and colleagues illustrate, wealthy private universities actually benefit from this arrangement, as endowment assets are heavily concentrated at these schools, despite the fact that they enroll relatively few students. Wealthy public universities are still okay, as borrowing costs are usually outpaced by funding increases from endowment investment returns. But less wealthy state universities serving larger shares of URS and low-income students are slammed by borrowing costs and lack substantial endowments.[14]

UC-Merced, with its opening in 2005, did not have time to grow endowment assets. And while UCM benefited from UC backing in the 2020 Project, the school was still impacted by its youth. It certainly did not profit from many decades of investment strategies shared among hedge fund managers and other "financial elite" that have shored up wealthier universities' endowment assets.[15]

Notably, the circumstances faced by UC-Merced may be unique, but the resulting structural and financial woes are not. Many public universities lack adequate and functional classroom, office, and research space, along with the capital to remedy these problems.[16] Schools around the country, even those built decades ago, are not necessarily in a much better position than UCM. Buildings decay without (and even with) sufficient maintenance. This is a looming crisis for Riverside, too, as previously state-of-the-art buildings have begun to crumble. Universities serving large numbers of URS are at particular risk given unequal and racialized access to financial resources in the postsecondary system.

WHITE FLIGHT

UCM was expected to serve a larger share of Latinx and low-income students than most other UCs because of its location. Indeed, when the doors to UCM's first non-residential building finally opened, the potential for a majority non-white student body was immediately realized. The undergraduate population was predominately Asian (37 percent), with a nearly even proportion of white and Latinx students (at 26.2 percent and 24 percent, respectively). This meant that the school, from its birth, met or nearly met numeric qualifications for two different Minority Serving Institution designations.

By 2016, however, the campus was half Latinx and only 11.2 percent white. This change was accompanied by a parallel increase in low-income students. UCM went from just under 40 percent of the student body being eligible for federal Pell Grants to just over 60 percent. These changes occurred at a much faster pace and on a greater scale than administrators might have predicted. Certainly, all UC campuses during this period experienced some growth in Latinx and low-income student populations, but none so sharply as UC-Merced.[17]

If UCR's transformation into a new university is a story about strategic utilization, UCM's new university status appears to be largely unintentional.

As a newly opened university, with no baseline student population, it would have been difficult for Merced leadership to accurately forecast what was to come. Still, the school could have paralleled UCR's approach from a decade earlier by ramping up recruitment in surrounding Latinx communities and schools.

Instead, UC-Merced initially focused on recruiting outside the San Joaquin and larger Central Valley. The first enrollment director, as one research staff member put it, "had an interesting philosophy. He said, 'It doesn't matter if I recruit in the Central Valley. I'll get [the same] amount of kids whether I spend a hundred dollars or a hundred thousand dollars.' He told his recruiters, 'If I ever catch you in a Valley school, I will ream you. You spend your time in the Bay Area and LA.'" The assumption was that a higher density of UC-eligible students in urban areas outside the Valley would create a greater yield at a lower cost. Later directors did not express this sentiment, but consistently over the years, only about a third of incoming students have come from the Central Valley. Changing this would require the kind of intensive effort that Orbach and his team used in inland California, as described in the previous chapter.

Another possibility is that Latinx students, who fueled the growth of the campus, crowded out white, and to a lesser extent, Asian students. However, the average acceptance rate between 2005 and 2016 was 79.8 percent and did not fluctuate substantially year to year. Yield rates have been relatively low, at 6 percent in 2005 and 13 percent in 2016. That is to say, most students who get in do not attend UC-Merced. It seems unlikely, therefore, that white and Asian populations have been increasingly unable to gain admission to the school.

The process of becoming predominately Latinx and low-income is better explained by what neighborhood and education scholars refer to as "white flight." As Douglas Massey and Nancy Denton argue in *American Apartheid: Segregation and the Making of the Underclass*, whites are often concerned about racial mixing because they perceive marginalized racial groups as a threat to social status.[18] Research on primary and secondary schools in the US suggests that white families draw on racialized beliefs about intelligence and success to read the presence of Brown and Black students in K–12 schools as a marker of low organizational status.[19] White families thus select into schools that are more heavily populated by whites. Although rarely recognized, a similar process may occur in universities. That is, when university populations include more Latinx and/or Black students, whites may begin to code the school as less desirable, accelerating demographic shifts.

At UC-Merced, white flight is most apparent after 2011. This year is an inflection point; the count of white students enrolled in the university drops—even during a period of growth (see figure 2.1 below). The dip coincides with UC-Merced's new status as the second Hispanic Serving Institution (or HSI) in the UC System, after Riverside. UCM's HSI standing was announced at the end of the 2010 spring semester. The first new class to be recruited under the HSI distinction arrived in 2011 and, for the first time, the number of white students was smaller than in prior years. Notably, a parallel dip in the number of Asian students attending the university occurred just a year later, despite the fact that UC-Merced became an Asian American and Native American Pacific Islander Serving Institution (or AANAPISI).

Administrators and staff involved in recruitment readily noted the decline in numbers of white students on the campus. They wondered about how to manage this challenge, particularly when it dovetailed with class dynamics. As an enrollment manager explained:

> I'm concerned about the Caucasian students.... It's just not that many white folks. They're not producing as many of them anymore. For those that are here [in California], universities back East and Midwest need more so they're recruiting.... Those folks want to be with people who resemble them, [and] there's places to go if you want to go. I used to call it white flight but now I just call it socioeconomic flight. They want to get away. They want to be with people like them.

He pointed out that affluent white students may be targeted by and selecting whiter universities out-of-state, as well as private schools. Like their racially marginalized peers, white students who remained on campus were more likely to have limited class resources. Similarly, the Asian population at UCM in 2016 included a substantial number of URS from subgroups that often have fewer educational and financial resources.[20]

White flight is also socioeconomic flight, in that it is typically affluent white families who have the resources to flee contexts where URS live and attend school.[21] At UC-Merced, the percentage of federal Pell Grant recipients (who are usually from households with an income of $30,000 or less) gradually converges with and then begins to surpass the percentage of non-Pell recipients around 2009 (see figure 2.2 below). This year also corresponds with the trough of the Great Recession in the US and a larger-than-usual jump in Pell Grants funded by the federal government. However, it is likely that, at least for UC-Merced, white flight substantially contributed to the relative growth of low-income students on campus.

UCM's accelerated demographic shift shaped the student population in

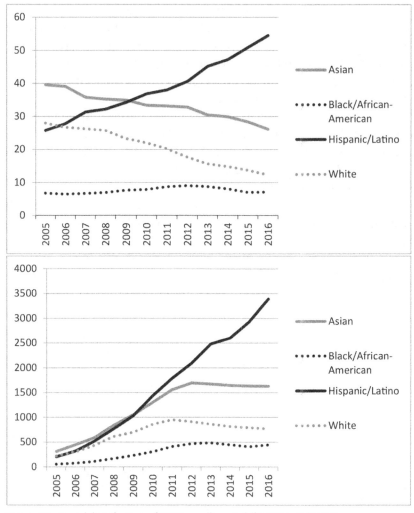

Figure 2.1. Racial distribution of UCM enrollment, fall 2005 to fall 2016.

Panel 1: By percent; Panel 2: By count.

Note: Data are drawn from the University of California Info Center, Fall Enrollment Headcounts.

ways that were consequential for survival in a postsecondary system heavily funded by student tuition. The interlinked processes of white and socioeconomic flight that increased the marginalized student population at UCM meant that the school could not turn to wealthy, white families as a primary source of financial support. Neither could UCR, but school leaders were better prepared to leverage commitment to the students that they intentionally admitted as a resource—first as a source of state funding and later as an or-

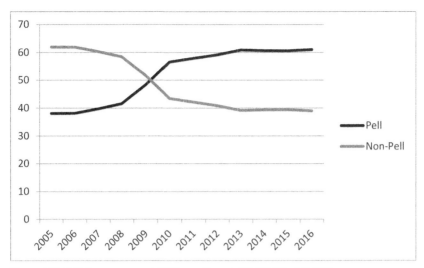

Figure 2.2. Pell Grant status of UCM enrollment, fall 2005 to fall 2016.

Note: Data are drawn from the University of California Info Center, Fall Enrollment Headcounts.

ganizational identity they could promote to granting agencies interested in student outcomes, philanthropists valuing equity in higher education, and corporate actors seeking to diversify their workforce (see chapter 7).

Thus, the degree to which campuses actively seek to enroll URS may be relevant in understanding how effectively and quickly the school can translate the student population into attention, status, and funding. We might surmise, therefore, that organizations going all in on the transformation from predominately white to new university, versus those that do so inadvertently, are better positioned for financial security. As the case of UCR also illustrates, deep commitment to conversion also means cultural transformation, which was happening, but still incomplete, at UCM.

ORGANIZATIONAL IDENTITY IN FLUX

A cohesive campus narrative about UC-Merced is still emerging. This is largely a function of youth. The university has had little time to develop a stable and unified organizational identity. There have been several attempts to project an identity to the public: for example, a *New York Times* piece about serving undocumented students, as discussed in chapter 7, and efforts to claim a "green campus" label (often foiled by the fact that rankings typically measure *improvement* in green technology, whereas UCM was simply built "green"). However, nothing has yet stuck as the defining feature of the school.

In contrast to the religious-like zeal and shared focus of UCR administrators, faculty, and staff, at Merced there were many who deeply cared about the student population but no widespread consensus about what UC-Merced is or does; for instance, a majority of interviewees never touched on the location of the campus in the San Joaquin Valley, the school's HSI designation, and the benefits (rather than the deficits) of the student population. There was not a seamless integration of the university's research aspirations with issues of access and inclusion. Rather, there were a lot of exceptionally supportive individuals and seemingly independent ideas about UCM rising to the surface.

If Riverside is any indication, claiming an organizational identity around "inclusive excellence" requires public recognition and incorporation of local marginalized populations into the university. At UCR, early partnerships with surrounding churches and community organizations, some formed in Chancellor Ray Orbach's era, have persisted, and new commitments have developed. Ties to the local community strengthened the university's position with the state and grounded the staff and faculty's recognition of their mission. In contrast, UCM's ties to the San Joaquin Valley, at least in the first decade of its existence, were less extensive and hard to recognize.

For example, UC-Merced funds a Center for Educational Partnerships (CEP), with the goal of increasing the college-going rate across the Valley. Data suggest that it has been successful. The CEP is, as an affiliated administrator noted, "*The* unit that has allowed the chancellor to be able to travel across the Valley and say, 'Hey, you know, this is the work that we do at UC-Merced for your community.'" Yet, very few people on campus are aware of the CEP. It is located in Fresno—over an hour away from Merced.[22] Furthermore, the grants funding the CEP require that it remain separate from the campus's admissions and recruitment efforts. Almost none of the students impacted by the CEP attend UC-Merced; among the UCs, UC-Davis and UC-Santa Barbara are the most likely to enroll these students.[23]

UCR's organizational identity is also a result of a lasting legacy of administrative engagement with marginalized student populations, which does not exist at UCM. Chancellor Orbach's unregulated, unscripted, and regular contact with students, which (as we explain in chapter 4) may be an artifact of a bygone era in higher education, never evolved at UC-Merced. Orbach's leadership also involved getting faculty and staff buy-in, at every level, with the agenda of supporting marginalized students. Chancellor Leland, like most contemporary university leaders, was more outward than inward facing. Under her leadership, the campus was oriented around a pressing need—survival.

The 2020 Project

When Dorothy Leland stepped into the role of chancellor in May 2011, she inherited a herculean task. The UC system had generously issued a new memorandum of understanding (MOU) guaranteeing a higher level of funding for UCM, until such a point that the school could become "self-sustaining" (i.e., function with the same amount of state funds per full-time student as its sister campuses). But the clock was ticking. UCM had until 2020 to reach the 10,000 students that analyses suggested would be the magical tipping point for self-sufficiency. Meeting this goal would require doubling the campus in size, without any obvious funding source in sight. As leadership reported, "There were still the drums beating out there that basically said, 'You … shouldn't be a research university.' There was some talk about becoming a branch campus of UC-Davis or something, and … that endangered the institution. It was not something that we could say, 'Well we can hang on,' because I wasn't sure we could."

Unable to devise a solution that would quell the ominous doubts surrounding the campus, university leadership turned to outside expertise. Chancellor Leland asked the chief financial officer of the UC system if he could recommend someone with experience in public-sector infrastructure finance. The chief financial officer suggested a relatively young Dan Feitelberg, a former employee of his at J. P. Morgan, the large banking conglomerate. Coming directly from private finance, Feitelberg was intimately familiar with P3s (public-private partnerships); in fact, he had helped engineer several of these deals.

There were not many alternatives. But once the decision to hire Feitelberg was made, it seemed likely that the campus would utilize a P3. Feitelberg was familiar with private-sector strategies from his time at J. P. Morgan, making a public-private partnership seem not only logical, but inevitable. He soon moved into the role of vice chancellor of planning and budget, where he had a great deal of influence. The chancellor relied on Feitelberg for the development of the 2020 Project, and UCM administration would dub him "Boy Wonder" for his ability to solve a seemingly intractable problem.

WHAT IS A P3?

At this point it is useful to provide more context on public-private partnerships, which are likely unfamiliar to many readers. P3s occur when local, state, or federal agencies contract private-sector entities in order to provide services or infrastructure for public use. Globally, P3s are used to provide education, food, water, housing, sanitation, and medical care to marginalized populations. They have become central to the agendas of large international aid agencies, such as the World Bank (WB), Organisation for Economic Cooperation and Development (OECD), and United Nations Children's Fund (UNICEF).[24] In the US, they reflect a long and growing reliance on private organizations for public social provision.[25] Medicare and Medicaid, for instance, have made payments to private providers since their inception.[26] Similarly, in the 1980s, the federal government withdrew from building affordable housing, instead utilizing private landlords, nonprofit providers, and vouchers.[27]

State lawmakers more recently have relied on P3s as a solution to repair and replace crumbling public infrastructure, such as major roadways, bridges, and transportation systems. P3s are a form of "backdoor borrowing," circumventing laws that require voter approval to accrue more debt.[28] Because the private sector can provide the financial backing necessary to complete a project, P3s may even appear to make money appear out of thin air. Ultimately, however, state entities must provide payments for the services provided by private entities, potentially in the form of tolls or taxes.

Advocates argue that features of P3s reduce time to completion and overall cost. Ideally, private investors are committed to quickly and economically finishing a project, as any unexpected expenses eat into profit. These consortia also bring together teams who are skilled at advancing different aspects of a project; designers and engineers can work with those responsible for operation and maintenance, such that the end goal is not just a complete project, but one that will continue to function at a reasonable cost for decades to come.[29] This is particularly appealing to governmental entities coping with the accumulating effects of deferred maintenance on prior public works projects. Arguments for P3s are also, not inconsequentially, consistent with the broader neoliberal project of limiting state intervention in the economy.

Those who are more critical point out that the outcomes of P3s may depend on the financial motives of private partners. Partnerships between nonprofit and governmental entities are more likely to take into account elements of social welfare. In contrast, the bottom-line goal of most for-profit partners is to make money. Ideally, profit and social welfare could both be achieved in a P3, but when profit is at stake, social welfare may not be a concern of private partners.[30] P3s offload short-term financial risks on private entities, and for-profit agents do not take these risks without the promise of significant returns. In short, there is money to be made off public needs.

Public-private partnerships have emerged in the US postsecondary sector to solve a very particular problem. They are a useful tool for college campuses seeking to update or build new student housing.[31] The revenue streams provided by student housing fees make these projects especially desirable for private partners. At the same time, decreased capital project funding, campus housing shortages, and increased competition for non-resident students, who often desire housing bells and whistles,[32] motivate campuses to pursue these partnerships.

P3 housing projects are anticipated, underway, or completed at many campuses around the country. UC-Berkeley's 781-bed Bancroft Hall, Columbus Avenue Student Apartments at Northeastern University, and the Greek Leadership Village at Arizona State University are three examples of projects with American Campus Communities (or ACC), which describes itself as "the nation's largest developer, owner, and manager of high-quality student housing and apartment communities."[33] Housing projects can, however, also fold in non-revenue-generating spaces, such as classrooms and cultural centers. This is an increasingly common way to meet space needs, without raising tuition or taking on new debt. In addition, some campuses are now pursuing other revenue-generating projects through P3s—including campus hotels, dining services, retail spaces, parking garages, and athletic fields.

These partnerships have been hailed by commentators as a new "silver bullet" for campus development.[34] The now-annual P3 Higher Education Summit website notes that "Public-private partnerships (P3s) are delivering critical infrastructure for colleges and universities across the country." The summit promises to bring together senior management from universities, along with representatives in architecture, construction, engineering, investment, and legal industries, to make these deals. The 2018 summit involved thirty-six private firm sponsors—including investment banking giant Goldman Sachs, private equity firm Alvarez & Marsal (A&M) Capital, the aforementioned ACC, and Plenary Groups (the parent company of Plenary Properties Merced)—and 123 featured schools, including new universities, community colleges, regional colleges and universities, and several large state flagships.[35]

The breadth of postsecondary organizations featured at the summit suggests that P3s are not just happening in new universities, or even in schools serving largely URS populations. However, these deals may be more rapidly evolving as an encompassing strategy for educational delivery, rather than as a solution for student housing, at the most resource-poor universities with the most-disadvantaged students. The Merced 2020 Project is a helpful illustration.

The Merced P3. The Merced deal deviates substantially from the typical student housing P3 formula. It is not only about building "extras" to enhance university status or to meet housing needs. Indeed, the project involves virtually all elements of a college campus—from the more glamorous competition swimming pool, to the less glamorous loading docks, parking lots, basic laboratories, and computational space. While housing and dining generate revenue, a majority of campus spaces will not. Instead, the P3 is creating the basic infrastructure needed for Merced to enroll even higher numbers of underserved California residents.

It is no understatement to say that postsecondary leaders and lawmakers across the country are watching intently. The school is a test case for the viability and limits of P3s in higher education. Indeed, with half of the campus built by more traditional means and half of the campus constructed via a P3, a natural experiment will be unfolding at UC-Merced over time.[36] As we detail later, the fact that this experiment is being carried out with low-income URS is not incidental. UC-Merced is taking a great risk, one that would be inconceivable to better-resourced universities, because it has few other viable options.

According to UCM leadership, typical approaches to developing infrastructure were too flawed or simply not possible. In the past, if the system wanted to construct a new building, it requested to have it itemized on the state budget, such that state funds would directly cover the project. The UC might also obtain tax-exempt bonds, which were eventually repaid to the state. However, in Merced's case, obtaining additional state capital financing was unlikely. Although the UC system contributed half of its limited funds available for capital projects until 2020, Merced did not have enough money to complete payment on the project within eight to ten years. UCM's ability to maintain the buildings once they were built was also in question.

Feitelberg, UCM's P3 architect, arrived at the conclusion that an availability payment concession approach would be the best way forward.[37] In this model, the university would contract a private entity for five different services bundled together. It would be faster than going service-by-service and dealing with five separate entities.[38] UC-Merced would then pay for the availability of functional buildings during the duration of the thirty-nine-year deal. The contract did not transfer property rights to the private partner or allow for the external collection of revenue. Feitelberg also concluded that the issue with two prior P3 deals in California that cost the public $300 million more than a traditional procurement method was the extent of funding provided by private entities.[39] Taking on 100 percent of financing raised the risk for private partners, who valued the risk transfer by inflating the cost. UCM instead opted for a 60/40 split, whereby the school took on more debt to lower the financing costs, but still obtained funds from the private partner, both out of necessity and to ensure that the private entity had "enough skin in the game for the contract to hold them accountable."

The details for acceptable building performance were also hashed out. If at any point during the contract buildings were not performing up to established criteria, the university would reduce their payments. For example, once construction was completed, the rooms "shall be lit, the temperature controls should be between 68 and 74 degrees, the elevators need to work, we can't have leaky roofs, and pavement cracks can't be more than a quarter of an inch."[40] If building performance fell outside of acceptable thresholds, then payments provided by the university would go down, presumably motivating the private partner to remedy the situation. Because UCM had faced expensive legal issues on prior building projects, another goal was to reduce financial risks associated with litigation. Feitelberg believed this approach would disincentivize legal action against the university, as the university could stop payment to the private partner until issues were resolved.

There were a number of hurdles to reach approval. The state legislature's consent was technically unnecessary, but it needed to go through system leadership. At one point, the UC system president reportedly told the chancellor that she was "banned ... from using the word 'innovation' because the regents [of the UC system] were afraid of innovation." There were also concerns from union workers. American Federation of State, County, and Municipal Employees (AFSCME) representatives were assured that existing union jobs would remain union jobs, and that UC employees would still conduct janitorial services. The developer was also required to pay prevailing wages to its workers. These assurances, however, came in the context of large numbers of private contract workers in the UC who work alongside career workers for years or even decades, only to receive a fraction of pay and benefits.[41]

Pulling off this large and unusual public-private partnership has made UCM leadership, especially Dan Feitelberg, mini-celebrities in the P3 field. The campus and the architects of the deal have won numerous awards.[42] Members of UCM administration have presented this model to interested audiences across the country, and it has significantly advanced the careers of several administrators. Most notably, in 2017 Feitelberg left UCM for a principal position at KPMG, one of the big four accounting firms in the US. In this job, he will continue to do strategic capital investment work with governments and higher education organizations—but from the private side of the equation. And when Chancellor Leland retired in 2019, the man who recommended Feitelberg for the job became interim chancellor.

UCM leadership has worked to manage the public image associated with the project, particularly surrounding its relationship with a private partner. The word "private" is almost nonexistent in university materials about the deal. As a high-level official strongly asserted, "It's not privatization." This is correct: UC-Merced maintains its own property and continues to collect its own revenue. In response to student protestors' charge that UCM is a "neoliberal institution," a top administrator noted:

> This is a misunderstanding about what I'm saying when I talk about the economic impact of this project. This is about job creation and [building] a very important entity. I know these people care about [that]. But framing it as a neoliberal issue means that it's putting money … in the pocket of Big Business or privatizing in a way that takes choice and flexibility … away from public entities and the public sector.

It is a fact, however, that this partnership moves services typically managed by state and university actors—including financing, operation, and maintenance of major building systems—to a private entity. More profoundly, the functionality and existence of the university will depend, in direct ways, on a relationship with a for-profit consortium, constraining the public's ability to put student welfare in the forefront. Recall from the introduction that restricting public demands for public goods is a primary aim of the larger neoliberal project.

WHAT COULD GO WRONG?

Only a handful of non-administrators were involved in planning the 2020 Project, and they were asked not to share information with others. This type of information vacuum is common with P3s, limiting the ability of the public to question, slow, or stop a deal.[43] It is important for involved communities and constituencies to know what might go wrong. Below we specify five ways that the contract may fail UC-Merced, potentially leading to higher costs and lower-quality experiences.

Faulty Assumptions. The UC-Merced project hangs on a series of budgetary assumptions. The school must be able to meet its payments to Plenary Properties Merced over the duration of the contract in order to ensure timely delivery of buildings, support, and services. Figuring out how to do this requires multi-year financial planning. Unfortunately, university budgeting is notoriously complex. At UC-Merced, this issue is compounded by the newness of the campus and membership in a system that is, itself, financially byzantine.

At the start of the 2020 Project development, the first task was to get a basic handle on the budget. This took several years. The information was then used to project out, building in assumptions about future cash flow. Several assumptions that became baked into the model, however, were highly improbable—for instance, a five- to sevenfold increase in non-resident students. A few staff questioned the assumptions. One noted:

> I kept raising my hand and said, "Does everyone realize this isn't gonna happen?" And the enrollment manager at the time, he was a great guy, he says, "We're doing this, and you're the only one who will ever look at this again. It's a political exercise, okay. So don't worry about realism. All right? This is Picasso. Just make some art." What they don't realize is Dan Feitelberg is sitting there saying, "Well, I got a great document to base 2020 on."

To be fair, it would have been difficult, potentially even impossible, to do anything but project a plausible fiction for this university, given the lack of stable trends. Yet, the inability to begin with accurate assumptions suggests that there may be some financial reckoning moving forward. Indeed, the university was doing deficit spending in the 2016–2017 academic year, when it had not expected to do so, and was encouraging employees to "identify new revenue streams" as a means to make up the gap.

Because P3 deals are financed across decades, errors in assumptions can be dramatically compounded, leading to serious financial shortfalls that are less likely to occur with shorter-term, more typical approaches to campus building. Financial shortfalls will necessarily lead to cuts in other areas of university expenditure, such as instructional support or financial aid—often the two largest flexible budget items. Cuts in these areas, as we argue in later chapters, are particularly damaging for racially and economically marginalized students.

Lack of Control and Limited Flexibility. Administrators readily admitted that "we lost some control" in the P3. A common illustration, provided by more than one respondent, involved colored tiles. As a high-level official explained, "We lost control of the way in which the detailed decisions that … end users or initial end users will make about a building [are determined]—you know, pink tile [or] blue tile, this or [that], but we substituted that for a very comprehensive … set of technical and design standards that the developer is required to meet."

This scenario downplays the degree to which university inhabitants lose the ability to tailor the physical environment. Private entities may fail to meet specifications if the subsequent savings outweigh the potential penalties of not staying within the contract. There is also room to push the edges of acceptability. For example, is a quarter-inch-wide crack still acceptable when it runs for fifty feet in the pavement along the foundation of a building? Even a contract that is as detailed as the UCM P3 cannot cover everything. When building inhabitants experience infrastructure issues that fall within (or even outside of) the range of specifications, there may be little that they can do. Infrastructure that would normally get fixed under a traditional model might be left unattended or generate additional costs.

Inability to Accommodate Change. Public-private partnerships can be thought of as "incomplete contracts," as they do not cover all possible aspects of infrastructure provision that may emerge during the contracted period.[44] For example, public entities may be held captive when previously unanticipated needs, such as for more space or technology, arise. And, because universities are evolving organisms, change is a given.

The equipment built into postsecondary infrastructure requires continual revising—sometimes on an annual basis. Universities often retrofit "smart" classrooms, rewire digital networks, and upgrade computing systems. New faculty members have specific needs: for example, a temperature-controlled space for sensitive archival documents or a lab with cutting-edge equipment. Pedagogical best practices shift over time, such that smaller, hands-on seminars with moveable furniture and space to interact are now viewed as more supportive of learning than traditional lecture halls.

Meeting these needs is important for the quality of the educational experience offered to students. Furthermore, with mounting pressure to obtain research grant dollars, the ability to update infrastructure is essential. However, private partners have no financial incentive to make alterations outside of contract obligations and may force universities to pay a high additional price for any changes. The incredible length of many P3s—for multiple decades, even half a century or more—raises the likelihood of universities encountering unanticipated needs.

Constraints on Future Funding. UC-Merced will be embroiled with the 2020 Project for nearly forty years. During this time, it will have fewer available funding streams to collateralize for future borrowing using more traditional, less risky borrowing vehicles. Merced's initial success, at least in building the 2020 portion of the campus, will likely encourage the UC and the state legislature to suggest that additional infrastructure needs be addressed in a similar fashion. Thus, the 2020 P3 deal could increase pressure for future capital investments to be done as similar public-private partnerships, further compounding any risks.[45]

Mismatched Interests. A final risk is rooted in a critical contradiction underlying postsecondary P3 deals. Mismatched interests between for-profit and public partners increase the likelihood of public interests being undermined. A brief illustration of another budding public-private partnership in the UC highlights the nature of this problem.

On a visit to the UC Office of the President, Laura intersected with three men in fancy suits representing one of eight developers who had been selected to bid on future P3 student housing projects in the UC system. They had a proposal for UC-Riverside's campus and were in the lobby chatting loudly among themselves as they waited to make their pitch. They repeatedly used the phrase "monetizing beds," which refers to converting student residents, or their "beds," into revenue. The developers concluded that with bigger rooms and more amenities, the housing units would be more desirable and, thus, more profitable.

Yet, the housing project at Riverside, as well as one at Santa Cruz, was part of a larger affordable housing initiative. While the developers' interests were in "monetizing beds," the UC was hoping to increase its supply of lower-cost housing—particularly in the wake of data revealing that many UC students cannot afford to live in the expensive areas surrounding their campuses.[46] This quick observation suggests just how mismatched the interests of universities can be with those of their (in this case, potential) private partners. The lack of a shared vision is problematic. We might expect that developers' interests in profit would, at a minimum, reduce the ability of the UC to address housing cost issues.

At UC-Merced, the carefully designed contract is supposed to serve as protection for the university—ensuring that the interests of developers remain balanced with those of university constituents. But the nature of the arrangement is such that the fundamental goals of the "partners" are at odds. Private entities aggressively pursue profit, while public university constituents, especially students and their families, often need access to high-quality, low-trouble, affordable infrastructure.

P3s for Disadvantaged Populations

UC-Merced will be higher education's guinea pig for large-scale, access-oriented P3 development. It is not surprising, we argue, that the school is located in an impoverished area and serves racially and economically marginalized students. UC-Merced may be part of an emerging pattern—one that is obvious in other arenas, such as medical care and housing—whereby P3s are concentrated among disadvantaged populations.

Notably, in 2019, Riverside began to think about following in Merced's footsteps by using an extensive P3 to provide the infrastructure needed for substantial growth over the next fifteen years. Outside of the UC system, we can also see examples of heavier P3 utilization among cash-strapped universities serving marginalized students. As an architectural and engineering firm involved in a P3 project at the University of Wisconsin-Milwaukee described:

> As with other universities nationally, the University of Wisconsin has seen decreased financial support and a tuition freeze from State government across its multi-campus system. Needing both new residence halls and space for the fine arts, the University of Wisconsin-Milwaukee looked at the historic Kenilworth Complex, a full-block, multi-building historic warehouse that it utilized for storage.... With no ability to finance the project itself, the University turned to the development community for financial solutions.... Familiar with the local market dynamics, the developer monetized the intrinsic value of the University's land, buildings, parking, and potential retail and rent from students to finance the renovation.[47]

UW-Milwaukee serves one of the poorest and most racially segregated cities in the country and is severely underfunded, especially given the needs of its student population.

A P3 is rarely ever utilized in a "best case" scenario. That is, schools that can avoid building this way have typically done so. It is unlikely that more elite schools with substantial endowments will undertake P3s for basic infrastructure provision. In contrast, public universities serving URS and low-income students in their states may be pushed to do so. As detailed in the introduction, postsecondary racial neoliberalism limits the resources available to these organizations. They are thus more vulnerable in interactions with private entities in a way that schools serving predominately white, affluent students are not.

Certainly, many predominately white public universities will eventually need to rebuild as Cold War structures crumble and climate change introduces new challenges. If current trends in postsecondary funding continue, they too may come to rely on P3s. However, we might predict that P3s will be most heavily concentrated in poor regions, in states with low postsecondary funding, and among universities filled with racially and/or economically marginalized students—schools that will struggle to extract support from middle-class white taxpayers. To confirm (or disconfirm) these predictions, researchers should be tracking the number, scope, and location of post-secondary P3s around the country to understand when and which universities turn to public-private partnerships, especially as an encompassing strategy for educational delivery.

The use of a P3 would not matter if these partnerships produced the same outcomes as other methods of financing campus growth and maintenance. Policy entrepreneurs often staunchly claim that "partnerships work" to solve issues of access, affordability, and opportunity that face marginalized groups and fail to point out downsides. However, it is difficult to say with any certainty that a P3 approach will improve conditions for disadvantaged individuals and families; in fact, the opposite may occur.[48] Research on housing, for instance, illustrates the potential for P3s to prove deleterious, in some cases providing remote living environments of insufficient quality while developers, nonetheless, profit.[49]

The limited evidence on the effects of university outsourcing to private companies, more broadly—for everything from grounds maintenance, dining, bookstore operations, food services, custodial services, and IT, to academic grading, curriculum design, assessment, classroom instruction, and organizational management—is mixed.[50] However, researchers have shown that there are risks associated with economic "opportunism," especially when outsourcing core university functions.[51] For example, stressed administrators may allow the quality of education to degrade if outsourcing appears to resolve pressing fiscal concerns or offer new sources of revenue.

Ultimately, the primary goal of private partners is profit, not social equity. Yet, it can be hard for the public to see how this may create potentially intractable conflicts. As Jacob Hacker concludes, privatized social welfare approaches tend to foster "subterranean politics," whereby public awareness of the costs and benefits of the arrangement is low, information is poorly distributed, and structures for mobilization are limited.[52] In short, the public is generally poorly informed about the potential risks and has few avenues for addressing them. At the same time, neoliberal ideology insists that private enterprise is the best possible means of achieving social equity, regardless of performance.

This is unfortunate, as it may only be through vigilance that the more troubling outcomes of P3s can be evaded. Detailed contracts are not enough to avoid the erosion of the social equity goals associated with public universities.[53] Advocacy groups can play an important and ongoing role in moving these partnerships in directions that are more favorable to public beneficiaries.[54] However, at UC-Merced, as in many contexts, those with concerns did not always have access to mechanisms for oversight or intervention. P3s make it exceptionally difficult to pin down who is responsible for and has the authority to fix problems.[55]

We do not yet know the full implications of P3s for public universities. At a minimum, however, P3s will further remove the state from the responsibility of providing higher education, especially for populations that have experienced systematic disadvantage.[56] It may be harder to extract public money when P3s appear to "solve" the problem of postsecondary infrastructure without upfront public investment. State leadership may point to public-private partnerships as alternatives to increasing postsecondary spending, reducing the pressure to act.

This chapter provided an organizational story that stands in stark contrast to the narrative in chapter 1. UC-Riverside has been able to leverage its advantages in ways that publicly challenge racialized status hierarchies. In contrast, Merced has quietly been moving up the rankings (from 165 to 136 in the 2019 rankings, and from 136 to 104 in 2020), as the school has instead been focused on survival. In many ways, though, these two new universities are more alike than different. Thus, the next chapter considers UC-Riverside and UC-Merced together, in the larger context of the University of California system. We argue that new universities often do the work of boosting the system-level image of diversity and equity. However, these schools are increasingly disadvantaged by changes in the funding structure of postsecondary education.

3 *Running Political Cover*

The One University (or 1U) Campaign was launched in 2018 by a coalition of faculty and students from across the University of Michigan's three campuses. The goal? To redistribute system resources more evenly. The Dearborn and Flint campuses, like Merced and Riverside, serve a disproportionately large share of marginalized students from within the state (Black and low-income students, in particular) but only receive a tiny portion of the financial resources available to the flagship Ann Arbor campus.[1]

As an open letter from Dearborn and Flint educators and community members states:

> There is a moral imperative for a public university to commit resources to its most economically and racially diverse student bodies. At Flint and Dearborn, these are the students we serve.... We work, both in and outside of the classroom, to provide life-changing opportunities that many of our students would not otherwise be able to afford or access.... And yet we frequently find our campuses unable to fully support ... this vision. On both campuses, transformational programs such as study abroad and music are underfunded. Scholarships that allow students to avoid crushing debt burdens are not funded to the scale of the problem. And money is difficult to find for things such as salaries for lecturers, professional development, and time for research and course improvement. At Flint, the College of Arts and Sciences, Flint's largest instructional unit, has no recourse but to run in structural deficit. All of this has negative effects on our students, staff, and faculty, disproportionately impacting the Michigan students that most need this support.

The letter voices frustration that the state and university system fail to adequately support campuses enrolling disadvantaged populations. Indeed,

Dearborn and Flint students pay 80 percent of Ann Arbor tuition, but the per-student state funding on these campuses is only about a quarter of Ann Arbor's per-student funding.[2] In addition, roughly half of the Ann Arbor campus is non-resident, bringing in extraordinary amounts of funding not available to the largely in-state Dearborn and Flint campuses.

The dynamics at play in the University of Michigan system are hardly unique. This chapter is about how public university systems distribute their student populations and resources across campuses—and the relationship between the two, especially in the context of postsecondary racial neoliberalism. State systems around the country are heavily segregated. Racialized organizational hierarchies determine both the distribution of limited state resources and access to valuable sources of private revenue. Universities that do the most to support historically underrepresented racially marginalized students (URS), particularly from low-income backgrounds, often face severe financial penalties.

The University of California system offers an ideal case to study intra-system resource distribution. In most states, regional universities make the largest contributions to equity and diversity for state residents, while flagship research universities are mostly exempt from this responsibility. The "different type of university" argument is thus frequently used as justification for the uneven resourcing of schools—even though all students, especially disadvantaged students, need access to quality instructional support, financial aid, advising, health services, and so on. In the UC, though, all nine undergraduate campuses are classified as research universities, and system leadership asserts that they are equal in importance. There is no explaining away funding inequities in the UC, therefore, by suggesting that we are comparing apples and oranges.

Furthermore, each UC campus currently receives the same amount of state funding per student—with the important exception of Merced heading into the 2020 Project; during this period, UCM received substantially more than her sister campuses. While we might focus on campus-to-campus differences in state contributions, increasingly funding disparities are not driven by inequitable distribution of state funds. State contributions are now so low that they often make up only a tiny fraction of overall system revenue. Our case, therefore, spotlights the devastating role that the move to private funding has for new universities and regional universities serving marginalized student populations.

We would also be remiss if we did not point out that the University of California system is a widely acknowledged mobility machine.[3] Even the most prestigious schools in the UC system enroll roughly double the percentage of students eligible for federal Pell Grant assistance as the University of Michigan-Ann Arbor. And although there is variation among UC campuses, UCs are generally more racially diverse than other research universities.

Yet, the vision of a unified University of California—1UC, if you will—is at risk. This system is also characterized by race and class segregation, matched by sharp differences in access to funding necessary for supporting students.[4] The two new universities in the system are, as a high-level administrator put it, "running political cover" for the University of California. That is, Merced and Riverside help produce favorable optics at the system level, allowing the university system to demonstrate commitment to serving in-state students, low-income students, and URS. But they do it with a fraction of the resources.

We argue that public defunding decreases the motivation for better-resourced schools to cooperate in a system and share revenue streams, as these schools have less need for state resources and their leadership may find the accompanying constraints from state legislatures to be too burden-some for too small a payoff. This threatens the stability of new universities, which rely on robust systems to support their important purpose. That this could be the case even in California suggests grim prospects elsewhere in the nation.

Institutional Diversity Work in the UC

Although individual schools in a public system may contribute equally to system-wide diversity commitments, it is more common for certain cam-puses to take on a larger share of what we refer to as "institutional diversity work." One of the most visible investments in diversity is the admission of historically underrepresented groups. The division of this work is often in-equitable, such that some universities get pegged as "doing diversity," while others do less.

Our notion of institutional diversity work draws on race scholarship, which discusses "diversity work" as the production and enactment of a vis-ible organizational commitment to diversity.[5] This work typically entails an overreliance on people of color.[6] We extend this concept by thinking of indi-vidual campuses as organizational actors that differentially contribute to the system-wide production of diversity. As scholars emphasize, diversity work is often utilized to craft a public image as racially conscious, diverse, and eq-uitable.[7]

In California, the state legislature has demonstrated interest in having its most prestigious university system serve in-state residents, low-income stu-dents, and racially marginalized students. But not all state legislatures emphasize diversity and equity; some state governments may directly penalize systems and universities that work toward these goals. Regardless of the political context, however, we contend that institutional diversity work is both important and unequal in systems around the country.

How does the University of California demonstrate commitment to state residents from disadvantaged groups? We argue that the system heavily relies on UC-Riverside and UC-Merced, its two new universities.

UC-Merced and UC-Riverside are key to the UC's efforts to serve state residents. The California Master Plan for Higher Education lays out access provisions for the state's primary academic research institution—the University of California.[8] The Master Plan initially indicated that the UC was to "select from" the top one-eighth (or 12.5 percent) of the California high school graduating class. Later revisions to policy changed this language. Instead of selecting from the top one-eighth, the UC needed to guarantee admission to every qualified student in the state who would be attending college for the first time.[9]

In 2016, nearly 25 percent of enrolled students on three campuses—Berkeley, Los Angeles, and San Diego—were non-residents. The percentage of non-residents at Davis and Irvine fell between 15 and 20 percent. Increases at these schools in the past fifteen years have left a smaller proportion of in-state seats for California residents.[10] Indeed, the percentage of California residents system-wide declined from around 94 percent in 2000 to 83 percent in 2016. This trend is concerning to state government representatives.[11] Merced and Riverside have eased tensions by continuing to enroll virtually all in-state students; the non-resident population is less than 1 percent at Merced, and less than 5 percent at Riverside—helping meet the system's responsibility to the state.[12]

The Master Plan also affirms the University of California's promise to ensure access for low-income California families via the principle of free tuition for state residents. Fiscal pressures have eroded this principle over time. However, when this book was published, the UC system maintained a guarantee that California residents with an annual family income of up to $80,000 would have their system-wide tuition and fees fully covered.[13,14] Thus, UC schools, in the aggregate, enroll a relatively high percentage of low-income students: around 38 percent of the system-wide undergraduate population in fall 2016 was composed of Pell Grant recipients.[15] This is 6 percent higher than the national average for *all* postsecondary institutions—including open-access and community colleges.[16]

There is, however, a difference in degree across campuses. Figure 3.1 makes this apparent. In 2016, around a quarter of students at Berkeley and a third

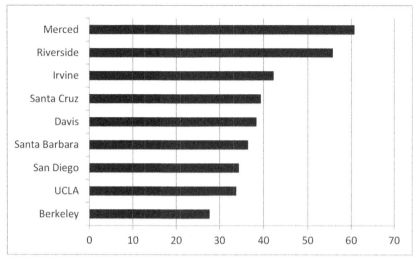

Figure 3.1. Pell representation by campus, 2016.

Note: Data are drawn from the University of California Info Center, Fall Enrollment Headcounts. Campuses are listed by descending Pell representation.

at Los Angeles, Davis, San Diego, Santa Barbara, and Santa Cruz were Pell Grant recipients. Notably, Irvine was over 40 percent. But Riverside was more than half Pell. Merced was 65 percent Pell. When the UC reports its overall statistics for Pell Grant student enrollment, these two campuses boost the system-wide average and allow the UC to boast that two of its campuses are majority Pell.

The UC also aspires to "reflect the diversity of California." In 2007, the UC adopted a diversity statement that called for the system to "achieve diversity among its student bodies and among its employees" and to recognize "the acute need to remove barriers to the recruitment, retention, and advancement of talented students, faculty, and staff from historically excluded populations who are currently underrepresented."[17] Evidence of movement toward these goals is frequently provided in university materials. For instance, the 2016–2017 budget for current operations reads:

> At the undergraduate level, UC has been very successful in expanding access to all Californians. Since the 1990s, UC has enrolled greater numbers of underrepresented minorities.... In Fall 1990, underrepresented minorities comprised 17.2% of all undergraduates, while in 2014, 29.7% of UC's undergraduate students were underrepresented minorities, and 38.3% were Asian American.[18,19]

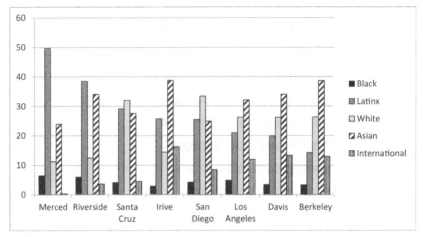

Figure 3.2. Racial representation by campus, 2016.

Note: Data are drawn from the University of California Info Center, Fall Enrollment Headcounts. Campuses are listed by descending Latinx representation. American Indian student representation is less than 1 percent at all UC campuses. Figures for the international population at UCM are altered to remove the campus's large undocumented population, as these students are from California.

UC-Riverside and UC-Merced have helped the system achieve its student body racial representation goals. The aggregate numbers reported above are, in part, a function of the massive growth of URS at Riverside over the last several decades and the later opening of Merced.

This is especially true for Latinx students. As figure 3.2 indicates, in 2016, Latinx students were heavily represented at Merced (over 50 percent of the student body) and Riverside (around 40 percent). Santa Cruz, Santa Barbara, and Irvine hovered around a quarter Latinx, and the other campuses were at (or, in the case of Berkeley and San Diego, well below) 20 percent. Still, Latinx students remain underrepresented in the UC, relative to the population of the state.[20]

While the percentage of Black students in the UC system as a whole is exceptionally low, between 2009 and 2013 Merced and Riverside, combined, contributed 25 percent or higher of the Black students in the entire UC system. This is notable, especially given the small size of the Merced campus. In fact, a 2017 infographic from the *New York Times* put the share of first-year, non-transfer students who identified as Black at Berkeley at around 2 percent—as low as it was prior to the civil rights movement.[21] Thus, as one Riverside official joked, "The University's diversity numbers aren't really bad—if you average us with Berkeley."

UC-Riverside and UC-Merced offer legitimacy for the system as a publicly funded entity. They demonstrate UC commitment to serving in-state residents, whose taxes contribute to the system's vitality, and provide upward mobility for economically and racially marginalized populations in the state. While not the only UC campus to do so, these two schools contribute the lion's share of student body diversity work for the system, proportional to their size, and in the case of Merced, newness in the postsecondary field. This makes Riverside and Merced essential to the UC, and critical to maintaining working relations with state leadership.

In return, Merced and Riverside are backed by the weight of the UC system. It is hard to overestimate the significance of belonging to a world-class university that maintains, at least in theory, equal commitment to and scholarly expectations for all campuses. Both schools routinely draw on their location in this powerful system to claim status or wield political clout.

An example from Merced illustrates the point. In 2010, the Carnegie Commission on Higher Education, which provides a classificatory system for postsecondary organizations in the US, was going to include the school for the first time.[22] The designation was going to be as a regional liberal arts school, but all other UCs are research universities.[23] According to a UCM staff member: "Keith Alley, who was provost at the time, went ballistic. Called Carnegie, kicked, screamed, threatened [laughter]. And basically, Carnegie says, 'OK, fine. If it's that important to you, we'll leave you out [for now].'" Finally, in 2016, UCM received its first designation by Carnegie—as a "doctoral-granting university with higher research activity," or Research 2 (R2) university. It seems highly unlikely that the school could have avoided classification for a decade and convinced Carnegie of the inevitability of Merced becoming a research university without the University of California name.

The system has also, at different points, provided substantial cash flow and financial backing to the two focal schools. The UC, as a whole, has good credit ratings and broad cash streams. All schools in the system benefit from the reputation and standing of the UC. Riverside and Merced, as less wealthy schools, must rely on the system, to a greater extent, to achieve campus goals. Riverside's growth and conversion in the 1990s was heavily supported by the system, as well as the state. Merced's 2020 Project depended on UC capital project funds—a commitment that a system-level leader described as "ironclad." In addition, even though internally the University of California disaggregates debt so that each campus rests on its own, "Externally, to the world, it's UC debt. In aggregation, the system is very powerful when we think about our credit rating or issuing debt."

Thus, while the larger UC benefits tremendously from the race and class composition of Riverside and Merced, the two schools benefit from the security that the system provides. This trade-off is not necessarily ideal, however, because it means that the larger system does not have to attend as intently to diversity within its individual schools. It can rely on certain campuses as a crutch. As one Riverside leader put it:

> In some ways our role on the national scene is easier than [in] the system for me. I'm going to be honest. In all candor, I'm a bit torn. I think the ethos and the culture that we've created here is special and has to be nurtured. But you can also make a case for a UC that's segregated, and I don't think that's good for the state.... That's not good for our students or for Berkeley students.... We can do better as a system.

And yet, this may be as good as it is going to get. In California, as well as in other states, system-wide commitment to equalizing the placement of qualified in-state, low-income, and/or racially marginalized students across schools is highly unlikely to occur.

The current arrangement could work toward improving postsecondary equity within the state if resources were dispersed fairly equally across the system. Given the higher cost of educating disadvantaged students, though, this would still result in disparities between campuses.[24] Even more ideal is a scenario in which campuses receive greater funding for students that have greater need and less funding for students that have less need. Under such conditions, majority-Latinx and majority-Pell campuses would receive the most funding. Additional resources would be needed to provide the same quality of education as at other UCs and to recalibrate educational practices in ways that take advantage of these students' strengths. However, as we detail below, increasing reliance on private funding in competitive markets — for example, from students, donors, and corporate entities — does just the opposite; it gives the most to those who need it the least. Schools serving Brown, Black, and low-income students are becoming increasingly resource poor.

A Changing Funding Structure

The UC, like most other state systems, has experienced dramatic reductions in state appropriations over the last several decades. As we illustrated in the introduction, between 1970 and 2014, the share of the state budget devoted to the University of California and California State University systems decreased dramatically, while funding for corrections spiked.[25] The share of UC and CSU funding was cut by more than half during this period, while the share of corrections funding more than doubled.

The average state expenditure per student for a UC education has declined by 22 percent in the past twenty-five years, going from $24,100 in 1990–1991 to $18,900 in 2015–2016. In the early 1990s, the state contributed 78 percent of the total cost per student, but this number was down to 41 percent by the 2015–2016 academic year. Reductions did not occur gradually but instead tracked fiscal crises. During these periods, tuition and fees spiked to partially offset state budget cuts. Despite periods of recovery, funding never returned to prior levels. Decreases have occurred as student enrollment at the UC has sharply increased—by 60 percent since 1990–1991, given system commitments to accommodating all UC-eligible residents in the state.[26] The UC has also seen a fundamental change in access to state capital financing, which is necessary for both building and deferred maintenance of existing infrastructure.

State leadership has pushed the UC on equity and public benefit, without offering the backing necessary for the system to fully achieve these goals. That is, the state wants to see the UC fulfill its obligations with less, despite a growing population of students that must be accommodated. These conditions have pushed the system toward a financing model heavily reliant on private sources of funding—which often leads to consequences like increases in non-resident students that frustrate the California state legislature.

At the same time, the system has pursued financial strategies that have weakened relationships with the state. As is the case all around the country, personnel from private investment have moved into public system leadership positions, bringing with them taken-for-granted assumptions of how to run organizations that emphasize profit and do not necessarily mesh with public equity goals. These individuals also come with deep ties and commitments to the world of corporate finance. Wall Street investment banks have thus, to a certain extent, moved into the (public) ivory tower.[27]

Changes are most apparent beginning in 2003, when the system retained Lehman Brothers, the fourth-largest investment bank in the US at the time. The firm recommended that the UC borrow more and place money in financial products (i.e., securities or investments designed to provide financial gain—what one report referred to as "increasingly exotic bond financing practices") in order to boost revenue.[28] The managing director of public finance for Lehman Brothers/Barclays Capital, who authorized bank sales of financial products to the system, was serving as a University of California regent, a vice chair of the regents' finance committee, and as a member, chair, and president of the UCLA Foundation board of directors.[29]

With the financial crash, investment personnel began to move more deeply into the UC. In 2009, a new chief financial officer position was created to oversee the increased borrowing. The regents hired the former managing director of Lehman Brothers/Barclays Capital. Similarly, the executive vice president for business services at the system level, and the next in line as the chief financial officer, had spent a decade at J. P. Morgan, where he became the top executive for its Western Region Public Finance Group, giving him authority over the sales of financial products to the system. These two men were followed by their former Wall Street employees, who would become, at least for a time, the vice chancellors of planning and budget at UCM and UCR. These hiring patterns reflect a change in financial logics internal to the UC.[30]

Between 2003 and 2015, the UC's debt more than tripled, from around $5 billion to around $15 billion. This increase was much larger than the national average; during roughly the same time period, public and community college debt in the US doubled.[31] Increases in UC debt are driven, in large part, by declines in state support; however, the debt increase also occurred during several periods of reinvestment by the state and reflects overborrowing by the system. Increases in debt would trigger a need for new sources of revenue, which were not coming from the state.

Indeed, UC system leadership assumed that the increasing debt could be handily serviced, even with state funding cuts. A common perspective, summarized by the credit rating agency Moody's in 2012, was that the UC could leverage its "powerful student market position" to "compensate for state funding cuts by raising tuition dramatically" and by "growing non-resident tuition, differentiating tuition by campus or degree, and increasing online course offerings."[32] These are private market solutions, which may come at the expense of students.[33]

The UC Office of the President (UCOP) also made the contentious decision to take over the system's debt from the state in 2013, as part of State Assembly Bill 94 (AB 94). The American Federation of State, County, and Municipal Employees (AFSCME) branch 3299, the UC Student Association, the Council of UC Faculty Associations, and the nonpartisan Legislative Analyst Office all opposed the restructuring and shifting of $2.5 billion in state public works bond debt to the UC. UCOP argued that the system's slightly higher credit rating would save as much as $100 million a year, but analyses suggested that the UC's credit rating would be downgraded after taking on the additional debt, negating the advantage.[34] This occurred only six months later.

AB 94 was likely appealing to UCOP leadership because it reduced state oversight over UC financial matters. Specifically, it allowed the system to use limited state general funds not only to pay off existing debt, but also for capital expenditures—without requiring the legislative approval necessary in the past. It would also limit the state's ability to stop the UC from further increasing debt service.

Critics pointed out that nothing in the bill prevented the state from decreasing UC appropriations in the future, despite the fact that the system took on this new obligation.[35] It also made it easier for Governor Jerry Brown to maintain his position and refuse to provide funding specifically for building or maintenance. Indeed, as UCOP leadership admitted, "[That money] could have gone to graduate student stipends or to more faculty lines, and instead we're using it to build buildings." To make matters worse, the system extended the period of debt service, significantly reducing any potential savings.

By the time that UC-Merced requested additional support from the system to build the second half of the campus, the UC was in a different financial position than in the past. The system offered generous time-limited support—but less than might have been possible under other circumstances. In recent years, the regents have reconsidered the heavy borrowing that occurred in the early 2000s.[36] However, an important symbolic separation was complete; the UC system was no longer granted the same degree of financial protection from the state. This move cemented the (already developing) turn to private market activities as primary generators of cash flow.[37] The shift toward private funding was thus a function of *both* state and system moves.

This change heavily disadvantages Merced and Riverside. As a system finance representative indicated, "It's a challenge for a campus like Riverside, almost a nonstarter for a campus like Merced [short laugh]." Both campuses are highly reliant on state support, in ways that their sister campuses are not. Abandoning a model of public education in which the state takes primary fiscal responsibility for its postsecondary system particularly hurts campuses that are not well positioned in private markets. These schools, not incidentally, also tend to serve racially marginalized students.

Private Sources of Revenue

By 2015–2016, state contributions were only around 10 percent of the UC funding "pie," as displayed in figure 3.3. Other revenue came primarily from private sources. Tuition and fees collected from students and their families, in particular, were essential. Of the permanent "core" funds used to run basic

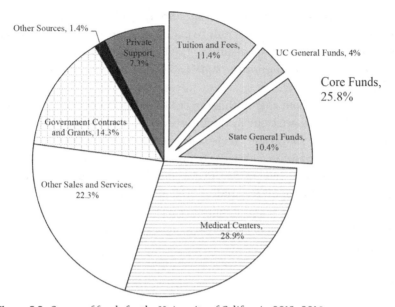

Figure 3.3. Source of funds for the University of California, 2015–2016.

Note: Data are drawn from the UC Office of the President (2016). Note that the portion of the pie devoted to medical centers mostly goes back into the operation and capital needs of UC medical centers.

university operations in 2015–2016 (see the pie pullout), UC tuition and fees plus UC General Funds (comprised heavily of non-resident supplemental tuition) covered the bulk of core UC funding.

Supplemental tuition collected from out-of-state and international students is an important revenue generator.[38] These students pay the same tuition as other UC students *plus* a supplement of more than two times the cost of tuition. Altogether, then, non-residents bring as much tuition as three or more California residents. As noted earlier, Merced and Riverside have miniscule non-resident populations. The two schools are ramping up efforts to attract non-residents, but it is unclear how successful they will be in these endeavors. More prestigious campuses currently capture the vast majority of the non-resident share.

In the UC system, the use of tuition and fees is highly restricted but there are other, more flexible, revenue sources that help diversify the funding stream. Research grants, for example, often include IDR, or indirect cost recovery. On a $3 million grant with 50 percent IDR, a university takes $1.5 million in IDR, minus costs to support the research. Especially in fields requiring large laboratories and expensive equipment, IDR can fail to cover university costs.[39,40] (Here, the payoff is largely indirect—via prestige, which translates to larger grants and donations.) In other fields, however, IDR itself can be a boon for the university. Merced and Riverside bring in only a fraction of overall UC grant dollars, despite both schools performing well for their size and, in Merced's case, newness.

Although federal funding agencies have been primary research funders, in recent years, private entities such as corporations and nonprofit foundations have played more central roles in grant funding.[41] Research activity also occasionally produces inventions that carry patent royalties—an additional source of funds.[42] Finally, sales and services revenue comes from entities such as bookstores selling university gear, campus catering, on-campus food markets, and sports-related enterprises; there is much greater potential for revenue at higher-status campuses with more visitors and events.

Among (relatively) flexible funding sources, private donations are dramatically increasing in importance. Public universities have been growing more dependent on alumni and philanthropic contributions over time. As a high-level campus finance representative explained:

> Other resources have dried up. The importance of delivering in private support has truly increased. In some respects, early on in my career, I almost felt like fund-raising ... was icing on the cake. Now it's become—Wow, if we aren't delivering here, certain programs, services, etc., could likely just go away, and so that adds some of the pressure to the work that we do.

This representative later noted that public universities are far behind privates in alumni giving, in part because, for decades, this was not the relationship residents had to their state systems. When state funding for postsecondary education was higher, students' families were already contributing to the UC system as tax-paying residents. Thus, universities did not ask for more and former students did not feel compelled to give in this way.[43]

Other UCs, located in wealthier communities and with more affluent student bodies, have more rapidly ramped up their donations. As a system official explained, "Our larger campuses generally have more flexible dollars because they've been established longer [and] they have philanthropy. UCLA is a great example of that.... They're able to look to the community and to very high-profile donors." In contrast, despite some donors who are drawn to the unique race and class composition of the student bodies at Merced and Riverside, both schools have "a limited pipeline for multimillion-dollar gifts." Merced, in particular, has not had the time to build up a pool of "legacies that have come through generations of graduates" that also tend to give back at higher rates.

We can see the difference in donations by comparing the success of UC funding campaigns. In 2013, UCLA and UC-San Diego both started funding campaigns. By June 30, 2018, UCLA had raised well over $4 billion and UC-San Diego over $1.5 billion. In contrast, Riverside's Living the Promise Campaign, which had begun two years earlier, in 2011, had only raised around $200 million by the same date.[44] Looking at donations that went directly to campus foundations in the 2017–2018 academic year, UCM and UCR's foundations received the smallest amounts. Merced's foundation received far less than 1 percent, and Riverside's foundation about 4 percent, of the private support that Berkeley's foundation took in that same year.[45]

The endowment assets of UCM and UCR are also among the lowest in the system.[46] At the end of 2016, Merced reported $1,370 per full-time student and Riverside $6,145. In contrast, at Berkeley, each student on campus represented $42,900 in endowment assets—approximately thirty-one times the amount at Merced. Endowments are often used for future investments, allowing schools with greater assets to more easily grow their funds than schools that start with less.[47] Over time, disparities become compounded.

Reliance on private funding, therefore, tends to hurt universities doing institutional diversity work for their systems. As leadership at UCR explained:

> This university struggles with how to fund everything. The president's office and others will tell you that in national comparisons we have more students in the UC on Pell Grants than many other universities; we have [relatively] more African American students, and so forth. So it takes more money. Unfortunately, we're at the place where many of those students are and we get less money. And this is a Merced kind of reality too. There's an imbalance between the funding mechanisms and the diversity of the students.

Merced and Riverside are not alone. In fact, new universities in most states, which tend to have a more clearly demarcated flagship, are often worse off. More prestigious flagships often have both the greatest potential to secure private revenue and the largest amount of (rapidly shrinking) state allocations.[48] Notably, community colleges, which serve even larger numbers of historically underrepresented students within a given state, have the least ability to claim either funding source.[49]

Campus Contestation over Resources

To a certain extent "co-opetition," or coordination combined with contestation, is a basic feature of the state system model.[50] As we will suggest, however, too much contestation, without cooperation, upsets the balance. Campuses within state systems are pitted against each other when forced to compete for private funding. With escalating competition, the coordinating aspect of co-opetition, on which schools like UC-Merced and UC-Riverside rely, begins to break down. Schools that are advantaged in economic markets have less incentive to continue supporting those that are not.

Mounting intra-UC competition is most evident in a 2009 letter to University of California leadership, penned by Andrew Scull, then chair of the Department of Sociology at UC-San Diego, and signed by twenty-two other department heads from physical and biological sciences, social sciences, engineering, and the humanities and arts. The letter came on the heels of an announcement of coming UC budget cuts, which would be felt at all campuses in the system. It asserted that the system included "four flagships (Berkeley, UCLA, UC[-San Diego], and—in its highly specialized way, UC[-San Francisco—a campus focused on graduate-level medical and biological training])" and argued that the UC should "establish different budget priorities for the profiles of different UC campuses."

As the letter continued:

> We propose that you urge the President and Regents to acknowledge that UC[-Santa Cruz], UCR, and UC-Merced are in substantial measure teaching institutions ... whose funding levels and budgets should be reorganized to match that reality. We suggest, more generally, that in discussions system-wide, you drop the pretense that all campuses are equal, and argue for a selective reallocation of funds to preserve excellence, not the current disastrous blunderbuss policy of even, across the board cuts. Or, if that is too hard, we suggest what ought to be done is to shut one or more of these campuses down, in whole or in part.... Corporations faced with similar problems eliminate or sell off their least profitable, least promising divisions.... It is simply not the case that all campus entities are of equal value to our goals.

This letter called for a radical departure from prior UC policy. It attempted to establish reputation, major grants, and entrepreneurial success (e.g., in spin-off companies) as primary factors of value, and proposed that the UC distribute resources in ways that cut out the schools doing the most institutional diversity work for the system.

The UC Academic Council, which advises the UC president on behalf of the system-wide Academic Senate, responded in a memo vociferously opposing the letter. In the memo, the council "affirm[ed] its commitment to one University of California where each campus is both a leading research institution in its own right and a respected part of the world-class University of California system, believing that each of our individual campuses is enriched and strengthened by its membership in the whole." However, the fact that the opposite sentiment coalesced so strongly on at least one UC campus, resulting in an explosive missive that required an official system response, is remarkable.

The letter continues to be remembered by many at Riverside and Merced as a threat to the survival of their campuses and an offensive dismissal of what these schools contribute to the system. One Riverside administrator remarked that it was horrifying to think that the response of some UC system members to the financial crisis was to stop serving disadvantaged students; this person was therefore skeptical of candidates for administrative positions coming from San Diego to Riverside. For Merced, occasional negative interactions with San Diego administration did not end with the letter. At a 2017 system-wide conference on undergraduate education, a San Diego delegate remarked to a room full of high-level administrators and staff that perhaps Merced found it easy to achieve its goals because administrators did not follow the rules. Merced administrators were frustrated and unsure of how to respond, but not entirely surprised. As one remarked, "What do you expect from them, given that they wrote that letter?"

Although there is a sense of kinship between Riverside and Merced, the pressure to compete with other UC campuses for resources generates some distance. As a UCR administrator noted:

> Merced is a campus that is the short end of the stick. I can kind of relate to them, because we've been a campus [in that position] and to a certain extent still get referred to as the diamond in the rough.... But I do kind of feel like, as a campus, people are [like], at least we're not Merced.

Merced administrators and staff understood this all too well. After the conference event mentioned above, Merced representatives noted that Riverside might be kin, but that Riverside employees were "glad that we [at Merced] are at the bottom now, as that moves them up."

While not as dramatic as debates about closing certain UC campuses in favor of others, intra-UC contestation is also visible in debates about non-resident tuition and fees. The 2009 letter, in fact, called for the immediate admission of 500 or more non-resident students per year, for at least four years, at San Diego—which would amount to over $20 million per annum. Individual UC campuses have continued to angle for a greater share of the UC-going non-resident population. Seemingly, every campus could get in on this game; however, there are strict limits on what the legislature will support. Despite sharp decreases in state funding, lawmakers still would like to see the UC adhere to the standards for serving in-state residents established in the California Master Plan.

In 2016, state representatives threatened to hold back $18.5 million in support to the public university system if it did not put a cap on students from outside of California.[51] In May 2017, the UC Board of Regents approved the first policy on non-resident undergraduate enrollment, which capped out-of-state and international students at 18 percent at five UC campuses, including Riverside and Merced. The four campuses where the proportion of non-residents already exceeded 18 percent (i.e., Berkeley, Irvine, Los Angeles, and San Diego) were capped at the proportion that each campus would enroll for the following academic year, in 2017–2018.[52] Allowing an uneven cap cemented a major advantage, as it ensured that these four schools could always access the most non-resident tuition and fees.

Private revenue is mostly kept at the campuses where it is collected, rather than pooling and redistributing across the system. Several years prior, in a process referred to as "re-benching," as a UCOP administrator explained (in a bit of an overstatement), "We [ensured that] any revenue that was generated on the campus stayed on the campus.... If you paid for business school at a campus it stayed there. [It is the same with] non-resident tuition [and] indirect cost recovery."[53] This official described re-benching as about achieving equity because it also equalized the amount of state funds per student across the system (except, in the short term, for Merced as it headed into 2020). However, when state appropriations are only 10 percent of the overall system revenue, equalizing state funds while allowing other revenue sources to vary can, over time, magnify disparities in campus resources.

Competition for private resources, and the concentration of these resources at more prestigious campuses, guarantees that Riverside and Merced will drift further away from their sister campuses in terms of available funding and resources. A non-resident referral pool system, which redirects applicants to other campuses upon being denied admission to a UC of choice, will help, but it is unlikely to dramatically change the percentages of non-resident students at UCM and UCR. Furthermore, it leaves the distribution of other campus income untouched.

In the past, the UC grew multiple, world-renowned campuses in part through the redistribution of funds across the system (albeit, not always in transparent or equitable ways). By not establishing a mechanism for shared private market–based revenue, however, the current UC has failed to give its less advantaged campuses an equal shot for development. For UC-Merced in particular, attempting to become established without long-term redistribution is a serious handicap.

Yet, this scenario is consistent with postsecondary racial neoliberalism, as market competition is favored over equitable redistribution. Thinking of the UC as a corporation in a competitive market, as suggested by the author of the inflammatory letter, is a clear expression of racial neoliberal principles. Racism may not be explicit in that letter, but colorblind racism still reduces the resources and opportunities available to URS, in favor of racially and economically privileged students and the organizations that serve them.

The ultimate form of resource concentration is the disbanding of a state system. In 2015, the Oregon University System ceased to exist. In recent years, Illinois, Michigan, Virginia, and Wisconsin have, to varying degrees, entertained conversations about fully privatizing state flagships. These proposals are often backed by the idea that universities outside of a public system will have greater success at drawing alumni and philanthropic contributions and may lobby more effectively around their own interests. As we suggest below, privatizing also frees universities from meeting state demands—whether they be diversity and equity goals or interests of conservative governing bodies.

It is nearly impossible to imagine the end of the UC. However, grumblings about being tethered to a state system are not uncommon. For example, at a 2017 conference at Berkeley entitled "The Future of Higher Education: Creating Opportunity, Assessing Value," panelists discussed how illogical it was for the UC, particularly its more powerful campuses, to answer to state authorities, given how little of the system's funding currently comes from the state. Similarly, a top-level administrator at UCR noted:

> The state places constraints on us: You need to take this many students. You need to take a certain ratio of transfer to freshman students. You can only take a certain number of out-of-state students. You need to review your curriculum with these goals in mind. There's a lot of things that the bargain with the state results in us having to do because the state says so. And I think some of these bigger, wealthier, more mature campuses are sort of like, gosh, is this still a big deal, you know? But I feel like you can't escape the history and all the [state] investment that went into these campuses.

As this person continued, "We're a long ways from ... a world in which the state really cuts Berkeley or UCLA loose and says, 'Fly [away]. We don't need you anymore. Go, be great.'" This statement is somewhat ironic, considering that virtually all programs in UCLA's Anderson School of Management became privately funded in 2014, when the MBA program converted from state-supported to self-supported.[54]

Tiny cracks in the UC system, therefore, are already visible. It is not an overstatement to say that the end of the UC would decimate Merced and Riverside. The existence of research universities that serve disadvantaged students depends, in part, on system support, protection, and resource redistribution.

As this chapter illustrates, the gradual move from publicly funded higher education concentrates resources at the most-advantaged organizations and thus among the most-privileged students. The breakdown of our public systems and the increase in system contestation for resources, rather than cooperation, hurts racially marginalized students and the universities that serve them. A segregated UC, where access to organizational resources mirrors racial hierarchies, therefore generates and maintains racial inequalities.

In the next section of the book, we focus on university responses to rapidly shrinking public support. We first examine the ways that new university leadership approaches fiscal austerity, again leveraging similarities at Riverside and Merced. Material limits are often inadvertently magnified by the assumption of future disinvestment and practices that lead to greater reliance on private funding. A chapter focused on resource-poor Merced then highlights the costs of university austerity to the frontline staff that serve students in new universities, as well as to the most-marginalized students within these schools.

Part 2

RESPONSES TO UNDERFUNDING

4 *Austerity Administration*

In 2015, Michael Crow, president of Arizona State University, published *Designing the New American University*.[1] The book offers a blueprint for public research universities serving disadvantaged students in an era of fiscal austerity. Some commentators have even suggested that Michael Crow is this generation's Clark Kerr,[2] the mastermind behind California's 1960 comprehensive plan for postsecondary education and leader of the University of California system during peak years of governmental support.[3] Crow similarly offers a bold vision for university management, but for the resource-starved public research university of the twenty-first century.

Arizona State University displays essential elements of the new university. Crow argues that universities should not draw prestige from exclusionary practices, instead promoting inclusive excellence. Like our focal campuses, ASU has expanded access to marginalized populations. Crow emphasizes college completion rates in a state that has long had some of the worst in the nation. His strategy intensifies research investments, with the goals of boosting the school's visibility in national rankings and bringing in more grant dollars. As the book claims, ASU is "the model for a New American University, measured not by those whom we exclude, but rather by those whom we include and how they succeed.... ASU seeks to provide broad accessibility to a milieu of world-class research and scholarship to a diverse and heterogeneous student body."[4] This should all sound familiar.

ASU is, however, an extreme version of the new university. Crow has executed his agenda in a series of audacious and hotly debated moves: a corporate partnership to provide online education for Starbucks employees,[5] a public-private partnership (or P3—see chapter 2) for a senior living center on campus, heavy reliance on contingent labor, and drastic restructuring of academic departments, among others. He has both devoted followers and vocal detractors.[6] The flash and exaggerated scale of his new university experiment can make it hard to see that what Crow is up to at ASU is not unique.

Administrative practices at ASU, in fact, closely parallel those at UC-Riverside and UC-Merced. UCR administrators were especially vocal about their admiration and emulation of Crow.[7] As one UCR administrator explained to Kelly, "I hope that you are going to be able to come to UCR and say, 'This is the future of American Higher Education.' ... UCR is one of those places that ... a lot of people thought was going to be [the next] Arizona State. Not only has [Crow] made real change in Arizona State, he is also a spectacular leader." Attracted by the Crow project and based on relevant experience at UCR, another top financial administrator would even move to ASU as the senior vice president of strategy. Network ties between the two schools were dense.

New university leaders share a reality. They are often in the undesirable position of administering austerity to their universities. Austerity is the reduction of public spending on social welfare that has hit public universities hard in recent decades.[8] In the introduction, we argued that postsecondary defunding was bolstered by racial resentment for people of color, who gained entry into predominately white research universities (PWUs) in the decades following WWII. We pointed out that today austerity has the greatest impact on universities that serve historically underrepresented racially marginalized students (URS).

Leaders at these universities face potentially insurmountable financial pressures. Yet, the practices of new university administrators, which we detail in this chapter, are not just pragmatic responses to material deprivation. They are enmeshed in a culture of austerity that is every bit as real and consequential as the conditions of austerity. In fact, the two go hand in hand. When an administrative decision is made, it is often driven, in part, by structural austerity—but cultural logics of austerity make the decision seem inevitable. These logics may intensify structural austerity by further weakening the abilities of administrators to solve problems via public channels, encouraging even deeper reliance on private markets.

Readers may wonder why we focus on university leadership in this chapter, as administrators are only one of many, often competing, constituencies in the "organized anarchy" of large public universities.[9] Even among administrators there may be sharp disagreement. Austerity, however, tends to change the decision-making structure. As organizational scholars point out, weathering adversity often boosts administrative power and leads to a more hierarchical structure.[10] This is certainly true in the case of Crow's ASU. Critics have pointed out, for instance, that his directive leadership style erodes faculty input in university governance.[11] Understanding why and how new university leaders operate is thus particularly important in the context of postsecondary defunding.

Administrative Culture under Austerity

Organizational leadership is, quite literally, a product of the times. University leaders often espouse logics that reflect both immediate fiscal conditions, as well as political and historical contexts.[12] By logics, we mean the cultural values, beliefs, and normative expectations that people within organizations use to organize their activities in time and space.[13] We argue that for administrators shaped by the golden era of postsecondary funding, it was easier to assume that public support is a basic requirement for postsecondary education, leading to requests of the state for more resources. In contrast, those whose entire careers have unfolded under austerity are far more likely to assume that public resources are not available and to adopt practices that may, in fact, entrench austerity.

Detailing the cultural logics of modern-day leaders necessitates brief reference to the mid-twentieth-century structural and cultural conditions that molded prior generations of public administrators. As noted in the introduction, public universities in the US benefited from unprecedented federal and state largesse as part of a larger project of Cold War state-building.[14] At the time, the University of California was perhaps the most resourced and prestigious public university system in the world. Leaders who emerged during this period, and especially in the UC, were indelibly imprinted.

For example, we can think about Ray Orbach (see chapter 1), who would later become chancellor of UC-Riverside. Shortly after he entered graduate school in physics at Berkeley during the mid-1950s, the Soviet Union launched *Sputnik* 1 into orbit. Describing the environment at the time, Orbach remembered:

> Berkeley was red hot. I mean ... things just happened. It was probably ... one of the most exciting periods in its history in physics. What we called the RadLab, now the Lawrence Berkeley National Lab, was just booming. There were Nobel laureates, Nobel prizes, and new discoveries almost every year. It attracted a wonderful group of very fine scientists. Things were going very rapidly.

In 1963, when Orbach took a job at UCLA, Clark Kerr was at the helm of the UC system, and the university "was growing ... just really developing." This was near the peak in federal spending on university research and development (or R&D). The share of the gross domestic product spent on R&D would only begin a long, multi-decade slide starting in the 1970s.[15] Moreover, the influential economist Theodore Schultz had developed and promoted a theory of human capital that posited education as a collective good—as opposed to an individual possession, later proposed by Howard Becker—that explained the exceptional prosperity of the mid-century US.[16]

Orbach came of age as a scholar during a moment of great infrastructure growth for universities around the country.[17] For instance, the chancellor of Riverside at the time, Ivan Hinderaker (1964–1979), walked onto a campus that was ready to go because it had been underwritten by the state. A publicly available interview with Hinderaker suggests just how typical this kind of commitment was; it is filled with references to dealings with the governor and state legislature, as primary gatekeepers for public resources.[18]

An abundance of governmental resources for public university systems and a tight relationship with state governance, therefore, characterized Orbach's formative years. He developed his academic career while the state-university partnership was still intact. When he became chancellor at UCR in 1992, this was no longer the case. Still, Orbach had been shaped by the Cold War era in higher education—as was likely true for many university leaders aging into top administrative positions in the 1980s and early 1990s. Orbach carried the culture of his formative years with him, even as the funding landscape began to radically change.[19] He assumed that the state would, and could, back public research universities.

This is, in part, what may have led Orbach to pursue projects that seemed like pie-in-the-sky proposals. For example, a large gamble was on the development of a medical school, which had faced decades of resistance from state and system leadership. In fact, the UC president had written a letter expressly forbidding the appointment of a dean of medicine, but Orbach ignored it— even though he could have been fired. The fact that Orbach imagined this as a possible course of action, via state-funded channels, suggests a mind-set not constrained by austerity. UCR would eventually get a medical school as a result.[20]

Administrators developing academic careers under austerity faced a different world. As detailed earlier, changes in postsecondary funding in the late 1970s and early 1980s were part of larger shifts in political and economic ideology. By 1989, Francis Fukuyama, political scientist and former State Department official during the Reagan administration, declared "an unabashed victory of economic and political liberalism" in an essay titled "The End of History?"[21] The election of neoliberal governments in Britain, Germany, the

US, and Japan reflected a growing belief in competitive private markets as the only way forward and a rejection of governmental "intervention" in the form of a developed welfare state.[22] As Britain's prime minister, Margaret Thatcher, famously quoted of the market economy, "There is no alternative" (or TINA).[23] Over time, even left-leaning political parties around the world adopted these basic tenets of political economy.[24]

The beginning of the end of history brought an intensified reliance on exchanges in private markets for organizational revenue—a process that would prove to be transformative for public service financing in the coming decades.[25] Reliance on private funding was fueled by austerity logics building through the 1990s and early 2000s and cemented in the Great Recession. Leading economists, in the panic of 2009, argued that governmental support of public services, such as higher education, hurt the economy and needed to be reduced.[26] Although others have strongly disputed this claim, it nonetheless reflects a culturally pervasive style of thinking.[27] Remember that austerity logics, as we argued in the introduction, have historically been associated with a lack of willingness to extend public support to racially marginalized individuals.[28]

Kim Wilcox and Dorothy Leland (chancellors of UCR and UCM at the time of the study) entered faculty positions during the 1980s. Both started in less prestigious public universities that were more likely to feel the crunch of defunding. They advanced to full-professor rank in the late 1990s and early 2000s, as a pattern of state withdrawal became notable. Wilcox and Leland took on leadership roles at Michigan State University and Georgia College & State University, where they established records of applying private market solutions to fiscal problems. Indeed, as the first sentence of a 2007 Association of American Colleges and Universities article by Leland states, "Today's higher-education environment has become increasingly competitive, and many public colleges and universities have begun to adopt market-oriented strategies as a result."[29] When Leland started as chancellor in the UC system in 2011 and Wilcox in 2013, financial advisors at both schools, per recommendation from system-level leaders, were part of the Wall Street financial crisis exodus. Notably, ASU's Michael Crow followed a similar track in terms of timing and a professional start in state schools: all three leaders belong to the same "cohort" of administration, one that is culturally and materially defined by austerity.[30,31]

Wilcox and Leland established their professorial careers in an academy where fiscal austerity was already the "unchallenged conventional wisdom" of higher education.[32] They successfully weathered the Great Recession as administrators of resource-challenged public universities. In their UC roles, they were awash in austerity logics—from legislators, governing boards, the general public, and even some of their own advisors, who arrived through corporate, rather than academic, trajectories. It would have been difficult to think differently.

Austerity logics suggest that a publicly funded higher education system is unaffordable. Embracing private market activities as a primary revenue source for universities is touted as the logical solution.[33] Administrators with long-term exposure to this logic thus tend to see a return to a heavily state-subsidized postsecondary system as not only implausible, but impossible. As a top UCR administrator passionately explained, "The model that got us here is not going to be what gets us into the future." The idea that "we have to dig our heels in and tell the state, the public, the legislature, the governor and so on, that we can't do any more until they give us more money" is misguided because "we're not as rich of a country as we thought we were." The administrator then launched into a description of the market-based strategies UCR would be pursuing to increase revenue (e.g., attempting to capture a greater share of highly desired UC non-resident tuition).

This statement is truly bizarre in a state that encompasses the wealth of both Hollywood and Silicon Valley. There is, in fact, a great deal of money concentrated in California, especially in particular regions and among certain individuals. More broadly, the claim that the US as a whole cannot afford public higher education has nothing to do with the wealth of the nation; it is simply austerity logic. Public policies shape how that wealth is to be distributed. As Democratic presidential candidate Elizabeth Warren's free college plan indicated, a 2 percent tax on "ultra-millionaires" with fortunes worth over $50 million would make it possible to create debt-free conditions for students who attend two-year or four-year public universities in the US. But if we believe that publicly funded public higher education is impossibly costly, these types of solutions are not on the table.

As Christopher Newfield argues in *The Great Mistake: How We Wrecked Public Universities and How We Can Fix Them*, austerity logics also reflect the widespread belief that higher education suffers from a "cost disease"—that is, universities will wastefully spend whatever money is available to them, regardless of need.[34] This is a myth; research indicates that tuition increases in the public sector have been driven primarily by sharp state funding cuts.[35] Nonetheless, such a perspective suggests that universities must learn to utilize limited public resources more efficiently and generate their own resources—and that such a goal is, in fact, well within reach, without dramatically compromising the quality of postsecondary research and education. Administrators may thus zealously pursue "excess," as if the central problem was university overspending, not public underfunding.

Pressures to accommodate current austerity and assume future austerity are particularly intense at new universities. These schools compete as research universities but without the resources available to PWUs. As a result, the new university is an ideal organizational form through which to study the administration of postsecondary austerity. In new universities, we may see some of the most-concentrated efforts to develop austerity practices. But these practices are also visible in many other resource-constrained publics.

As we detail below, contemporary administrators act in ways that are inflected by austerity logics; they seek to make their universities leaner, more efficient, and more productive, weaning these organizations off state support. The rest of the chapter emphasizes four general austerity practices: 1) grow big; 2) cut costs; 3) be market-smart; and 4) think (inter)nationally.[36] These practices, we argue, tend to undercut the experiences of new university students in general, and URS in particular. At times, such practices are even counterproductive to organizational goals of survival and prestige production. Leadership may set into motion a self-fulfilling prophecy, inadvertently undermining claims to public resources by suggesting that public universities are "just fine" without substantial state support.

Austerity Practices

Below we describe four austerity practices shared by UC-Riverside and UC-Merced, relying on Crow's ASU for more exaggerated examples.

GET BIG

As Riverside leadership explained: "In these budgetary [times] and [looking to] the budgetary future, you've got to get big. You've got to get big in your enrollment, because we're all increasingly tuition dependent." Big meant 25,000 students at UCR in 2020, up 7,000 students from 2008. Future plans set even higher goals: 35,000 students by 2035. This would push UCR closer to the size of many prestigious flagships, and aspirations among campus leadership looked far beyond that.

Getting big is important for new universities: tuition, student loans, and need-based financial aid are the most reliable sources of revenue that these schools can secure. When the state places limits on tuition increases, getting big is an obvious way to increase tuition revenue. Indeed, for Merced, growing big(ger) was nothing short of an imperative. As detailed earlier, the school would need to rapidly admit more students in order to become fiscally stable.

Given pre-existing infrastructure, though, Riverside was better positioned to get big than UCM, whose growth was expected to slow (at least temporarily) at around 10,000 students.

Getting big is also a strategy pursued by public schools seeking to compete on the basis of research. Research universities use undergraduate student tuition dollars to bolster the research that generates grants, awards, and organizational status. The Carnegie Classification for Research 1 (or R1) status heavily weighs research and development expenditures, especially in science and engineering. This leads to incredible pressure to enroll more students, particularly outside of the most elite and well-established universities, as there may be no other way to compete.[37] Thus, UCR's goal of joining the prestigious American Association of Universities (populated by elite research universities) was, by the estimation of UCR leadership, predicated on increasing numbers. As a top official explained, "If you take the AAU public universities ... the average enrollment is something like 45, 46,000 students."

The behemoth of Arizona State University is a useful illustration of a new university striving for the AAU distinction. Since Crow's arrival in 2002, enrollment at ASU has nearly doubled to over 100,000 students, due in large part to heavy use of online curricula.[38] The Tempe campus has, under Crow's leadership, often held the distinction of the largest single-campus enrollment in the nation, and currently remains one of the top five biggest universities in the US. Crow argues for a "scaled up" approach to higher education in his book, suggesting that the "academy might even learn from the Cheesecake Factory," which has reengineered the gourmet culinary experience for "affordable delivery to millions."[39]

What are the limitations of getting big? Under current conditions, the approach creates a status problem. "Gourmet" is defined by its eliteness and exclusivity. It is a form of cuisine that, by definition, is not equally available to all restaurant-goers. Prestige may thus be particularly elusive with a mass-production approach.[40] New universities may be able to build access into what it means to be a high-quality public university, as discussed in chapter 1, but they cannot appear to "take everyone" and still claim elite status. This is why gaining students through the UC referral pool process, whereby applicants to other UCs could be offered admission to UCR and UCM without having applied, was so stigmatizing. Even the strong reputation of the UC system could not overcome the reputational hit. As an admissions representative at UCR explained, it was not until UCR moved off the referral pool that "the attitude [began] shifting" and the campus started "to shed a little bit of that stigma." Scaling up also introduces potential for reduction in the quality of the experience provided. Large cohorts of students within states are, in fact, associated with lower public subsidies per student and relatively lower undergraduate degree attainment.[41] Resources effectively become diluted.

At ASU, leadership has responded to issues posed by scaling up with a tiered system of delivery that allows the school to still attract sought-after applicants. The Barrett Honors College provides a highly tailored residential college experience—but only for a subset of 5,000 "select" students. This suggests awareness among ASU leadership that the Cheesecake Factory version of higher education is not necessarily ideal and may not draw students who have other postsecondary options.

ASU's growth strategy has been to consolidate more students on fewer mega-campuses, using economies of scale to reduce costs. But this strategy may not work as well in larger states and those with significant geographic boundaries. Indeed, seam-busting campus sizes have not been a feature of the UC. UCR leadership argued that this is a fiscal disadvantage: "California's model has been, when in doubt, add a campus.... But it's ten infrastructures, it's ten heating and cooling plants, it's ten admissions offices, it's ten development offices.[42] And so I've been pretty vocal about the fact that we need to ... stop adding campuses and start growing campuses." But California is the third-largest state in the nation, after Alaska and Texas. At its longest point, California is 1,040 miles from north to south, and at the widest point, 560 miles east to west. The Central Valley is also bounded by mountains on all sides, meaning that entry and exit occur through "passes" that can be congested and are subject to weather conditions. With only one UC campus (Merced) built since 1965, and no plans for another, many demographic groups and areas of the state remain underserved by the UC.

The impact of rapid campus growth is also much different than in the past. In the mid-twentieth century, the adage "If you build it, they will come" rang true. That is, postsecondary infrastructure typically preceded or accompanied growth. Students often entered campuses capable of accommodating them. By the 1990s, however, the situation was reversing: If enough students came, the state might support the building of infrastructure. Thus, as discussed in chapter 1, Orbach could strategically enroll more students than the university could manage and make a plea to the state for funding to support them. Austerity administrators are, however, as UCM leadership frequently put it, flying the plane while building it. That is, they use the funding offered by new cohorts of students to remedy problems facing prior cohorts, such that current students constantly lack functional space and resources.

This was immediately visible on our focal campuses. During our study year, both were grappling with the realities of getting big. UCR had overshot their already ambitious enrollment target because of state pressure to admit more students than they had planned—pressure that was not backed with resources. Typically, campuses attempt to limit "summer melt," or the loss of committed students over the summer. But at UCR, several staff members told us that they were busy trying to do the opposite and "melt" students—for example, by being strict on deadlines for paperwork. They were anxious about what would happen if they did not succeed.

At UCM, the increase in students was occurring on an already cramped campus. Classes were meeting late into the evenings, student rooms that were once doubles had become triples, triples had become quadruples, and students could be found studying in odd spaces (including a little-used elevator). Growth at both campuses thus preceded the development or maintenance of basic infrastructure, such as classrooms and dormitory spaces. Consequently, new or improved spaces often proved inadequate by the time they came online. It was a constant game of "catch up" in which neither campus could succeed.

Some may argue that these growing pains are worth it, as increasing the size of UCR and UCM means more access for URS to higher-status public universities in the state of California. Students that might otherwise attend less prestigious regional or community colleges have greater odds of matriculating to a UC because of Merced and Riverside. However, the alternative to increasing enrollment at these new universities should not be that disadvantaged students are shut out of the UC. The growth of Merced and Riverside, as the previous chapter illustrates, takes the heat off other UC campuses to admit greater numbers of racially and economically marginalized in-state residents.

The extent to which getting big is a last resort—not a desirable strategy—is visible when comparing with elite privates. Harvard University, Stanford University, Princeton University, and other Ivy League schools, for instance, have not significantly increased available slots for many decades. They have instead dramatically grown in endowment dollars, not students, allowing for astronomical increases in per-student expenditures.[43] This helps concentrate resources in the most-privileged schools serving the most-privileged students.

In contrast, when new universities like Riverside and Merced need more resources, they are pushed to grow rapidly. But they cannot comfortably accommodate the needs of their students. As a UC-Riverside faculty member of color passionately articulated in a town hall addressing administrators' austerity practices:

Unchecked growth undermines the pursuit of being a world-class university. A world-class university is not one in which new students arrive without housing accommodations, face panic with course registrations and financial aid, or attempt to get appointments with overburdened advisors and staff. It is not one in which students come to class stressed out because they've spent an hour or more trying to find parking. And it is not one in which students avoid the restrooms, if at all possible, because they are, in my students' words, disgusting. Only then to go into classrooms with broken furniture, missing ceiling tiles, dust-encrusted air vents, wires coming out of walls, floors covered with dirty footprints and leaves, and filthy desks and chairs. They have to contend with unstable Wi-Fi access because the system is overburdened, and several student centers are overwhelmed. The message students get is that once they've scored target numbers and have contributed to UCR being named a Hispanic Serving Institution and recognized as one of the most diverse campuses in the nation, is that it is then unimportant that they, at a minimum, receive instruction in adequately appointed labs, classrooms, and lecture halls. This is not world class, it is third class.

This faculty member emphasized the racialized element of getting big, as so much of the growth was driven by tapping into the state's Latinx population. The explosion of disadvantaged students in new universities with limited resources runs parallel to the concentration of excessive resources at elite universities for small numbers of privileged youth.

CUT COSTS

Austerity administrators operate under the assumption that, along with boosting revenue, they must shave organizational costs and stretch available resources. At Merced, where there was little to shave and stretch, administrators promoted what they referred to as "tolerable suboptimization." This policy was based on awareness that staff could take on extreme workloads only if they let the quality of their work slip to "tolerably" suboptimal levels. In this way, the university could continue to operate with insufficient staff. We address the suboptimal experiences of students and staff under tolerable suboptimization in chapter 5.

Riverside administrators had a bit more wiggle room. They argued that the campus could do more with less, through a few cost-saving measures. To a certain extent this was true. Describing UCR's iconic citrus orchards, a top administrator noted, "We have all these citrus groves, right? Low-hanging fruit sitting on the ground waiting for you to pick them up. That was my sense of UCR." As a visual reminder to be vigilant of easy savings, he used a picture of an orange orchard as his computer backdrop. Low-hanging fruit included things like rescheduling chemistry lab maintenance and changing costing procedures for waste removal. Both changes saved money with little negative impact.

But not all cuts are painless. In a resource-scarce environment with intense status pressures to produce research, instructional costs are the most flexible budget lines. The "dirty secret," according to an academic official at UCR, was that "If [a university] wants to pour more money into the research mission, the only way it's going to come about is shaving it off from tuition.... You figure out how to do the teaching in a way that leaves you something to scrape off to subsidize research." Although the reappropriation of undergraduate tuition is a standard practice, it takes on new meaning when schools are scraping from already thin instructional budgets dedicated to educating marginalized youth.

UCR, like many other universities, has employed corporate strategies to cut its instructional costs. This, in itself, is not new; universities have long adopted the latest "management fads."[44] However, recent management tools are being employed under great financial strain to remedy the "cost disease" thought to be rampant in universities.[45] It is in this context that Chancellor Wilcox and Riverside's chief financial officer piloted a program for activity-based costing (or ABC). ABC involves developing measurements of per-unit costs for any given activity to produce more accurate data. These data are then ideally used within the organization to reduce costs, plan better, and maximize quality relative to the level of spending.

The mandate to pilot ABC at a UC was a response to conflict between the governor and the UC president over funding.[46] Interestingly, the pilot was conducted at a new university, rather than one of the better-resourced UC campuses, where there may have been more pushback over cutting costs. ABC is supposed to reduce both seemingly unnecessary instructional costs and thus reliance on state funds. UCR administrators seemed to embrace the challenge. As a UCR white paper about the project asks: "How can a cutting-edge university continue to deliver a superior education to a growing student population, in an era of reduced state funding?" ABC is their answer.[47]

To be clear, there are good reasons to engage in more explicit costing. University budgeting is notoriously complicated and opaque. Existing approaches do a poor job of helping leadership make strategic, cost-informed decisions about desired outcomes, such as student success. Universities should know how much it costs to run classes or grow particular departments, if only so that they can better predict what resources will be needed.

Furthermore, state legislators regularly look at K–12 cost data, but do not have similar information for higher education. As a result, they may question if requests for funds are necessary.[48] It is useful to strategize about how to secure greater appropriations.

Embedded in ABC, however, are assumptions about the nature of organizational activities that may not fit many academic situations. For instance, the idea that learning activities can be measured and priced per unit is perplexing. Would that unit be an idea? A student? An email? A meeting? How would walking a distressed student to psychological services be priced? There is also an assumption that workers operate solely on financial incentives—and surprise that this does not appear to hold in the university. As a financial administrator at UCR remarked, "Even though [UCR] had been successful in student success [previously] … it's actually surprising given how poor the incentives were for that. It's like you could tell people were actually just doing it based on their values because financially they weren't incentivized at all." Austerity administrators at new universities may, in fact, implicitly rely on the assumed "psychic benefits" of the work, and/or altruistic goodwill, to motivate staff and faculty as working conditions deteriorate. Moreover, by attempting to replace values with financial incentives, austerity administrators may actually undermine effective teaching.

At UCR, a decentralized budgeting model accompanied ABC. Often referred to as Responsibility Center Management (or RCM), this approach disperses budget and revenue production to individual units while maintaining centralized control over goals and standards. Units are pushed to meet these goals through a series of financial incentives and disincentives.[49] RCM may "work" in that it can cut costs and boost revenue.[50] However, it may also create perverse incentives to provide lower-quality instruction.

For example, in the past, schools internal to UCR requested additional funding for teaching support when the number of students in need of a class exceeded available seats. Leadership assumed that this "created an incentive for [schools] to underprovide because if they underprovide then they get more money." The provost decided to fund courses from a fixed sum determined by administration and distributed to school deans upfront. As a result, the supposed incentive to initially underprovide (as a means to get more funding) was gone. Now schools were purportedly incentivized to meet demand in a cost-effective way, as any additional money could be pocketed and put to other purposes. This approach, unfortunately, built in incentives to skimp on teaching costs.[51]

Common tactics to shrink the instructional budget include raising class sizes, using technology to reach mass audiences, and shifting to lower-cost non-tenure-track labor. The last two, in particular, are core features of the scaled-up university proposed by Crow.[52] Around 30 percent of the student population is enrolled in ASU online and does not set foot on a physical campus. In addition, the student-to-tenure-track-faculty ratio at ASU is among the worst in the nation, as the school relies heavily on contingent labor.

Strong evidence suggests that these changes are not beneficial for students—especially the populations that attend new universities. Larger class sizes are harmful for first-generation, Black, and Latinx college students, who connect better to professors and peers in smaller-scale settings.[53] Online courses, as they are currently implemented at most universities, tend to slow progression for low-income students who benefit from face time with their instructors.[54] Finally, relying on contingent academic labor to cut costs creates an exploited underclass of academic workers who have fewer resources, including time and energy, to teach effectively.[55]

Attempts to cut costs are also rarely constrained to instruction. The research mission of a university is also impacted. During the study, both UCR and UCM hired faculty via interdisciplinary research clusters. A "big science" model drives the push for interdisciplinarity, particularly in highly competitive research universities; these schools can integrate larger teams of researchers across disciplinary divides in order to address more complex problems and apply for larger grants.[56] In the new university, however, interdisciplinarity is often also a direct response to severe resource constraints. The UCM provost, for example, readily admitted that interdisciplinary cluster hiring was a way of prioritizing a limited number of upcoming faculty positions. Instead of having to decide between a hire in sociology, political science, and economics, for instance, he imagined having one hire as part of an "Inequality, Poverty, and Social Justice" research pillar speak to all three disciplines.

Arizona State University best epitomizes interdisciplinarity as an austerity management strategy: Crow exploded traditional units and reestablished them in "a federation of unique transdisciplinary departments, centers, institutions, schools, and colleges"—saving millions of dollars as a result.[57] But this move is not unique to ASU. Universities around the country are reorganizing into interdisciplinary units, often in response to funding shortfalls.[58] For example, in 2016, Plymouth State University announced aggressive changes to its organizational structure. The school moved from twenty-four academic departments to seven interdisciplinary areas—resulting in a number of staff layoffs and faculty retirements.[59]

Interdisciplinary reorganization, when done well, can break down traditional disciplinary barriers that keep academic fields from intellectual cross-fertilization and increase faculty racial diversity.[60] Yet, scholarship suggests that positive outcomes require considerable investments in infrastructure—including research centers, advisory panels, and incentives.[61] Productive clusters also tend to center on a well-defined problem, start with researchers who were already publishing together or citing each other's work, and depend on having a few highly productive and skilled leaders to harness the talents of the group. Success is more likely in natural science and engineering fields, where team science is well established, and less likely in fields where independent research is more common.[62] In short, successful interdisciplinarity is potentially quite expensive, context specific, and far from a guarantee. It is certainly not a silver bullet for postsecondary financial woes.

BE MARKET-SMART

Austerity administrators seek private funding, beyond undergraduate tuition. As one how-to guide for university leaders clarifies, "Market-smart institutions exploit opportunities to gain revenue."[63] This may sound like modern-day leadership embodies what Gordon Winston refers to as the "car dealer" model of the university, in which commerce and profit extraction are the primary goals.[64] However, Winston notes that the charitable flipside, "the church," which collects donations in service of a social and religious mission, is also part of the university. In fact, many austerity administrators see themselves as using revenue from the car dealership to build the church; that is, they believe that schools must be "market-smart" in order to both survive and achieve goals that are "mission-centered."[65]

What do market-smart schools do? They sell what they can (i.e., monetize assets), develop new assets, identify corporate partners, and direct resources to what are thought to be the most profitable units in the university. Market-smart practices are not always "smart" or even executed in ways likely to yield profit. Yet, neither are these practices inherently detrimental for racially and economically marginalized student populations. Rather, practices that divert resources from these students or extract profit from them have the greatest potential to do harm.

Being market-smart requires considering elements of the campus that can be marketed as assets. For example, while patrons of universities have long been thanked for their contributions with a titled building, space, or school, UC-Merced leadership explicitly discussed naming rights to new buildings as financial products to hawk. As one administrator noted:

I would love to see more named buildings on this campus, and certainly the 2020 Project is only going to expand our portfolio, our menu of options.... In this area the right donor could get a bargain because you could name a building on this campus for a hell of a lot less than naming a building at Stanford or Berkeley.

Here, the language of "portfolio" and "menu of options," as well as the "bargain" available to donors (i.e., the ability to get a named building on the cheap), suggests a more aggressive and strategic approach to the donor relationship. In this administrator's estimation, buildings could be sold as appreciating assets on a prestige market, much like the equivalent of a penny stock of prestige, but backed by the UC: "It is a University of California campus that holds nothing but promise for the future, so an investment now will in twenty years.... Can you imagine having your name on a building on this campus then?" Investors would, they hoped, be motivated to gamble on UCM by the promise of future ROI (return on investment).[66] On a smaller scale, student respondents also told us about how Merced was selling bricks to graduating students. They joked that they were, quite literally, building the school.

Campuses may also seek to produce new goods or services to sell. For example, in 2018 ASU broke ground on its Mirabella Senior Living Project—a twenty-story facility on the Tempe campus, offering assisted-living apartments, skilled-nursing suites, and a secured memory-care section. Leadership clearly expects that Mirabella will appeal to aging adults (who are also potential donors), as well as produce profit.[67] This gamble may work. However, as one analysis of the industry concludes, "Not all nursing homes will make it. The survivors in the sector likely will be chains, along with a handful of small, often high-end, niche operators."[68] ASU is aiming to be one of those high-end, niche operators. But Mirabella may end up costing more than it makes—especially for patients that need extensive care. This is one example of how the push to be market-smart can lead universities into producing goods that non-university entities have far greater experience in providing.

The above examples are relatively neutral in their impact on marginalized populations. But market strategies can also target racially and economically marginalized students as consumers or market these students as assets for private corporations. Both strategies are ethically ambiguous and potentially exploitative. These kinds of market-smart approaches are desirable to administrators because they leverage something that the new university can attract in spades—URS, often from low-income households.

During a budgeting meeting in 2016, for example, UC-Merced administration suggested the development of "self-funding" graduate degrees, which have been referred to as a "cash cow for struggling colleges."[69] In contrast to a model in which postsecondary schools heavily subsidize graduate study, the self-funding model generates funds that can be reinvested in the program and university. With graduate degrees dubbed the new growth industry in higher education, the potential to earn revenue is irresistible to many universities and encouraged by some academic leaders.[70] The strategy shifts the costs of graduate education away from universities, which instead profit from students and their families. Unfortunately, prospective graduate students most likely to enter self-funded programs may be historically marginalized, in part because these students have less knowledge of how graduate school typically works in many fields. This can lead to vastly disparate levels of graduate school debt for Black and low-income students, in particular, who may enter self-funding programs at higher rates.[71]

New universities can also pursue partnerships with corporations and firms that are explicitly focused on gaining access to Black and Brown workers. For instance, administrators at both UCR and UCM intentionally cultivated financial relationships with companies that desired educated workers from historically underrepresented racial groups to diversify their predominately white organizations. As a Merced representative described, "A lot of large tech firms … are not seeing any kind of change in diversity recruitment. We, on the other hand, are a campus that may be able to assist with that.… But we're gonna need some assistance. The opportunity [is there] to open up that pipeline." We explore these corporate partnerships, as well as the ethical quandaries they introduce, in greater detail in chapter 7, with a close look at the relationship between UCR and PepsiCo. As we show, students clearly benefit by gaining jobs from such partnerships; however, they may not have access to the most desirable or highest-paying positions—instead being employed to corner racialized markets.[72]

Universities may also attempt to follow market-smart principles by internally directing resources to seemingly profitable units. Typically, this practice is executed on the basis of a faulty assumption that, as we will show, ends up having racial consequences. The notion that the natural and physical sciences, engineering, and computing always "pay," while the humanities and social sciences do not, is pervasive in the academy.[73] For example, in 2009, then-president of the UC system Mark Yudof stated on national public television:

> Many of our, if I can put it this way, businesses are in good shape. We're doing very well there. Our hospitals are full, our medical business, our medical research, the patient care—so we have this core problem: who's going to pay

the salary of the English department? We have to have it. Who's going to pay it, and sociology, and the humanities, and that's where we're running into trouble.[74]

Yudof's language here—referring to research and patient care as "businesses"— reveals an intense concern with profit production. He sounds more like a chief financial officer of a corporation than a leader of one of the nation's most-revered public universities.

Yudof's statement is also factually incorrect. After outcry, President Yudof issued a clarification that the overhead (or indirect cost recovery—see chapter 3) collected in the process of university-sponsored research often does not cover the actual costs of supporting that research. Many low-cost and high-enrollment departments that do not require research labs, equipment, and intensive support are, in fact, less expensive. Social science departments are good examples, as much research in these fields is done by a single individual, in a single office. These fields can also educate large numbers of students in lecture halls or basic classrooms without special equipment.

Nonetheless, decisions on faculty hiring and salaries, as well as departmental resources and staffing, are often made with the assumption that grant-producing fields are more profitable. These units may also receive greater organizational support.[75] University representatives described this process at UCR:

> The School of Social Sciences, Humanities, and Arts gets shunted to the side. And resources.... I mean it's like the school is seen as a distant second or third to the other schools.... The things that have become important in universities are who brings in the funds. And [the] splashy science stuff and engineering—that brings in the funding.

The same was true at UCM:

> Engineering got a lot of funding.... They got things and so their staff grew quickly.... The same with Natural Sciences. [I have] for years been working with [human resources], showing them the Social Sciences, Humanities, and Arts staff chart and the other school charts. [I] actually had [a high-level official] tell me [in order to justify disparities], "Well, it's apples and oranges, they're the sciences and [this is] the humanities."

At UCM, differences in staffing across schools were indeed sizeable, as detailed in the next chapter. None of these disparities were explicitly about race.

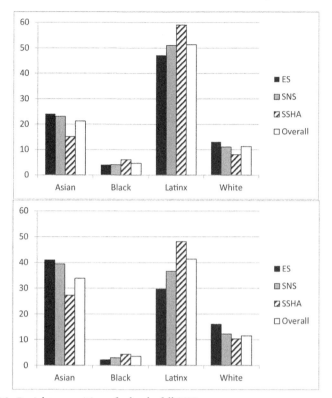

Figure 4.1. Racial composition of schools, fall 2017.

Panel 1: UC-Merced; Panel 2: UC-Riverside.

Note: Data are drawn from UC-Merced Institutional Research and UC-Riverside Institutional Research. These campuses use different measurements for racial and ethnic categories than the UC Office of the President. In particular, the figures above categorize Hispanic Blacks as Hispanic or Latinx, lowering the percentage of Black students relative to system-wide figures.

However, when combined with racial patterns in school enrollment internal to campuses, differences in organizational support can translate into inequalities along racial lines. In fall 2017, this was the case at Merced and Riverside (see fig. 4.1). At both universities, the School of Social Sciences, Humanities, and Arts (SSHA) served more Black students and a greater share of Latinx students, whereas white and Asian students were underrepresented, relative to the overall population. In addition, at Riverside in particular, there was stark underrepresentation of Latinx students in the Engineering School (ES) (around 10 percent lower than the percentage of the university population that was Latinx) and Black students (only 1.7 percent of students in ES identified as Black). Both white and Asian students were overrepresented in ES. These patterns also existed in Merced's ES, but they were not quite as pronounced. At Riverside, the School of Natural Sciences (SNS) showed similar, but less dramatic, gaps as the Engineering School.[76,77]

Riverside and Merced are not unique in this regard, although it is perhaps surprising to see patterns that exist in predominately white universities also reflected in new universities. Racial disparities across fields (often heavily inflected by gender) are visible in national data for four-year colleges and universities: Asian and white men are heavily clustered in engineering and computer science fields, while Black and Latinx women are overrepresented in the social sciences.[78] If the schools and fields that the most-marginalized students enter are systematically underfunded and understaffed, these students are likely to have a less enriching and less supported experience than their more advantaged peers in other units.

When new universities take a market approach to resource distribution they are, ironically, reproducing the same dynamics that disadvantage these organizations in competitions with more prestigious universities. Recall from chapter 3 that faculty at UC-San Diego used market principles to propose shutting down UCM and UCR during the Great Recession. They argued that "Corporations faced with similar problems eliminate or sell off their least profitable, least promising divisions." Similarly, we see competition in private markets guiding the distribution of resources internal to new universities. Because market-smart approaches are colorblind, they do not account for the uneven distribution of racial groups across high- and low-resourced fields. Racial disparities in access to resources *within schools*, as we indicate here, are the predictable result.

THINK (INTER)NATIONAL

New universities draw students from surrounding regions and build a reputation for serving their states. In some ways they are profoundly local. But the gaze of austerity administrators is consistently drawn outward, away from their campuses and communities. Crow, for example, begins his book by positioning ASU in a global context, remarking on ASU's rise in the Shanghai Academic Ranking of World Universities, from not even the top 200 in 2002 to eighty-eighth in the world in 2014 (notably, this spot is higher than ASU's rank among US universities in the *U.S. News & World Report*). In 2018, ASU announced an expansion program in the Los Angeles area. In truly global fashion, the university already has outposts in China, Vietnam, Mexico City, and Dubai.[79]

How do we make sense of this seeming contradiction between the local roots of new universities and their expanded gaze? Public research universities, in general, have been stretching outside of state lines and reaching overseas to court patrons and clients, a pattern that has intensified with shifting funding streams.[80] When state resources dry up, universities seek revenue elsewhere. Private funding markets are not constrained by boundaries, and status competitions are decidedly not local. Universities are ranked on national and international levels, and their peers are typically not within the state. In many ways, therefore, new university administrators are acting no different than any other leaders under austerity.

There are also unique pressures on new universities. As we demonstrated in chapter 3, under austerity, relationships with sister campuses internal to a state's postsecondary infrastructure can become less cooperative. In the University of California system, therefore, while it was once possible to stake a claim for state resources on the basis of presumed equality with Berkeley, other UCs have now become outsized competitors for market resources. New universities may need to make claims for status and resources beyond state lines. Although they seek to gain status on the basis of local actions (i.e., access and completion for state residents), they do so on a national stage.

UCR leadership, for example, was clear about the importance of a national focus. Chancellor Wilcox "wasn't there very long before he realized that in the mind-set of people of the State of California, we were always going to be at the bottom of the totem pole." Wilcox knew Riverside could not yet compete in the global arena; what he did instead was focus on national platforms for attention and prestige. He reportedly claimed, "We're not going to be a hero in California until we are a hero in the rest of the country." Berkeley was no longer the model. UCR administration planned to raise the profile of the school by working in partnership with like-minded university leaders around the country. As a top administrator at UC-Riverside explained, "I think the recognition is catching up, and I think the national priorities are catching up. Our work with the University Innovation Alliance, the national network, is a reflection of [the fact that] we're not the only ones thinking this way." UIA membership identified Riverside as unique in the UC system (no other campuses are members) and linked it with the global vision of partner universities such as ASU and Purdue University (see chapter 1).

The only problem is that new universities are different than predominately white research universities. For example, new universities typically cannot successfully court significant numbers of wealthy out-of-state and international students. One of the flaws with thinking (inter)nationally is that it can lead new university leadership to attempt practices that just do not work for their organizations. For instance, Merced has the smallest nonresident population in the UC system. Yet, as noted in chapter 2, Merced's financing plan moving into 2020, when special remittances to the campus from the system were slated to end, built in a rapid increase in this population. According to university leadership, "There is a plan that, by 2020, about 5 percent to 7 percent of our undergraduates will be non-California residents." In reality, by 2018, there were still only twenty-three out-of-state and fifteen international students on campus (out of 7,881 total undergraduates).

The outward focus of new university administrators also has potentially troubling effects on leadership style that may be most consequential at new universities. The change can be seen in how and with whom administrators consult. Thus, over time, Chancellor Leland reportedly spent less time with the council of school deans and more time with individuals involved in the P3, who were focused on financial, rather than academic, planning. At UCR, faculty noted an increasing number of outside hires into top administrative positions, rather than promotions from within. As one faculty member colorfully noted in reference to a James Bond movie, "Some [on campus] even mutter variations of Goldfinger's famous adage, 'One outside administrator is happenstance. A second is coincidence, and a third is enemy action.'"

Turning attention to the national or international stage has the effect of removing leadership from campus, local, regional, and state arenas. This is a break from past approaches. For instance, former UC system president Clark Kerr's list of qualifications for a university president, presented at a talk at Harvard University in 1963, started with "a friend of the students, a colleague of the faculty, a good fellow with the alumni, a sound administrator with the trustees, [and] a good speaker with the public" before moving farther afield. As we showed in chapter 2, Chancellor Orbach, who entered the UC during the Kerr era, was a stalwart friend of the students, a faculty colleague, and deeply rooted in the Riverside community throughout his tenure.

In contrast, high-level austerity administrators are located almost entirely off-campus and away from immediate constituencies.[81] As a senior administrator noted, Chancellor Wilcox began "going around the country spreading the gospel," which meant that "like any modern university president or chancellor, his function is almost exclusively external to the campus." The administrator continued:

> [Take] Gene Block at UCLA or Pradeep Khosla down at San Diego. Those folks are not walking around campus shaking people's hands because they flat-out don't have the time. I think people don't understand. There's nobody on this planet that works as hard as Kim [Wilcox] does. He's got no life other than this job and he's working his ass off. I mean … every evening, he's on

airplanes. We don't have a university airplane. Gene [Block] flies around on some university airplane. Kim flies Southwest coach.

While UCR leadership sought to continue in the tradition of Orbach, much of the on-the-ground work had to be delegated further and further down the line.

The story was much the same at Merced. Under the strain of financing and planning the 2020 P3 project, Chancellor Leland all but vanished. Her absence was so conspicuous that students circulated a flyer with Leland's picture and the words "Have you seen her?" The last reported location was in Washington, DC, "with lobbyists." The irony is that Leland's lobbying efforts were for one of UC-Merced's most vulnerable student populations. She was active with the Congressional Hispanic Caucus in advocating for undocumented students under the Trump administration. In some cases, when she was not on campus, she was knocking on the doors of Congress members and pressing them to pass legislation that would support the so-called "Dreamers" on her campus.[82] Yet, the reason for any particular absence was less noticeable to students than the mere fact that their chancellor was often not present.

Not being local enough may have consequences for new university administrators' relationship with the state. If they are constantly looking outward for support—and do not see the system or the state legislature as the first places to turn—it may be increasingly difficult to depend on those relationships. This kind of drift does not matter for prestigious publics that, as we detail in chapter 3, can afford to exist on their own. New universities do not have this luxury. While new university leadership may seek national attention, attending to the local connections that sustain the university is of paramount importance.

Perhaps not surprisingly, austerity administrators often face considerable backlash from faculty, staff, and students. Those implementing austerity practices, just a step or two down from chancellors and presidents, tend to be most at risk. In fact, during our study, a threatened vote of no confidence among faculty resulted in the resignation of UCR's provost. One faculty member pointed out that faculty put pressure on the provost because he was someone with whom everyone was familiar; Chancellor Wilcox was less visible and thus less of a target. As UCM's then provost noted, "I could've taken that article that was written about [UCR's provost] in *The Chronicle* [of *Higher Education*], unplugged his name in Riverside, and plugged in my name in Merced, and it was basically the same story. . . . So I'm thinking I'm next."[83]

Removing particular individuals, however, tends not to stop austerity practices. These practices are not grounded in the actions of any single person—even the university chancellor. They tend to be motivated by pressures from the state legislature, system leadership, university governing boards, financial advisors, and public constituencies who argue that universities are spending irresponsibly and push them to become more self-sustaining. Once particular types of responses are established, it can also be difficult to undo the infrastructure, personnel, and regulations that accompany them. The conditions motivating administrators to adopt austerity logics and strategies remain firmly in place.[84]

In *Austerity: The History of a Dangerous Idea*, Mark Blyth argues that austerity may be a response to structural conditions, but it is also an ideological process that constrains responses to fiscal shortage and motivates further cuts to public spending.[85] Austerity is bad for states, Blyth argues, because it attempts to solve economic problems on the backs of the most vulnerable members of society and ultimately deepens the very financial crises that austerity is intended to address. Looking at higher education, we can see that austerity penalizes universities serving marginalized students—leading administrators to employ austerity practices, some of which are detrimental to students.

By engaging in austerity practices, administrators may also undermine claims to public resources. For example, shifting focus outward, rather than maintaining heavy engagement with local and state actors, may fray relationships with state governing bodies. Claiming that ABC is the answer to running a public university with reduced state funding only cements austerity logics; it suggests that even resource-poor universities spend too much and can do more with less. Universities that are looking for new profit centers may direct less attention to requesting funds from and demonstrating needs to the state. These approaches may help produce the conditions that disadvantage new universities and their students in the first place.

In the next chapter, we examine the on-the-ground consequences of a particular austerity policy at Merced for staff members' provision of basic services required by college students. This detailed account helps demonstrate, more concretely, how university-level austerity practices filter down to the experiences of students. Not only are new university students, as a whole, more likely to be negatively impacted by austerity practices; we argue that marginalized populations within new universities are at a heightened risk.

5 *Tolerable Suboptimization*

The administration of austerity has a direct impact on those who occupy new universities. Cost cutting, attempts to increase efficiencies, and decreases in the quality and quantity of services are not just top-down, disembodied organizational practices; many university constituencies experience, react to, and even push back against these constraints.[1] Given the relationship between racialized hierarchies and resource distribution, new university occupants are particularly likely to encounter austerity practices. In this chapter, we zoom in to examine the everyday functionality of three core services—academic advising, mental health, and cultural programming—under austerity. We focus on the cost to historically underrepresented racially marginalized students (URS), along with the staff that serve them.

We intentionally highlight frontline staff workers, who represent an often-overlooked group in educational research. Understanding university infrastructure requires taking seriously the staff members whose day-to-day interactions with administration, faculty, and students help reproduce the organization.[2] Students routinely rely on university staff to meet basic needs and perform functions required for their enrollment. Staff members' abilities to do this, and do it well, are a function of the context in which they work. But at UCM, resources were exceptionally scarce. As one administrator crudely put it, "UC-Merced is already the leanest machine that exists in the public higher-ed world.... We can't get any leaner without being diagnosed with an eating disorder."

We focus specifically on "tolerable suboptimization"—an official policy proposed at higher levels as a stopgap measure to reduce UCM staff overload without hiring more staff or increasing compensation. As we will demonstrate, staff members were urged to reduce performance, but only to (undefined) "tolerable" levels. This organizational practice, to a certain extent, was already occurring informally, out of necessity. However, the official promotion of less-than-optimal service highlighted just how sparse resources were at UCM. The high stress of attempting to do a job with inadequate support was particularly intense for the student-facing employees at the heart of the university.

Even highly skilled and well-intentioned staff members faltered under the weight of high caseloads and insufficient resources, while rejecting the notion that it was acceptable for them to do less for students. Pushback against the efforts of management to decrease the quality of service may be a unique feature of care work, in which employees self-select into fields that require a high level of concern for the populations they serve.[3] As a result of the pressures facing staff members, students often failed to receive the support that they needed. This outcome was especially problematic when considering the new university context: These students required more—not less—organizational support. Furthermore, within the university, resource cuts and service reduction hurt marginalized student populations the most.

Tolerable or Intolerable?

During the 2016–2017 academic year, Merced leadership engaged in extensive workforce planning (WFP, as it was referred to at UCM). The goal was to figure out how to staff and run the university in the four years leading up to 2020. Student enrollment and campus space would be rapidly growing, creating the need for more staff and faculty than in the past, but the resources to fund current and future positions were scarce. On October 4, the assistant vice chancellor (AVC) of human resources and another member of the administration recorded an informational webcast about staff WFP. Staff members around the university were asked to pause their work, tune in, and submit questions, which were answered live and also in a document that was circulated after the webcast. Given concerns about budget cuts and potential layoffs, the webcast was widely and anxiously viewed.

During the webcast, the AVC indicated that workers should practice "tolerable suboptimization." He defined the term as follows: "Absent an allocation of X resources, then we must accept Y level of suboptimization." Examples of tolerable suboptimization included making faculty wait longer for their travel expenditure reimbursements or extending the time it takes to categorize new positions for hire. As the AVC noted, the long-range budget model only allowed for funding about a third of the requested staff positions identified during the WFP process, but "we must live within our means." Consequently, he determined that the university must "accept a standard of output that may not be ideal but is necessary so that we do not overwork and overtax our valued staff." However, as he warned multiple times, "Tolerable suboptimization is not an invitation—or permission—to abandon responsibilities.... I personally abhor uncorrected underperformance and find it intolerable."

For staff toiling under exceptionally high workloads with little relief in sight, these warnings came across as insulting. Indeed, the tersely worded questions that staff submitted during the webcast revealed a high level of concern about institutionalizing tolerable suboptimization as not only a suggested, but mandated, practice. As one staff member wrote, at times "yelling" in all capital letters (and setting a trend): "Tolerable suboptimization is fine, but then EVERYONE needs to know the wagon wheels ARE going to fall off and replacement wheels will be several weeks out. This place is breaking and no one seems to mind." Staff also emphasized the huge negative impact of understaffing on students and faculty. As another question read: "If your function is 'administration' maybe this doesn't matter as much but those of us on the FRONT LINES serving our faculty (and students) are DYING out here.... Can we expect WFP to ... actually provide some help WHEN THE FACULTY AND STUDENTS ARRIVE expecting service?"

"Tolerable suboptimization" became a campus catchphrase. Faculty who were aware of the webcast used the term to signal criticism of UCM's administration, or to point out the effects of insufficient staffing. Staff rolled their eyes when employing the phrase to (sarcastically) describe delays, disruptions, or simply the contradictory state of working at UCM. One high-ranking Student Life staff member explained:

> They did a webinar talking about what's to come and ... about tolerable suboptimization. I thought, okay we're going to get T-shirts made because that's kind of the model we'd been working with: you know, do more with less. And [the AVC] said we're still a University of California and we expect excellence. We're not going to tell you that you need to work eighty hours a week to achieve that. Because they can't say that. I've been saying since I came here that we've got all the needs, but not all the resources. But I've never worked on a campus with more folks committed to serving students. We're going to do what we need to do in service to them to make sure that they have an amazing, powerful, productive, life-altering positive experience. But my mother used to say, you can't get blood out of a turnip. There's only so much you can do. I think right now we're in that era of we've got to figure out how to make this work. We got to figure out how to do more with less again.

These comments suggest that official endorsement of tolerable suboptimization was not experienced as a relief. As this person emphasized, UCM staff were already doing all they could to support students with the time and resources available to them.

News of the new administrative stance even reached students. At the opening of an undergraduate student cultural space, discussed in more detail in the next chapter, a faculty speaker pointed out that the university encouraged tolerable suboptimization, as evidenced by insufficient cultural programming on campus. He urged students to think about what such a practice meant for their education—and to question tolerable suboptimization particularly when applied to a largely non-white, first-generation student body. As one student ethnographer in the audience recorded: "[This faculty member] said that the university thinks we are stupid and thought they could get away with it since 70 percent of the school is first generation, but that is not the case.... Students were snapping, clapping, and looking at each other with the 'ohh shit [I can't believe he said that]' look in their eyes."

The AVC's official endorsement of tolerable suboptimization was not motivated by devious calculations about hoodwinking the student body. Rather, austerity logics, as discussed in the previous chapter, were at play. Regardless of the AVC's original intent, however, the faculty speaker was correct to point out the potential impact of tolerable suboptimization on students' educational experiences. Marginalized populations, in particular, often need the university to offer support, information, and guidance that affluent white students can more easily access from their parents, social networks, and communities—as well as demand from their universities.[4] Thus, as we show below, tolerable suboptimization was particularly damaging for URS at new universities.

Academic Advising

It is difficult to determine what an ideal caseload for an academic advisor should be, as many factors can affect advising delivery, including the larger political and economic context, specific features of the campus racial climate, and the typical student's access to cultural, material, and financial resources. However, we can look to the numbers of academic advisors across the country as a general guide (see fig. 5.1). According to a recent national survey of academic advising, the median caseload per full-time academic advisor at a public doctorate-granting university was 285. Caseloads are much higher at two-year public universities (441), and much lower at private bachelor's-granting universities (100).[5]

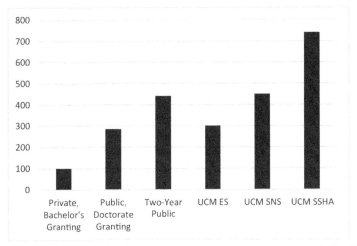

Figure 5.1. Academic advising caseloads by university type and UC-Merced school.
Note: National data are drawn from Robbins (2013). UC-Merced data are provided by campus institutional research.

At the time of the study, full-time advisors in the UC-Merced School of Social Sciences, Humanities, and Arts (SSHA) had an average caseload of 740, including the lead advisor, who also had managerial responsibilities. This is roughly 2.5 times the national median for advisors at similar schools. The only other academic advisors on campus with a similarly high load were those advising biology students (the most popular major on campus). In contrast, advisors in the School of Natural Sciences (SNS) had caseloads closer to 450—still over the national median, but far below SSHA numbers. The caseload for advisors in the Engineering School (ES) was around 300 for full-time advisors and a low 150 for the lead advisor.[6] School-based inequities in access to advising *internal* to the campus were, therefore, greater than differences between the median caseload for two-year public schools and four-year private schools.

The situation in SSHA was compounded by several other factors. First, SSHA advisors were doing tasks that, in other schools, were assigned to separate staff. For example, SSHA academic advisors, but not ES advisors, were also in charge of course articulation, or the process of determining credit that would be assigned to course content from transfer institutions.[7] One SSHA advisor even reported working nights in order to revolutionize the course articulation system, moving it from hard copy to a streamlined digital system—all while managing a personal caseload. SSHA also had the largest number of minor areas of study on campus, and thus did the minor advising for a significant proportion of students in other schools.

This extra labor was particularly difficult to manage due to compensation issues. UC-Merced advising staff were typically paid between $37,000 and $47,000, without the ability to receive extra pay for the labor they did outside of typical work hours. The local community colleges reportedly paid more, and primary and secondary school workers could take summers off or receive additional pay for working during the summer. These factors made it hard to keep UCM advising staff, leading to regular disruptions in students' relationships with their advisors. In SSHA, where the workload was highest, turnover was greatest, contributing to periods in which caseloads were even higher than 740.

Seeing a SSHA advisor was not an easy task. A student first checked into a small, nondescript waiting room separated from the suite of advising offices by a locked door. It was impossible to simply "stop by." On busy days, the waiting room got stuffy as students continued to crowd in. The door was cracked open, and the line snaked out of the room and down the hall. The wait time to see an advisor could be hours. As a result, students who spotted the crowd would sometimes turn the other way. Managing the flow of students was challenging in part because a previous SSHA administrator, unlike administrators in other schools on campus, had declined to purchase online appointment software that would help manage the flow of students and get them to their assigned advisors.[8] As a result of scheduling issues and limited numbers of advisors, students often had to see any available advisor. Due to advisors' high caseloads, most requests of first-year and second-year students were filtered to peer mentors located in a shared office down the hall. These were often missed opportunities for advisors to identify problems, offer general advice, and bond with students.

SSHA advisors worried about their lack of availability to students. They had been drawn to this career and to UCM, specifically, with the desire to support the types of students who attend the university. Many advising staff were Latinx and grew up in the surrounding area. Not being able to meet the needs of students was deeply disappointing. As one advisor noted with a sigh, "We want to be available more, [but] we just can't. I know that's another frustration our students particularly have. We're not as available as they would like us to be.... They're frustrated, and I think it's a very valid frustration that they have." The realities of advisors' jobs, however, meant that even the interactions students had with advisors were often not reflective of advisors' training or full abilities.

Laura spent a day shadowing each of the three full-time SSHA advisors and the one contract worker (an advisor employed on a year contract) during their advising sessions. The average advising session that she observed lasted between seven and eight minutes. As she noted at the end of one day, "Interactions are clearly designed to check boxes and get business done. They are friendly but brisk. This is not an environment in which a student is likely to unload unless they are really struggling and it is spilling over easily." Even when the line was not long, advisors' interactions struck this tone. This was, in part, because an advisor's work was not limited to meeting students, but also because advisors—in response to heavy workloads—had established an efficient routine for their interactions with students. They were effectively practicing tolerable suboptimization; it had become part of the habits of workers in an organization operating under intensified austerity.[9]

The following field notes are from a typical session between an advisor and a Latina student that was focused around course planning for the next semester. The conversation is summarized as closely as possible. The session lasted five minutes, including the student's signing of the consent form.

> **Student:** I failed calculus and I don't know what to do.
> **Advisor:** What happened?
> **Student:** I failed it.
> **Advisor:** I mean, what was the primary issue? Time management, the professor, et cetera?
> **Student:** Time management.
> **Advisor:** So, you think this time around you will do things differently. Is there a reason that you are taking psych[ology] statistics? Because you could substitute econ[omics] statistics for that [since you have already taken it], and it will be one less stats class. Unless you really want to take psych statistics. It's not guaranteed, but you can petition to have that count. My recommendation, but it's totally up to you.
> **Student:** [nods in assent]
> **Advisor:** So, you have two other options [locates them on the screen and lists them to the student].
> **Student:** The problem is many upper-division classes [in psych] are all taken and closed at this point.
> **Advisor:** [Pauses, scanning the list online], you should keep checking if students drop, but I see that this [one class] has six spots. You could also find soc[iology] or other courses that are still open with no prerequisites. Anything else?
> **Student:** No.

The advisor takes the time to ask the student why she struggled in calculus, but the pace of the interaction and the request to consolidate an answer into a "primary" cause of failure likely discouraged her from elaborating. The student picked the first option provided to her, which may or may not have been accurate. The advisor's proclamation that the student would do things differently in the future closed the conversation. This advisor did not offer advice on how to better manage time, direct the student to relevant campus resources, or open a discussion about why the student struggled to manage time. The advice about not needing to double up on statistics was likely helpful, given the student's past history with calculus, but it may have also come across as doubting her abilities to manage the class. The closing of "Anything else?"—although technically a prompt for more questions—felt final.

This advisor utilized an interactional style that elicited and transmitted relatively minimal information, without engaging in in-depth conversations likely to become more time consuming. Others did the same. For instance, another advisor ignored a student's repeated offhanded remarks about her baby (the challenges of motherhood may have been competing with academics) and did not ask a sophomore student why she wanted to take more than a full load to get ahead. All advisors in SSHA displayed a high level of awareness of the need for high-touch interactions with their students, but simply could not execute this under the stressful conditions.

Students' own reports of experiences with SSHA advisors mirrored Laura's observations.[10] For example, as a first-year Latina explained in her second semester of college, she could not get in to see her assigned advisor:

> **Student:** I've only gone once.... When I did go, I didn't have eye contact with my student [peer] advisor because she was on her computer, and she's just talking to me. So, it made it really tense and awkward.
> **Interviewer:** You have a student advisor and then also another advisor too?
> **Student:** Yeah. I was told that we're not allowed to talk to our actual college advisors until we're like third years or fourth years.
> **Interviewer:** I wonder why that is. Did they tell you why?
> **Student:** Well, I don't know. They just assigned me a student advisor, but my roommate, she's a psych major and she's also in the same department I am. I guess she went and she said that she wanted to talk to … our advisor, but they told her that she couldn't talk to her because she had to be a third year or fourth year, [because at that point] you could talk about your career and [you are] getting close to graduation.

This student experienced peer mentors as a barrier from accessing professionally trained academic advisors and was discouraged that she would need to wait years to connect with her advisor.

A fourth-year Latino student was able to see his advisor, but was frustrated with turnover, the quality of his interactions, and rapid growth in the student population without a parallel increase in advisors:

> It's like a runaround.... There's a switch-up in advisors. I had [one advisor]. [Then] I got an email that [this advisor] is no longer with us so I went back to [another advisor whom I had in the past] and [who is] very busy all the time.... I've been trying to get [this advisor] to know me, but I know [this person] is very busy with a lot of students, so it's kind of a difficult situation. It feels like [the advisor] doesn't have time, but I hope that [this person] can make time because, if they feel more personally involved, then they will probably do a better job at being an advisor. I feel that's like a major issue. In the past the advisors used to be more hands-on, but now that we have more students I feel like it's less hands-on. I hope that it gets better.

When academic advisors were not accessible, marginalized students in our sample often tried to figure things out on their own. Without necessary information, they made mistakes. Thus, the student above explained that he worried about doing something that would prevent him from graduating. Previously, he had unknowingly taken many courses that did not count toward his major—and was not advised of this until later. As he pointed out, "I've taken enough classes to have like six associate's degrees already [laughs]."[11]

As noted earlier, in the Engineering School (ES), caseloads were low—due in no small part to the dean's support for hiring advisors out of the (more substantial) school budget. Although walk-ins were accepted, on the engineering advising web page students were also invited to "Make an appointment! See your advisor's hours for their availability." The space and building also had a much different feel. As Laura's field notes indicated:

> I had the joy of heading into engineering's new digs today. You literally feel transported to another campus—a much richer campus. Everything from the quality of the contemporary wood encasing the elevator, to the seating, and the opaque glass and silver doors, also designed to write on, screams money. There is even a lovely outdoor deck overlooking the grasslands on one side of campus, which feels lush and comfortable. It is not overcrowded because hardly any of the gen[eral] pop[ulation] on campus heads out this way (in fact, a SSHA faculty member showed me this the other day, as it was his "secret" working spot).

Inside the building, the advising office was not locked. Students checked in at the front desk and waited in a seating area that allowed them to actually see the advisors' offices—and even wave if doors were open. A rack of science magazines, general info on internships, and a number of specialty publications, such as *Diversity and Democracy* and some from the Society of Hispanic Professional Engineers, were prominently displayed.

Because the school was able to provide enough advisors, peer mentors were not necessary. As an ES advisor explained, this was ideal. "I feel like students should be connected to an advisor, should be connected to someone else that's going to guide them the whole entire process.... I feel like that's a lot of pressure to put onto a student worker as well." The advisor also described a more holistic style of advising:

> I think mainly what we're looking for is, academically if they're not doing well, then we need to do a little bit more of exploration. Is it learning style? Is it time management? Is it just major fit? Then we look at the personal as well.... We ask about their community that they're currently building on campus ... How they're feeling in the dorms? Are they on campus, off campus? How's that going? And so we look at how their interactions are with the rest of the student population.... Like, for example, we had a case where a student was being harassed by another student and the student just didn't want to talk to anybody, didn't really want to say anything. I required her to come in for first-year advising. I'm like, "How's it going?" She's like, "It's fine." And I'm like, "No, really how is it going? What's going on? You seem a little upset. Are you upset about anything?" She's like, "Well, I didn't come in for this reason." I'm like, "It doesn't matter the reason you came in. You're here."

This advisor coordinated with several offices to provide "wrap-around" services geared toward addressing the student's experiences of harassment and improving her psychological well-being—as both issues were also affecting her academic performance. This approach was the opposite of that occurring in SSHA. ES advisors indicated that they had time and space to probe deeply on matters that might be impacting their students.

We were unable to observe advising sessions in the Engineering School and directly confirm ES advisor reports. However, our random sample of students indicated that students had more positive than negative experiences with ES advising. As a first-year Black student noted of his encounters with his ES advisor:

> I've only been to the one advisor that I've been assigned to, of course, and it's been really, really helpful. My academic advisor has told me essentially what I should be doing and what classes I should be taking, what recom-

mendations if the worst-case scenario were to happen — like if I were to fail a class. She even gave me options for doing research or being able to apply to internships as fast as possible to build up as much of my resume as possible, so when it comes to the real world or looking for jobs it would be a lot easier than if I were not to be doing anything at the moment.

As this student suggests, ES first-year students often have access to their assigned advisors, assume this is the norm, and begin building a working relationship. His advisor not only went through the basic registration process, but also helped the student see that even in the worst-case scenario he had options to move forward. Career planning began early, so the student would have the experiences necessary to reach his goals by graduation.

It was thus not surprising that an external review report on UCM academic advising singled out SSHA, in particular, as providing inadequate services to students. Advisors were deeply hurt by the report. As one explained, near tears:

I had a lot of emotions and thoughts going through my head at the same time because of how our unit was called out.... I kept playing in my head that we are "cold, aloof, and unwelcoming" — the exact three words that were used to describe SSHA's advising environment.... Knowing how much we all work so hard to serve our students and get what they need as fast as we possibly can, it's very frustrating.... But, I mean, at the same time I get where they are coming from, right? It's almost mission impossible to get back here [and see an advisor].

SSHA advising was critiqued for the lack of an appointment system, the locked space, and the reliance on peer mentors. But these factors were beyond the control of advisors. The first two decisions had been made at a higher level. And the third — the peer mentoring system — was implemented "just for survival mode. We had to. There was no way we were going to be able to survive this semester if we were at three advisors and didn't require first-year students to go see the peer mentors."

Perhaps the most hurtful aspect of the external report for advisors was the fact that, as one advisor explained, "Findings were not suggesting that more advisors be hired. It was more of change your processes and everything should be fine. Our ratios are already much higher compared to the national average, and we're gonna keep growing." This message was consistent with the campus focus on tolerable suboptimization. We disagreed, however, with the reviewers. It was clear to our research team that the problem was not rooted in process, effort, or advisor skill, but the sheer lack of resources devoted to SSHA advising. Students paid the price for this arrangement, in which SSHA advising staff were forced to downgrade the services they provided. And things were only likely to get worse.

Stark differences between SSHA and ES academic advising also reflect racial inequities that can develop within college campuses. As noted in the previous chapter, UCM displayed a typical pattern: SSHA was disproportionately Latinx and Black, and ES was disproportionately Asian and white.[12] When students are sorted by race within universities, then resources can fall along racial lines. The shift toward private market funding, characteristic of austerity, only exaggerates resource inequities existing within public universities—as it tends to favor units that do the least "diversity work" for the university. Resources are frequently diverted from schools like SSHA, which disproportionately serve URS. As a result, the students who encounter overworked, under-resourced staff are more likely to be racially marginalized.

Mental Health Support

In recent years, mental health issues among the college-going population have been growing in both number and severity.[13] Between 2010 and 2015, counseling center usage at colleges around the country increased at around five to six times the rate of enrollment.[14] As a result, some observers have described a mental health "crisis" or "epidemic" occurring on college campuses.[15] Postsecondary schools around the country are struggling to respond, as meeting the needs of students requires significant investments in mental health services.

The International Association of Counseling Services recommends a ratio of one counselor to 1,000 students at schools where there are concentrations of students with severe mental health conditions or a need for behavioral threat teams, as is the case for all University of California campuses.[16] At the time of the study, a staff member reported that the student-to-psychologist ratio at UC-Merced was around 1,500 to 1—similar to other UC campuses. This ratio, however, was particularly problematic in the context of Merced. Geographic features of the campus and characteristics of the student population significantly intensified the need for mental health care support.

UC-Merced is located in a health care desert. There are only a few qualified mental health practitioners in the vicinity. UCM students are also less likely to have access to good parental health insurance coverage and a car, both of which would allow them to visit highly qualified providers in urban areas hours away. Thus, Merced students that sought mental health services had to lean heavily on available on-campus supports. As one practitioner explained, "We're kind of it.... At all the other campuses ... if they have a student that has what we consider to be a severe mental illness or something that is going to require more chronic care, they can refer them to a provider because they have 200 different clinical psychologists in the community." Other campuses were able to set eight-visit limits for students because they could refer out to other care providers. Counseling and Psychological Services (CAPS) at UCM, in contrast, had nowhere to send its students and could not set visit limits. This significantly increased the number of visits per student.

In addition, the percentage of students utilizing CAPS services at UCM was around 20 percent—double the national average for postsecondary organizations. This was, in part, a function of the student body composition. Research suggests that individuals who hold subordinate positions across several systems of stratification are at greater risk for experiencing anxiety, depression, and other mental health issues.[17] Staff reported that stressors faced by UCM students were often compounded:

We have a lot of first-generation students here. It's the pressure ... especially, I think, within the Hispanic population. You can even break it down further, if you're the eldest female and so on and so forth. The pressure that my success really is not just for me but it's for my whole family. Like, the burden is on me to do this. And otherwise, how's my family going to get out of poverty? How are they going to be able to buy a house? All of the things they've sacrificed have to be for something. And it's got to be for my degree. I think that [burden] is so much for them.

This example suggests that race, social class, and gender intersect in ways that magnify mental health issues for students.[18]

As one support staff noted in reference to national data on college student mental health, "Not only do our students experience more stress, but it has a more significant impact on them when they do experience it. Instead of, for example, getting a lower grade in the class, more of them would say I had to withdraw from a class or I got a D or an F in a class." Staff described UCM students' experiences with stress as a house of cards: "We're seeing students that have ... gone through something traumatic. They've had a lot of obstacles.... There are still things that they haven't dealt with.... So, if one thing goes bad then everything crumbles." Dealing with the fallout often required intensive care, but this need could not necessarily be predicted by the intake visit, which might flag a poor grade on a test or a fight with a roommate as the issue at hand. More serious problems could quickly surface.

During the 2016–2017 academic year, aspects of the larger political and social climate, in particular the election of Donald Trump, also intensified existing pressures for UCM students. Undocumented students feared for their safety and worried about the dismantling of policies that made college more affordable and citizenship attainable. Many students, even if not personally undocumented, worried about friends and family members who were. Trump's commentary about Mexicans as rapists and drug dealers highlighted and promoted anti-immigrant, racist ideology that was painful to Latinx students. Black students described increased encounters with anti-Blackness on and off campus. Students who identified as LGBTQ+ (i.e., lesbian, gay, bisexual, transgender, queer/questioning, with the plus encompassing other marginalized sexual identities), most of whom were of color, organized on campus to counter discrimination.

Administrators and staff suggested that a more workable ratio of psychologists to students at the university might be closer to 700 to 1—less than half of the current caseload. Under existing conditions, CAPS workers were flooded with students. They reported an average of seven clinical hours, or hours of face-to-face contact with students, a day; this did not include any other duties, such as the managerial labor of running CAPS, note-taking on existing cases, or emergency care. Quality assurance and risk management programs—which exist at many of the other UCs—were not viable, as practitioners were doing everything they could "just to take care of the students that we need to take care of."

Rather than seeing all students in a timely fashion, psychologists were forced to triage and identify the students at greatest risk. When a student called or visited CAPS, they were asked a series of questions that related to "suicidality and homicidality, which would of course get you in immediately." Students who did not meet these criteria, or who were not comfortable answering in the affirmative, were given an appointment that could be as far out as a month or more. This meant that many students at or near crisis points were forced to wait for a long time to receive help. As a Black woman in her third year described:[19]

[The CAPS intake worker] said, "Are you having an emergency?" I said, "Well, what's an emergency to you?" Because it could be different. And he basically asked me if I'm gonna kill myself, then at the end he says am I gonna hurt someone else? I was like, "No, but that's not the only emergency." And then they were like, "Oh, sorry. We can give you [an appointment in a month]."

Appointments also got shorter as CAPS got busier. As a practitioner indicated, "Our schedules get full and that's where we go to these very abbreviated [sessions, asking:] ... What's going on? Can we do some solution-focused problem-solving as to what's going [to work] for you?"

Students also complained about the limited representation of people of color in CAPS. This issue came to a head in 2015 after campus police shot Faisal Mohammad, a student of color who had attacked several members of the campus with a knife. The stabbing victims survived, but Mohammad did not. Racially marginalized students at UCM at the time of the event often connected the police killing of Mohammad with the broader threat of racialized police violence to their communities. The event, and the subsequent increased police presence on campus, was therefore particularly traumatic for many URS—and in a different way than for other members of campus whose fears were calmed by seeing more police.[20] As a faculty member noted, "I had students of color come to my office saying, 'I am fucking terrified. I'm not terrified by Faisal Mohammad or by violence from students. I'm terrified from these police.... I go the long way to my classroom now because there's police standing there.'"

This faculty member highlighted the shooting as a critical event that "revealed the way in which African American students, but all students of color, wanted counseling services to be more diverse." As a Latino student organizer explained:

> Where are our psychiatrists of color, right? We have these folks who might be trained in cultural competency, but it's really different when you have someone who looks like you. How could you talk to someone who doesn't understand, or you don't feel will understand? We had a student [of color] who tried to stab a couple of folks [and] who got shot and killed on our campus. How is that not an indicator that like, hey, you know, maybe we should have some psychiatrists of color?

We have no way of knowing whether psychiatrists of color on campus would have stopped this specific event from occurring, but it was important for mental health support staff to understand how students of color, who were more likely to experience violence at the hands of the police, interpreted and experienced the shooting. Without appropriate university support, as a senior staff person indicated, students "were looking out for each other, supporting each other."

At the time of the interview, mental health support staff and administrators were somewhat hopeful that conditions would improve. The University of California had approved an increase in annual student service fees to expand mental health services across the system. This approach relied on private family resources, rather than on state, system, or university funds, to address student mental health needs. Regardless of the funding source, this initiative was expected to decrease campus psychologist caseloads to 1,000 students, offer more access to psychiatric care, and focus on "recruiting diverse mental health providers with cultural competency and special skill sets to care for vulnerable populations."[21] If achieved, these goals would significantly reduce the UC-Merced CAPS workload and improve the quality of care obtained by students.

Yet, the limited resources available to combat the challenge of recruiting qualified practitioners to UC-Merced were worrisome. School representatives worked hard to achieve hiring goals—for example, placing advertisements with multicultural organizations and sending postcards to every one of the few licensed clinicians in the Central Valley. One administrator even "went knocking door to door [at private practices] through Merced, Atwater, and surrounding areas."

These tactics were ineffective in part because the school, located in Prison Alley, competed with the Department of Corrections (DOC) but failed to offer the same level of pay or even similarly decent working conditions for similar positions, as DOC hours were more regulated. As a staff member (who had experiences with both workplaces) noted to a coworker, "Being here [at UC-Merced] is much more emotionally draining and tiring than working for a prison. And prisons pay like twice as much." Unfortunately, incentives to significantly increase pay for mental health practitioners—and draw talented workers from the DOC and also outside of the region—were nonstarters. In the workforce planning process, every salary above the average potentially meant one less staff position overall.

Cultural Programming

Cultural centers were established in the late 1960s and early 1970s as a safe haven for students of color at predominately white universities (PWUs), typically in response to student activism and protest. These spaces provided an avenue for students of color to explore their racial and ethnic identities, create academic and social networks, resist harmful stereotypes, demand university attention, engage in social justice activism, and connect to local communities. Cultural centers and their dedicated staff members continue to support these functions. Recent research suggests that the presence of cultural centers increases the comfort of Black and Latinx students on college campuses, which can improve student retention.[22]

However, cultural centers may now be on shaky ground. Increasing numbers of racially marginalized students, limited financial resources, and categorization as social rather than academic programs can lead cultural programming on many campuses to be treated as lower priority.[23] At UCM, for instance, cultural programming around race was exceptionally limited. This was, in part, because of the faulty assumption that Minority Serving Institutions are not in need of special supports for historically underrepresented groups. As detailed in the next chapter, several administrators noted that the group-based cultural centers that developed during the civil rights era at some PWUs were not relevant for UCM. Certainly, some students of color—specifically Latinx students—could look around campus and see other students like themselves. However, the "institutional whiteness" of relatively prestigious postsecondary spaces is not just about students.[24]

Even new universities where students of color are the majority can be experienced as white spaces when staff, faculty, and administrators are primarily white and practices and policies are modeled after PWUs. Students of color must also continually interact with other social institutions, such as the labor force and criminal justice system (even in the surrounding community), which reflect and maintain racial inequities. Furthermore, not all marginalized populations are equally positioned on new university campuses. Some groups are still numerical minorities, as was the case for Black students on UC-Merced's campus. These students were most likely to report experiencing racial discrimination and harassment at the hands of administrators, faculty, staff, and peers—even other students of color.

At the start of 2016, UC-Merced's resources devoted to race-focused cultural programming could be summed up in one word—Deo. Deo was one of two staff members on campus hired to support historically marginalized populations (the other being a coordinator of women's and LGBTQ+ programs). Deo's office structure and placement were perhaps a fitting metaphor for the resources the university granted to this work. As Laura's field notes recount:

> Deo is located in the bowels of the library building, where the decorative niceties give way to a concrete labyrinth of sorts. This is, of course, where the Office of Student Life is located. But then Deo's own office is way in the back of that suite, next to the women's programs and LGBTQ+ coordinator. The two are in an open-air shared cubicle—divided only by a wall, which, at the top, has a frame (no glass) and allows for sound from outside to freely

filter in, as well as across offices. This is particularly problematic for two staff members who are supposed to be offering "safe space" for vulnerable populations on campus. In reality, they can't even offer privacy in their "offices." These spaces are also tiny. Deo has stacked stuff upon stuff to make all the snacks and binders/papers fit. In fact, these spaces weren't even supposed to be offices. They were only converted to meet campus space needs.

Deo's office was a function of extremely constrained space at the university, and the goal was to relocate Deo as more space opened up. However, in the calculus of who most needed private and accessible space, Deo lost—even though the office was frequented by a steady stream of URS looking for mentorship and support.

Deo's official job description, as the "social justice coordinator," was also exceptionally broad, making it difficult to meet all of the demands placed on the position. Deo described:

> [I am] really looking at what students are talking about and what is going on locally, nationally, and globally. Currently with Black Lives Matter, with the North Dakota pipeline, socioeconomic class [issues]—especially the makeup of our students as first generation, low income—and we have, you know, a good number of undocumented students. And then also campus climate.... As an office of one, I would get a phone call of "What are you doing for Black History Month? What are you doing for Native American Heritage Month? What are you doing for Hispanic Heritage Month, right? What are you doing for Pride Month?"

Not surprisingly, Deo was spread very thin. As one concerned staff member put it, "What a burden that's placed on that position. I definitely think that we absolutely could be doing more.... I just don't think right now we have the people resources to do it and do it right.... And who suffers because of it?" The implied answer was marginalized students.

On many campuses, a staff member like Deo would be housed in a cultural center of some kind. The year prior to this study, a delegation of UCM students attended the UC Students of Color Conference, where they learned that cultural centers and dedicated staff were a resource available on all other University of California campuses—but not at UCM. A Latino student leader explained:

> We're talking about these issues that we're facing on campus, [and] when it came to campus climate [and the] lack of resources, they're like, "Why didn't

you go to your multicultural center?" These are other students from other [UC] campuses telling us this. And our students were obviously confused.... We're like, "What is a multicultural center? I don't know what that is." ... Toward the end of the conference, we were able to congregate and talk for real. [We asked,] "What are we going to do, having come to this conference, with the [shooting of a student of color] incident ... on our minds? ...[As] we spoke, we [realized that we] need a space for students to exist as who they are. Why don't we have these resources? We're first-generation students of color, marginalized, and [in] this super-conservative community.... How can [the university] not have this support?"

A movement to demand multicultural space was born. Notably, Black students had already been demanding cultural space for years. However, the accounts of students, staff, and faculty suggest that administration did nothing until Latinx student activists raised the issue at a system-wide meeting. One activist explained, "We spoke up in public comment, asking about multicultural centers and really highlighting the fact that we don't have any, and we're advertised as [a] diverse [campus] ... that [is] first generation and low income. And then the system board was asking questions ... and that's when things started moving."

In response to students, administrators indicated that cultural spaces were always "in the plans" for the 2020 Project, but that space allocation was in flux and thus nothing had been definitively labeled. For student activists and their allies, however, the absence of existing cultural space and the lack of commitment to putting cultural centers in otherwise detailed 2020 building plans were sources of deep frustration. As one faculty member explained, from his perspective, leadership made a serious mistake in not immediately finding space:

At the very least [the university could] do the kind of paternalistic liberal thing of, we're gonna give you these things. In an ideal world you don't give people things, you make them part of the process, and they give them to themselves. But [leadership is] even fucking up the symbolic stuff. Bestowing a room on students is not really that big of a deal. It's a symbolic gesture, and at the end of the day the administration still holds the power to bestow that room upon them. It doesn't change the power arrangements of the university. It doesn't threaten the status quo at all. [University leadership] fucked that up.

An external report on diversity efforts, commissioned by the university, less harshly concurred that leaders had made mistakes: "While the institution appears to take minoritized students' concerns [about the lack of cultural centers] seriously, the follow-through is perceived as inadequate at best."

Why did administrators blunder in addressing students' cultural space needs? Students, particularly low-income, first-generation URS, are often disenfranchised in the university context. The relatively low power of students, compared to other constituencies (like faculty), was magnified by the perception that UCM students, in particular, "do not complain." For instance, as Chancellor Leland explained in a media piece in 2015, "These students by and large are grateful for the opportunity to be here.... They weren't born with silver spoons in their mouths." The chancellor's surprise at the 2020 student protests, documented in chapter 2, suggests that she, like many other university leaders, had assumed that racially and economically marginalized students would not be the squeaky wheel requiring major concessions.

Leadership was also coping with other pressures that required (or were seen as requiring) greater attention. As a staff member explained:

> In order for UC-Merced to continue to grow and for UC-Merced to place itself on the map, emphasis has to be given to the academics and the research.... Now the chancellor, that's her responsibility, to continue to build UC-Merced, get the financial support, get the academic recognition that we're now starting to see in these rankings and so forth. But somewhere in the priority—a multicultural center or a student center is not on that list. It's not on the immediate list. There are discussions about even having a natatorium [indoor swimming pool], but there's no discussion about a multicultural center.

A swimming pool would help attract wealthier students and bring competitive aquatic sports to the campus—both of which could contribute to UCM's financial self-sufficiency. The pool was soon written into the plans. The choice to commit to a pool before a designated space for cultural programing is a great example of how the needs of URS may be set aside, especially when resources are scarce.

Certainly, there is nothing new about structural racism in postsecondary organizations: It was only through forms of "spectacular speech," such as hunger strikes and extended protests, that students at other UC campuses were able to build and retain some key cultural spaces during the 1990s.[25] However, just as austerity is bolstered by racism, racial inequalities (regardless of intent) may be magnified by austerity. When market logics are employed, the battle for cultural space may become difficult. What are framed as needs or enhancements for revenue streams are often automatically granted precedence. More often than not, these developments support the interests of advantaged white student populations who tend to bring in more financial resources, rather than URS.

After continued pressure, UCM leadership responded by offering temporary spaces. The first space to open was the Graduate Cultural Resource Center (GCRC). However, after only two months the GCRC was shut down for renovation. It was a poor choice for a cultural center, as it had been designed as a storage unit, with no ventilation system. Only a few students could be in the space with the doors closed because the carbon dioxide levels became dangerously high. The concentrated chemical off-gassing from paint, furniture, and new carpet also resulted in itching, coughing, and other unpleasant symptoms for those who occupied the space. Graduate student activists created protest posters reading "Unfit for Humans," "Enviro-racists," "Shame Merced," and "We want oxygen for culture!"

The second space was the undergraduate Intercultural Hub. It was at the opening of this space that the faculty speaker introduced students to the term "tolerable suboptimization." The Hub was a very small room that had previously held a conference table and some chairs. All groups that sought a "safe space" on campus from racial or other microaggressions would need to share the Hub; this would prove problematic, as we detail in the next chapter. Like the GCRC, it was also unstaffed. Student organizers, who were expected to run the undergraduate cultural center, explained in an online public statement: "Unfortunately the Hub does not have professional staff with quality experience and knowledge specifically hired to serve the needs of the students of color on campus, and we hope students continue to ask our administration to provide the campus with a bigger space, funding, and resources that reflect the needs of students of color on campus and those with intersecting identities."[26] They posted this statement after finding it impossible to support all of the students who wanted to use the Hub. Austerity practices, as we highlight in the next chapter, implicitly rely on student labor to meet community and individual needs that go unaddressed by overstretched staff.

Academic advising, mental health support, and cultural programming are only three examples of tolerable suboptimization occurring at UC-Merced. With only four financial aid advisors (who also processed all necessary paperwork), accessing a financial aid advisor at certain times of the year was near impossible. In student housing, new off-campus housing did not have a designated residence life coordinator on-site to provide support and afterhours assistance. The increased number of students in university housing taxed existing housing staff. The availability of IT services dropped dramatically; even though new buildings came online and more students arrived, there were few changes in IT staffing.

The university also had one of the highest student-to-tenure-track-faculty ratios in the system. In the 2016–2017 academic year, the ratio of undergraduate students enrolled at Merced to tenure-track faculty was 32 to 1. The system average that year was 28.9 to 1.[27] This meant that Merced had fewer faculty with tenure or who were on the tenure track, per student, than is typical in the UC. UCM students were thus more likely to be taught by adjunct faculty with higher teaching loads, whose time and energies are necessarily more divided. And while UC-Merced has been remarkably successful in moving undergraduates into PhD programs (second in the system only to UC-Berkeley),[28] faculty described not being able to meet student demand for research opportunities and being overburdened in writing letters of recommendation for employment and graduate school.

Tolerable suboptimization, which occurred despite staff (and even faculty) intent, thus detracted from the university experience for most students at UCM, across multiple areas of the university. Yet, student groups were affected differently. As we demonstrated, areas of the university that dealt with higher concentrations of URS, or were particularly needed by racially and economically marginalized populations, were most likely to experience heavy resource constraints. Targeted grants for marginalized student programming could bring relief, but they were typically temporary, thrusting responsibility back on the university for maintaining these services. Thus, as one staff member, who had chosen to leave UC-Merced due to poor working conditions, noted, "When [our first-generation student program—which is also almost entirely Latinx] was grant funded, there was a lot more flexibility to do things; now it's very [much] like just keep the house standing."

UC-Merced may be unique, even among new universities, in the official endorsement of tolerable suboptimization, but it is hardly alone in the use of austerity practices as a means of organizational survival. Public universities around the country, especially community colleges, are operating at bare-bones levels. Students, and the dedicated staff members supporting them, feel these cuts acutely. In addition, when universities are forced to scale down or limit services, the students that are most harmed are frequently those that require the greatest support. These inequities occur both *across* higher education organizations—as the least-resourced universities have the largest URS and low-income populations—but also *within* universities.

Internal to a given university, there are pressures to siphon resources from marginalized student populations and apply them to more advantaged groups. For example, campuses may endorse tolerable suboptimization at the same time that they build recreational facilities appealing to white students from out-of-state, develop honors programs (which typically serve more privileged students at higher rates), and expand graduate research capacity—all three of which were occurring at UCM.[29] The same conditions that produce tolerable suboptimization thus encourage resource-strapped schools to invest in the populations and functions that have the greatest potential to bring needed funds or status.[30] This can mask the extent to which new universities are struggling to stay afloat and magnify the impact that limited resources have on marginalized undergraduate student populations.

In the next section of *Broke*, we argue that the experiences of URS in new universities are also shaped by colorblind diversity logics. Diversity logics are central to racial neoliberalism. They frame race as only one dimension for individual identity expression and make group-based racial remediation difficult and possibly illegal. Austerity pressures on universities, changing legal contexts, and a general refusal to address systematic oppression of racially marginalized groups foster the development of diversity logics. We explore the consequences of these logics for the labor involved in producing safe and comfortable postsecondary environments for URS. The final empirical chapter explores the relationship between new universities and predominately white corporations. In the search for private support, new universities offer educated Brown and Black workers to "diversify" the workforce—but this exchange introduces complex ethical quandaries.

Part 3

DEALING IN DIVERSITY

6 *Student Labor and Centers of Support*

WITH VERONICA LERMA

UC-Merced student leaders were passionate, direct, and angry with the university about what they called "student labor"—their efforts to create a safer, more welcoming campus environment for marginalized students in the absence of sufficient university support. As Gabriel, a Latino member of the Multicultural Student Council, explained, "This school is run on student labor.... We have very weary ... student leaders that feel tied to communities [of color].... Administration definitely needs to step up their game." In a separate interview, his council-mate Alex, a queer, white student (one of very few in this study and a strong ally for racially marginalized students) shared similar sentiments: "I think [the administration has] come face-to-face with the fact that they are exploiting [student leaders]. I hear stories about how funds are getting used elsewhere on our campus, and I feel it's a slap in the face to students who are performing the student labor, [both] physical and mental.... The administration benefits off of that."

Gabriel and Alex's remarks reflect a larger trend. In recent years, historically underrepresented racially marginalized students (URS) around the country have demanded change from their universities. We are entering a new period of student activism—following the campus "hotbeds of activism" in the 1960s to 1970s and protests in the 1990s, which focused on preserving earlier gains.[1] In fact, national data now show the highest numbers of students, especially racially marginalized students, who indicate there is a "very good chance" they would participate in a protest since the beginning of data collection in 1967.[2]

Reading the demands of student protestors across the nation—many of which were once catalogued online at TheDemands.Org—reveals the extensive, but little recognized, labor undertaken by marginalized students to address the racial climate in higher education. For example, a 2015 statement by Black students at the University of Missouri reads:

It is important to note that, as students, it is not our job to ensure that the policies and practices of the University of Missouri work to maintain a safe, secure and unbiased campus climate for all of its students. We do understand, however, that change does not happen without a catalyst. [We have] invested time, money, intellectual capital and excessive energy to bring to the forefront these issues and to get administration on board so that we, as students, may turn our primary focus back to what we are on campus to do: obtain our degrees.

This statement echoes the sentiments of UC-Merced students, whose extensive labors left them tired and frustrated with the lack of university efforts to make campus comfortable for racially marginalized students. Notably, URS are not alone in their efforts. They often work alongside, and even receive direct support from, faculty and staff of color—who, research suggests, experience a similar sort of depletion.[3]

We define racialized equity labor as "the struggle of organizational actors, from a variety of positions, to address race-based marginalization and inequality."[4] We describe this labor as racialized in part because it is not evenly shared across race. Racially marginalized people shoulder the burden, occasionally with the support of white allies like Alex. These efforts usually go undercompensated, uncompensated, or even punished by university officials.[5] It is thus more accurately "labor" rather than work, which implies payment.

Labor is also racialized because the "institutional whiteness" of research universities ensures that historically underrepresented individuals feel like outsiders.[6] Indeed, a large body of scholarship documents how predominately white universities (PWUs) can be uncomfortable, even hostile, for racially marginalized students.[7] These students frequently experience racial microaggressions and encounter infrastructure that best supports the needs and interests of affluent white students.

Simply changing student body composition, however, does not fix the problem.[8] Even new universities can be problematic spaces for racially marginalized students. As noted in the previous chapter, staff, faculty, and administrators are often primarily white and draw on PWUs to model policy and practice.[9] Most new universities also started as predominately white, and former organizational structures are not easily shed. Additionally, some URS will remain numerically minoritized in new universities. In our focal schools, this was the case for Black students on their majority-Latinx campuses.

In this chapter, we focus on the, perhaps counterintuitive, role that "diversity" plays in producing high levels of racialized equity labor among racially marginalized students. Diversity, or a shallow commitment to difference in all of its forms, is now the dominant cultural logic of race in contemporary postsecondary organizations.[10] Most US universities have developed a "diversity regime," or "a set of meanings and practices that institutionalizes a benign commitment to diversity."[11] Diversity regimes are highly compatible with austerity: When resources are perceived to be limited, diversity regimes offer a relatively affordable "solution" to race—one that is also consistent with anti–affirmative action legal frameworks.[12]

Unfortunately, as race scholars have argued, diversity regimes fail to redistribute power and resources in ways that support racially marginalized groups.[13] They do not eliminate, and may even help produce, the need for racialized equity labor. Insufficient organizational change creates conditions under which URS often feel compelled to address the racial environment. But efforts to remedy problems that remain are often ignored, resisted, and eventually appropriated (in diluted form) by university leadership.[14]

In what follows, we detail the development of diversity regimes at both of our new universities, highlighting some of the problems. We then offer an illustrative contrast. At UCM, diversity was the only cultural logic addressing race and a diversity regime the only infrastructure attending to race. Students' racialized equity labor emerged as a way to tackle the troubling campus climate. At UC-Riverside, a competing logic—that of equity—was at play. The school was a national model for cultural centers that took a collective approach to race, oriented around history, positionality, and community. Group-based centers were the backbone of efforts to support marginalized students and secure additional infrastructure. As a result, student labor was reduced and reconfigured in positive ways. Table 6.1 offers a summary of these competing cultural logics of race, which are detailed throughout the chapter.

Diversity Regimes

Recall from the introduction that diversity is a colorblind ideology.[15] It obscures race as a system of oppression by focusing on individual identities, with little attention to structural inequalities that divergently position students from different racial groups. As a consequence, diversity regimes tend to support one-size-fits-all infrastructure—a single center, training, and/or administrator that is expected to address all diversity-related issues on campus, without singling out any particular group for "special" treatment. This is appealing to resource-poor public schools. But it is difficult to enact widespread change without more extended university contributions and attention to the unique needs of particular URS.

The UC system's Diversity Statement highlights the limitations of diver-

Table 6.1. Comparing organizational cultural logics of race

Cultural logic of race	Diversity	Equity
Definition	Recognizes a variety of personal experiences, values, and worldviews arising from different cultures and circumstances	Recognizes the pervasiveness of race as a system of oppression across societal institutions and internal to organizations
Perspective on race	Colorblind	Communal and collective
Level of focus	Individual	Structural
Type of infrastructure	Multicultural centers and programming	Multiple group-based centers collaborating on programming
Relationship to austerity	Compatible	Incompatible
Racialized equity labor	Increased labor for racially marginalized students who are focused on meeting basic needs and preserving past gains	Decreased overall labor; racially marginalized students can be proactive and oriented to change

sity in addressing racial inequities. It defines diversity as "the variety of personal experiences, values, and worldviews that arise from differences of culture and circumstance. Such differences include race, ethnicity, gender, age, religion, language, abilities/disabilities, sexual orientation, gender identity, socioeconomic status, and geographic region, and more."[16] Especially with the open-ended addition of the word "more," this is a very broad definition. The definition risks, as Wendy Moore puts it, "construct[ing] race as an amorphous concept with the same consequence as experiences like growing up in a rural area, developing expertise at playing an instrument, [and] participating in rodeos."[17]

When race is described as but one of many, equally important identities, administrators may see devoting targeted attention to URS as in opposition to campus diversity and inclusion goals. As a UCM administrator explained, "The struggle that we deal with is: How do we keep a more overall inclusive campus environment while simultaneously supporting individual student identity development around their race and ethnicity? A lot of that work is done when you have discrete centers and programs, but the moment you do that ... the less inclusive the overall campus environment is."

This quote can be read as a suggestion that directing resources to URS is a form of separation that hurts everyone—but especially white students, who may no longer feel included. As such, the development of cultural centers is framed as disrupting the harmony of an inclusive campus. This is a common idea and one that we heard at both focal campuses. Thus, a UCR administrator used the language of "silo-ing" to discuss perceived inclusion issues with cultural centers focused on serving particular racial groups. This person argued that "we need to do more to break [these silos] down."

The UCR administrator also raised another worry—the potential for white student groups to demand special accommodations for white students when group-based centers are in place: "I hope this doesn't come out the way it sounds, but once Black [students] do it [get a cultural center] and [Latinx students] need one and then, you know, it goes on down the line. Where do you stop? [Kelly: Then you have white students who want white student spaces.] Exactly." This was a particularly salient issue on a campus where white students were, in fact, a numerical minority. As the administrator continued, "And, again, the irony is that I think white students on our campus could make the argument for it [laughter]."

As these quotes reveal, the colorblindness of racial neoliberalism is at direct odds with racially marginalized students' efforts to claim space and resources. Creating an explicitly Black or Latinx space is seen as hostile to inclusivity and is perceived as antagonistic to white students. In a diversity regime, race cannot be the basis for "special" treatment. This, of course, ignores the fact that universities—even new universities—are experienced as white spaces. These spaces are normatively white and, without intervention, remain so. Normative whiteness does not violate diversity-based policy, though, because whiteness is not officially articulated. Pushing back requires making the racialization of space visible and claiming space for racially marginalized students. But this is, of course, not a colorblind approach. Furthermore, URS may be blamed for "introducing race" when race was there all along.

Administrators' concerns were, to a certain extent, rooted in the larger legal context. As a UCM administrator explained, "I think our struggle is how do we [manage] in a post–Prop[osition] 209 environment. That becomes interesting." Prop. 209 is an anti–affirmative action amendment to the California state constitution that limits the abilities of state employees to consider "race, sex, color, ethnicity, or national origin in the operation of public employment, public education, or public contracting." The amendment is ambiguous about what exactly this means for universities and to what degree it extends beyond admissions policies and procedures. But Prop. 209 does open up California universities to potential legal action, especially from conservative (and predominately white) anti–affirmative action groups in the state.

Because UCM started afresh with cultural programming in the era of Prop.

209, it is not surprising that the university settled on a single multicultural center, rather than several group-based centers. (As discussed in the previous chapter, however, even securing a single center was an uphill battle for students.) The administrator responsible for selecting the form of cultural programming on campus argued that forward-thinking universities were moving away from a civil rights–era model of individual centers:

> I talked with a colleague. She used to be the director of [a cultural center] at [a top 100 PWU], and she's now a vice president there. She said one of the first things she did as vice president was start to eliminate the individual cultural centers and create more of a combination of a community center around culture and identity that was much more integrated because she had so many students that were feeling like they didn't have one place to belong.

At the example university, student cultural organizations retained some separate spaces on campus, although not staffed centers. The centers were shuttered.

There is a national tendency toward "multicultural" initiatives that replace or supplant group-based centers.[18] This is, after all, a more budget-friendly approach that fits well within a diversity regime.[19] However, experts on cultural centers urge administrators to avoid assuming that multicultural approaches are adequate replacements for discrete cultural centers. As one group of authors points out, "Institutions should be aware of the risks of a multicultural center that serves as a 'one-stop shop' for all [racial] minority groups. In providing one support center.... They run the risk of diluting the services and the potential impact of a culture center."[20] We illustrate this problem empirically in the next section.

UCR, in contrast, had a rich cultural center infrastructure, established in a different historical era, as detailed below. But some high-level administrators shared a similar perspective as UCM leadership. In particular, they argued that maintaining a Chicano center on a Latinx-majority campus was not contributing to diversity, as it provided resources to an already well-represented group. A UCR administrator noted:

> We're [eventually] going to be over 50 percent Latino, and ... well, the argument could be made, I would never make this unless I wanted to find myself on the street the next day, but the argument could be made, or question could be asked—do you need the program? If the reason for having it was because you were bringing in an alienated, disenfranchised community that

needed support to transition and thrive on campus, that argument is no longer there.

This comment is grounded in the idea that student body representation is an adequate measure of student marginalization. It does not consider the ways that Latinx students might feel alienated and disenfranchised by their white faculty members, administrators, and peers who maintain racial privileges both on and off campus. Nor does it address the racism that students encounter outside of the university, which may also impact their academic success.

Diversity regimes frequently include multicultural and diversity training. Both campuses provided this programming for new students. UCR offered training during new-student orientation, and UCM in a session for a required first-year class. The trainings were designed to be time-limited interventions (running approximately an hour) that could reach a broad audience. Although different in structure, they shared a focus on individual identities and recognizing differences of many kinds among the student body.

At UCR's "Building Common Ground" activity, hundreds of students arrived and lined up against the walls of a large ballroom. Orientation leaders read a series of statements, and students were supposed to step toward the center of the room if they related to the statement. They were asked to look around before resetting for the next question. The process was to be conducted in silence. The activity began with the statements "I identify as a woman" and then "I identify as a man." There were a series of statements about racial/ethnic identity (although white was not included, which had the effect of establishing it as the norm), as well as about religious identities and sexuality. Finally, students were presented with statements about experiences (e.g., "I personally experienced, or know someone who has experienced, sexual assault") and beliefs (e.g., "I am uncomfortable interacting with people who have a different racial identity than my own"). After the activity, students broke into groups of ten for a short discussion with a group leader. The room was loud, making it difficult to record conversations, but students appeared to be focused on processing their feelings and observations about the activity.

At UCM, students in a 300-person auditorium participated in a "Speed Diversity Dialogue." They first learned about the "Big 8 of Diversity": race, culture, age, disability, sex/gender, religion, sexual orientation, and socioeconomic status. Students received a packet going into more detail—for example, explaining intersections between personal identities. The packet also provided material to guide the main event, including a series of potential prompts to kick off the "speed dialogue" (which was designed to be like speed dating).

Examples included "Based on my culture/race/ethnicity, something that people believe about me that is not true is ..." Students were asked to discuss "diversity-related issues" with partners they did not know for two minutes at a time, for a total of three rounds. Afterward, they listened to a lecture about diversity. The first slide of the presentation was titled "Why should we care about diversity?" The one reason students were given was because of hate crimes. They were also asked to work on their "multicultural excellence" (by developing awareness of differences, knowledge of other perspectives, skills to interact across differences, and strategies for social change). Other highlights included a definition and examples of microaggressions and a group singing of Michael Jackson's "Man in the Mirror," which takes a very individualized approach to social change. (As the lyrics go: "If you want to make the world a better place, take a look at yourself, then make a change.")

Each campus had thought carefully about its programming. UCM's Speed Diversity Dialogue (SDD) is rooted in psychological research finding that greater social contact with people who are different than oneself leads to greater acceptance. It is used at universities around the country. Similarly, UCR's "Building Common Ground" activity was designed to show students that they could relate to people whom they may have thought were very different. UCR even offered an additional, and more intimate, set of voluntary cultural awareness workshops for staff and student organization leaders, with the hope that information would diffuse person by person from the workshop throughout the campus community.

It was troubling, however, that the only programming on race received by most students on either campus was not only brief (literally speedy at UCM), but also rooted in a diversity framework, where the focus was intentionally individualistic. In both first-year trainings, racial identity was framed as only one of many identities, all of which were equally deserving of university validation and support. Racism was not discussed as both a historical and contemporary system of oppression that continues to shape access to social and material advantages. Without this structural lens, it can be hard to understand why URS on college campuses might need additional organizational resources or why cultural centers devoted to white students and white racial identities would be problematic.

Another feature of diversity regimes is a new class of workers—chief diversity officers (or CDOs), administrators whose charge is to manage all diversity-related issues for the campus. Campuses typically have only one CDO. At the time of the study, Merced had not yet hired a CDO, but Riverside had. A CDO is a visual representation of a campus's commitment to diversity. Research, however, suggests that they struggle to create meaningful change.[21]

As a recent study of US universities indicates, hiring a CDO does not positively impact racial diversity at student, faculty, or administrative levels.[22]

At UCR, it was easy to see why. The CDO at the time of the study was initially appointed at a 50 percent position (in which only half of their time was spent on diversity issues) and had limited power. As this person noted, "My difficulty with my function to partner up with other senior administrators is [that] I only have the sort of power to suggest and to advocate or lobby with them. Ultimately, it's in their jurisdiction to make these kinds of decisions.... I can only do so much." The CDO was also relatively junior and frustrated by "all kinds of resistance in terms of diversity and inclusivity" among more "senior colleagues and other administrators."[23] This person noted, "These are all administrators who are [at least outwardly] committed to the cause of diversity and inclusion. I guess they all have their own positions to consider. And the tension and politics of their positions affects how much collaboration you can have with them."

At UCM, equity advisors (faculty members who supervised diversity in academic hiring) elaborated on issues that university-sanctioned diversity workers, like a CDO, faced. In particular, they noted the difficulties of working through diversity to achieve racial justice:

> Because of Prop. 209, I can't say we want to give special attention [to under-represented racial groups] [or that] our role as a university is to rectify these historical inequities. Because that's not what it's about. On paper, it's about diversity, so there's that. [I am] trying to play around that line.... It gets complicated. And I stumble because I don't want to get in trouble. Actually, [a colleague] and I were talking about this, that it's actually problematic that I'm even put in that position. Why am I putting myself in a position where I could get sued or lose my job?

As this quote suggests, equity advisors who raised awareness about racially marginalized groups were, ironically, in a more tenuous position than faculty who refused to consider the importance of racial diversity in hiring. In a diversity regime, characterized by colorblind dynamics, just focusing on racial marginalization (but not other forms of "diversity") is often coded as a problem. Diversity workers who raise concerns about racial equity may be severely limited in a diversity regime—particularly one with legal teeth.

The broad inclusiveness of diversity can even make it a useful tool for faculty and administrators to advocate, albeit often indirectly, for white individuals. As an equity advisor noted: "Faculty will try and use the language [of diversity]. They try to use it to their benefit. For example, say they want to bring in a [white] person who is from Germany. They bring diversity to the table, [noting that] they're from another country. And you're like, okay, well, yeah." The German scholar could be seen as legitimately contributing to diversity on campus because diversity is not supposed to be about racial marginalization alone. Diversity becomes an inadequate tool to address racial inequality, in part because it can be leveraged (both intentionally and unintentionally) in ways that work against remedying racial inequalities.

Diversity and Racialized Equity Labor

Diversity regimes produce racialized equity labor for URS and their campus allies. Merced offers a useful case to illustrate this point, as there was no other pre-existing logic for race at the university. Below, we show that multicultural initiatives and a lack of targeted organizational supports for URS increased student labor (also see table 6.1 above). We highlight the eventual appropriation of student labor for university benefit—in ways that do not necessarily support the welfare of racially marginalized students.

THE PROBLEM OF INCLUSIVITY

Cultural infrastructure typical of a diversity regime is often so broadly "inclusive" as to be ineffectual, and potentially even unsafe, for marginalized populations.[24] A single multicultural center welcoming everyone is a good example. We use the case of the Merced Intercultural Hub to show how inclusivity can create more racialized equity labor for URS, as they cope with the damage done in inclusive spaces.

As Vesta, the Latina student leader featured at the start of the book, put it, "Even though we're a majority Brown school, we still go through microaggressions every single fucking day." She, and other Hub founders (mostly Latinx and queer), strongly desired a space only open to people of color, queer people, and their allies. After a long battle with administration, detailed in the previous chapter, the Intercultural Hub was secured. But administration wanted the space to be inviting to everyone, expressing concerns about the exclusivity of the initial proposals, particularly around race. Angered by this, Vesta noted, "This university is a safe space for white folks.... It's only when marginalized folks [try to organize, it's] like, 'Oh look at them, they want to be alone.' And, it's like, no."

The inclusivity of the space quickly produced problems for URS seeking to use the Hub. Vesta was informed by several Hub users, for example, of a racist incident:

There were white folks there that were talking bad about Black professors on our campus. In the Intercultural Hub, while there were Brown folks at the table. And they were talking about the Drag Show too.... [After the incident] I saw two queer women of color outside, and they looked really sad. One of them looked like she was ready to cry.... This is not what we had planned. This is not going how we wanted it to go ... [The white students] probably didn't see that as violence, but it is violence because that is [supposed to be] the only space on campus that we could unapologetically be ourselves, whether it be Brown, Black, or whatever fucking color or fucking sexuality or gender.

The administration's insistence that the Hub be a multicultural student space meant that the marginalized students using the space, both queer students and URS (with much overlap in these categories), were subject to racism, homophobia, and transphobia in the very space they had fought to create.

After this incident, the organizers, who had engaged in a large amount of racialized equity labor just to get the university to open the Hub, now felt they had to monitor interactions within the space. Vesta explained, "So now this also falls on us. It's on us to be like, 'Hey, don't say that stuff in here,' you know." This was a huge responsibility, demanding of organizers' time, and also potentially placed them in conflict with their peers. Furthermore, they could no longer be in the space without being on duty.

The student leadership group convened multiple times to develop guidelines for the Hub space—although they could not enforce them without university support. They requested a permanent funding stream for the Hub so that student organizers did not have to beg for money annually through the student government process. They also asked for full-time staff and paid student interns who would have "not just cultural competency training, but [instruction on] how to navigate certain conversations," such as the problematic discussions that occurred in the newly opened Hub. More space was high on the list. Students were still engaged in protracted negotiations with administration several years after our study concluded.

LACK OF ORGANIZATIONAL SUPPORT

Because diversity regimes tend to produce broad, multicultural initiatives, targeted supports for specific racially marginalized groups may be limited. At UCM, this posed a particular problem for Black students, who reported race-based discrimination at even higher rates than their Latinx peers and from a wider array of demographic groups (i.e., not just from white students and university employees). We briefly provide examples of Black students' reports, as they highlight a need for university support that was not provided.

Several Black students described difficult interactions with professors who held preconceived notions about them because of their race. For example, Janella explained that a professor drew on stereotypes of Black single mothers when he pointed her out in class and asked, "How did it feel being raised by a single parent?" As she noted, "I wasn't raised by a single parent.... I thought that was really insulting [to assume], and I almost snapped, but I held myself back." Students also described weathering outright hostility in the classroom. Kamaria, who was in a class with her Black friend, reported a teaching assistant (TA) who would "intentionally ignore us, not answer our questions [when no other hands were raised], not help us, [and] throw papers at us." The TA even refused to hand Kamaria and her friend quizzes (which were timed), while passing out quizzes to the students around them. The women missed out on five of the ten allotted minutes and did poorly on the quiz.

Encounters with administrators were often fraught, as well. A few students were stunned when they heard university leadership explain, without nuance or attention to structural racism, that it was hard to attract Black psychologists because these workers were drawn to places where there was a higher concentration of people "like them"—the local prisons. Students indicated that these situations happened in part because the university employees, from administrators to faculty and staff, were predominately white and almost never Black. There were, for example, no high-level Black administrators, who would have been more likely to understand why that statement was so offensive. At the time, there were also fewer than five tenure-track Black faculty members on campus. Students only knew of five Black staff members, "and one was a cook [in the dining hall]."

Some of the most painful instances of anti-Black racism, however, came from other students. Four Black students separately recounted a scarring event involving their family members. As Nikki remembered, "When we had our [student-organized] Black Family Day and our parents are here, [we received so] much backlash on Yik Yak [a no-longer-existing social media app]. It was [all] racial slurs and racial comments. My mother's there and she's looking like whoa, so this is the kind of school you go to?" Tiffany, one of the event organizers, explained:

On Yik Yak, there [were things like], "Why are all these Black people on our campus? They just want to be ratchet[25] and make noise. Why are they playing all of this music? Nobody cares about Black history," because it was also during Black History Month. Then it went into completely hypersexualizing

Black women, and they were just like, "I'll never like date a Black woman...."
It lasted more than twenty-four hours.... We felt like we had nobody to talk
to. Everybody who was planning it, we were all in tears. I was just like, "Do
we do this again? Did we make a mistake by even bringing this idea up?"

Comments on Yik Yak were local (within a five-mile radius) and anonymous,
so students could not pin down from whom the racial hatred was coming.
It could have been the students sitting next to them in class. Not knowing
made it harder to be comfortable on campus.

Black students responded to these experiences, and the ineffectiveness of
the developing diversity regime, by collectively mobilizing and engaging in
racialized equity labor. In fact, it was difficult for entering Black students to
avoid being recruited into one or more student-led efforts. The most labor-
intensive was the creation of AFRO Hall, or Afrikans for Recruitment and
Outreach Hall, a living and learning community spearheaded by two enter-
prising Black women. Tiffany and Tasha's efforts illustrate the high degree of
racialized equity labor that students of color often undertake when university leaders do not work to directly counter racism.

Like the Hub organizers, Tasha and Tiffany would initially contend with
the accusation, from both administrators and peers, that AFRO was being
exclusionary in promoting a space specifically for Black students. As they explained in a joint interview: "[There were] a lot of questions of like ... 'Why
are you trying to seclude all the Black people?'" They were reportedly told,
"'[UCM is] fine. We're the most diverse campus, and we don't need something
like this. You're gonna make the campus climate worse.'"

Once they got approval for AFRO, the two women engaged in an extraordinary amount of labor. As a university housing representative confirmed, Tiffany and Tasha met weekly with leadership and staff to deal with space provision, room assignments, and other housing issues. They recruited students at
orientation and other events, acting as a liaison between Residence Life staff,
students, and parents—even fielding phone calls. The women wrote grant
proposals, hosted study sessions, and conducted workshops and other events.
Tiffany and Tasha created a book-loan program that operated out of their
own residence, formed a partnership between AFRO and the local Boys &
Girls Club, and hosted the Black Family Day described above. Expenses often
came out of their own pockets, despite the fact that both women were from
low-income households.

Without sufficient university support, Tasha and Tiffany often turned
to racially marginalized faculty and staff. As a faculty member noted, "They
heard that there was a new Black faculty on campus [laughter] and, I believe

you know they were excited.... It's like people know who I am before I know them." This faculty member was quickly pulled into the work of AFRO, even during a leave, and agreed to meet with all AFRO students individually, in order to give them "face time with a professor." These activities, typically not engaged in by white faculty, would take time from research, the single biggest component for academic tenure.

In addition, two Black staff members, whose support was legendary, would hold open office hours once weekly, between 5 and 7 p.m. (after paid hours ended), so that Black students, including Tiffany and Tasha, could seek help. These individuals interfaced with administrators on behalf of Black students and introduced Black student activists to networks of Black leaders in the Central Valley. When necessary, they shared cell phones and provided home-cooked meals, interview-appropriate clothing, and shelter. As these examples suggest, students' racialized equity labor is also often the labor of many people of color in a university.

The tide began to turn in 2015 when the Black Student Union issued a list of demands to the university—including a call for a Black cultural center. Black students on campus also protested what they described as a "hostile, anti-Black campus climate." After these events, the university hired an external consultant to evaluate the schools' strengths and challenges in relation to diversity and inclusion. University officials began to take notice of AFRO Hall. They even promoted the program to the consultant—but failed to mention that it was an entirely student-led effort. As Tasha and Tiffany recalled:

> People actually assumed this was a paid [position] or program on campus. But it was still student run.... That's one of the things [the consultant] commented on. She was like, "Oh, I thought this was a university program because [I was] asking what [university] support [is available], [so] why is this student org[anization] coming up?" ... And we're like, "Maybe we should reintroduce ourselves [laughter]. We are AFRO Hall. It's us." At that point, we started realizing like, okay ... people are seeing us.

The consultant produced a report calling for university action. As the report stated, "UCM students are excellent and primarily responsible for leading efforts to hold UCM accountable and push the university to enhance its diversity efforts. While some faculty and staff have been supportive (particularly in light of recent campus protests), the students are leading in ways that might be expected or required of professional staff on some campuses." She advised that multiple, well-staffed cultural spaces were needed in part to lighten the load on students.

Shortly after the consultant submitted her report, the university started to publicly promote AFRO Hall as an appealing housing and cultural option for Black students. The housing unit, however, continued to lack sufficient resources—making it impossible to achieve the vision of its founders. At one point, the university even combined AFRO and non-member students on the same floor, with some in the same rooms. There was no dedicated staff person or housing representative for the program. It was not attached to a Black cultural center or other grounding unit on campus. This was the consequence of austerity and diversity logics, combined. AFRO's existence was a major win—but it simply existed.

UNIVERSITY APPROPRIATION

During our study, Intercultural Hub organizers led a number of digital protests organized around provocative and effective hashtags such as #Exploited StudentLabor. They argued that the university, while initially blocking student efforts, had appropriated their labor in order to produce better optics around race on campus. In doing so, the university made invisible the racialized equity labor of students.

Organizers pointed to the initial announcement of the Hub opening, sent via email to the campus community. Leadership not only changed the name of the space (to the Multicultural Center), they also made no mention of the student labor that went into planning and, as we learned in this chapter, running the space. As Vesta reported, "They took everything, but [didn't] even acknowledge that it was students, you know? This was announcing it as if it [was a vice chancellor's] initiative or something.... Way to invisiblize all the years of student work." It would take some time for an acknowledgment of the student labor involved in creating the Hub to be included on the university website.

The duo behind AFRO were also erased from the narrative. Not only did administration fail to tell the external consultant that AFRO was a student venture, a campus climate official attempted to sell Tiffany and Tasha's own creation to them as an example of university-provided support. As AFRO Hall's faculty advisor recalled, "[The official] said, 'What is the university doing for you guys, to help?' And Tasha and Tiffany were basically like, 'Nothing, the university is not doing anything.' And then the campus [climate] person was like, 'Well, I've heard about this housing that they have for [Black] students.' And [the two women] were like, 'No, we do that for ourselves. [Recently] the university has supported us, but this is our mission, our idea. It's not the university giving to us.' They were really upset by that."

Following the evolution of the Intercultural Hub and AFRO allowed us to map out what we describe as a cycle of racialized labor appropriation.²⁶ The cycle is also apparent in five other student-led initiatives not detailed in this chapter, suggesting a clear, not idiosyncratic, pattern. First, people of color identify problems in the racial environment of the organization and work to solve them. Next, leadership responds by blocking these efforts, often by arguing that they run counter to diversity. Finally, leadership appropriates racialized equity labor to solve an organizational problem, often as a diluted diversity initiative.

University appropriation was widely acknowledged by student activists and their advocates. As Carmen explained of a student-founded organization supporting undocumented students of color, "It was really hard trying to work with the students, us trying to do the work that the university should be doing.... And it's ridiculous for us to be doing so much for the university to only take credit for it." Similarly, a staff member passionately remarked that the university "just bled ... out" marginalized students to meet its diversity goals.

What kinds of organizational problems prompt the appropriation of students' racialized equity labor? In the case of the Intercultural Hub, public shaming at a system-wide meeting prompted UCM to act. For AFRO Hall, it was Black student protest. Universities may draw on racialized equity labor when seeking to quell student activists, save face in the media, smooth relations with state legislatures, or address accountability issues. In these cases, the racialized equity labor that leadership once blocked suddenly becomes useful for the organization. As Sara Ahmed articulates, "The commitment of champions can be how the university itself appears to be committed.... The university might even appropriate their commitment 'as its own.'"²⁷

Racialized equity labor is a boon for universities. It reduces the cost of climate initiatives, as equity labor is often free and lessens the likelihood of negative attention from events such as protests or boycotts. The resulting programs and infrastructure may help leadership bolster claims of providing a positive, diverse, and multicultural environment. The university may profit from the ability to meet racial representation goals and to effectively market the school to students of color. AFRO Hall organizers, for instance, provided unpaid recruitment services. They called all potential incoming Black students to promote AFRO (and thus UCM) and provided infrastructure that made UCM appear more welcoming to Black students. In short, this labor offers financial and reputational benefits to universities.

University appropriation, however, rarely leaves the intent and scope of racialized equity projects intact. Leadership tends to favor diversity initiatives that maintain the status quo. Thus, the Intercultural Hub and AFRO were left unstaffed, severely under-resourced, and incomplete articulations of the founders' goals. They were also made to be friendly with the campus's multicultural approach to diversity. The Hub had to welcome all students, even those that did not respect the space, and AFRO Hall could not always exclude non-members. These hurdles created more work for student leaders, reinitiating the cycle of racialized labor.

This cycle takes a toll on student leaders. They reported high levels of emotional stress and strain.[28] As Alejandra stated, "Mental health is a big issue in our [Latinx student] community. Especially when you're constantly giving and giving and giving so much because you care about the organization … it starts to affect you." The time and resource demands of racialized equity labor often competed with the student role. As Nikki reported, "I'm pleased with the work that we did. But there's costs … [especially to] academics, trying to balance both. That took a toll on me.… I didn't know how to handle it right." Career development could be impacted. Reflecting on her college experience, Tiffany noted, "My family [is] like, 'You didn't do any research; you didn't do any internships.' And I'm like, 'I had AFRO [and] that [took up all] my time.'" Because she spent most of her years at college engaged in efforts to support other Black students, Tiffany was unable to gain the research experience seen as valuable for graduate school or a career in her field of biology.

These costs are not inevitable. URS should not need to engage in high levels of racialized equity labor just to comfortably exist—labor from which universities ultimately benefit. There are other models. In fact, below we offer a promising alternative. We argue that semiautonomous centers of support for specific racially marginalized groups introduce a racial equity logic and provide material supports that impact the level and nature of students' racialized equity labor.

Collective Action through Centers of Support

UC-Riverside has perhaps the nation's most-developed cultural center infrastructure. It is home to a total of eight group-based cultural centers—five of which serve specific racial/ethnic groups. Chicano Student Programs (CSP) and African Student Programs (ASP), on which we focus, are rooted in the Chicano and civil rights movements of the mid-twentieth century. These centers promote racial equity through the empowerment and support of groups systematically disadvantaged on the basis of race. Both are grounded in communities of color inside and outside of the university. In this section, we describe the equity logic around which these centers operate, which is also summarized in table 6.1. We argue that ASP and CSP reduce and recalibrate Black and Latinx students' racial equity labor. Finally, we discuss the risks that postsecondary defunding and diversity regimes pose to these centers of support.

EQUITY-ORIENTED CULTURAL CENTERS

UCR has made a material commitment to its cultural centers. Each of UCR's distinct racial/ethnic centers has designated space in the heart of campus, paid professional staff and, at least for now, a secure funding stream from the university. Four of these centers are located in Costo Hall—this includes ASP and CSP, along with Asian Pacific Student Programs and Native American Student Programs. Costo Hall is also home to the LGBT (Lesbian, Gay, Bisexual, and Transgender) Resource Center, Undocumented Student Programs, and the Women's Resource Center. The newest center, the Middle Eastern Student Center, founded in 2013, is in the nearby Highlander Student Union building. Below we offer a synopsis of ASP's early years, before doing the same for CSP.[29]

Pinpointing an exact date for the founding of ASP is difficult. In 1968, and toward the end of the civil rights movement, a group of sixty student activists founded the Black Student Union. This group also helped form the Black Studies Department. A center of social, cultural, and intellectual activity quickly emerged around "Black House," an off-campus, university-owned structure. Black House also engaged directly with the surrounding community—running programs for tutoring, drug abuse, and other areas of need. The agreed-upon founding year for what would eventually be ASP is 1972. That same year, Black House was the target of what was most likely a hate crime in the form of racially motivated arson. The Riverside Fire Department found signs of forced entry, gasoline-soaked papers, and an empty ten-gallon gas container.

Despite this setback, Black student activists and their allies within and outside of the university continued to fight for recognition. They formed five National Pan Hellenic organizations—historically Black fraternities and sororities that often provide a safe haven for Black students on college campuses. In 1979, Black Student Programs was established as an official campus entity. It joined forces with CSP, along with community and state leaders and union representatives, to unsuccessfully fight the closing of Black and Chicano Studies. The two academic programs were dissolved and absorbed into Ethnic Studies. In 1988, students voted to change the name of the cultural center to African Student Programs.

CSP grew out of Chicano Studies (initially Mexican American Studies) and an Early Academic Outreach Program (EAOP) serving nearby Latinx communities. When the chair of Mexican American Studies left his position at Riverside, the incoming chair, UCR history professor Carlos Cortes, had one condition: The student services unit needed a dedicated staff member. This led to the formation of what is now known as Chicano Student Programs in 1972. CSP was also supported by a small group of alumni and Latinx students (only 0.5 percent of the student population at the time, despite the racial composition of the surrounding area), a handful of Latinx university employees, and community leaders.

When CSP was founded, the Chicano movement was thriving. This energy fueled the program's early years. CSP collaborated with Movimiento Estudiantil Chicano de Aztlán (MEChA) and local community colleges to host transfer days—decades before such activities became commonplace. Cesar Chavez came to campus as a guest speaker. Inspired by his leadership, student groups promoted workers' rights. CSP-affiliated students held most positions on the editorial board of the student newspaper, the *Highlander*, and published many stories of resistance and advocacy. The campus's Latinx/Chicanx paper, *Nuestra Cosa*, was formed—and is still going nearly fifty years later.

As these brief histories suggest, ASP and CSP are a result of collaborations between student activists, university allies, and communities of color. There are also strong connections to group-based programs of academic study. The cultural centers are a source of creative and intellectual energy. They are deeply connected to and facilitate social activism, starting from the movements in which they have their roots and into the modern day.

This history is manifest in the equity logic around which the two cultural centers are organized. As Uma Jayakumar and Samuel Museus argue, an organizational culture of equity involves "Recogniz[ing] the pervasiveness of persisting institutional racism, historic and current exclusionary institutional practices, and disparities.... These cultures recognize how institutional practices have historically legitimated and valued the knowledge, perspectives, and strengths of White middle- and upper-class students over students of color, economically disadvantaged students, and other marginalized populations, as well as the reality that they often continue to do so."[30] Equity-based efforts thus contribute to the uplift of marginalized communities and challenge oppressive structures rather than maintaining the status quo. Achieving equity requires social change and collective action.

ASP and CSP are actively committed to supporting more than students' individual racial identity exploration; they also do the collective work that is needed to shift racial dynamics within the organization, as well as in larger social structures. Therefore, the centers' work is not just about students or any given individual. The project reaches well outside the bounds of the university. As one director noted, "The work revolves around [the students'] needs and, not just theirs, but the community. Because we are part of the community. Because we are working with the community." The idea that cultural centers are primarily for individual identity development, as the UCR administrator quoted earlier suggested, is entirely misleading; it is a way of erasing the collective character of the centers' work.

The collectivism of centers was immediately observable. For example, the annual Chicano/Latino Youth Conference brought over 1,000 younger students and their parents from the whole state, with the goal of increasing college enrollment—a long-standing focus of CSP. A Black Lives Matter town hall organized to prevent police violence on campus, as discussed below, drew many Black community members, as well as UCR students. Even events that seemed, at face value, to be more individualistic were grounded in collective goals.

For example, as a UCR administrator explained, Black Graduation was not just about particular students getting degrees. It was initially designed to be:

A celebration of achievement of [an] individual as well as a community. For every one of these students who graduated, it wasn't just—you got your degree, congratulations. It was another potential doctor coming from and serving that African American community. Another potential attorney serving that African American community. Another opportunity that came to that community. It was very intentional to celebrate in that manner, that this was an achievement for our community—an achievement by our students for our community.

The event had a feeling of group euphoria. As Kelly described of the processional—which did not take standard form:

A hip hop song began playing loudly and a moment later a group of graduates emerged ... doing a choreographed dance, and the arena erupted with cheers. Friends and others in the audience jumped up and began dancing alongside the graduates, creating a carnival-like atmosphere. By the time they were dancing down the center aisle to the empty seats at the front reserved for the graduates, nearly everyone was on their feet. People were singing along to the music, dancing, clapping, cheering, whistling, and taking pictures and videos.

Other highlights included spoken word about Blackness, attention to specific African cultures, history of Black graduates at UCR and in the US, and a call to action: "These degrees don't mean anything if you don't use them to help our communities."

UCR's centers do not stop at collective commemoration. Making changes also means calling out discrimination and protesting university policies. Center staff understood that as university employees they walked a thin line. They could not, for example, personally take up protest signs with their students. At the same time, they noted that, unlike diversity personnel at universities around the country, they did have slightly more freedoms given the different history of cultural centers at UCR:

> The student affairs model does not incorporate this special space, because we do not operate within those confines.... We operate in a different way. Our founding is different.... I couldn't work here, I couldn't do my job successfully, if I wasn't engaged in the politics of our students. My role is not to cultivate activists. It is for our students to be engaged and to know, to whatever level they would like to know, the issues in our community, but also the successes. If that produces students that are very passionate, then I think that the legacy of our student programs has done [its job].

An equity approach does not require or allow dispassionate distance from the students served by a center, lest staff support one group over another (a worry when coming from a diversity approach). Instead, staff worked alongside URS to achieve victories important for the collective well-being of Black and Latinx students on UCR's campus.

The above quote also points to another important feature of UCR's cultural centers. In some ways, they operated semiautonomously from the university. That is, while center staff were on the university payroll, centers of support were also accountable to the larger communities that helped found them. This is why administrators were often leery of challenging CSP, in particular, but also ASP. There were local communities attached to the centers that could be mobilized against the university.

Together, the eight centers and staff members also formed an important campus constituency, often working together. As one staff member explained, "If your department succeeds, her department succeeds and hers succeeds. If yours fails, then we're next ... so we're here to make sure that everybody's department is flourishing and supported." The operation of these programs was anything but exclusive or "silo-ed." Another center staff member described,

"We now have up to eight ethnic and gender offices in our *familia*. We're able to collaborate so effectively together." This was aided by co-location. "Our physical structure is that we are [mostly] all in the same building, Costo Hall, so there are a lot of collaborative projects." Centers shared funding streams to support each other. They co-hosted events.

Events and programming were also frequently intersectional. Individuals in CSP brought up (unprompted) their efforts to get Chicano Studies courses to include material about queer Chicanx/Latinx communities. ASP staff talked about their Black Queens Week, which honored Black women, and the potential development of a week dedicated to Black Male Excellence. The specific needs of undocumented Latinx students were at the center of CSP and Undocumented Student Programs collaborations. ASP and CSP staff also thought carefully about how first-generation status shaped the experiences of their target populations.

At UCR, the idea that multiply marginalized students would be poorly served by discrete cultural centers seemed entirely unfounded. As one staff member explained, it was helpful for students to have more, not less, discrete physical space and resources dedicated to supporting the various communities with which they identified. It also made it easier to nudge students who would not otherwise engage in intersectional conversations. The process was far less threatening if students could start from a safe place, one that was not in competition, but rather in collaboration, with other marginalized groups.

REDUCING AND RECONFIGURING STUDENT LABOR

At UCR, cultural centers operated as umbrella organizations under which a great deal of race-based support was provided. For example, ASP worked closely with Pan-African Theme Hall (PATH) and CSP with Únete a Mundo (Mundo)—group-based living learning theme halls. Recall that at UC-Merced, AFRO—the Black student housing community—was an almost entirely student-run operation. Having designated cultural centers to help coordinate housing communities at UCR meant that this work was not done by students. It also allowed housing communities to dramatically expand the cultural events, academic programming, and social functions they offered.

Both centers also managed a large number of related student organizations. As an ASP member noted, "We do a lot of student org support.... I counted it recently. We have about seventeen student orgs that we advise." With centers acting as primary advisors for student organizations, students had regular space to use and staff to which they could turn. It also meant that non-center faculty and staff of color would not be (as frequently) asked to perform similar functions, reducing that particular burden on racially marginalized employees.

As noted earlier, group-based graduations are also run out of these centers. The year of our study, CSP was organizing the forty-fifth annual "Chicano/ Latino graduation ceremony, Raza grad, which is the culmination of all of the achievements and all of the years [of graduating Latinx students at UCR]." An ASP staff member noted that Black Graduation was their biggest annual event. In the early 2000s, the event could be held in a room seating 500, and it was not even full. "Now we can go over to the rec[reational] center. One year when I was working here we had over 3,000 people in the rec center, to the point where they kind of told us, 'You're gonna have to stop letting people in or we're gonna have to shut it down because we were over capacity [laughter].'" At UCM, these two graduation events were run primarily by students. That is to say, if students failed to organize details (e.g., speakers, space, and funds), the graduation ceremonies would not happen.

Mentor programs offered by these centers connected older students to younger students. For example, the Chicano Link Peer Mentor program was in its sixth year and included about 350 students. The center had piloted an undocumented student component to this peer program. ASP and CSP also connected existing students with UCR alumni who could provide a source of help and inspiration. As an ASP staff member noted, "I'm programming with [the Black Alumni Chapter], giving our students opportunities to network and connect with ... like, hey, this person graduated from UCR and is now a doctor; I am bringing them back to speak about their experiences." Most center staff were themselves also UCR alumni, and thus were able to leverage their personal ties and knowledge.

The two centers ran numerous cultural, musical, social, and art-based events. For instance, ASP organized a barbecue social to connect new Black students with Black faculty and staff. CSP hosted a festival featuring Chicanx/Latinx music on the campus radio station. The centers also served as symbolic and material commitments to the needs of Latinx and Black students. As center staff explained in a group interview, "There are students who will come here every day. There are students who will come here twice a week, once a quarter. There are so many combinations of how often they come in. [Other staff: Once in four years. Like I'm about to graduate, I want to participate in graduation.] They might need a letter of recommendation or just some advice or whatever. But however frequently they come ... they know that this center does exist. I believe [it] is a comfort to them."

Center staff engaged in a high degree of emotional labor—labor that at

UCM racially marginalized students offered to other racially marginalized students. As a center staff member explained:

> Students have to navigate dozens and dozens of microaggressions all the time, whether it's on or off campus. Coupled with the historical facts of [URS] in education in this country, it poses a challenge on a daily basis. To help students get through those challenges … we're here to serve in various capacities. We're not trained clinicians, but we have life skills and understanding. We're capable of letting our students know … this is what it is [that you are dealing with], and this is how you're going to [get by]…. We can refer them to other folks on campus. But sometimes they prefer just to come to talk to [us] and that's it. That's a responsibility that we have.

This labor is often an invisible and draining aspect of care work. But it matters.

Cultural centers can do heavy lifting for URS, but it is equally important that students have a voice in how their needs are addressed. ASP and CSP therefore worked in collaboration with students. This was clear in how staff discussed what programming was offered and how it was organized. For instance, ASP staff explained that students were excited about the high school outreach event, previously titled Afrikan Unity Day. As a result, the center planned to "really give students the [opportunity to] … plan out the day. They've made the decision to change the name to My Black Excellence, and are kind of putting the Pan-African lens on the student experience, putting students through workshops that will help them understand more [of] their Black culture … while still giving them the tools they will need [to navigate applying to college]."

Center staff did not mean that Black students would be responsible for the event and all planning details. Instead, students served in an advisory capacity and were asked to suggest how it should be run—not to run it themselves. What students were doing was still racialized equity labor, but it was also organizationally supported labor. As a consequence, the amount of work students had to do was reduced and the type of labor was reconfigured.

When students took on heavier amounts of racialized equity labor, it was also of a very different nature than at UCM. The existence of ASP and CSP made it possible for students to engage in proactive, rather than reactive, work and to direct efforts away from meeting basic needs to making larger-scale social change. A great example of this is the Black Student Task Force (BSTF), grounded in the larger Black Lives Matter movement. The task force was formed at UCR after the Black Student Union protested in solidarity with Black students at the University of Missouri, in particular Jonathan Butler. Butler went on a hunger strike to protest racism on his campus and to call for accountability from administration. As a consequence of this event, Allison, president of the UCR BSTF, explained, "There was a meeting hosted in ASP [including several members of administration], in which there was a discussion about our needs, and those needs turned into demands."

The BSTF came out of this meeting. It had not only the backing of ASP, but (given center advocacy) the ear of administration. As Jason, another BSTF officer, told Kelly:

> We talked about what happened at UC-Davis, with the Black student that was assaulted … [on campus] and the administration didn't really do much about it. And the Compton Cookout [a racist-themed party organized by a fraternity at UC-San Diego].… It's just lucky we have not seen anything on UC-Riverside's campus [like that], but I don't ever want to. I feel like the Black Student Task Force … one of the words that describes us [is that] we're definitely proactive, you know. Proactive in trying to prevent this from ever actually occurring.

One of the immediate goals of the BSTF was to host a town hall in which students and community members could share their concerns with the campus police and also potentially come up with some solutions. This came on the heels of media coverage of numerous police shootings of Black people. As Allison put it, "This summer it just seemed to happen back to back to back. Every time I turn on the news or get updates on my phone, it was always someone else getting shot."

The police event, like many of BSTF's ambitious goals, involved a massive amount of work. Allison and Jason had to coordinate with the police force, community members, students, and administration to make the town hall happen and manage what was likely to be an explosive event. But it was also a high-impact event, with the kind of university support that could motivate police participation, even absent any particular grievance or wrongdoing. It was difficult to imagine a similar town hall occurring at UCM, or most other universities. As a senior administrator noted about the event, "I posited to [the BSTF] that I agree, we have problems across America, we have problems here on campus. But I think it's also the case that we're better off here on campus at UCR than most, many places.… So, what are we going to do about it? Let's do some things that others can't do."

LOOMING THREATS

We have shown how important UCR's equity-oriented cultural center infrastructure is for moderating and supporting the racialized equity labor performed by URS at the university. But this cultural infrastructure exists alongside a diversity regime and is constrained by postsecondary defunding. This context posed some challenges to the unique ecology of organizational support for racially marginalized students.

Many center staff brought up concerns about the trend toward multicultural centers. As one cautioned, "When you go to the model of a multicultural center, that ship is gonna sink, especially when it comes to really celebrating the diversity that we have here." Similarly, a sympathetic administrator remarked, "I think it's important for us to strengthen our cultural center programming and outreach and support structures and resources that we have in place. UCR is unique in that we have separate and distinct centers and not a collective where everyone is kind of [lumped together]. There are distinct populations that we are serving." Others pointed out that UCR's accolades could easily slip away, if the school was to remove or reduce the infrastructure that made them possible.

Staff made these comments because threats against the discrete cultural center model were implicit in the university's administration of austerity (see chapter 4). One-size-fits-all diversity initiatives typically cost less than the kind of cultural infrastructure built by UCR. And there are social and legal pressures to move away from equity-oriented models that emphasize group-based collective action. Center staff felt these pressures acutely.

For instance, staff members noted that organizational resources were being devoted to diversity-related infrastructure and likely coming at the cost of additional supports for ASP and CSP. As one staff member described, "In their attempt to increase programs and initiatives and create other offices, like diversity and inclusion, we have not invested in the original spaces that have cultivated this work in the first place. And that is the office of Chicano Student Programs and African Student Programs, in many respects." This person explained that their "center has been staffed in the same way, shape, and form that it was in the '90s."

As the campus has continued to rapidly grow in size, simply maintaining existing infrastructure is not sufficient to support students at the same level as in the past. For every staff member, there are increasingly more URS to serve. For CSP, the issue has been compounded by drastic changes in the percentage of the population that identifies as Chicanx or Latinx. Staff remarked that "the support and the investment in the center has not grown to be able to support the large number of Chicano/Latino students who have, since the existence of CSP, grown to be 35 percent of the undergrad population." With sharp increases in what are effectively staff caseloads, we might expect that some racialized equity labor will fall back on the shoulders of students. Indeed, even with support, BSTF activists grew tired from shouldering more work than might have been necessary with more ASP staff.

UCR's cultural centers have also had to change how they operate to deal with the repercussions of Prop. 209, California's anti–affirmative action statute. An administrator explained, "When Prop. 209 was first implemented, one of the immediate things that happened was [that] we took a hard look at what programs we were offering and how we were advertising them. Was there language in there that said this is something for Black students only?" This required scouring phrasing on all flyers and also tempering the tone of Black and Raza graduation ceremonies so they read as more "inclusive."

Another difficult issue post–Prop. 209 was financing cultural center events. As the administrator continued:

> We began to be very cautious about funding sources and resources spent on the celebrations. And so with Black Graduation, for example, rather than using … fees that were paid by students to the University of California or from the state of California to UC Riverside, we began looking at foundation accounts and community contributions and donations, which had more flexibility. This was not state money, and so it's not under the limitations set by Prop. 209. We started looking at the role that student fund-raising could play in funding these events and were successful, but we also began to see the cost of participation rising for students.

This placed financial obligations on marginalized students, and UCR has worked to partially "relieve that burden" by securing other streams of funding.

Yet, in the 2014–2015 academic year, students on UC-Riverside's campus voted for the Highlander Empowerment Student Services Referendum (or HESSR). This referendum involved the collection of student fees ($14 per academic quarter for five years) that were directly allocated to support and enhance seven of the eight cultural centers. (Undocumented Student Programs had a direct funding stream from the University of California Office of the President.) This show of support indicates just how much UCR's cultural centers are valued by students. But the funding mechanism, in which URS are asked to pay for their own equity-based cultural infrastructure, is reflective of postsecondary racial neoliberalism, as the costs of inclusion are shifted onto students.

Public unwillingness to fund vital supports for URS is even more pronounced in other states, where attacks on funding have been targeted directly at programs for racially marginalized students. For example, an Arizona state law, in response to a popular Mexican American Studies program in a Tucson school, banned public courses that "are designed primarily for pupils of a particular ethnic group" and "advocate ethnic solidarity instead of the treatment of pupils as individuals."[31] Funding cuts were used to force compliance. This law was overturned in 2017, when a US district judge banned it. The judge noted that the law "was enacted and enforced, not for a legitimate educational purpose, but for an invidious discriminatory racial purpose."[32]

Such attacks seem unlikely in California's current political climate but reflect the challenges that new universities, in particular, may face in serving their students. Diversity regimes and postsecondary austerity work hand in hand to remove essential programming for URS. Without this programming, students engage in higher levels of racialized equity labor, which can take a toll on well-being and academic progress. Universities around the country should be looking to UC-Riverside to see how equity-oriented infrastructure works, even in a difficult legal and fiscal context. However, these centers will not continue to exist, at least not in the same way, without strong organizational support.

Dealing in diversity is not just about cultural programming. The next chapter shows that new universities creatively leverage the racial composition of the student body in exchange with predominately white organizations seeking to craft "diversity." We argue that austerity pushes these schools to consider any possible source of revenue, recognition, and support for their students. Although this approach has clear benefits for students, it also comes at a cost because of the racialization of market exchanges: Students attending new universities are racially marked and devalued in ways that wealthy white students attending predominately white universities are not. As a consequence, URS in new universities may transition into careers that demand racialized equity labor and offer racially calibrated pay.

7 *Marketing Diversity*

We have a very aggressive diversity agenda,
and we want to look like the people we serve.
—STEVE, A PEPSICO REPRESENTATIVE

Everything is for sale in the contemporary research university. Campuses offer scientific research to corporations, academic programming and social experiences to students, named buildings to potential donors, causes to nonprofit organizations, sporting events to fans, and swag to university enthusiasts, among a host of other commercial goods. There has been a shift in logic, in which the primary value of a university feature is rooted in its perceived contribution to the financial bottom line, not its consistency with nonfinancial missions of the university. Students are no exception. They too can be peddled for profit.[1]

There is nothing about "selling students"—the title of a provocative piece by Daniel Davis and Amy Binder—that is unique to the new university.[2] There are incredible pressures on all research universities to utilize any assets in competition against more resource-rich organizations. Students not only bring in money as consumers, they are also valuable in securing donations, corporate sponsorships, nonprofit foundation support, and other sources of funding. The process is not always purely extractive: Students can benefit from these transactions, for instance, via jobs or better-supported university programming.

But the selling of students is also racialized. Predominately white universities (PWUs), implicitly and explicitly, leverage the racial privilege of the student body in attracting private funds. These students' social networks, which concentrate race and class privilege, can be tapped for financial contributions, and students themselves are likely to be wealthy alumni donors in the future. Prestigious PWUs also rely on the racial and class composition of existing student bodies as a signal of prestige when targeting new waves of affluent, white families desperate to pay exorbitant tuition rates so they might secure elite status for their offspring.

The new university's strategy must be different. Leadership seeks to utilize one of the organization's greatest resources—a substantial number of academically successful racially marginalized students. Administrators hope to capitalize on the ability to help other organizations produce racial diversity. The goal is to exchange a predominately non-white student body for attention, respect, and funding by offering white-dominated organizations racial heterogeneity and/or the appearance of commitment to diversity—in what we refer to as a "diversity transaction."[3] Because segregation concentrates historically underrepresented racially marginalized students (URS) at new universities, these schools offer a one-stop shop for external entities seeking to boost their multicultural image and increase their profits by breaking into new markets.

New universities benefit from marketing diversity. To an extent, the students attending these universities do as well. But diversity transactions occur in the context of racial hierarchies that devalue URS and the schools that serve them, while elevating other students and universities. Thus, when high-status organizations, such as corporate firms, seek to reproduce their high status, they turn to elite PWUs to recruit what are presumed to be the "best" candidates—a majority of whom are white.[4] In contrast, new universities are not sought out to create corporate prestige, even though these schools also offer excellent job candidates.

Instead, corporations may use new universities for a very narrow set of purposes: in particular, to secure historically underrepresented candidates that help address diversity-related issues and market products to non-white consumer groups. Therefore, new university students may be funneled into relatively lower-status positions that require engagement with and knowledge of economically disadvantaged communities of color, helping corporations corner racialized markets. Corporations also benefit from the unpaid efforts of these workers to recruit and retain underrepresented workers and develop products that appeal to particular racial and ethnic groups.

We illustrate how new universities "market diversity" by first examining a partnership between PepsiCo, Inc. and UC-Riverside, later turning to other examples. Interviews with key actors in both organizations help us demonstrate what is being exchanged.[5] Through the partnership, Pepsi gains access to an excellent non-white labor pool, maintains an exclusive contract for product sales with the university, demonstrates commitment to communities of color, and powers the corporation's race-based sales and development think tanks. UC-Riverside benefits financially from Pepsi's financial sponsorship and the placement of UCR students in solid jobs that enhance the university's reputation.

Our case illustrates the power of racial differentiation and marginalization as a material resource for organizational survival and profit.[6] Although much economic sociology on markets does not consider race,[7] we document the centrality of racial privilege and disadvantage to the structure of markets. In particular, we demonstrate the ways that race shapes the market for college-educated labor—where employers go for which workers, for which jobs, and for what pay.[8] We also highlight the racialized processes behind corporate actors' efforts to create and secure stable niches for the sale of goods and services.[9] What we reveal are key features of racial neoliberalism, more broadly: As public goods retract, consumer markets expand to include marginalized groups, which are pushed to compete in racially hierarchical labor markets in the place of economic justice.[10]

Race and Corporate Partnerships

Corporate partnership programs are a little understood, but rapidly increasing, feature of research universities.[11] Typically, these programs offer corporate hiring departments differing levels of access to student labor pools. Corporations are eager to participate because they hope to reduce recruitment costs and may negotiate other benefits with their university partners (e.g., brand advertisement, product exclusivity, and first rights to use new university-developed technology). Universities charge fees and extract various forms of sponsorship from corporate partners. Both parties may benefit from mutual blessing; corporations may boast that they hire heavily from prestigious universities, and these universities can claim to offer an inside line to desired corporations.

Scholars have noted that the corporate head-hunting model of employment treats students as a commercial good for exchange.[12] Its spread among research universities is, in part, a function of the defunding of public higher education. Universities are eager for any source of outside financial support. Defunding has also contributed to rising costs for students and their families, leading to accountability pressures and efforts to measure the employment and earnings outcomes of university graduates that only increase the importance of career placement. This model is in direct tension with more traditional career counseling focused on developing individual student career interests.

There are differing levels of corporate commitment to universities that correspond with well-established terminology. A "target" university is where an employer might turn for specialized needs—for example, to acquire mechanical engineers or nanotechnology majors. "Core" status, however, is the most desired by university officials. A core university provides "non-specialty" students to work in units that do not require a high level of scientific expertise, such as management, accounting, development, human resources, and advertising. The demonstration of loyalty is considered higher because the employer could go almost anywhere to meet these broad needs.[13]

Research on corporate partnership programs, or other preferential hiring arrangements, typically focuses on elite universities where students are more likely to be racially and economically advantaged. Elite PWUs tend to partner with elite firms in high-wealth, high-status occupational sectors, funneling students into a narrow swath of jobs, primarily in finance, consulting, and technology. This obscures the racialized nature of hiring. As Lauren Rivera explains in *Pedigree: How Elite Students Get Elite Jobs*, these kinds of partnerships allow high-status employers to argue that their hiring processes are "race neutral."[14] When limited numbers of Black and Latinx students end up in the pool of potential candidates, very few will be hired. These employers typically do not partner with new universities because they believe the best candidates come from the most prestigious schools. Elite firms' presence at diversity job fairs around the country, Rivera argues, rarely leads to hiring. The goal is instead to signal visible commitment to equity—but not to act on it.

The schools that Rivera and others focus on are, however, only a tiny fraction of the four-year university sector. Corporate partnership programs exist outside of the elite Ivies and the top tier of public research universities favored by competitive firms. On the West Coast, in particular, many schools populated by URS from low-income households have also developed, or are aggressively seeking, these kinds of partnerships.[15] How can we make sense of corporate partnerships with new universities, or other universities serving disadvantaged populations? What role does race play in these partnerships?

PEPSI AND UCR

UC-Riverside is a "core" campus for Pepsi recruitment efforts. It shares this status with several other schools in the region, most of which are part of the California State system—making UC-Riverside, as a University of California campus, the most elite of the bunch.[16] The majority are Pepsi-exclusive campuses, which sell only Pepsi products. They tend to be located near Pepsi plants. A large Pepsi facility, for example, is located right in Riverside, about a ten-minute drive from the campus. All of the schools are demographically similar to UC-Riverside in that they enroll URS from low-income households.

At UCR, the relationship with Pepsi is the result of careful cultivation by the university career center. As one Riverside official explained, the school was focused on "leveraging UC-Riverside's diverse profile and looking for companies that really have a commitment to diversifying their workforce." UCR's interest in addressing corporate diversity needs was a perfect match for Pepsi. As Reggie, a former UCR student and current Pepsi manager, indicated, "The reason we want to go to UCR is because it's a diverse school. We look at that and say, 'Well, this where the fish are, right? We're gonna spend our time and resources there.'"

The company was particularly interested in building its executive pipeline program, which helped move racially marginalized individuals into field leadership positions. Steve, another former UCR student turned Pepsi manager, played a key role in the development of this program. He described himself as an "ambassador for UCR. I'm all about UCR. I talk about UCR with the organization.... I worked with [the director of UCR's African Student Programs] on that partnership and on my executive team here to say, 'Hey, why don't we pour in and invest in and hopefully hire these candidates to come on board.' We have had some success for sure."

This partnership indeed involved investments in UCR's students. For example, Pepsi ran resume preparation and interviewing workshops at the university that were open to all students. Such training was a valuable resource, particularly for first-generation college students. Pepsi also offered much-needed funds to African Student Programs (see chapter 6), although the amount was relatively low considering the wealth of the company. As Steve explained, "I partnered with Pepsi to donate $5,000 a year to UCR's African Student Programs." From Pepsi's perspective, the ultimate goal was "so that we have exposure and we start to groom these students that one day will come and be a part of our organization."

The partnership was born out of genuine interest in supporting UCR's racially marginalized students. The fact that, on the Pepsi side, this agenda was pushed by former UCR graduates who had a deep personal interest in the school and its students was not incidental. Furthermore, as we documented in the last chapter, the campus's cultural centers are incredibly supportive of URS and their interests. Securing jobs that require a bachelor's degree and offer economic security for Black and Latinx students is important. Thus, there were good intentions on each side of the partnership.

But Pepsi was looking to UCR to fill particular types of jobs—field leadership positions in local communities that required interfacing with the stores and clientele buying Pepsi products. As Steve explained:

> We want to look like the people we serve … [from] the people that purchase our product to the consumer that takes it home. If I'm selling to a Korean business owner, I have folks on my team that are Korean that can speak to them in their language. Being in LA, being in a melting pot right here in Southern California, it's critical that we have a competitive advantage over our competition. It's big. It's key. There's some multicultural teams. We used to have a team of reps that spoke nothing but Spanish, and they would call on some of these multicultural big supermarket stores, some of these stores that are becoming more and more common in Southern Cal. Culturally, having folks that understand the dynamics of our surrounding communities, it adds a lot of value.

For leadership roles that were closer to the products frequently consumed by communities of color, the company focused on placing managers of color.

The match did not have to be perfect. The two Southern California managers we spoke to were Black men. What seemed to matter most was not having a white person in a field position leading a team in a non-white area. The implication was that white employees might hurt the company's ability to establish ties with stores in marginalized communities, closing off avenues for profit. This is likely true and highlights the limitations of white workers in particular markets. But this form of racial matching, as we illustrate below, could also cut off substantial opportunities for workers who were not white.

Field leadership positions required managing large teams of people who were racially and economically marginalized. Pepsi thus stationed field leaders in bottling plants and near the manual labor that fueled operations. As Kelly noted when waiting for an interview with Steve:

> There is another door across from the main door that leads back to the offices and production/distribution facilities. Along one of the walls, there is a glass case with memorabilia, including trophies, Pepsi signs, and old bottles of soda. Apart from the Pepsi stuff, it felt like the waiting room at an oil change shop.

Having shared life experiences, both inside and outside of the office, made the job easier. As Steve noted, "If you're managing a team of folks that drive trucks, they're going to bring a lot of problems to you that are very blue collar, and you have to understand their work and be able to talk [to them]. We hire from the geography we service, right, so I serviced Compton [a heavily Black, low-income area] a lot. I service part of East LA [which is 96 percent Latinx and low-income]. We like to hire from within our communities, so you have to be able to deal with these kind[s] of personalities."

UCR was a sweet spot for recruitment into field leadership positions. On one hand, it was prestigious enough to produce what Pepsi representatives considered to be leadership material. Thus, when Kelly asked Steve about recruiting for the pipeline at the Cal State campus closest to that particular plant, Steve responded: "I just interviewed a guy yesterday from there for this executive pipeline program. And what we're seeing in those campuses, they're great because they're very diverse—we want to focus on densely populated diverse campuses—but we want a high caliber of student as well. So, not only African American or Hispanic, but they also have to be very … you know, future leaders."

On the other hand, UCLA or elite private University of Southern California (USC) were too far up the chain. As Reggie explained, UC-Riverside students brought "the work ethic and [did] not come in with all these high expectations that aren't going to mesh well with the veteran people within the organization…. If you're going to bring in campus hires, that's contentious enough, it creates enough resentment just having the campus tag on you. And you don't want to have a bad attitude on top of that." He continued, "Look at UCLA, you're around a lot of rich kids. The path that got them into that school was pampered. They didn't have to work [in college]. It's a different type of candidate that you're getting. Which is fine, they're going to be well suited for a variety of different things, and then go on to do great things. But for this particular program, it requires a lot of work, a lot of commitment, and [Pepsi leadership] feels like, given the background of the students at UCR, given the diversity, given the economic status coming into it, [it is a good fit]."

His narrative highlighted the class disadvantages that often accompany racial marginalization as essential for field leaders in positions closer to the lower-paid workers in the company. The implication is that racially marginalized workers from less prestigious research universities like UCR are not going to balk at less than glamorous working conditions or demand more from the company. These students are expected to be grateful for the job and thus work hard without complaint and without acting "better than" lower-rank workers.

Steve noted that the company had actually experienced issues attempting to recruit for field positions from more elite campuses:

One thing that Pepsi does is to just understand a Berkeley student and a UCLA student. The kind of companies that already recruit from there are ... not a higher caliber, but the work we do is very blue collar. We are in the field operational element of Pepsi. So, a lot of what we do here is field-based stuff. Pepsi [has] made the analysis to say, "Hey, [it] may not make the most sense for us to recruit out of UCLA and Berkeley." Also at USC, based on experience. They've hired a lot of students at a lot of those schools, and they've quit. They come, they say, "This is too blue collar for me, this is not really what I ... I went to a really top percentage of school."

He explained that schools like UCR are "good big schools, but they're not, you know, Harvard. We don't go to Harvard. We probably recruit from those schools, but for different kind of roles. Headquarter, strategic [work], just different analytical roles, not more of our field leadership roles. A lot of [our favored] schools [for field positions] are commuter schools. People are working full-time and going to school, so it just kind of is calibrated that way."

What these managers are describing is a hierarchy of recruitment, tightly linked to university rankings. Students at open-access universities are seen as not "selective" enough for field leadership positions, while students at elite universities are deemed too "selective" and may instead be considered for higher-status positions within Pepsi, which are likely related to finance and marketing.[17] Economically disadvantaged students of color at new universities like UCR thus experience both benefits and costs from their middle position. They are given preference for Pepsi's field leadership positions. These are good jobs. Both of our managers were exceptionally proud of their career trajectories.

Yet, field positions are also viewed as "blue collar" and are likely lower paying than many non-field-based leadership positions. When corporations increase overall diversity by matching managers to "look like" their consumers and laborers, then Black and Brown students are less likely to find themselves working in the most-advantaged positions in the company. Indeed, the flipside of this logic is that only white workers from affluent families should hold top leadership positions that involve interfacing with other white individuals—for example, other corporate leaders, financiers, and politicians—on behalf of corporations.

Pepsi and other companies turning to new universities to diversify their workforce could make a significant impact on the racial pipeline into corporate leadership by continuing to expand opportunities for URS in *all* segments of the company.[18] Racial and class hierarchies are behind the assumption that students from more prestigious organizations deserve higher-status and higher-paying jobs. Elite four-year universities with low representation of URS from low-income households do not produce inherently "better" candidates than other schools. Corporate partnerships that place high-performing URS on all career tracks—not just secondary, racialized career tracks—send an important signal: Successful companies secure greater numbers of high-quality candidates when they widen the net to universities like UC-Riverside.

ERGS AND NEW UNIVERSITIES

In recent years, UCR officials have expanded their efforts to market diversity. They have reached out to race-based corporate Employee Resource Groups, or ERGs. ERGs often evolve from corporate affinity groups that bring together individuals around any shared identity (e.g., Black, Latinx, woman, disabled, queer, parent, or pet lover). While affinity groups tend to be loosely coordinated social associations, corporations are now encouraging the development of organizationally supported ERGs that utilize the talent, knowledge, and experiences of employee subgroups to achieve corporate goals.[19]

ERGs have been around for decades and are now a common feature of the corporate landscape. Ninety percent of Fortune 500 companies have at least one ERG.[20] As a UCR representative explained:

> Among Fortune 500 firms, when they designate something as an Employee Resource Group, [or] ERG … they're really talking about a more formal structure for these [affinity] groups. They're going to be given a budget, anywhere from $30,000 to $50,000 for a local site. And these are national organizations with a governance structure that takes it down to the local site. They will be charged with doing a couple things. One would be community engagement. Second could be training and development for their members; you know, leadership development, retention.… And then these Employee Resource Groups also play a role in recruiting talent into their companies.

The representative used Pepsi as an example: "Pepsi will come to our career fairs and recruit, but they will bring members of their Employee Resource Groups from Mosaic, which is their African American group, to PAN, which is their Asian group, to [Adelante], which is their Hispanic group, and they'll use those members to help with recruiting." Mosaic is not just at Pepsi, so when UCR makes ties with this ERG via Pepsi, it opens up connections to the Mosaic ERGs at a number of other corporations. This dramatically increases UCR's reach to other corporations interested in diversifying their workforce.

UCR's ERG strategy developed, in part, through relationships with Pepsi's Mosaic ERG. Initial connections to Mosaic came through Steve and Reggie. The executive pipeline program tended to funnel employees into ERGs, as taking a leadership role in a relevant ERG was seen as a way for employees from underrepresented groups to build an "internal resume." Pepsi employees could then run university diversity recruiting efforts through the ERG. As Reggie noted, "I was doing that [handling campus recruiting for Pepsi] as a representative of UCR and just figured we'd create some sort of synergy within Mosaic. I would handle Mosaic's workforce recruiting initiatives, at least as they relate to UCR's campus." Mosaic did a lot of the work involved in "build[ing] connection with the African community [and the] African American community at UCR."

UCR leadership described ERGs as "untapped. We're the only career center that I am aware of in the UC system, or even in the country, that is focused on developing our relationships with ERG group leaders, as well as their executive sponsors." For several years, the university had hosted the National Employee Resource Group Summit, in combination with other partners. The school was actively "bringing together leaders from Employee Resource Groups and basically helping them develop ERGs in their companies. This is working at a very high level, at executive levels, with companies." The payoff was a potentially longer-lasting relationship with a corporation. As the UCR official explained, "I'd rather spend my time developing executive-level contacts, which are going to be more consistent within companies, than [with] the college recruiter that probably spends two or three years [at the company before moving on]."

UCR recently entered into an ERG-focused collaboration with UC-San Diego's Rady School of Management, California State University-Fullerton, and Spectrum Knowledge, called Elevate. Elevate is an academy that brings together corporate leaders from around the country with the goal of expanding ERG activity. Pepsi is, of course, involved. As Reggie noted, "We're doing ERG strategy sessions … [where] other companies bring their ERG leaders and we share best practices. We're starting to expand Mosaic's reach, not only internally, but with other outside affiliates. And trying to build it." This also benefited UCR, as the greater the reach of Mosaic, the better the chance that more UCR students might be employed through the connections that started with Pepsi's Mosaic ERG. Furthermore, UCR's role in Elevate meant it would be one of the first universities that companies involved in the academy would turn to for hiring college-educated Latinx and Black workers.

Elevate promotes ERGs to corporations primarily by focusing on their financial benefits. As the web page notes, "According to our research, if ERGs are optimized and leveraged effectively, they can yield thousands of percent in annualized Return-on-Investment (ROI) for their organizations. This mostly stems from their workplace, workforce and marketplace engagements."[21] Exactly how do ERGs produce financial returns? There are at least three mechanisms through which organizations profit.

ERGs play a central role in boosting corporations' visible commitments to diversity. Corporations, like universities, must establish a diversity regime (see chapter 6) that involves policies and infrastructure signaling a multicultural, inclusive environment. Scholars argue that, increasingly, "appreciating and capitalizing on diversity is a winning strategy."[22] Corporations compete for spots in *Diversity Inc.* magazine's Top 50 Companies for Diversity, *Black Enterprise* magazine's 50 Best Companies for Diversity, and *Fortune* magazine's 100 Best Workplaces for Diversity, among others. The presence of ERGs helps win these kudos. In fact, ERGs' sheer existence is a data point considered in the calculation of these rankings, along with the many functions they perform (e.g., mentoring, recruitment, and increasing supply to businesses owned by people of color).

Workers in ERGs also do a significant amount of racialized equity labor for their corporations. Recall that racialized equity labor refers to the struggle of organizational actors, typically from racially marginalized groups, to address race-based marginalization and inequality.[23] Students of color often do this labor at new universities; they may then move to corporations where racialized equity labor is conducted and organized through ERGs. Typically, employees are not paid more for their participation in ERGs, although it may boost their career trajectory within the company. ERG workers may be doing labor that is not directly related to their position within the company and/ or may go well above and beyond the expectations associated with their position. Steve and Reggie's extensive efforts to foster close relationships with the UCR career center and African Student Programs, through their roles in Pepsi's Mosaic ERG, are one example of this type of labor.

Finally, ERGs also function as race-based think tanks that commodify knowledge about particular groups and communities. The goal is to sell targeted products to new consumer groups. A wider client base equals greater sales and profit. But selling to non-white consumers requires understanding the marketing and products to which communities of color will respond. ERGs have long offered these insights to corporations. As entrepreneurship scholars explain, "To date, the innovation work that has been done [in ERGs] is focused on the particular ERG characteristic. An automobile manufacturer wants to sell cars in India so asks the members of the Indian culture ERG to help. A food company wants to launch a product that is directed to the Hispanic community, and it involves the ERG Latino members to test out new concepts with their families and provide feedback."[24]

Pepsi has experienced great success in harnessing the cultural knowledge of ERGs for corporate profit. For instance, Adelante, Pepsi's Latinx ERG, was involved in the development of Flamin' Hot Cheetos and Tapatío-flavored Doritos and Ruffles for Frito-Lay—a division of PepsiCo. These products have been wildly successful with Latinx consumers in the US. As a top-level Pepsi executive noted upon receiving the 2011 Latina Style Employee Resource Group award on behalf of Adelante, "Adelante has a long legacy of helping to impact sales at PepsiCo.... It's amazing what a little passion and networking can create."[25]

Employees involved in ERGs are thus valuable for corporations. They help effect an image of corporate diversity, which can be leveraged for positive attention, awards, and sales. ERG workers engage in free racialized equity labor that saves money for corporations. For instance, rather than turning to external firms for racial climate, recruitment, and retention supports, internal talent performs much of this labor. Additionally, ERGs help corporations extract profit from marginalized communities that were previously untapped by predominately white corporate development and sales units.

In her book *The Enigma of Diversity: The Language of Race and the Limits of Social Justice*, Ellen Berrey offers insight into the problems with ERGs. She includes a case study of a corporation transitioning from social affinity groups to an ERG-like structure. A speaker was informing workers involved with affinity groups of the change. In her presentation, the speaker was "constructing racial and gender inclusion according to a corporate logic ... [whereby] diversity management activities were acceptable only if they seemed to directly support the company's ... goals of cost cutting and profit maximization." Pitching the message that affinity groups would need to bring in greater profit or disband "the company's best-mobilized racial minority, female, and GLBT employees" suggested that "the social networking and socializing practices of these groups was of low value." The only rationale for these groups' existence had to be oriented in the company's business interests. Berrey describes this as "the extreme appropriation of racial minority inclusion."[26] It follows the same market logic as calls to shut down or defund the "least profitable" universities (see chapter 3) or campus units (see chapter 4), regardless of their contributions to producing racial equity.

The primary, and perhaps only, reason that ERGs exist is profit production. That is to say, corporations are signaling little interest in supporting affiliations of disadvantaged workers unless that disadvantage can be leveraged as a valuable corporate resource in market competitions. Marginalized employees' abilities to receive organizational supports, and to locate other workers who share a similar background, hinge on their financial utility as racialized workers to the corporations for which they work. University partnerships with ERGs, as a means to place URS in solid jobs, thus position students in neoliberal markets through their marked racial statuses.

Pitching Adversity

The Pepsi-UCR partnership, and UCR's broader engagement with ERGs, offer intriguing examples of diversity transactions. However, there are numerous other ways in which new universities attempt to exchange the racial composition of the student body for organizational resources. In the context of postsecondary racial neoliberalism, this may, in fact, be one of the few resources available to organizations serving URS. And universities may act with the explicit purpose of supporting the student body. At the same time, as the discussion above suggests, there can be costs to these exchanges. Below we offer an additional illustration of a diversity transaction before further exploring the ethical complexities.

MEDIA COVERAGE AND UCM

Positive coverage in the *New York Times* is highly coveted by college campuses. The newspaper is a widely respected media outlet, with a wide readership, particularly among wealthy individuals who might be generous donors or send their offspring to the school. Simply being mentioned in this newspaper may also raise visibility and name recognition—boosting the university's status and rankings. There are good reasons for universities to leap at the opportunity to broadcast their successes in the pages of the *NYT*.

In 2017, UC-Merced leadership worked with the *NYT* on an article entitled "Creating a Safe Space for California Dreamers." It highlighted the experiences of several undocumented Latinx students on the campus. They were on a path to permanent residency through Deferred Action for Childhood Arrivals (DACA), the program housing the DREAM Act—hence the label of "Dreamers." This path requires university attendance. Without meeting this requirement, students could lose their legal status and be subject to deportation.

The article featuring UCM relied on the use of "adversity narratives"—accounts of hardships faced and overcome (or likely to be overcome) with the help of the university.[27] For example, as the article reported, "From fifth grade onward, [one undocumented student] was out until almost midnight helping her single mother mop, sweep and clean the counters of a bakery before moving on to scrub the tile floors of a nearby Italian restaurant." Another "saved up money for college by picking plums alongside his mother, who raised three children by rising at 4:30 a.m. six days a week to work in the fields." A third "fled the violence in El Salvador, sleeping on his grandmother's dirt floor until he could join his parents, whom he knew only through photos and phone calls."[28] The piece implied that admission into UC-Merced would save each of these students from a future much like their difficult past.

Adversity narratives are typically discussed as something that racially marginalized individuals may deploy in competitive contexts. A recent piece in *The Atlantic*, for instance, describes ways that students are encouraged to use adversity narratives in the college admissions process. Nonprofit organizations often provide a bullet-point list of potential essay topics for disadvantaged students, such as "English is not your first language" or "You've been homeless," that are expected to help admissions officers better understand the challenges particular applicants have faced. These exchanges can be deeply fraught for individuals. As the author of the piece points out: "If I were to succeed, I would need to leverage precisely the circumstances that had, conceivably, held me back." Individuals may use adversity narratives to help transform past hardships into benefits, but the benefits are rarely sufficient to outweigh previous disadvantage. The exchange itself may take a mental toll.

The *NYT* article celebrated UCM's efforts to serve undocumented students and also highlighted the plight of "Dreamers" around the country. But in this case, the university, as an organization, also stood to gain from the use of adversity narratives. In fact, a representative at the UC system level was very direct about how the university could benefit from such coverage:

> I'm sure you saw the *New York Times* article about the Dreamers there. I sent it to a number of people, like my friend [well-known political consultant and strategist], and I said, "Have you ever been to Merced?" He's like, "No, I'd love to go." I think philanthropic money can start coming to Merced, especially because of its mission. That also takes a long time to build up, but I do think that that's one opportunity and [the UC Office of the President] can also help ... the chancellor in those areas.

As this quote suggests, UC representatives were thinking primarily about how UC-Merced could translate the coverage into private funding—support that the university direly needed. Donors could make a major difference for UCM's unique student population.

This is a diversity transaction; the university offered coverage of its marginalized student population to the *NYT*, which also benefited by indicating to readers that the newspaper cared about this particularly vulnerable subgroup. The coverage was symbolic given the political context in which it occurred, just months after the election of Donald Trump, who campaigned on a promise to rescind DACA. Students' adversity narratives were used to up the emotional appeal of the piece. This made for a more gripping read, but it also provided compelling evidence of UCM's efforts to provide access and opportunity for undocumented students of color, whose life chances might be measurably improved by the university.

As is often the case, the exchange involved some complicating factors. The *NYT*, perhaps in the effort to create a vivid narrative, provided identifying information for undocumented students profiled in the piece. The newspaper included not only these students' full names, but also their residence hall names, dormitory room numbers, and pictures. This is a level of detail that is difficult to imagine in a piece featuring any other college students. At the time, the newly elected Trump had promised to scale up deportations and conservative provocateur Milo Yiannopoulos had threatened to publicly name undocumented students at UC-Berkeley. On UCM's campus, several conservative students held up "ICE ICE Baby" posters with the phone number for US Immigration and Customs Enforcement (ICE). The publication of the article thus put undocumented students and their families at risk.

Discussions with UC-Merced administration indicate that they were not aware that identifying information was going to be provided. The newspaper should not have put students at risk. But the university could have proactively stepped in to protect students. They might have more closely monitored the newspaper's coverage of a vulnerable population. After the publication, they could have immediately pushed the *NYT* to pull the identifying information. But, to our knowledge, they did not. As one frustrated faculty member, who was involved in discussions with administration about the piece, put it, "[University administrators] are trying to do their best, but other times … to get that philanthropy you have to sort of—in a derogatory sense—pimp out this campus and their students. Like … we're just gonna sort of use them to promote the campus and get national attention."

Commodifying Social Inequalities

Diversity transactions are ethically complex. Both of our empirical cases illustrate the tensions that university officials face in making these exchanges. On one hand, there are obvious, pragmatic benefits that accompany diversity transactions. New universities gain recognition, financial resources, and other forms of sponsorship, all of which are often denied to these excellent and striving schools. On the other hand, marginalized students are used as organizational currency in market exchanges—exchanges that do not always uniformly benefit these students.

When new universities offer workforce diversity to corporations, these schools are providing job training and economic security for many of their racially marginalized graduates. This should not be overlooked. It was, after all, a focus of the well-intentioned UCR officials and Pepsi managers involved in the partnership. At the same time, they facilitated a chain of diversity transactions, whereby the racial marginalization of non-white students and employees became resources for companies to save and make money. This chain connected the university and corporations in a racialized exchange of labor and talent.

Similarly, UCM's efforts to serve California's youth—most of whom are Latinx and many of whom are undocumented—are crucial. The school deserves positive media coverage. As UCR's efforts to change criteria for prestige suggest (see chapter 1), claiming support of undocumented students as a point of pride may even help push back against stigma attached to serving marginalized students. In this particular case, UC-Merced leveraged adversity narratives for organizational gain—benefits that were also expected to trickle down to the student population. But school administrators did so without sufficiently protecting the safety and well-being of their undocumented students.

In her study of for-profit higher education, Tressie McMillan Cottom argues that postsecondary organizations can "commodify social inequalities"—that is, use the experiences and aspirations of racially marginalized students to produce profit.[29] She argues that most for-profit universities prey on racially and economically disadvantaged individuals, leaving these students with high levels of debt and little to show for their time in school.[30] What Cottom describes is the intentional and aggressive organizational exploitation of marginalized students. The gain described in her research is almost all on the side of the for-profit university. Not all cases, however, are so clear-cut.

New universities commodify social inequalities, but they do so in part to support disadvantaged populations. UC-Riverside and UC-Merced offer an important social good—a four-year college degree—at a very low cost to URS from low-income households. These universities, and their leaders, do not get rich from diversity transactions. UCR has made very little from its partnerships with Pepsi. UCM might have attracted some philanthropic support from the *New York Times* coverage, or none at all. In either case, however, any funds acquired directly or indirectly from diversity transactions fell into already depleted coffers.

Commodification of URS is a predictable feature of postsecondary racial neoliberalism. The withdrawal of support for public higher education, combined with racialized university hierarchies, poorly positions new universities in market exchanges. That these organizations utilize the one resource they have in abundance—racially marginalized students—is not surprising. Predominately white universities, after all, are also selling students, although the nature of the exchange and degree of harm that can be done are different. So are the financial returns; in racialized markets, racially advantaged students, especially from affluent households, carry more status and funds to the universities that depend on them.

New universities make diversity transactions so they can continue to keep the doors open. When organizational value is measured primarily by the ability to extract private funding in racialized markets, new universities are devalued and under-resourced. It is difficult for these organizations to exist in a political, fiscal, and cultural context in which racially marginalized youth are treated as a threat or a drain on public resources, rather than a promising resource worthy of substantial investment. In the concluding chapter, we consider policy solutions that may help break down higher education's racial neoliberal cycle so that schools like Merced and Riverside may thrive.

Breaking the Cycle

Throughout *Broke: The Racial Consequences of Underfunding Public Universities*, we have focused on postsecondary racial neoliberalism. In the introduction, we illustrated links between broadening access to predominately white research universities and defunding public higher education. Once postsecondary austerity was established, a vicious cycle was set into motion. We argued that racially and economically privileged students have been concentrated in universities that amass an increasing amount of private resources to support their students. In contrast, historically underrepresented racially marginalized students (URS) seeking economic mobility have been heavily represented in the least-resourced universities. These inequalities give the false appearance that elite predominately white universities and the students they serve are higher "quality"—justifying continued resource disparities.

The new university, a competitive research university that has evolved to serve marginalized populations, offers a useful vantage point to understand higher education's racial neoliberal cycle. These universities are a pressure valve that keeps our racially segregated and unequal system from facing uncomfortable scrutiny and pressure.[1] New universities offer URS from low-income households substantial access to top 200 research universities. The University of California system includes two such schools, UC-Merced and UC-Riverside. Case studies of these focal schools provided the empirical material for the book.

We started with the "Battle with the Rankings"—highlighting the racial bias built into assessments of student "merit," which have been used to justify postsecondary segregation and the devaluing of universities serving URS. The tentatively successful challenge that new universities have made to existing rankings demonstrates that a new organizational form is emerging—one that prizes access over exclusivity in the service of a research mission. In chapters 2 and 3, we examined the link between racialized organizational hierarchies and the unequal distribution of organizational resources. "P3 Paradise" focused on the financial realities that face new universities serving large numbers of marginalized students. We argued that these organizations are in vulnerable positions in relation to for-profit actors and may pursue potentially risky strategies to fill the gap caused by state retraction. "Running Political Cover" contended that resource disparities between public universities in the same state system intensify with the shift to private funding. Schools with whiter, wealthier student bodies are able to draw private revenue streams that are largely blocked for schools serving URS from low-income households.

The book then took a hard look at what austerity means for the operation of new universities. "Austerity Administration" argued that the efforts of new university leadership to grow big, cut costs, be market-smart, and think (inter)nationally can entrench austerity and inadvertently harm URS. "Tolerable Suboptimization" walked readers through the detrimental impact of underfunding on academic advising, mental health services, and cultural programming for racially marginalized students in new universities. As the subtitle of *Broke* suggests, these chapters detailed the racial consequences of underfunding the new universities that do important work for their systems and states.

A final pairing of empirical chapters focused on the colorblind logic of "diversity" and its relationship with austerity. In "Student Labor and Centers of Support," we demonstrated that a budget-friendly, "inclusive" approach designed to support all students equally increases the racial equity labor that URS undertake to make campus safe and welcoming for people of color. "Marketing Diversity" explored ethical quandaries that arise when new universities obtain much-needed funding by exchanging URS with predominately white organizations seeking diversity. We argue that the attack on civil rights–era cultural programming and the commodification of non-white students for private support are undesirable but predictable side effects of our failure to acknowledge and combat structural racial inequalities in higher education.

As a whole, the book highlights the cyclical, mutually reinforcing nature of postsecondary racial neoliberalism. Devaluing students of color makes it possible to legally segregate them into different postsecondary schools, which are then disadvantaged in the postsecondary field, and to systematically deny those schools the kind of support that was granted to public universities when these organizations were predominately white. New universities are thus set up to struggle.

A racial neoliberal cycle, however, is not just happening in US higher education. As Raewyn Connell points out, universities in the US and Western

Europe possess the vast majority of material and cultural resources in the global higher education system.[2] These include celebrity researchers and research funds, top academic journals, and a monopoly on the languages of modern knowledge, particularly English. While US and European scholarship is routinely cited by scholars around the world, research conducted in Africa, Asia, Latin America, the Middle East, and elsewhere is largely invisible outside those regions. During the Cold War, the US invested in higher education in developing countries, but this came to an end in the 1970s and 1980s. Universities in other parts of the world have been forced into competition against the resource-rich universities of the global north. This inequality is reflected in international ranking systems, which Connell argues "were *designed* to highlight the elite Anglo-American research universities,"[3] and the growth of private higher education organizations in place of public colleges and universities.[4]

Nor is this cycle confined to higher education. Research on banking and housing in the US provides parallel examples. Mehrsa Baradaran shows how, under Jim Crow segregation, Black banks necessarily relied on Black customers who were unable to patronize white banks. The need to depend on relatively disadvantaged customers meant that Black banks were less able to invest and accrue profits. White banks worked together to ensure liquidity during crises, but these organizations refused to lend to Black banks. Today Black banks still have less access to capital and are more likely to fail.[5] Similarly, Keeanga-Yamahtta Taylor describes a process of "predatory inclusion" whereby policies meant to end redlining and incorporate Black people into the housing market led to exploitative lending practices, widespread foreclosures in Black communities, the decline of property values, and the demonization of Black people as unfit for homeownership.[6]

We recognize that reading *Broke* can be difficult because it suggests that the problems we have identified are pervasive and beyond repair. We do not believe this to be the case. Thus, our concluding chapter is devoted to action. We ask: What policies, practices, and approaches may challenge postsecondary racial neoliberalism? Social scientists, especially sociologists, are not typically trained to answer questions like these. We are instead inclined to document inequalities and reveal the mechanisms producing them. Indeed, the empirical chapters of *Broke* highlight this craft well. But the book also contains glimmers of hope and kernels of potentially effective policies, some of which come from the vibrant, creative, and motivated constituencies that populate new universities. Here we draw out these possibilities.

Tackling racial neoliberalism in higher education is going to require hitting it at multiple points, simultaneously. That is, any one of the solutions below, on its own, may not be enough. As we suggested in the introduction, racially advantaged groups quickly develop new "opportunity hoarding" strategies, finding different ways to maintain (or increase) existing advantages.[7] Thus, creating social change necessitates repeatedly breaking the racial neoliberal cycle—disrupting the cultural understandings (e.g., racialized hierarchies) and material consequences (resource flows on the basis of those hierarchies) that reinforce and reproduce each other.[8]

One of the limitations of our suggestions, however, is that they are geared toward addressing *proximate* causes of racial disparities. As Victor Ray and Louise Seamster argue, race is itself a "fundamental element of social stratification."[9] Structural racism is remarkably stable across time and place, and deeply resistant to disruption. The tight links between race and social class, as illustrated in this book, also make consistent linear racial "progress" unlikely, even in a single societal domain. We can tackle proximate causes but still see stubborn patterns of racial inequality. History offers numerous examples. For instance, opening up research universities to racially marginalized students gave these students access to higher-prestige organizations, but it did not provide them with the same resources available to their white peers in predominately white research universities.

Higher education is not the "solution" to racial inequality. It is not the great equalizer. Even as a proximate mechanism for social change, it is deeply flawed. The history of postsecondary education in the US is exclusive, violent, and based on racial subjugation—from the slavery profits that helped found many private universities, to the federal claiming of indigenous lands to form land grant universities, and the coercive pressures on Historically Black Colleges and Universities that were designed to limit their power.[10] Yet, in the US, higher education is often, and quite ironically, expected to do the work of a functional welfare state—build economic security, serve as an engine for mobility, and create greater well-being for all who pass through the college gates.

Higher education could contribute to these goals. But we need to give up on the idea that higher education can be the *sole* (or even primary) lever for addressing societal inequalities.[11] Just like we need to tackle postsecondary racial neoliberalism at multiple points, we need to work through many, interlinked societal institutions to help create change. Postsecondary recommendations should thus be implemented alongside policies that address racial differences in wealth and debt, access to health care, K–12 educational quality, protection against environmental pollution, and freedom from incarceration—among others. They must grow our capacity to act collectively across these issues.

Five Recommendations

We focus our efforts where we have expertise, offering five interlinked recommendations that will work against postsecondary racial neoliberalism: challenge diversity logics, abolish the SAT, combat organizational hierarchies, encourage collaborative public systems, and reinvest in public higher education.

CHALLENGE DIVERSITY LOGICS

As we have argued throughout the book, diversity is a colorblind logic that makes it difficult, if not impossible, to attend to the needs of racially marginalized students. It focuses on individual differences, rather than structures of oppression that impact students and their communities differently, and treats collective efforts to center race as divisive and unfair. Universities build infrastructure around diversity that can potentially make campuses less, rather than more, comfortable and safe for racially marginalized students.[12] Thus, as Sara Ahmed astutely puts it, "Diversity becomes about *changing perceptions of whiteness rather than changing the whiteness of organizations*. Changing perceptions of whiteness can be how an institution can reproduce whiteness, as that which exists but is no longer perceived."[13]

Equity-oriented logics, in contrast, attend to history, positionality, and power. They emphasize the collective empowerment of communities systematically disadvantaged on the basis of race.[14] Equity logics may be present on many new university campuses—although the spaces where they thrive can be threatened. One way to combat diversity logics that stall or prevent meaningful change is to devote university resources to strengthening equity-oriented infrastructure and communities.

UC-Riverside's cultural centers offer an exceptional model. As we detailed in chapter 6, these centers are powerful sites of resistance within the university. But rather than creating tense racial dynamics on campus, harming administrators' abilities to work with racially marginalized communities, or creating cultural "silos," UCR's cultural centers are sites of communication, healing, and cooperation across divides. They are, in our estimation, key to the university's exceptional success in supporting marginalized students. These centers help create what is, arguably, one of the most racially harmonious campuses in the UC system. Yet, underfunding has left UCR's cultural centers under-resourced. They have not grown with the student body—a problem that is likely to worsen, as massive growth is a key aim of UCR's austerity administrators. The university has also increased its commitment to diversity programs, spreading resources more thinly and bolstering diversity logics as solutions to racial inequities.

A perceived and real barrier to heavy investment in equity-oriented infrastructure is anti–affirmative action legislation. This legislation casts uncertainty over university initiatives that address racial inequality, leaving administrators feeling as if their hands are tied. There have been efforts to push back. In 2014, Latinx and Black lawmakers led efforts to repeal Prop. 209 in California, which impacts not only universities, but any form of public education, employment, and contracting. State leadership immediately got mired in debates about affirmative action in college admissions, which operated as a political third rail. Even though Prop. 209 would be unlikely to pass in today's California, and despite the fact that repeal efforts quietly won Senate approval, the topic was shelved by the Speaker of the State Assembly after conflict erupted.[15]

This controversy highlights an important point: College admissions is holding universities, and the public sector in general, hostage—blocking efforts to organize around equity, not diversity. After all, "diversity" as the dominant organizational framework for race was solidified in Supreme Court college admissions cases. It is reasonable to conclude that challenging diversity logics is going to require tackling admissions head-on, possibly by completely revamping the process.

One way to move out of this gridlock is to leave behind the idea that affirmative action is the only way to address racial disparities in college access. Affirmative action was an important and necessary remedy at a crucial historical moment, and it may still have a role to play. But it is an imperfect solution. Rather than addressing the racial bias built into the way students are evaluated, and consequently, how universities are ranked, affirmative action made it possible to create exceptions based on race. Unfortunately, this also left intact the system that required exceptions to be made in the first place.[16]

ABOLISH THE SAT

As historian and anti-racist thinker Ibram X. Kendi argues, "The use of standardized tests to measure aptitude and intelligence is one of the most effective racist policies ever devised to degrade Black minds and legally exclude Black bodies." He explains that scientific attention devoted to measuring the race-based "academic-achievement gap" is the "latest method in reinforcing the oldest racist idea: Black intellectual inferiority."[17] His observation puts obsessive focus on the SAT into historical perspective. We have long tested and probed people of color to justify racial hierarchies based on assumptions of intellectual difference.[18]

The SAT is the epitome of this phenomenon. As noted in the introduction, the SAT bears little relation to actual college performance.[19] But it has an oversized impact on how we assess student "quality" and thus that of the universities that students attend. It is a powerful mechanism for legitimating racialized hierarchies, without directly invoking race, and is shrouded in inaccurate science with white supremacist roots.[20] If our goal is to tackle postsecondary racial neoliberalism, our sights should be on the standardized testing at the heart of the social construction of "merit." It is on the basis of this testing, and other related measures of merit, that educational resources flow.

The announced, and quickly abandoned, "adversity score" offered by the College Board, the company that administers the SAT, is an example of growing recognition of problems associated with the test.[21] The adversity score distilled the challenges students face in their school and neighborhood environments (e.g., crime and poverty) into a single number. The idea was that this could be used by universities to counterbalance the advantages available to affluent white applicants. After controversy, the College Board indicated that it would not include this score with student test results, but instead provide aggregate-level school and neighborhood hardship scores to admissions officers. At no point did the adversity score include the education and income of students' parents—meaning that advantaged parents could still attempt to leverage school and neighborhood inputs in their favor.

The adversity score, and other similar efforts, are a Band-Aid for a deeply flawed and racially biased effort to quantify "intelligence" in a single test score. We need to abandon the college testing regime entirely. There are a number of other ways to assess candidates that are not as problematic for racially marginalized youth: High school GPA, class rank, transcripts (with attention to course offerings available in the school), essays, samples of class work, science projects, and letters from teachers and mentors are some options. Currently, there are several "test-optional" or "test-flexible" schools, to which applicants can choose to not send test scores. There is, at the time of writing, only one test-blind university in the US—Hampshire College in Amherst, MA. The school will reject all score reports. As the school's policy reads, "Unlike 'test-optional' institutions, we will not consider SAT/ACT scores regardless of the score. Even if it's a perfect score, it will not weigh into our assessment of an applicant."[22]

Change may need to come from the top, as elite schools are the least vulnerable to status hits and thus have the greatest room to maneuver. Some have even suggested that elite universities could move to a lottery admissions system to radically democratize opportunity. Most proposals are not for true lotteries but require minimum entry qualifications or matching between student and university preferences. This is not an implausible suggestion: Entry processes with some elements of built-in randomness are a reality in many parts of the world—the Netherlands, Turkey, and (for some courses of study) the UK. In the US, the process by which medical students are matched with residency programs is another model.[23]

Any admissions system, of course, can be gamed by privileged families and university gatekeepers. But the greater the randomness, the less chance for tinkering in ways that preserve racial and economic privilege. Greater randomness in admissions also reduces wealthy white people's investment in particular universities, which can reduce competition between schools for a limited pool of resources.

If we reject the notion that "merit" actually measures students' capacities to achieve, rather than their privileges, then it is easier to see access to well-resourced universities as a social good that should be more evenly distributed and that can be fully utilized by a wide variety of deserving students. There is real-life evidence to this last point. The Posse program, which enrolls groups of marginalized youth in elite universities, indicates that many students can go on to be successful in this context. Even students who might not have met existing admissions criteria can be at the top of their college graduating class.[24] This program suggests the importance of sufficient organizational support for student success.[25] It also pushes back against racialized notions of student intelligence and ability that are mapped onto organizational hierarchies.

COMBAT ORGANIZATIONAL HIERARCHIES

We also need to combat the racialized organizational hierarchies that penalize new universities and other schools serving racially marginalized students. This project has been embraced by UC-Riverside and the University Innovation Alliance (or UIA), as highlighted in chapter 1. Recall that the UIA is a political coalition of "public universities with a public mission" focused on graduating students from all race and class backgrounds.[26] As we concluded in that chapter, there are a number of barriers that limit the potential of the UIA's current strategy for radically reconfiguring organizational status accumulation.

Part of the problem is that UIA schools are still working within typical status arenas—for example, the *U.S. News & World Report* rankings—and with the overarching goal of member schools joining elite predominately white research universities in the highly coveted Association of American Universities (or AAU). This means the UIA's approaches can easily get co-opted by universities with greater resources and less sincere commitments to supporting the marginalized students of their states. Coalition schools are also bound by the desire not to take too great a status hit in their efforts to keep or achieve AAU status.

We suggest a more radical move. First, dramatically expand the UIA. There are new universities all over the country. There are also numerous other university leaders who see the writing on the wall and would be willing to make a change, if they were joined by their peers and competitors. As we highlight below, there is power in universities acting together. This strategy offers more than one voice. The risk is shared. And a large coalition of organizations is a political bloc not to be underestimated.

Second, these schools should refuse to submit information to the *U.S. News & World Report* indefinitely, or at least until the rankings more directly reflect a public mission. Measures to capture this mission include the percentage of the student body that is Pell Grant eligible, the percentage of URS enrolled (relative to the state or regional population), and graduation gaps between racially marginalized and racially privileged populations. These metrics would require other schools to reconfigure whom and how they serve in order to compete with new universities. Additionally, if enough schools drop out of the *U.S. News*, its monopoly on university ranking will be challenged. This opens up possibilities for new alternatives to take hold and could force a larger change in the *U.S. News*.

Finally, the UIA could launch a challenge to the AAU. "America's leading research universities" are not, and cannot be, just predominately white. Currently, membership is only by invitation. Schools are evaluated by the "breadth and quality of their programs of research and graduate education."[27] The primary screening criteria—federally funded research expenditures, membership in National Academies, faculty awards, fellowships, and citations—disadvantage new universities that have more limited resources. These schools are then excluded from the AAU, which subsequently makes it harder to build the research infrastructure necessary to meet the screening criteria. The AAU should consider ways to increase representation of universities that do excellent research *and* meet public needs.

The ultimate goal is to dramatically disrupt the notion that Black and Brown students go to lower-quality colleges and universities while affluent white (and often affluent Asian) students attend higher-quality research universities. Racialized organizational hierarchies, in combination with racialized notions of "merit" embedded in the SAT, are the basis for the differential resourcing of new universities relative to predominately white schools. Redistribution will require recognizing the vitality and importance of new universities.

ENCOURAGE COLLABORATIVE SYSTEMS

Public university systems have an important role to play in redistribution. Systems need to develop mechanisms that pool and share resources, so that universities serving the most-disadvantaged populations are not the least re-sourced. Motivating public reinvestment in higher education, as outlined below, is going to require within-system collaboration, rather than a scramble to pick up the scraps. Public universities should view other campuses as allies—not drains on their potential resources.

The University of California system could be a leader. Conversations about another "re-benching" exercise, where the system reconsiders the distribution of state funds across schools, are bubbling to the surface. Leaders at UCM and UCR, as well as some other UCs, are interested in proposals that grant more state money, per head, for Pell Grant–eligible students—in other words, those from the lowest-income families. Should this type of approach succeed, UCM and UCR will receive a greater share of state monies than their sister campuses. Other campuses may then have more incentive to enroll Pell Grant students.[28] In a non–Prop. 209 universe, the system could also directly address racial representation.

But in most state systems outside of the University of California, the starting point for redistribution is more politically complicated. Most other systems are composed of a flagship research university, alongside teaching-focused regional schools. Funding disparities from private sources, like those we explored in chapter 3, are even sharper. States also tend to offer far more per-student funding to flagships; as a consequence, URS at new universities may be paying similar tuition but receiving only a tiny fraction of the funding that goes to their more advantaged peers in more prestigious research universities.

The research versus teaching university comparison highlights an interesting puzzle. Research universities need access to research support. Both research and teaching universities need access to funds for student support. There is no reason why a low-income student of color at a new university, or even a teaching university, should have a less rigorous or less organizationally supported experience. But research universities have grown accustomed to thinking about undergraduate students as a source of funding for research, which complicates conversations about pooling and redistributing student-based resources.

Jason Owen-Smith argues that underwriting research with tuition and fees is a "distasteful and untenable" "shell game."[29] He instead highlights funding proposals that develop a postsecondary division of labor. The basic idea is that research and graduate education could be covered by the federal government and undergraduate education on public research campuses could be supported by states, encouraging federal and state collaboration on higher education. There are many possible variants that would similarly disentangle the different potential functions of universities. Such approaches would have the benefit of directly addressing a common justification for student funding disparities internal to state systems—the notion that not all schools are the same type of organization. It could also be used to dramatically improve new universities' access to funds for both research infrastructure and the education of racially and economically marginalized students.

Postsecondary leaders need to recognize the downsides of fighting system peers for available public and private resources. Competing in an increasingly cutthroat postsecondary market only tends to bolster austerity. It may seem like the only way to survive. However, in the long run, intra-system competition has the effect of increasing reliance on private market resources and making it more difficult to make claims for public funding. In contrast, when public universities within a state work together, they can convincingly demonstrate that higher education is addressing a wider array of public needs. This is a crucial move for public reinvestment in higher education.

REINVEST IN PUBLIC HIGHER EDUCATION

Our country made a choice in the last decades of the twentieth century to withdraw funding for higher education, just as waves of racially marginalized youth gained greater access. This was likely not coincidental. But it is reversible. What conditions would motivate reinvestment? And what do we need to do in order to avoid ending up in the same place?

Reinvestment requires convincing the public that higher education is a public good, from which all of society benefits, and not solely a private commodity that promotes individual gain. The public is not motivated to spend money when the returns are perceived as going to only some members of society—particularly when those individuals are socially marginalized.[30] We can look to the Cold War era, when higher education began to open up to new populations, for an example of a moment in which higher education was thought of as a social good. But the Cold War University was a war machine—driven by military spending and fears of falling behind Soviet scientific development.[31]

War and militarization are not the only causes that can fuel public investment. Anything that is perceived as a potential public threat or societal need that can be addressed through higher education could qualify. For example, scientific consensus indicates that the devastation that will be wrought by climate change in the coming decades is a rapidly unfolding crisis. A version of the Green New Deal legislation, as initially proposed by House Representative Alexandria Ocasio-Cortez and Senator Ed Markey, could serve this purpose; universities are a major source of the science behind renewable energy, and research on policies to deal with upcoming natural disasters, public health crises, environmental pollution, and population migration is generated in universities. These problems require collective action. Research universities can be both models for and sources of collective efforts to deal with climate change.

Assuming the political will for reinvestment, we would also have the chance to recalibrate the funding mechanisms that have fueled postsecondary racial neoliberalism. Offloading university funding onto students enabled austerity, as individuals and their families were expected to absorb costs no longer covered by the public. Family wealth thus financed services that the state once provided. The racialization of wealth ensured that this would be most damaging for URS and their families, who would need to take on enormous amounts of debt (or opt out in order to avoid debt).[32] Some scholars have therefore referred to racially marginalized students' movement into higher education, under these conditions, as a form of predatory inclusion.[33]

We need to detach the funding of higher education from individuals and their families and put higher education back in the purview of the public. Many states are moving this way by adopting versions of "free college" programs. For example, a California provision recently expanded community college fee waivers to all first-time, full-time students graduating from California high schools. The New York Excelsior Program eliminates tuition costs at two-year and four-year postsecondary schools for state residents whose families make up to $125,000. These, and other similar programs, are experiments in what is likely to be an evolving, multiple-decades-long project.[34]

Not surprisingly, therefore, early "free college" plans are imperfect. They fail to adequately address non-tuition costs, such as room and board, books, and transportation.[35] Many are applicable only to community college students, even though these schools tend to have exceptionally low graduation rates.[36] Some are means-tested, as they apply only to low-income families, excluding part or all of the middle class and also running the risk of public unpopularity. Perhaps most centrally, existing state plans are still rooted in student-based funding models. These are "last dollar" programs that require students to first go through the confusing and problematic Free Application for Federal Student Aid (FAFSA) process and then offer a supplement top-off that results in no tuition.[37]

In order for states to radically break with the status quo and fund postsecondary organizations directly, we will need to dismantle the federal funding apparatus and recapture revenue from Pell Grants, Supplemental Education Opportunity Grants, work-study funds, and other federal aid sources. Currently, private schools receive a disproportionate share of federal dollars relative to the number of students that they enroll.[38] For-profit universities are largely fueled by Pell Grants, military education programs, and federally subsidized student loans.[39] This money could be poured into public education. As several presidential candidates (across a few elections) have pointed out, universal "free" college could also be underwritten with a tax on the ultra-rich. In this kind of model, student costs, from the first dollar, could be covered by federal and state provision directly to public universities.

A big question, of course, is which organizations get what amount of aid. Difficulties in resolving this are what led to the punting of institutional aid in amendments of the Higher Education Act, as discussed in the introduction.[40] Barriers are obviously political, but they are also logistical. Because scholars and policymakers have long measured postsecondary "quality" by the presumed "merit" of who attends a given university, we have not yet devoted as much effort to measuring the ways that universities, as organizations, give back to the public.[41] Our postsecondary data apparatus was built in the Cold War era to capture individual human capital acquisition and is best suited for painstakingly measuring individual student educational and occupational attainment. If we are interested in funding organizations, not students, we need to think more about postsecondary organizations as relevant units of study.

Our work suggests some possible ways to disperse aid across schools. States might offer greater funding to public universities serving higher proportions of in-state residents, URS, and low-income students, and to schools that can demonstrate positive impact on local and regional health, education, and economies. There is also a great deal of variation in how successful public universities, even those with similar student bodies, are in graduating marginalized populations.[42] Or in moving their marginalized student populations into graduate school. In addition, the research contributions of higher education are crucial and may be concentrated at particular universities.

Contributions that fit state and national agendas—such as green technologies that help with drought prevention and response—might receive high levels of support.

Primary and secondary school funding can also offer us a cautionary tale in devising useful metrics. The No Child Left Behind Act, in place for over a decade, placed an obsessive focus on a problematic measure of success—student test scores—and severely penalized schools that did not show improvements. Many negatively impacted schools were under-resourced and serving marginalized populations.[43] Whatever measures of organizational success are applied in the postsecondary sector, they cannot be colorblind; that is, measures should recognize structural disparities that confront organizations serving URS and reward, rather than penalize, schools that enroll and support these students.

Reasserting Public Interest

Why should policymakers, educators, and taxpayers support these radical changes? Currently, higher education is central to the neoliberal project. The postsecondary sector is the competitive arena in which to "earn" protection from unemployment and poverty.[44,45] Those who desire stable, decent-paying jobs with access to medical and other benefits must move through it.[46] In the US, there is virtually no other safety net. For marginalized groups, in particular, universities offer a form of partial insurance—one way to push back against the uneven distribution of income, wealth, occupational status, and respect.[47] In other words, we should care because higher education, while not the great equalizer, is highly consequential for conditions of basic security in a market-based economic system.

Higher education is also a key battleground to reassert public political demands for equitable redistribution. Students from a wide variety of racial and economic backgrounds should have access to well-resourced universities—not just racially and economically privileged students, along with small numbers of the marginalized. Higher education, unlike many other social institutions, still retains much of its public character, but this may not always be the case. New universities, for example, will be forced to lean into their worst tendencies, or may even cease to exist, if public funding continues to decline. Like other public workhorses, they depend on public investment and system support.

New universities are, in fact, remarkably well positioned to recover the promise of public higher education. These schools have taken up the challenges posed by postsecondary racial neoliberalism with commitments to principles of access and inclusion. They have broken the mold for public research universities by asserting that this type of organization does not have to be predominately white or affluent. The students that populate these schools are vibrant, resilient, and full of potential. We can see seeds of a different way of evaluating value—one that is more collective, communal, and focused on challenging structures of oppression—in student efforts to resist austerity, racism, and exploitation.

It is an astounding waste, and a misuse of resources, not to invest more in students like Vesta, whom we met at the start of *Broke*. In the years after our interview, Vesta would graduate and begin working for an organization in LA that collects and shares schooling data to advocate for Black and Brown parents and their children to receive a high-quality K–12 education. In effect, Vesta went back to her community and offered protections to kids from backgrounds much like hers, as they are often overlooked, criminalized, and deprived of valuable educational supports.[48] The resources that UC-Merced provided for Vesta, despite the school's financial challenges, are going right back into supporting the future of California.

The changes that we have proposed are political—yet not intervening is also a political decision with political consequences. The inequalities generated by racial neoliberalism are not a natural or inevitable outcome of impersonal "market forces," but rather a result of social structures designed to benefit a small fraction of the populace.[49] Leaving higher education to brutal colorblind competitions between students for spots in well-resourced universities, and between public universities for scraps from the state or donor largesse, is not good for any but the wealthiest schools and the most-privileged individuals. The current system comes at a high cost for many young people and their families. Change it.

Acknowledgments

Every book is the product of larger intellectual communities. We have benefited immeasurably from scholars who are building race theory and conducting research on racial inequalities in education. As we detail in the methodological appendix, we wish to thank those whose work inspired and grounded *Broke*. We are particularly humbled by race scholarship attending to intersections between white supremacy and neoliberalism, as intertwined systems of oppression. The book also benefits from a resurgence of organizational postsecondary scholarship that has occurred over the past two decades.

We are grateful for the insights of Elizabeth Armstrong, Prudence Carter, and Brian Powell—all of whom read multiple drafts of the book and provided detailed commentary. Each of these scholars imparted important lessons. Elizabeth pushed us on the analytical contributions of the book as the central claims of *Broke* came into view. Prudence urged us to keep clarifying the racial neoliberal cycle and weaving it through the empirical chapters. Brian helped us think about how to report the struggles of the new universities we studied, while also protecting these vulnerable organizations and reporting their successes.

We shared our findings with three groups that provided formative feedback. Laura workshopped difficult ethical issues related to the book with cohorts of William T. Grant Foundation Scholars during an annual conference. This exercise provided clarity on how to move forward and led us to take a direct approach to our own positionality. To Berkeley Sociology, Laura presented an earlier version of "Running Political Cover." She found an engaged audience who provided a useful perspective from what is, alongside UCLA, the most prestigious school in the larger University of California system. A trip to the University of Wisconsin-Madison, during which Laura presented a version of "Austerity Administration," helped us articulate the role of social class without pushing race from view.

Jordan Conwell, on that visit to UW-Madison, shared his understanding of W. E. B. Du Bois's insights regarding political-economic context. Jacob Lederman, at the University of Michigan-Flint, provided information about the IU campaign in the University of Michigan system and urged us to think more about how state systems outside of California work. University of Michigan graduate student Jared Eno is working on a phenomenal dissertation project focused on the racialization of organizational classification schemes. It is, in many ways, the temporal precursor to *Broke*. In the process of working with him, Laura gained greater clarity on our central argument. With regard to our historical and comparative lens, we have Mitchell Stevens to thank for the continual reminder that we need a historical and political sociology of education.

Veronica Lerma, coauthor of "Student Labor and Centers of Support," as well as first author on "Racialized Equity Labor, University Appropriation, and Student Resistance" in *Social Problems*, played a key role in theorizing the labor that student activists of color provide to make their universities safe and comfortable. She also conducted a large number of student interviews and offered comments on the entire manuscript. The data quality and contributions of this book are sharper for her involvement. We also wish to thank Maria Duenas, an excellent qualitative researcher who provided interview and ethnographic support, along with Michelle Yeung and Christina Acosta, who took field notes at a key event.

A team of UCM undergraduates were also involved in this research. These students include Jovita Angel, Ashley Bennett, Dakari Finister, Rosa Hernandez, Reginald Nelson, Ana Padilla, Patrick Pascual, and Mayra Ramirez. Their input and emerging talent as researchers is evident in *Broke*. We would have missed a great deal of the student perspective without them. Jovita Angel, in particular, took on a central role in the project. We wish to thank her for her commitment to sharing voices of resistance.

The dedicated, skilled, and caring staff members at both UC-Merced and UC-Riverside also inspired this book. They welcomed us into their worlds at some risk to themselves and their units. We hope that we have managed to protect these workers and have successfully articulated the need to support their tireless efforts. A special shout-out goes to the SSHA advisors at UCM, who allowed Laura to shadow them for months and provided a read of the "Tolerable Suboptimization" chapter. We also wish to thank African Student Programs and Chicano Student Programs at UCR. We tried to do justice to the rich history and crucial work that goes on in these, and other, cultural centers on UCR's campus. Finally, we are grateful to Ekpeju Ed E-Nunu and Gerry Medina for including Kelly in their work, for two valuable lunches in which they helped us think through emerging findings, and for modeling the exceptional cultural accomplishments of UCR.

Administrators at both universities were also open and welcoming of this research project. This was also true of system-level administrators. We are grateful for their willingness to share information, insights, and perspectives. While we are sometimes critical of university and system leadership, our goal was to situate these actors in a larger context. And we worked to remind readers that the UC system is an exceptional public institution. There is no other system in the world like it. The UC's contributions to mobility are central to its past and very much a part of its current and future role in the state and nation. We are proud to be affiliated with the UC and wish to see *Broke* motivate even greater public investment in the system and its new universities.

We would be remiss if we failed to mention the support of our families. Laura's husband, Kyle Dodson, did far more than his share of childcare while Laura was collecting data and sharing ideas in various forums. Lane and Sage kept her grounded. Her parents, Melody and Ed, offered love from afar. Kelly could not have made it through the researching and writing of *Broke* without the tremendous patience and generosity of Malena and Oliver. His parents, Paul and Heather, supported him more than he could have ever hoped. Leah and Craig gave him a home away from home. Anna Garber Hammond was a kind and gracious partner.

Finally, we would like to thank our trusty editor, Elizabeth Branch Dyson. When we began collecting data on the project, we knew she was a perfect fit for the book we would eventually write. She has carefully shepherded *Broke* though the publication process and given us valuable space to be bold in our ideas. The book would not exist—certainly not in this form—without her support.

Methodological Appendix

ON BEING WHITE AND STUDYING RACE

The single greatest methodological challenge for us in producing *Broke* has been thinking carefully and intentionally about our whiteness. We went into this project convinced that white scholars should write about race in the academy. The work of changing racist structures should not be shouldered solely by colleagues of color. Racialized equity labor (as discussed in chapter 6) is damaging to the careers and well-being of racially marginalized scholars. In contrast, white scholars typically profit from the ability to move through our careers with the privilege of never thinking about the racial dynamics of the environments in which we work. We do not wish to continue supporting this inequity.

At the same time, we are also aware that well-intentioned white people can do a great deal of harm while they are attempting to support communities of color. We recognize that our whiteness gives us a platform to make bold claims about racial stratification in the academy that will not be diminished as "me-search" or "too political." This platform has not historically been granted to Asian, Black, Brown, and Indigenous scholars, as well as those from other marginalized racial and ethnic groups. From the outset, we understood that we could misstep by attempting to speak for, instead of, and about these groups. Thus, we made efforts, at every stage of the project, to reduce the harm that we might cause. At the same time, we recognize that these efforts were likely not always enough—and that we might not necessarily know if, how, and when we inflicted harm.

In what follows, we discuss how our positions in a "matrix of domination" shaped all stages of the research project. Patricia Hill Collins explains that a matrix of domination binds systems of oppression together, such that race, class, gender, heterosexuality, and other systems are mutually constituted in a web of power.[1] As a white woman in a more senior position in sociology, and a white man of a similar age but in a less senior position, Laura and Kelly, respectively, were differently located in the matrix of domination. Yet, both of us could draw on racial privileges that enhanced our other statuses and, in some spaces, afforded us a great deal of power. We thought about what this meant as we envisioned, conducted, and wrote up the study, but we also learned a number of lessons along the way.

Developing Research Questions

Both of us had been working on research projects focused on student experiences prior to our joint project. Like most postsecondary scholars, we drew conclusions about the educational infrastructure in which students were embedded based on student reports. This was, in fact, one of the limitations of *Paying for the Party: How College Maintains Inequality*, which played a key role in bringing attention to the structure of postsecondary organizations.[2] With *Broke*, we wanted to more thoroughly and directly study organizations.

Prior to this point, Laura had spent a decade and a half interviewing white women attending a predominately white university. This research, with Elizabeth A. Armstrong, focused primarily on social class. Over time, Elizabeth and Laura gained greater understanding of how the students they studied benefited from white privilege, and the degree to which Midwest U (the university at the center of *Paying for the Party*) depended on this privilege. More recently they have considered the ways in which white women are actively complicit in shoring up the matrix of domination.[3]

The initial seeds of *Broke* were planted when Laura accepted a tenure-track position at UC-Merced. In her early years at the university, she probably learned more from her undergraduate students than they did from her. They immediately challenged the binary comparisons (i.e., white vs. Black, with Black in the deficit) that characterize decades of educational research. Students demanded scholarship that recognized the rich racial and ethnic tapestry of the US—which was patently obvious in California. Laura became increasingly curious about her students' limited access to university resources and the ways this was linked to student body racial composition. She was also intrigued by the fascinating organizational environment around her. UC-Merced is, after all, the first—and quite possibly last—public research university of the twenty-first century. After about five years at the school, Laura started to plan the new project in earnest.

Kelly came to this project after 3.5 years studying the experiences of poor women in the Riverside Community College District. His data collection was part of a larger research study that placed class and poverty, in particular, at the center of the study design and analysis. It emphasized the position of single women, many with children, because of their greater likelihood of being poor and leaving college without a degree. As Kelly looked carefully at the larger context of the women's lives—the local labor market, neighborhood demographics, transportation systems, childcare arrangements, and interactions with police—race emerged as a key factor.

The Inland Empire, which encompasses Riverside and the surrounding region, was impacted by the broader race relations and urban development that reshaped Los Angeles during the late twentieth century.[4] Women's college experiences of choosing classes, picking majors, and imagining career trajectories were inseparable from growing up in communities like "Little Tijuana," living with immigrant family members, or learning how to style Black women's hair as children. Like Laura in *Paying for the Party*, Kelly relied on student reports to understand the role that the higher education system in and around Riverside played in producing raced, classed, and gendered outcomes. With *Broke*, Kelly was able to bring his understanding of the region and local community—key pieces of the UC-Riverside story—to enrich the project's organizational approach to inequality in public higher education.

We decided to focus the project specifically on the racial consequences of austerity, asking research questions about organizational practices under defunding and the impact on students who attend new universities. As two white scholars studying universities led by mostly white leadership but populated by historically underrepresented racially marginalized students (URS), we recognized that we were in some ways better positioned to study those in positions of power. Doing so is important. Research on advantaged actors helps us understand how systems of inequality are maintained. At the same time, because organizational narratives tend to privilege the perspectives of leadership, we did not want to rely solely on the reports of system and school administrators.

Our research questions thus required involving a wide array of university constituencies and researching all facets of the university—even those that are often overlooked. We thought seriously about how to include staff in the project, as we suspected they had unique perspectives on how the university operated. We did not presume to write an intimate or complete account of URS experiences in new universities. At the same time, we did not want to exclude the voices of racially marginalized students, paint them as passive victims of racial neoliberalism, or give the impression that URS are a monolithic group.

Attention to the power dynamics of the new university was also complicated by the vulnerable position of UC-Merced and UC-Riverside. We needed to take into account the racialized location of these schools in the UC system and the postsecondary field. We did not want research coming out of this project to be read as an exposé or indictment of UC-Riverside, UC-Merced, or the University of California system. It was important not to damage schools doing critical work to support and educate URS. Rather, we hope an outcome of the book will be to increase state funding for the UC system overall and to put pressure on the system to move toward a distribution of resources that helps UCM and UCR thrive.

Collecting Data

We made the decision to split the field sites, with each of us leading data collection at one university. We looked at other examples of multisite, team ethnography and realized that communication would be key. A shared online depository where we posted all of our field notes and interview notes allowed us to comment on and read every document that came through either site. We kept up a steady stream of emails, which were eventually logged as data, and had regular team meetings over the phone and in person. Both of us made a visit to the other campus so we might understand what it felt like to be in the space.

Initially we had concerns that Kelly's status as a postdoctoral fellow might hamper his ability to connect with the leadership at UCR while, in contrast, Laura's status as a faculty member would place her at the heart of her field site. However, we failed to anticipate the degree to which being a white man overrode any other criteria. Once administrators realized that Kelly was a man (as the name is commonly used for women), Kelly experienced relatively unfettered access to men at or near the top of the UCR hierarchy. They joked with him openly. The meetings seemed casual and relaxed. In one case, a white scholar and administrator, who knew both Laura and Kelly, ignored Laura and talked directly to Kelly, despite Laura's more senior position in the academic hierarchy.

Experiencing firsthand the differences between being a white man and a white woman interacting with powerful university actors helped us think about what these experiences might have been like for a woman or man of color. We had an unusually high degree of entrée with administrators—even Laura. We had been warned that leaders of universities would only provide us with "sound bites" and that these interviews would be shallow and overly calculated. Talking with administrators, however, produced surprisingly rich data. They were, of course, worried about presenting a positive image of the university, but we were interested in what image they wanted to project. It may have helped that we asked a host of questions about their biographies and day-to-day aspects of their jobs that, as it quickly became clear, they were not often asked to share. This may have put them at ease. And, as we have hopefully made clear throughout *Broke*, both universities have done many good things for public higher education, which may have emboldened these leaders to speak openly.

But race mattered. In conversations about race and racially marginalized students, administrators (who were almost all white) likely saw us as sharing similar perspectives. When we asked them to tell us how their schools supported and failed to support students of color, several steered the conversation to what they perceived as hostilities from students of color. Some felt comfortable enough to share their concerns that white students were being harmed through neglect or by too much support for URS. In meetings with UC system leadership, our ties to other white individuals who vouched for us greased the wheels.

We suspect that administrators in our sample would have been more guarded and careful in their language choice had we not been white. Scholars of color might have been perceived as a threat to university image and as having a racial "agenda," regardless of what they conveyed. Although leadership immediately responded in the affirmative to our requests for interviews, they may not have so readily found time for racially marginalized scholars.

Our conversations with faculty and staff were different. Many were scholars of color and/or vocal advocates for URS. Over the years, Laura had built trust with these faculty and staff, at least enough to make interviews possible. Kelly had to work harder. In particular, the cultural center staff at UCR were understandably weary and cautious of what Kelly, as a white man, wanted from and for UCR's cultural centers. Kelly attempted to set up interviews with one specific center and was deflected both over email and in person.

The interview became possible only after center staff saw Kelly observing the "Building Common Ground" activity and participating in multiple cultural workshop trainings. Center staff whom Kelly had met through these trainings advocated strongly for Kelly with the resistant director. They scheduled a time for the interview and kept the interview going long enough for Kelly to convince the director of his intent—at which point the director became an active participant. As we learned more about the ways in which cultural centers were threatened on UCR's campus, we gained a better understanding of the need for protection. We intentionally included as much of the rich history and achievements of UCR's centers as we could, in order to recognize, celebrate, and protect these vital spaces.

We focused our student interviews on Black and Latinx students because they were at opposite ends of representation on our campuses. Random samples of students in their first and fourth years (with the fourth-year students split between those on track and not on track to graduate on time) were drawn from within each racial group. In this process, we came to understand that the organizational reporting of racial statistics is a political project. The designation of "Hispanic," which is often collected and treated as an ethnicity indicator, offers a useful example. When translating "Hispanic" into marginalized racial categories, university staff and administrators could choose to use Latinx either to override Black, or to have Black override Latinx. (This is, in part, why some race scholars argue for the importance of "white Hispanic" and "Black Hispanic" as distinct ethnoracial categories.) What option universities use and when depends on specific political objectives.

In our case, we opted to include the very small number of Latinx students who also identified as Black in our random sample of Black students, based on how they reported others on campus as interpreting their racial background. Occasionally, we found students whom the universities coded as either Black or Latinx but did not report identifying or being routinely identified as either (e.g., a Middle Eastern student coded as Black). These students were interviewed but not counted in the random samples. We intentionally sampled from among those who had US citizenship, given the particular vulnerabilities of undocumented students—especially on UC-Merced's campus.

We thought a lot about including students from a wider variety of racial backgrounds in the random sample process. In particular, UCM and UCR have a high number of Asian students from subgroups that are URS—but the campuses also enroll Asian students that are not considered to be underrepresented. Ultimately, we decided we could not expand the scope of the sample much further and hope to adequately convey the depth and variety of URS experiences and responses to austerity. Our targeted interviews with student activists and leaders also helped introduce some variation in race and documentation status.

We were angry when the Institutional Review Board (IRB) at UCM initially responded with a request that we include a random sample of white students in the study, as a basis of comparison for URS. We explained that we had a comparison, grounded in degree of representation, and scolded the IRB for assuming that white students should be the automatic "control group" in every research project. Notably, Laura was never asked to include URS in her prior research on white students. We saw this as clear evidence of the normalization of whiteness and its construction as a "race-free" category.

At UCM, Laura worked closely with Veronica Lerma, who is a coauthor on chapter 6 and the lead author on a paper about racialized equity labor.[5] She and Maria Duenas, who are both exceptionally talented qualitative researchers, were paid research assistants who conducted the majority of UCM interviews with Latinx students and, to a lesser extent, Black students. Both women identified as Latina. Maria speaks fluent Spanish and also assisted in observing Spanish orientation. Student interviewees frequently expressed relief that the interviewer was a person of color and not a white faculty member—but retained suspicions about the project in general. The political context was tense: Interviews were occurring after the publication of the *New York Times* piece about UCM Dreamers (see chapter 7), and there was widespread distrust toward faculty studying Latinx and undocumented populations on campus.

Veronica and Maria fielded a number of questions from suspicious student activists, including: "How is this study going to benefit students and not exploit them?" and "Why are white people involved?" They were frank with students about the goals of the project and the desire to represent student narratives of action and resistance. It was not always enough, though—especially for students who had been hurt by the university or used as research subjects in ways that they felt supported the goals of researchers but not communities of color.

Laura also did a number of interviews herself. She wanted to conduct student interviews in which there was a trusting relationship already established, so as to reduce the likelihood of placing student respondents in an uncomfortable situation. Thus, Laura's interviews were with students whom she knew personally through classes or to whom she had been vouched for by other students in her networks. This primarily included Black students and student activists, as well as some Latinx and white activists.

At UCR, Kelly conducted all of the student interviews himself. The political context was less fraught, but we imagine that URS were less comfortable reporting racist incidents and negative racial dynamics to him than they might have been with an interviewer of color. One of the interesting things about UCR, though, was that the more positive relationship between administration and students, as well as the outreach infrastructure, meant that Kelly could connect to student activists through his ties to leadership. For instance, administrators set up the initial interviews with the Black Student Task Force, which was at the heart of the local Black Lives Matter movement at UCR. This would have been unthinkable at UCM. Activists had also seen Kelly at Black Lives Matter events and noted that it mattered for their willingness to participate in this project.

Our research also involved ethnographic methods. At UCM, observations were spearheaded by a team of eight undergraduate researchers from a variety of racial backgrounds. Laura had invited them to join the project after they excelled in her classes. These students included Jovita Angel, Ashley Bennett, Dakari Finister, Rosa Hernandez, Reginald Nelson, Ana Padilla, Patrick Pascual, and Mayra Ramirez. The team met weekly, and students received credit for an independent study. After training in qualitative methods, the team conducted most of the study's ethnographic observations on the UCM campus; for instance, data about the groundbreaking ceremony in chapter 2 come from student ethnographers. They also took notes in spaces where Laura would have been conspicuous and unwelcome. Laura observed primarily in spaces where faculty status was necessary or helpful (e.g., events for incoming students) or where faculty were the primary participants (e.g. campus-wide budget meetings).

Over time, the research group evolved into an advisory panel. They suggested fruitful interview subjects, among both university employees and students, and often provided the contacts and recommendations necessary for these interviews to occur. The research group helped devise interview guides. Laura floated key themes past this group, who told her when she had it right and when she was wrong. Jovita Angel would continue to work with Laura after the research team meetings were over, as a paid research assistant. Her imprint on this book is substantial. Jovita, who was a major activist on campus, reminded Laura and Kelly of the importance of taking URS efforts to create a new university that meets their needs and agendas seriously, and not to prioritize administrative organizational narratives.

Kelly also engaged in ethnographic observations at UCR, only some of which made it into *Broke*. Many of these observations, like the Spanish-language orientation, were paralleled at UCM. But others were not. For instance, along with numerous cultural programming events and diversity fairs, Kelly attended remedial math classes at UCR. These were held in a lecture hall and were among the worst learning experiences Kelly has ever witnessed. Students who come from underfunded high schools where they receive little college preparation are often slotted into these classes. We decided it would be near impossible to make progress under such conditions.

Over the course of data collection, racist and discriminatory comments were made in front of—although not to—us. The racially marginalized individuals that we interviewed, in contrast, reported being on the receiving end of such comments and actions. One of the benefits of being white is that these experiences, while disturbing, were not personally traumatizing for us, as they might have been for a racially marginalized scholar. Our engagement in this research topic also never required us to foreground or share difficult aspects of our biographies.

A useful example of the different costs to white scholars versus scholars of color occurred when Kelly was going through cultural awareness training. Like other participants, he was asked to recount experiences of marginalization. It was hard for Kelly to think of things that could be taken seriously in that moment, whereas for multiply marginalized individuals, workshops like this can represent yet another arena in which they are expected to dredge up painful experiences and recount adversity narratives. We recognized the false equivalencies that diversity logics promote—equating Kelly's first-gen status (as a cisgender, heterosexual white man) with the marginalization experienced by others in the room. Notably, private conversations with training organizers indicated that they understood this too (and future iterations of the training incorporated greater focus on structural inequality), but they were bound by the expectation that this training be inclusive, comfortable, and welcoming to all.

Analysis and Writing

We took a deep dive into race theory as we were collecting and analyzing data. We were not unfamiliar with race scholarship, but we did not yet realize that race scholars like Sara Ahmed, W. E. B. Du Bois, Eduardo Bonilla-Silva, Prudence Carter, Patricia Hill Collins, Jordan Conwell, Tressie McMillan Cottom, John Diamond, Roderick Ferguson, Ruth Gilmore, Amanda Lewis, Ian Haney López, Wendy Moore, Michael Omi, Victor Ray, Cedric Robinson, Louise Seamster, James Thomas, Karolyn Tyson, Howard Winant, and others had already developed the arguments and analytical approaches central to our book. Throughout *Broke*, we have done our best to cite and credit the race scholarship upon which we build.

We were initially struck by the limited treatment of race in neoliberal scholarship; in many cases, the word "race" does not even appear in the text. If race or racial resentment is discussed, it is often confined to a few pages or is dismissed as insufficiently causal and thus unimportant. There is also a strong tendency (one to which we have contributed in the past) for higher education scholarship to zero in on social class inequities without recognizing racial inequities—or to see social class as the primary system of oppression, and race as secondary. Quantitative scholars often discuss, for instance, the extent to which racial differences can be "accounted for" by disparities in social class, without recognizing that race is integral to the distribution of educational, financial, and many other social goods.

We did not want to fall into these traps, which we recognize as particularly appealing to white scholars. Our goal was to force readers to "see" race—even if they did not want to and even if they tried to turn away. Earlier drafts of the book were perhaps too successful in this endeavor. When Laura gave a talk at the University of Wisconsin–Madison in fall 2019, Jordan Conwell remarked that we should do a better job of articulating the role of class (even though, as Jordan noted, he is almost always in the opposite position of reminding educational scholars to think about race). He offered the insight, detailed in the introduction, that racial projects often sweep up poor whites and urged us to think about how race and class operate together as systems. We owe this and other insights in the introduction (particularly regarding Du Bois) to Jordan.[6]

Unlike neoliberal scholars, race scholars have led the way in articulating how race is related to economic systems of oppression. Cedric Robinson, in his 1983 book *Black Marxism: The Making of the Black Radical Tradition*, took issue with Marx for failing to recognize the racial character of capitalism, an analytical mistake that was likely also methodological; Marx was narrowly focused on movements within Europe. Robinson argued that capitalism was not a negation of feudalism, but rather an evolution from feudalism reliant on slavery, imperialism, violence, and genocide. Proletariats were racial subjects, whose societal position was justified by racial myths.[7] More recently, Michael Omi and Howard Winant, whose understanding of racial neoliberalism is central to the book, pointedly explained the ways in which race as a system of oppression has fueled the rise of neoliberalism in the US.[8]

We approached our analysis assuming that the allocation of educational resources in the US is inherently political and is in part about maintaining, as well as challenging, white supremacy. We considered how racially advantaged groups, in the aggregate, use higher education to maintain their privilege— both intentionally and through force of habit. At the same time, we considered the efforts of marginalized actors (students, families, and universities) to change the status quo. These efforts sometimes succeed, at least in part, despite serious positional disadvantages. Yet, as work on the development of academic tracking (which was a response to racially integrated schools) shows, gains by the marginalized are often met by new efforts among the privileged to re-establish advantage.[9]

Our multilevel approach was also inspired by race scholars. Du Bois helped us understand that the micro-level educational inequalities faced by URS in our sample were, in fact, deeply determined by the larger political-economic context (what he referred to as the "peculiar environment")—in this case, racial neoliberalism.[10] Victor Ray's exceptional piece on racialized organizations led us to think about relationships among the organizations that comprise the larger University of California.[11] We focused on the ways in which racialized cultural beliefs inherent in a race-based hierarchy shaped access to financial and material resources. We applied this same analytical lens to the internal distribution of resources within each of our focal universities.

This approach required us to think across a wide span of time (from the beginning of the Cold War University and into the present moment) and to move back and forth fluidly between micro, meso, and macro levels of analysis, in both directions. We had rich empirical examples to guide us—for example in the work of both Prudence Carter and Karolyn Tyson.[12] Each of us read interview transcripts and notes, ethnographic notes, and historical documents about both cases, alongside scholarship on racial neoliberalism and racialized organizations. We pieced together a historical narrative for each of our cases, thought about how they were similar or different to other universities in the postsecondary field, and arrived at the notion of the "new university" as a historically unique phenomenon. Then we began to consider why new universities have developed and how they might continue to develop in the future.

Throughout this process, we wrote a series of analytical memos on particular themes (e.g., "de facto racial segregation in higher education" and "organizational management of 'diversity' without meaningful change"). Early on, these themes informed our data collection. For instance, as we considered the vulnerabilities of new universities in relation to for-profit actors, we realized that we needed to better investigate the public-private partnership developing at UC-Merced. After data collection ended, we began to think about how some of our themes fit together in the racial neoliberal cycle described in the introduction. It took many iterations to move from a laundry list of traits to a clear cycle, and to separate out preconditions for the cycle (e.g., broad access and defunding) from the cycle itself.

As equal authors, Laura and Kelly worked through the core challenges of the book together. The structure of the book was a particular puzzle. We did not want to jump around in time too much, so as to offer readers a more linear narrative. It was hard to determine whether we should introduce our readers to the specific cases first, or to the system in which UCM and UCR are embedded. We ultimately determined that readers needed to understand the similarities and differences between our cases before considering them together. The center of the book—around austerity logics and practices—came together very quickly, especially after reading Michael Crow's manifesto, *Designing the New American University*.[13]

The final section took some time to develop. During our last round of major revisions, we cut a chapter on the "New U-PD," which examined policing at new universities, as it did not fit with the rest of the book. However, almost from the moment that Kelly conducted interviews with PepsiCo employees (a thread that we followed after intuiting its importance), we knew that the book would end with the new university job pipeline. A growing body of research on "diversity" by scholars such as Sara Ahmed and James Thomas helped us see the different ways that new universities managed and were limited by diversity, as well as how they might commodify URS to offer diversity to predominately white organizations.

We see *Broke* as a way to promote the work of race scholars that is often overlooked and marginalized in the sociology of education. At the same time, we will likely profit from its publication—accruing tangible benefits in our careers, such as status and some marginal financial benefits. We recognize that this is a problem. Our goal is to continue reminding readers, scholars, and audiences of all kinds that there is a wealth of existing knowledge that should be front and center in crucial conversations about higher education, racial inequality, and social change. A new generation of scholars addressing these issues, many of whom are themselves racially marginalized, will lead the way.

Notes

INTRODUCTION

1. Bilingualism in the US is highly racialized and, depending on the class status, national origin, and specific language of the speaker, schools may treat bilingualism as a deficiency. As such, the linguistic abilities of racially marginalized students are often marked as inappropriate and in need of remediation (Flores and Rosa 2015).
2. Berg (2012).
3. Feagin, Vera, and Imani (1996); Lee and LaDousa (2015); Ray and Best (2015); Strayhorn (2013); Watkins, LaBarrie, and Appio (2010); Wilkins (2014).
4. See Patton (2010).
5. See Deil-Amen (2015). Also Carnevale and Strohl (2013); Cottom (2017).
6. See the literature on MSIs (Minority Serving Institutions): Conrad and Gasman (2015); Garcia (2019); Wooten (2015). Hispanic Serving Institutions (HSIs), in particular, serve nearly 60 percent of Latinx college students and 16 percent of Black college students. Students at HSIs also tend to come from lower-income households, with 48 percent of students at HSIs receiving Pell Grants (Postsecondary National Policy Institution 2015).
7. See Eaton et al. (2019) for more on state-to-state variation in need-based grant aid.
8. We have chosen to use the term "historically underrepresented racially marginalized students" (URS), rather than "underrepresented minorities" (URM), to recognize that marginalization occurs even when groups subject to racial discrimination represent a numerical majority, such as on many new university campuses (see Benitez 2010).
9. Zambrana (2018).
10. Pell Grant recipients typically come from households with income of $30,000 or less and represent the bottom 30 percent of the college-going population (U.S. Department of Education 2014a, 2014b).
11. Connell (2019).
12. Allen and Jewell (2002).
13. Conrad and Gasman (2015); Wooten (2015).

14. Vargas and Villa-Palomino (2018).
15. The Morrill Acts of 1862 and 1890 granted federally controlled land to states for them to establish and endow "land grant" colleges that evolved into large public universities. These schools benefited considerably from the government-sponsored Cold War expansion of higher education after World War II.
16. Douglass (2007).
17. It is important not to view the Morrill Act as unambiguously positive. As Lee and Ahtone (2020) point out, the Morrill Act was "a massive wealth transfer masquerading as a donation." The land that was distributed by the federal government and sold by states to endow land grant universities was acquired for a fraction of its resale value or, in many cases, through confiscation from Indigenous people. The dispossession of Indigenous land for public higher education is part of the broader American settler colonial legacy.
18. See Crow and Dabars (2015). We return to ASU later in the book as an extreme version of the new university.
19. See Grawe (2018) on the coming demographic changes in higher education.
20. See Stevens and Gebre-Medhin (2016) for a broader historical picture. Mitchell, Leachman, and Masterson (2017) describe funding cuts since the Great Recession.
21. Blyth (2013, 2); Gilmore (2007).
22. Evans and Sewell (2013). Also see Fourcade and Healy (2007); Hall and Lamont (2013); Mudge (2008).
23. For examples, see Connell (2019); Fabricant and Brier (2016); Geiger (2004); Lambert (2014); Molesworth, Scullion, and Nixon (2011); Newfield (2016); Slaughter and Rhoades (2004).
24. See Armstrong and Hamilton (2013); Hamilton (2016).
25. Notable exceptions are Cottom's (2017) excellent examination of for-profit universities and Ferguson's (2012) history of how higher education incorporated minority difference in response to post–World War II activism.
26. Omi and Winant (2015, 211). Also see Hong (2015).
27. Du Bois (1898, [1935] 1999). See Conwell (2016) for a cohesive account of the Du Boisian framework for the sociology of education. Carter's (2012) *Stubborn Roots: Race, Culture, and Inequality* offered an empirical model.
28. Slobodian (2018). Also see Friedman (1951).
29. Slobodian (2018, 16).
30. See Tooze (2018); Slobodian (2018, 22).
31. Slobodian (2018, 22).
32. Slobodian (2018, 151).
33. Slobodian (2018).
34. Cooper (2017, 229–30).
35. Becker ([1957] 1971). Friedman ([1962] 2009) argues that there is, in fact, "an economic incentive in a free market to separate economic efficiency

from other characteristics of the individual" (109). He even goes so far as to suggest that racial discrimination as the expression of taste is really not different from other kinds of preferences: "Is there any difference in principle between the taste that leads a householder to prefer an attractive servant to an ugly one and the taste that leads another to prefer a Negro to a white or a white to a Negro, except that we sympathize and agree with the one taste and may not with the other?" (110).

36.   In a detailed history of Buchanan's role in the rise of neoliberal ideas and policies in the US, MacLean (2017) documents how Buchanan founded the Virginia school of political economy, developed public choice economics as a counter to "the collective order" (xxv), and proposed a "constitutional revolution" to "ensure that the will of the majority could no longer influence representative government on core matters of political economy" (pp. xxvii–xxviii). MacLean connects Buchanan's core ideas to the intellectual legacy of John C. Calhoun, a staunch critic of popular democracy and vociferous defender of slavery.

37.   For example, in 1972, Rothbard wrote, "Biology stands like a rock in the face of egalitarian fantasies" (Slobodian 2019, 9). MacLean (2017) points out that, like James Buchanan, Rothbard drew inspiration from John C. Calhoun.

38.   Cooper (2017, 132).

39.   Blyth (2013, 2).

40.   Fligstein (2001); Mirowski (2014); Prasad (2006); Slobodian (2018).

41.   Omi and Winant (2015, 215).

42.   Cooper (2017).

43.   See Cooper (2017), in particular her account of the Volcker Shock and its consequences. Also see Loss (2012); Mettler (2011, 2014).

44.   Cramer (2020); Gilens (1995, 1999); Haney López (2014); Van Doom (2015). Also see Prasad's (2006) account of the uneven rise and spread of neoliberalism, although she downplays the role of racism.

45.   Cooper (2017).

46.   Omi and Winant (2015, 215).

47.   Poterba (1997).

48.   Omi and Winant (2015, 214). Also see Cooper (2017); Gilens (1999); Haney López (2014); Kotsko (2018); Van Doom (2015).

49.   See Black and Sprague (2016); Douglas and Michaels (2004); Haney López (2014); Inwood (2015); Omi and Winant (2015); and Quadagno (1994) for Reagan's usage of the "welfare queen." Despite the alleged proliferation of such individuals, media networks could only find two women to publicize as examples. The "welfare queen" is thus best understood as a political and discursive tool—what Collins (1990: 77) describes as a "controlling image." Controlling images are "designed to make racism, sexism, poverty, and other forms of social injustice appear to be natural, normal, and inevitable parts of everyday life." Also see Adair (2002); Kohler-Hausmann (2007); Lubiano (1992).

50. See Prasad (2006, 86–89).

51. Haney López (2014).

52. Omi and Winant (2015) anchor the obsessive focus on individual competition in the broader ideology of producerism — that is, the notion that members of society engaged in tangible wealth production are of the greatest value to society. Producerism has a racist history, drawing on white supremacist ideas about biological differences in intelligence, motivation, responsibility, and work orientation. Also see Cooper (2017); Kotsko (2018).

53. Bonilla-Silva (2010); Hirschman and Garbes (2019).

54. According to Kotsko (2018), an example of this cycle of demonization and greater market exposure is welfare reform. The demonization of welfare recipients supported welfare reform, which exposed welfare recipients to increased competition in the labor market. Also see Hays (2003).

55. Haney López (2014).

56. Cooper (2017).

57. See Gilmore (2007); Matthew (2015); Pager (2007); Pettit and Western (2004); Seamster (2019); Shedd (2015).

58. Taylor et al. (2011). Also see Hamilton and Darity (2017); Jones (2017).

59. Omi and Winant (2015, 230).

60. Labaree (2017); Loss (2012); Stevens and Gebre-Medhin (2016).

61. Horowitz (1987); Roksa et al. (2007); Skrentny (2002); Trow (2005).

62. Higher Education Act of 1965 (HEA) (Pub.L. 89–329).

63. Best and Best (2014).

64. See the original California Master Plan for Higher Education (California Department of Education 1960).

65. A 1962 picture of the University of California system president Clark Kerr — then at the height of his power, with President John F. Kennedy in UC-Berkeley's Memorial Stadium on the university's Charter Day celebration — captures the relationship between the government and the UC system during the first half of what Stevens and Gebre-Medhin (2016) refer to as the "National Service" period (see Loss 2012, 166).

66. Some of the earliest challenges to segregated schooling came in response to undergraduate and advanced education, well before the affirmative action era (see Byrd-Chichester 2001). These cases were important for the landmark 1954 *Brown v. Board of Education* decision.

67. Preer (1982).

68. Notably, efforts at desegregation threatened the existence of Historically Black Colleges and Universities (HBCUs) that had evolved in response to racial exclusion — especially because HBCUs were recognized as "racially identifiable," whereas predominately white universities were not. See Samuels (2004).

69. Reuben (2001).

70. Moore (2018).

71. See Anderson (2010); Lewis and Diamond (2015); Tilly (1998); Tyson (2011).

72. See Clotfelter (2017); also Carnevale and Strohl (2013).
73. Clotfelter (2017); Davies and Zarifa (2012). For a discussion of persistent inequalities in global higher education, as well as points of resistance, see Connell (2019, 95–114).
74. Loss (2012).
75. Omi and Winant (2015, 219) discuss the reframing of racism as a "race-neutral" matter that could "affect anyone."
76. Allen and Jewell (2002).
77. Affirmative action was viewed as infringing upon the rights of "innocent Whites" (*Gratz v. Bollinger*), and race was officially established as but one "plus" in diversity calculations (*Grutter v. Bollinger*) (Moore 2008, 2018).
78. See Haney López (2014).
79. See Crenshaw (2007); Gomer and Petrella (2017); Rai and Critzer (2000).
80. Samuels (2004).
81. From Reagan's 1980 campaign, as quoted in Gomer and Petrella (2017).
82. Loss (2012).
83. Baker (2019).
84. Moore (2018).
85. UC Office of the President (2003); Bleemer (2020). See HoSang (2010) for more on the racial implications of California's propositions.
86. For more on legacy admissions, see Espenshade, Chung, and Walling (2004).
87. Loss (2012); Cooper (2017). Also see Buchanan (1970) for a neoliberal critique of student movements.
88. Loss (2012). Antagonistic relations with the UC system continued after Kerr's dismissal. On "Bloody Thursday" in 1969, Governor Reagan sent the California Highway Patrol and Berkeley police officers into protests in People's Park, right next to UC-Berkeley. Police shot and killed a student spectator, and over 100 Berkeley students were admitted to local hospitals with injuries inflicted by police. Later that evening Reagan sent in the National Guard, who patrolled the streets of the city for several weeks.
89. Loss (2012).
90. Eno (2019) discusses this crucial decision.
91. Gladieux and Wolanin (1976, 48).
92. See Eaton (2020a).
93. Stevens and Gebre-Medhin (2016).
94. Gilmore (2007) details the political and social forces producing the prison boom in California. Also see Eason (2017).
95. Mitchell, Leachman, and Masterson (2017).
96. Webber (2017); also see Deming and Walters (2017).
97. Clotfelter (2017); Davies and Zarifa (2012); Eaton et al. (2016).
98. See Fryar (2015) for a discussion of resource differences between flagship and regional state universities and Goldrick-Rab (2016) for more on how this works in Wisconsin. Kahlenberg (2015) addresses community college funding.

99. Bound et al. (2016); Curs and Jaquette (2017); Jaquette, Curs, and Posselt (2016).
100. See Krogstad and Fry (2014). Prior to 1975, Historically Black Colleges and Universities (HBCUs) might have absorbed increases in Black students. However, by this point, fully three-quarters of Black students were enrolling in what were once predominately white universities (Allen and Jewell 2002).
101. Ashkenas, Park, and Pearce (2017); Berrey (2015); Carnevale (2016); Moore (2018); Stancil (2018).
102. See Berrey (2015) on "selective inclusion."
103. Carnevale and Strohl (2013); Cottom (2017).
104. Cottom (2017) discusses ways in which organizations can commodify inequalities, capitalizing on the educational aspirations of marginalized populations.
105. Douglass (2007).
106. King (2018).
107. The tenth UC, UC-San Francisco, offers graduate-level medical and biological training.
108. Data on specific origins of Asian students in the UC is not publicly available, and we do not have permission to report percentages for subgroups. However, the top ten metros in the country where Hmong are concentrated include Fresno, Stockton, and Merced, all near UC-Merced. Laotians are similarly concentrated near Merced (Sacramento and Fresno), while Cambodians are predominately located in and around Los Angeles, a short distance from UC-Riverside. On Filipino representation across the UC, see Fang (2014).
109. Lee and Zhou (2015) and Kao and Thompson (2003) discuss Asian subgroup variation in educational attainment.
110. Hinderaker and Hinderaker (1998).
111. Vargas and Villa-Palomino (2018).
112. For more on the prisons in this area, see Gilmore (2007).
113. See Armstrong and Hamilton (2013); Hamilton (2016).
114. See Nielsen (2015).
115. We are informed by an "inhabited institutions" approach (see Hallett and Ventresca 2006), in that we see postsecondary organizations as populated by people who do things together, rather than as characterized by disembodied, top-down macro-logics.
116. Fourth-year samples were split by those on track and not on track to graduate "on time."
117. Random sample participants had US citizenship. We chose not to intentionally sample undocumented students, as this group is vulnerable and, in the context of the UC, already the subject of research (see Golash-Boza and Valdez 2018; Valdez and Golash-Boza 2018). However, some student respondents were undocumented, and many more students in both targeted and random samples had undocumented family members and friends.
118. Response rates were very high for targeted interviews, as we were often

introduced to participants through student, staff, faculty, or administrator allies. Recruiting random sample participants proved more challenging. The response rate for these interviews at UC-Merced was around 33 percent. It was slightly lower at UC-Riverside. Laura's position as a faculty member at UCM made it more likely that students would respond to her inquiries. However, we came to realize that students do not read email very often. Students not connected to us personally may have also been reluctant to respond to white representatives of their universities.

119. Kelly conducted UCR student interviews, while Laura and two graduate students conducted UCM interviews. Students received a $25 gift card in compensation for their time. University policy prohibited us from compensating university employees.

120. See Bonilla-Silva (1997); Golash-Boza (2016).

121. See Liddell (2018) for a useful discussion of capitalization.

122. White supremacists capitalize "white" to emphasize white racial solidarity. To emphatically reject the notion of whiteness as a source of a collective identity or pride, we do not capitalize it. However, we recognize and support the choice of critical race scholars who capitalize "white" to highlight the ubiquity of white participation — consciously and unconsciously — in projects of white racial domination.

123. Latinx appears to be a term that is primarily in usage on college campuses and has evolved from the Latinx LGBTQ+ community. The term may impose a value system on the linguistic grammar of a language that genders nouns. Yet, Spanish is richly varied in usage around the world and is constantly evolving. Also, many Latinx individuals do not speak Spanish, so arguments about linguistic purity can be problematic.

124. Intersectional scholars of color have long understood the ways that systems of oppression are deeply intertwined (see, e.g., Anzaldúa 1987; Collins 1990, 2004; Collins and Bildge 2016; Combahee River Collective [1977] 1983; Crenshaw 1991; hooks 1984; Hurtado 1996; Wingfield 2009). In *Black Marxism: The Making of the Black Radical Tradition*, Cedric Robinson ([1983] 2000) argued that capitalist society developed around racism, as a way of organizing labor relations.

125. See Du Bois on the "wages of whiteness" ([1935] 1999). Lewis and Diamond (2015).

126. Ray's (2019) racialized organizations theory highlights the link between racialized schema and the racialized distribution of resources between and within organizations.

127. See Ochoa (2013) and Tyson (2011) for an illustration of how this cycle might work in K–12 schools.

128. See Karabel (2005).

129. "Merit" is a form of "within market classification" as described by Fourcade and Healy (2013). It comes in contrast to "boundary classification" that cleanly includes and excludes different groups from a market.

130. Adkins (2012, 625). See Konings (2018) on speculative worth.
131. See Aguinis, Culpepper, and Pierce (2016). Similarly, a study of students at thirty-three "test optional" schools found "virtually no difference" in the grades and graduation rates of students who submit scores and those who do not. Non-submitters were more likely to be non-white and first generation (Hiss and Franks 2014).
132. See Price (2019).
133. Patel (2019) offers a history of the SAT's racist roots.
134. See Brigham (1923).
135. See Freedle (2003); Santelices and Wilson (2010).
136. Stevens (2007).
137. Seamster (2019).
138. Owens (2017); Reardon (2016); Ryan (2010).
139. Carnevale and Strohl (2013).
140. Jack (2019).
141. See Garcia (2019) on the racialization of postsecondary organizations in the US.
142. As Espeland and Sauder (2016) note, rankings are social constructions that shape the hierarchies they purport to assess.
143. See Davies and Zarifa (2012).
144. Bowen, Chingos, and McPherson (2009); Clotfelter (2017); Fryar (2015); Reyes (2018).
145. Carnevale and Strohl (2013). Chen (2012) discusses the importance of student services spending for completion. On organizational differences in advising support, see Habley (2004). Beattie and Thiele (2016) discuss the importance of small class sizes for disadvantaged students.
146. Carnevale (2016).
147. Ahmed (2012); Moore (2018). Warikoo (2016) discusses the way white students at elite universities understand racial diversity—primarily as a commodity or selling point to enhance their own college experiences.
148. See Bradley et al. (2018) for research suggesting that chief diversity officers have no impact on increasing faculty racial diversity.
149. Ahmed (2012); Thomas (2018).
150. See Lerma, Hamilton, and Nielsen (2019).

CHAPTER ONE

1.   UC-Riverside (1954). It should be noted that this vision of "peace and friendship" sits uneasily with the development of the Cold War University.
2.   See Douglass (2000) for a discussion of the motivating beliefs of California Progressives that shaped the development of the University of California.
3.   Hinderaker and Hinderaker (1998). Not only was the infrastructure suitable for growing UCR's research mission, it also made an attractive futuristic

backstop for Gene Roddenberry, the creator of *Star Trek*, who used the campus in a 1973 television pilot, *Genesis II*.

4. Ray (2019).
5. A detailed breakdown of the category "Asian," especially for this time period, is not available, but faculty who were at UCR in the 1990s reported that many of these students were of Southeast Asian descent, often refugees from countries such as Vietnam, and typically underprivileged.
6. Soja (1987, 1996); Starr (2004).
7. Brown (1995); Ringquist (2005).
8. See Winston (1999).
9. Malkiel (2016). Also see Lowen (1997) on how Stanford University utilized students to build research capacity.
10. The shift from a focus on affirmative action to outreach in the UC system began in the mid-1990s when senior administrators first commissioned a directory of UC programs dealing with pre-collegiate education and later published guidance for campuses to conduct outreach (Mohr and Lee 2000).
11. Traub (1999).
12. HoSang (2010).
13. UC Office of the President (2003).
14. UC Office of the President (2003).
15. Martin, Karabel, and Jaquez (2005).
16. UC Office of the President (2003). Also see Bleemer (2020).
17. UCR set a number of leadership firsts. Rosemary Schraer (1987–1992) was the first woman and France Córdova (2002–2007) the first Latina to serve as chancellor in the UC system.
18. Despite having started the Chicano Studies program at UCR in the 1960s, Rivera also has the ignominious distinction of having temporarily dismantled this program, as well as the Black Studies program, due to low student numbers.
19. Reinhold (1992); Sheffrin (2004).
20. See Abbott (1991) and Clemens (2006) on historical contingency.
21. Grawe (2018).
22. Mitchell et al. (2017); Webber (2017).
23. Traub (1999).
24. Allen and Jewell (2002); Byrd (2017); Karabel (2005).
25. Clark (1960); Karabel (2005); Stevens (2007).
26. As Mohr and Lee (2000) point out, even affirmative action, which moderates the merit system, is based on an individualist logic that maintains the exclusion of larger communities of marginalized people.
27. Karabel (2005); Stevens (2007).
28. Berrey (2015).
29. See Jack (2019) on the "privileged poor."
30. Ahmed (2012) describes this as the "conditional hospitality" of universities:

It is predicated on the abilities of people of color to integrate into the organizational culture and their willingness to allow universities to profit from their contributions to institutional diversity.

31. See Berrey (2015); Garcia (2019). Holland and Ford (2020) analyze the ways that universities represent racial diversity to prospective students and find that elite institutions highlight diversity, whereas less selective schools (with greater numeric diversity) are less likely to do so, precisely because of the status hit associated with this approach.

32. There is, for instance, a robust literature on the racialized expectations and perceptions that teachers apply to students (see Cherng 2017; Irizarry 2015a, 2015b).

33. See Brint, Riddle, and Hanneman (2006) for more on university presidents' reference sets. Bastedo and Bowman (2009) also point out that university reputations are heavily impacted by prior USN ranking.

34. Bowen and Bok (1998); Soares (2012).

35. See *U.S. News & World Report* (2014) for more on how rankings were compiled.

36. Although a *U.S. News* diversity index existed, it remained separate from the overall rankings. Thus, schools could serve a small number of URS, or fail to graduate marginalized subpopulations at acceptable rates, without taking hits to overall prestige. Increasing the representation of URS, on the other hand, could threaten school rank.

37. See Garcia (2019) on the racialization of prestige and Hispanic Serving Institutions (HSIs).

38. Roksa and Arum (2015).

39. Ramirez (2018).

40. Ramirez (2018, 91).

41. This rally involved a protest in the hallway of the chancellor's office. According to Orbach, he went out in the hallway to discuss what was happening with the students. When people started to shove, he sat down in hopes of calming the situation. But to the police watching from the stairwell, it looked like Orbach had disappeared, and they poured in, ultimately arresting fifty-five students.

42. UC-Riverside (2010, 4).

43. Williams, Berger, and McClendon (2005, 3).

44. Ahmed (2012) and Thomas (2018, 2020) provide clear critiques of what Thomas refers to as an organizational "diversity regime."

45. It is useful to point out that as a UC campus, UCR is accessible only to the top 12.5 percent of California students. Although far more accessible than other top research universities, it is not as accessible as the regional California State University system.

46. Anderson (2015).

47. Nichols and Evans-Bell (2017).

48. Watanabe (2017).

49. See Sherkat (2016).

50. Bickel and Lake (1999); Lake (2013).
51. Chetty et al. (2017).
52. University Innovation Alliance (2019).
53. *Washington Monthly* Editors (2014).
54. Hamilton (2016).
55. Gaddis (2014) used an audit study design to determine the effect of college selectivity and race on responses to job applications in 2011. He included UCR as a less selective university along with UMass-Amherst and UNC-Greensboro. Applications from elite universities were 1.7 times more likely to get any kind of response than applications from less selective universities. While response rates also varied by race, college selectivity was more consequential. Black applicants from elite universities were more likely than white applicants from less selective universities to receive a response. Moreover, Gaddis finds that applicants from elite universities receive responses from jobs with higher listed salaries.
56. Chen et al. (2012, 302). Also see Lounsbury and Rao (2004); Malter (2014); Washington and Zajac (2005).
57. Baker (2014).
58. Ray (2019). Also see Thomas (2018); Vargas and Villa-Palomino (2018).
59. Espeland and Sauder (2016).
60. See Hoxby and Turner (2019).

CHAPTER TWO

1. See Kuang (2017).
2. California Department of Education (1960).
3. Like the Inland Empire, discussed in the previous chapter, the San Joaquin Valley was wealthier in the 1960s than it is today. Although largely rural, the population of the San Joaquin Valley was demographically much more similar to communities in the nearby San Francisco Bay Area. Beginning in the 1980s, however, the socioeconomic status of Valley residents started to decline relative to people living in coastal areas, a phenomenon Moretti (2013) calls the "Great Divergence."
4. In 2000, the National Science Foundation noted a major discrepancy in research investment between coastal California, where most UCs are located, and the San Joaquin Valley. The difference was vast: $140 versus $7 per person (see Alley 2007).
5. Merritt and Lawrence (2007). Recall from the previous chapter that UCR did extensive outreach to grow the campus during this period and had to put direct pressure on the governor through local community leaders in order to fund campus growth.
6. For more on the California "electricity crisis," see Weare (2003).
7. Walters (2002).
8. Desrochers (2007); Olivares et al. (2009).

9. Hong (2004).
10. UC president Gardner initially planned to open three new UCs—in 1998, 1999, and 2000. This plan was reduced in the late 1980s to the one additional campus.
11. UC-Merced is technically the tenth UC campus; however, UC-San Francisco is dedicated to graduate-level and advanced medical and biological training.
12. There are thirteen state prisons and four federal prisons in the area.
13. See Krippner (2011); Also Brown (2015); Cooper (2017); Konings (2018).
14. Eaton et al. (2016).
15. Eaton (2020a).
16. Fabricant and Brier (2016).
17. In 1990, the number of Latinx individuals living in the state was half that of whites, but by 2014 the Latinx population had edged out whites to become the new majority (Panzar 2015). High school graduation rates among Latinx students went from 68 percent in 2009 to 80 percent in 2016 (California Department of Education 2017).
18. Massey and Denton (1993).
19. Olzak, Shanahan, and West (1994); Renzulli and Evans (2005).
20. See Kao and Thompson (2003); Lee and Zhou (2015).
21. For example, see Fairlie and Resch (2002).
22. The CEP preceded the opening of UC-Merced, and running the CEP out of Merced would have been too cost prohibitive. For example, staff mileage necessary to reach more populated areas would eat into the budget.
23. Also, in 2016 UC-Merced relaunched the Blum Center with a focus on promoting access to healthy food on campus and in the region.
24. Verger (2012).
25. Eaton and Weir (2015).
26. Morgan and Campbell (2011).
27. Eaton and Weir (2015); Erickson (2009); Morgan and Campbell (2011).
28. DiNapoli (2013).
29. For a review of potential benefits and limitations of P3s, see Kwak, Chih, and Ibbs (2009).
30. Kuang (2017).
31. Blair and Williams (2017).
32. Jacob, McCall, and Stange (2018).
33. See P3 Higher Education Summit (2018).
34. For instance, the model has been endorsed by the National Association of College and University Business Officers (NACUBO) in an article entitled "Public-Private Partnerships: It's the Right Time." The author? A CEO of a private student housing company (see Bernstein 2017).
35. See P3 Higher Education Summit (2018).
36. Seltzer (2017).
37. This is also known as a "Design-Build-Finance-Operate-Maintain" (DBFOM) model.

38. Government-funded deals often take the form of "Design-Bid-Build" (DBB) or "Design-Build" (DB) contracts, in which campuses hold responsibility for procuring individual services to build. DBB budgets on a service-by-service basis, whereas DB bundles design and construction into a single capital project. The DBB approach, while very common, is often slowed by the need to separately employ different entities for different work. Estimates suggested that the fastest the Merced project could be completed using this approach was 2024—four years after the infrastructure was needed. The 2020 deadline was not a problem for the DB bundle design, but financing remained a serious barrier.

39. See California LAO (2012) on the expensive P3 deals for the Presidio Parkway in San Francisco and a new courthouse in Long Beach.

40. This quote by UCM leadership does not provide the exact terms of the contract. However, it does illustrate, broadly, the types of specifications that were agreed upon by the university and Plenary Properties Merced.

41. AFSCME 3299 (2018). Contract workers are also disproportionately people of color. For instance, at UCLA and Berkeley, where contract workers were surveyed, 96 percent and 93 percent, respectively, were non-white.

42. The Merced 2020 Project was named the "2016 North American Social Infrastructure Deal of the Year" by Infrastructure Journal Global and "America's P3 Deal of the Year" for 2016, as part of the Thomson Reuters Awards for excellence in the global financial industry. In 2017, the school was titled the "P3 Social Infrastructure Project of the Year" and received a silver medal on behalf of the UC regents for the "Best Governmental Agency of the Year" at the annual P3 Awards in Washington, DC. The prior year at the same awards ceremony, Feitelberg was granted the "Best Individual Contribution Award" for the person who "most successfully progressed P3 infrastructure and innovation," as well as the "Public Sector Champion Award" from the Performance Based Building Coalition and InfraAmericas.

43. Hacker (2002); Mettler (2011).

44. Hart (2003).

45. There is a tendency for organizational actors to address market-created problems with market solutions (see Mirowski 2014).

46. UC Office of the President (2017a).

47. Shields (2017).

48. See Miraftab (2004); Sagalyn (2011); Verger (2012).

49. Miraftab (2004).

50. See Wekullo (2017) for a review of existing evidence.

51. See Connell (2019); Edwards, Crosling, and Edwards (2010).

52. Hacker (2002); Mettler (2011).

53. Miraftab (2004, 98).

54. Eaton and Weir (2015).

55. Morgan and Campbell (2011).

56. Also see Verger (2012).

CHAPTER THREE

1.   See Harring and Lawrence (2019).
2.   Hertel and Hoadley (2019).
3.   The University of California fares exceptionally well in Chetty et al's (2017) mobility report card.
4.   The UC is not as racially segregated as lower levels of education in California. Notably, however, there was an uptick in Latinx-white dissimilarity after the opening of UC-Merced. See Baker, Solanki, and Kang (2019).
5.   Ahmed (2012) discusses "diversity work" as done by individual faculty, staff, and administrators within a university. However, when looking at a university system, it is possible to imagine individual campuses as organizational actors that contribute in this way.
6.   Internal to an organization, people of color are often asked to be the face of diversity initiatives (see Ahmed 2012). External to an organization, diversity work may take the form of connections to people of color, such as when a predominately white corporation is a patron to Black arts and cultural groups (see Banks 2019). Diversity work is typically thought of as something done by marginalized individuals or groups.
7.   Ahmed (2012); Thomas (2018).
8.   The Master Plan, initially formulated in 1960, created a comprehensive and multilevel state infrastructure of postsecondary schools with differentiated functions. See Douglass (2007) for more on UC commitments to state residents.
9.   Details on access provisions for the Master Plan can be located at UC Office of the President (2017b).
10.   See Curs and Jaquette (2017) for more on this trend nationwide.
11.   Laura met with California legislative representatives who voiced this concern, and it is at the center of battles over non-resident student caps, as detailed later. The idea is that state funds should go toward serving students from the state.
12.   The UC Master Plan also specified that eligible California community college transfer students be enrolled at a ratio of one transfer student for every two first-year students (UC Office of the President 2017b). At the time of the study, UCR and UCM only enrolled small percentages of community college transfers; in this way they relied on other UCs to help meet the transfer ideal. However, community college transfer students are not representative of the overall community college population—or even the college-going population. Having successfully completed a few years of college, these students often persist at high rates.
13.   In 2017–2018, the cost of in-state attendance at a UC was $11,502 in systemwide tuition and $1,128 in student service fees—all of which would be guaranteed for students under the income ceiling. UCR campus-based fees were $1,239 (for three quarters), and UCM campus-based-fees were $968 (for two

semesters). The Cal Grant and the Blue and Gold Plan, described in the note below, do not cover campus-based fees.

14. The largest share of low-income student funding comes from the publicly funded California state Cal Grant program. The Blue and Gold Opportunity Plan offered by the system fills in any gaps for individual students.

15. For more information on low-income student access and the degree of inter-generational mobility provided by US colleges and universities, see Chetty et al. (2017).

16. College Board (2018).

17. UC Board of Regents (2007). This statement was adopted in 2007, but later amended in 2010.

18. UC Office of the President (2016, 70).

19. The task of increasing racial diversity in the student body has been compli-cated for the UC; as noted in the introduction, from 1996 forward California Proposition 209 prohibited race-conscious admissions and hiring practices. However, system and campus administrators have continued to seek ways to achieve the same goals. In 2015, the system issued what was essentially a "how-to" booklet, designed to help employees increase the representation of people of color in ways that do not directly violate Prop. 209 (UC Office of the General Council 2015).

20. The Campaign for College Opportunity (2015).

21. See Ashkenas, Park, and Pearce (2017). This infographic uses a different racial classification system than the UC internal reports, which indicate higher numbers of Black students (due to how students who identify as both Hispanic and African American are coded). The *New York Times* infographic puts UCLA, UC-Merced, and UC-Riverside in 2015 at the highest rates in the system, with 4 percent of Black students. While double the percentage at Berkeley, and four times the percentage of Black students at San Diego, these numbers are still lower than the percentage of Black individuals in the state, which is around 6.5 percent. (UC internal figures, however, put UCM and UCR at right around the state average in 2017.) The UC system has a long way to go to achieve Black representation equivalent to the population of the state.

22. For more on the Carnegie Classifications, see www.carnegieclassifications.iu .edu.

23. UCR was initially classified as a liberal arts institution but abandoned this designation in the late 1950s as it developed into a research university.

24. See Armstrong and Hamilton (2013) on the costs of maintaining a robust "mobility pathway."

25. The UC and CSU are the two public four-year systems in the state.

26. UC Office of the President (2016).

27. See Eaton (2020a) and Eaton et al. (2016) on the financialization of higher education, which is most intense among private organizations. Also see Krippner (2005); Van der Zwan (2014).

28.   See Eaton, Goldstein, et al. (2013).
29.   For a more detailed account of the UC system's promotion of investment bankers to top system positions, see Eaton, Goldstein, et al. (2013) and Eaton, Habinek, et al. (2013).
30.   See Eaton (2020a); Eaton, Goldstein, et al. (2013).
31.   Eaton et al. (2016).
32.   As quoted in Eaton, Goldstein, et al. (2013).
33.   Furthermore, the benefits of increased borrowing would not be equitably shared across campuses. Critics argued that money went to auxiliary enterprises and projects designed to attract non-residents, like Berkeley's art museum and Memorial Stadium rebuild (see Eaton, Habinek, et al. 2013). The stadium project, in particular, has been described as a financially disastrous decision, given the overall cost to the campus and the system (Redford 2017). There is less evidence to suggest that funds were channeled into the basic infrastructure and services necessary to increase UC enrollment.
34.   AFSCME 3299 (2012).
35.   AFSCME 3299 (2012).
36.   Murphy (2016).
37.   Notably, the California State University system would experience the same change in financial relations with the state, seemingly without the full backing of CSU leadership. Such a move makes even less sense for the CSU system, which does not share the same "powerful student market position" as the UC system.
38.   High-level system and campus administrators frequently point out that non-resident tuition is used to subsidize the education of low-income in-state residents. Yet, postsecondary systems around the country, like the University of California, have rapidly increased the percentage of non-resident students while decreasing the share of in-state students, who are also more likely to be from low-income backgrounds and underrepresented racial groups (Jaquette, Curs, and Posselt 2016).
39.   See Newfield (2008).
40.   In figure 3.3, most IDR is included in the "Government Contracts and Grants" portion of the pie. However, a small portion of federal and state contracts and grants is included in the UC General Funds.
41.   As Owen-Smith (2018) notes, the share of science and engineering research expenditures covered by federal grants dropped precipitously between 2005 and 2015.
42.   Berman (2012a). A report by the Brookings Institute (Valdivia 2013) shows that only a handful of universities (the UC system is listed among them) make money through the current license to the highest-bidder patent model.
43.   Eaton (2020a) shows significant gaps in donations per student by university control, with the wealthiest privates receiving far more than even the wealthiest public schools.

44. University of California (2018).
45. University of California (2018).
46. The endowment assets per student at UC-Santa Cruz tend to fall between UC-Merced and UC-Riverside.
47. This is, in fact, one of the major advantages that elite private schools have over publics, even prestigious publics like Berkeley (Eaton et al. 2016). Several elite privates have endowment amounts that are in the millions per student.
48. See Goldrick-Rab (2016) for more on how this works in Wisconsin.
49. See Kahlenberg (2015).
50. Brandenburger and Nalebuff (1996).
51. Exactly how this would be enacted, however, was a source of great debate. Holding some schools at low non-resident numbers could generate a system-wide cap of 20 to 25 percent, while others continued to enroll high numbers. The legislature would not be satisfied with a system-wide cap, however.
52. UC Board of Regents (2017).
53. Although re-benching increased the localization of resources, not *all* revenue stays internal to each campus.
54. See Rivard (2014).

CHAPTER FOUR

1. Crow and Dabars (2015).
2. See Dirks (2015); Stripling (2015).
3. See California Department of Education (1960); Kerr ([1963] 2001).
4. Crow and Dabars (2015, 60–61).
5. Crow engineered an aggressive deal with the corporate giant Starbucks on a scale and of a nature previously unseen in public higher education. The Starbucks College Achievement Plan is a college tuition reimbursement plan, in which Starbucks will cover costs beyond federal and institutional aid for any worker who averages at least twenty hours a week—but only for the new digital program offered through ASU Online. It replaces a previous, albeit less generous, tuition reimbursement program whereby the company covered a portion of workers' tuition at any accredited university, including brick-and-mortar organizations. This deal captures a seemingly bottomless revenue stream (the Starbucks workforce), monetizes new assets (students who would not have otherwise attended ASU), and uses the Starbucks brand to sell the university. It opens up a new market for fiscal gain through recruitment of disadvantaged populations employed by corporate actors.
6. Brint (2018) offers a critical, but evenhanded, analysis of Crow's administrative approach.
7. UCR is not alone in this. Cintana Education is a recently formed public benefit corporation that capitalizes on the popularity of the ASU new university

model. It draws on ASU's expertise to support the development of new universities in an international context (see Fain 2019).

8.   Blyth (2013).

9.   Cohen, March, and Olsen (1972); Kerr ([1963] 2001).

10. Cohen et al. (1972) argue that decision-making in universities involves so many actors with varying preferences, shifting technologies, and fluid participation that it is best simulated using a "garbage can decision process." They note, however, that, especially in the case of large universities, resource constraints and interrelated problems (flowing from these constraints) increase administrative power and lead to a more hierarchical structure of decision-making.

11. See Brint (2018).

12. Barley and Kunda (1992) argue that managerial discourse is tightly tied to both the cultural and material conditions of the time. Here, we make a similar argument for university administrators.

13. See Haveman and Gualtieri (2017).

14. Stevens and Gebre-Medhin (2016).

15. American Association for the Advancement of Science (2019).

16. Cooper (2017, 219–27) distinguishes between the human capital theories of Schultz, who viewed investment in education as a way to grow national income and benefit the public as a whole, and Gary Becker and Milton Friedman, who emphasized the private returns to education. According to Cooper, Schultz was influential in government policymaking, due to his strong ties with Walter Heller, the chairman of the Council of Economic Advisers under Kennedy and Johnson. Heller promoted a more direct and generous role for the federal government in higher education, which inspired President Johnson's efforts to make higher education a major policy agenda, culminating in the Higher Education Act of 1965.

17. Loss (2012); Stevens and Gebre-Medhin (2016).

18. Hinderaker and Hinderaker (1998).

19. As Reinhold (1992) reported, "The State of California ran out of cash today and began to pay its bills with I.O.U.'s for the first time since the Great Depression." Steep cuts to higher education funding were expected.

20. It is important to point out that Orbach was not ignorant of fiscal constraints or habitually profligate. In some cases, he displayed a frugality that stemmed from his lower-middle-class upbringing. For example, when Orbach arrived as chancellor to UCR, he not only decided to live in the chancellor's residence instead of commuting from his home in the exclusive Pacific Palisades community, he also furnished the chancellor's residence with furniture from a Holiday Inn that was being converted to house the UCR extension program. As Orbach noted, "Nobody could say that we were extravagant."

21. Fukuyama (1989, 3).

22. Slobodian (2018). Also see Connell (2019) for a discussion of the spread of neoliberalism to postsecondary systems around the world.

23. Scholars view blind adherence to TINA as a central feature of neoliberalism; for example, see Queiroz (2016).

24. Mudge (2018).

25. For more on this change in higher education, see Arum, Gamoran, and Shavit (2007); Connell (2019); Eaton (2020a); Fabricant and Brier (2016); Molesworth et al. (2011); Slaughter and Rhoades (2004); Stevens and Gebre-Medhin (2016).

26. For an example, see Cochrane (2009).

27. See Blyth (2013).

28. See Haney López (2014); MacLean (2017); Omi and Winant (2015).

29. Leland and Moore (2007).

30. Crow did, however, spend time at an elite private university—Columbia University—between his time at Iowa State University and Arizona State University. At Columbia, Jonathon Cole, Columbia's provost between 1989 and 2003, mentored him. Cole, in response to shifting economic conditions, wrote a powerful defense of the US research university in *The Great American University* (published in 2009). Crow rapidly moved up Columbia's administrative ranks. He started at ASU in 2003, before the Great Recession hit.

31. For a discussion of culture and cohort effects, see Small (2002). Small's cohort-based theory of narrative frameworks provides a model for understanding how shifting contexts can affect how different cohorts of people narratively frame a given situation or environment, such as a neighborhood or organization.

32. Dow (2015, 29).

33. See Berman (2012b) on how the changing fiscal environment, not an institutional entrepreneur, changed the dominant cultural logics in higher education.

34. Newfield (2016). Also see Bowen (1980).

35. Webber (2017).

36. A useful accompaniment to this chapter is Brint et al.'s (2016) piece "Surviving and Thriving: The Adaptive Responses of U.S. Four-Year Colleges and Universities during the Great Recession." Also see Berman and Paradeise (2016). In summarizing papers in the volume, they argue that universities have responded to increasing financial pressures and competition by cutting costs, becoming more entrepreneurial, intensifying administrative control, and expanding the adoption of rationalized management tools.

37. See Eaton et al. (2019). The paper includes a figure that maps undergraduate enrollment growth at public universities by research category since 2000. While the top tier remains largely flat, every other category has increased considerably in a short span of time. These schools are likely attempting to increase their research standing via student enrollments. This dynamic sup-

ports the growth of what *The Chronicle of Higher Education* recently referred to as "mega universities," including striving postsecondary organizations like ASU (Gardner 2019).

38. Ryman (2018).
39. Crow and Dabars (2015, 139) quote Harvard physician Atul Gawande, who used the Cheesecake Factory as a prototype for an alternative health care model, one that is assumed to reduce costs and provide better services to a larger swath of the population.
40. See Connell (2019) for a discussion of the link between exclusivity and prestige in higher education around the world. According to Connell, the necessity of exclusion to produce elite status has undermined efforts at producing more egalitarian postsecondary organizations, for example, in China.
41. Bound and Turner (2007).
42. There are, however, only nine University of California campuses that serve undergraduates.
43. See Clotfelter (2017); Eaton (2020a).
44. Birnbaum (2001).
45. Newfield (2016).
46. In 2015, in order to resolve disagreements about state funding for the UC system, UC president Janet Napolitano and Governor Jerry Brown formed a "committee of two" to consider cost reductions and other systemwide issues. The plan to pilot ABC at UCR developed from these negotiations.
47. UC-Riverside (2018).
48. Wisconsin Hope Lab (2015).
49. Hearn et al. (2006).
50. See Jaquette, Kramer, and Curs (2018) on the positive effect of RCM on tuition revenue.
51. A UCR administrator favorably compared this approach to the system of welfare block grants to states after the 1996 welfare reform.
52. See Crow and Dabars (2015) and Brint's (2018) commentary.
53. Beattie and Thiele (2016).
54. For a review of research on online education, see Jaggars (2011).
55. House Committee on Education and the Workforce (2014).
56. Brint (2018).
57. Crow and Dabars (2015, 62).
58. Olsen (2010).
59. Seltzer (2016).
60. Urban Universities for Health (2015).
61. See Townsend, Pisapia, and Razzaq (2013).
62. Brint (2018) provides a useful review of the conditions under which interdisciplinarity works. Also see Dahlander and McFarland (2013).
63. Zemsky, Wegner, and Massy (2005, 59).
64. Winston (1999).

65. Zemsky et al. (2005).
66. Brown (2015) emphasizes the extent to which value in neoliberal markets can be about prospective prestige or gain, rather than immediate returns.
67. Faller (2018).
68. Rust (2016).
69. Marcus (2017).
70. See Policano (2016).
71. See Pyne and Grodsky (2019).
72. As we explore in chapter 7, this contrasts with the benefits that accrue to privileged students attending prestigious universities that partner with elite finance and consulting firms. See Binder, Davis, and Bloom (2016).
73. Hollinger (2013); Reid (2013).
74. Both Newfield (2016) and Reid (2013) quote this statement.
75. Berman (2012a); Benneworth and Jongbloed (2009); Hollinger (2013).
76. Acronyms for the schools at UCR and UCM are different than those used here. We used the same labels for consistency.
77. At the time, only UCR had a standalone business school. Asian students were overrepresented by 17.3 percent in this school, while all other groups were underrepresented.
78. Dickson (2010); Lewis et al. (2009). See Riegle-Crumb, King, and Irizarry (2019) on the exclusion of Black and Latinx youth in STEM fields.
79. Vincent (2018).
80. Stevens, Miller-Idriss, and Shami (2018).
81. Kerr ([1963] 2001, 22) as quoted by Marginson (2016, 23). As Kerr continues, "an astute bargainer with the foundations and federal agencies, a politician with the state legislature, a friend of industry, labor, and agriculture, a persuasive diplomat with donors, a champion of education generally, a supporter of the professions (particularly of law and medicine), a spokesman to the press, a scholar in his own right, a public servant at the state and national levels, a devotee of opera and football equally, a decent human being, a good husband and father, an active member of a church. Above all he must enjoy traveling in airplanes, eating his meals in public, and attending public ceremonies. No one can be all of these things. Some succeed at being none."
82. Under the Development, Relief, and Education for Alien Minors (DREAM) Act, undocumented youth who arrived in the US as children could gain a pathway to permanent legal status by achieving several milestones, including attending or graduating from an education of higher learning. President Trump has repeatedly threatened the status of Dreamers in the US.
83. See McMurtrie (2017).
84. The volume edited by Bastedo (2012) offers a rich understanding of the impact of university leadership, but also addresses organizational and environmental constraints on the actions of leaders.
85. Blyth (2013).

CHAPTER FIVE

1. As inhabited institutionalists remind us, people do things together in institutions (Hallett and Ventresca 2006; Hallett 2010).
2. Seeley (2016).
3. Staff responses to tolerable suboptimization are, in some ways, the opposite of Burawoy's (1979) notion of "making out," in which workers treat the labor process as a game that requires "play[ing] all angles" in the attempt to reduce effort and maximize benefit. Nor is it entirely consistent with Bourdieu's (2000) observation that workers derive some internal rewards from doing good work, despite the low status of certain jobs. The workers in this chapter are instead (or also) motivated by the need to not let students suffer, to the extent possible, due to limited organizational resources. Gastón (2019) offers a useful corollary. He describes the historical emergence of a "caring class" of hospital workers who defined themselves by a sense of moral obligation to care for their patients. Gastón also illustrates how moral obligation can be utilized for effective collective action against market pressures to reduce the quality of care.
4. See Hamilton (2016).
5. Robbins (2013).
6. Some acronyms for schools internal to UCM are different than those used here. We used the same labels for consistency in making comparisons across our focal schools.
7. SNS also handled course articulation, but not in as high volume as SSHA.
8. Shortly after the study concluded, the SSHA website was updated to include appointment scheduling software. However, during busy times of the semester (e.g., approaching registration), advising shifted to walk-ins in order to serve more students. As a result, the waiting room was crowded once again.
9. Emirbayer and Johnson (2008) have applied Bourdieu's notion of habitus to organizational analysis to suggest how microprocesses of individual behavior build up into organizational structure. For tolerable suboptimization to function as a routine way of operating, it has to become part of workers' durable principles of judgment and practice. The concept of habitus helps explain how austerity logics become part of daily practice even among constituencies that do not embrace those logics.
10. Questions about experiences with academic advisors were part of our interview guide for a random sample of full-time Black and Latinx students in their first and fourth years at UCM.
11. Notably, biology majors who were in the School of Natural Sciences had similar reports, likely because of advisors' similarly high caseloads.
12. See Riegle-Crumb, King, and Irizarry (2019).
13. Hunt and Eisenberg (2010); Winerman (2017).
14. Center for Collegiate Mental Health (2017).

15. For example, see *Psychology Today* coverage of the issue (Henriques 2014).
16. See the Regents of the University of California (2015).
17. For examples, see Grollman (2014); Rosenfield (2012).
18. Intersectionality scholars, such as Collins (1990, 2004) and Crenshaw (1991, 2016), emphasize the importance of attending to positionality in multiple systems of power.
19. This woman was part of a targeted sample of student leaders. We did not ask all students to reflect on their experiences with CAPS, as seeking mental health support is often a sensitive issue. Instead, we addressed this only if students raised the topic.
20. As (2019) notes, US law enforcement is a race-making institution. It has played a central role in justifying unequal racial arrangements via colorblind and seemingly neutral appeals to legality, safety, and morality. Under racial neoliberalism, the criminalization of people of color has become a primary mechanism for social control (see Anderson 2012; Wacquant 2001; Western 2006).
21. Rosenberg (2016).
22. See the volume edited by Patton (2010) for both historical overview and recent research on cultural centers.
23. Hefner (2002).
24. Ahmed (2012); Brayboy (2003); Brunsma, Brown, and Placier (2012); Ray (2019); Urciuoli (2018); Vidal-Ortiz (2017).
25. Armbruster-Sandoval (2017).
26. For more on "the Hub," see Lerma, Hamilton, and Nielsen (2019).
27. University of California (2019a).
28. For more information on graduate outcomes across the University of California campuses, see University of California (2019b).
29. On internal university stratification and honors or advanced programming, see Bastedo (2009); Bastedo and Gumport (2003); Hamilton, Roksa, Nielsen (2018).
30. Armstrong and Hamilton (2013).

CHAPTER SIX

1. See Armbruster-Sandoval (2017); Rhoads (1998); Rogers (2012); Van Dyke (1998).
2. Eagan et al. (2016).
3. Ahmed (2012); Hirshfield and Joseph (2012); Matthew (2016); Moore (2017); Zambrana (2018).
4. Lerma, Hamilton, and Nielsen (2019, 2).
5. See Lerma et al. (2019) for more on the concept of racialized equity labor. Racialized equity labor is a type of "racial task," as theorized by Wingfield and Alston (2013). Racial tasks are a wide array of ideological, interactional, and physical forms of labor that people of color must perform in white spaces

(e.g., management of self-presentation, emotion work, and efforts to smooth interactions with white peers).

6. Ahmed (2012); Brayboy (2003); Brunsma, Brown, and Placier (2012); Ray (2019); Urciuoli (2018); Vidal-Ortiz (2017).

7. For examples, see Feagin, Vera, and Imani (1996); Lee and LaDousa (2015); McCabe (2009); Nenga, Alvarado, and Blyth (2015); Ray and Best (2015); Smith, Allen, and Danley (2007); Strayhorn (2013); Watkins, LaBarrie, and Appio 2010; and Wilkins (2014).

8. Ahmed (2012); Brayboy (2003); Urciuoli (2018).

9. See Vidal-Ortiz (2017). Also, Vargas and Villa-Palomino's (2018) study of Hispanic-Serving Institutions (HSIs) suggests that even in these schools, Latinx students are rarely centered in HSI Title V programmatic efforts — despite the fact that it is Latinx students who qualify HSIs to compete for these funds.

10. See chapter 4 for a definition of cultural logic.

11. Thomas (2018, 141; 2020).

12. For a K–12 illustration of the links between austerity and diversity logics, see Turner (2020).

13. Ahmed (2012); Anderson (2005); Jayakumar and Museus (2012); Thomas (2018, 2020).

14. See the cycle of racialized labor appropriation as documented in Lerma et al. (2019).

15. See Bonilla-Silva (2010).

16. UC Board of Regents (2007).

17. Moore (2018, 56).

18. This tendency fits with neoliberalism's framework of multiculturalism and individual responsibility that masks race and racism in both policy and practice (Inwood 2015; Melamed 2006).

19. Hefner (2002); Patton (2006); Princes (2005); Shotton, Yellowfish, and Cintrón (2010).

20. Shotton et al. (2010, 56).

21. Ahmed (2012).

22. Bradley et al. (2018).

23. The previous CDO was a more senior academic and was well respected for their work in this role. While this does not suggest that the previous CDO was more effective or empowered, it is important to point out that this role was not reserved only for relatively junior faculty.

24. On the limits of multiculturalism, see Bell and Hartmann (2008); Cobham and Parker (2007); Lewis (2003); Shotton et al. (2010).

25. "Ratchet" is a term that originated as a racialized (and typically gendered) rap insult, meaning "ghetto ... gutter, [or] nasty." This is the meaning suggested by the speaker. However, the term has also been reclaimed by some and can mean "cool ... sleek, or flashy." See Ortved (2013).

26. See Lerma et al. (2019).

27. Ahmed (2012, 135).
28. At UCM we conducted twenty-two targeted interviews with student orga-
    nizers and thirty-three random interviews. Ten of these random interviews
    were of students who also happened to be student activists and leaders,
    most of whom identified as Black. This paragraph thus refers to the thirty-
    two students in our sample engaged in organizing on campus. See Lerma
    et al. (2019) for more details on the toll that racialized equity labor took on
    UCM student leaders.
29. Ramirez's (2018) dissertation and case study of UC-Riverside's cultural cen-
    ters provided many details regarding the history and operation of this infra-
    structure.
30. Jayakumar and Museus (2012, 16).
31. State of Arizona (2010).
32. Strauss (2017).

CHAPTER SEVEN

1. Berman (2012a); Bok (2003); Davis and Binder (2016); Morphew and Eckel
   (2009); and Slaughter and Rhoades (2004) discuss increased commercialization in the university.
2. Davis and Binder (2016).
3. Here we extend the work of legal scholar Nancy Leong (2013), who refers
   to "racial identity markets," along with Patricia Banks's (2019) notion of
   "diversity capital," to think about how the ability to aid in the production of
   "diversity" can be leveraged as an organizational resource. The notion of a diversity transaction is also inspired by Viviana Zelizer's (2011) understanding
   that economic exchanges are a pervasive part of intimate life and often do
   not resemble the prototypical exchange between a merchant and customer.
4. See Rivera (2015); also Binder, Davis, and Bloom (2016).
5. Kelly interviewed two Pepsi employees, both of whom were former UCR students and, in their new roles, involved with recruiting students from UCR.
6. Robinson ([1983] 2000). Also see Omi and Winant (2015).
7. For examples, see Fligstein (2001); Zelizer (2011). However, for a recent cor-
   rection, see Hirschman and Garbes (2019).
8. Also see Rivera (2015).
9. As Fligstein (2001) points out, even using the example of Pepsi versus Coca-
   Cola, market strategies are not about shutting down competitors, but rather
   creating stable control over the markets in which corporations sell their
   products.
10. See Omi and Winant (2015).
11. Davis and Binder (2016).
12. Binder et al. (2016); Davis and Binder (2016).
13. Davis and Binder (2016).
14. Rivera (2015).

15. Davis and Binder (2016).
16. In the 2019–2020 academic year, posters began to appear around UCM's campus that suggested a similar partnership was developing or in place.
17. See Fligstein (1990) for more on how workers with finance and accounting backgrounds rose to the top of corporations and how positions dealing with labor became lower status.
18. Pepsi has taken some steps to diversify the very top of the organization. The CEO of PepsiCo Foods North America, Steven Williams, is a Black man who went to the University of Central Oklahoma for his BA and appears to have risen up from the bottom. He later went to Harvard University for the Program for Leadership Development, but it is not clear whether that was before or during his time at Pepsi. The Pepsi website says he "has held leadership positions of increased responsibility in sales, general management, customer management, sales planning and shopper marketing."
19. Douglas (2008); Welbourne and McLaughlin (2013).
20. Huang (2017).
21. Elevate (2015).
22. Douglas (2008, 11).
23. Lerma, Hamilton, and Nielsen (2019).
24. Welbourne and McLaughlin (2013, 41).
25. HispanicPR (2012).
26. Berrey (2015, 250).
27. See Courteau (2016) for the use of adversity narratives in admissions.
28. Brown (2017).
29. Cottom (2017).
30. Also see Gelbgiser (2018); Houle (2013); Looney and Yannelis (2015). Eaton (2020b) offers insight into which for-profit entities are likely to be the most exploitative.

BREAKING THE CYCLE

1. The idea of a pressure valve in the US higher education system goes back to at least the mid-twentieth century. In particular, community colleges assumed the role of "cooling out" student aspirations as large numbers of underprepared students began to enter higher education and compete for limited positions at the top of the education system and labor market (Clark 1960). Brint and Karabel (1989) argued that community colleges adopted a gatekeeper role in order to cement their own status as functional organizations in the broader postsecondary field. This preserved the elite status of four-year universities. In the college-for-all era, community colleges have encouraged, rather than discouraged, four-year-degree attainment (Rosenbaum, Deil-Amen, and Person 2006), thus diminishing their role as a pressure valve. Other points in the system have subsequently evolved to release pressure from growing postsecondary demand.

2.   Connell (2019).
3.   Connell (2019, 85). Emphasis is in the original text.
4.   Buckner (2017).
5.   Baradaran (2019). Also see Ray's (2019) discussion of this book.
6.   Taylor (2019).
7.   See Anderson (2010); Lewis and Diamond (2015); Tilly (1998).
8.   See Ray (2019); also Sewell (1992).
9.   Ray and Seamster (2016, 1361). They build on Link and Phelan's (1995) notion of the "fundamental cause."
10.   Boggs et al. (2019) offer an excellent history of the university from a critical studies perspective. Also see Ray (2019).
11.   See Labaree (2010).
12.   Also see Lerma et al. (2019); Thomas (2018, 2020).
13.   Ahmed (2012, 34). Emphasis is in the original text.
14.   Jayakumar and Museus (2012).
15.   See Mehta and Mason (2017).
16.   Reuben (2001).
17.   Kendi (2019, 101).
18.   See Jackson and Weidman (2006).
19.   See Aguinis, Culpepper, and Pierce (2016); Hiss and Franks (2014).
20.   See Kendi (2019); Patel (2019).
21.   See Hartocollis (2019) for coverage of the "adversity score" controversy.
22.   Hampshire College (2019).
23.   Kamenetz (2019).
24.   For coverage of Posse, see Rosenberg (2012).
25.   See Armstrong and Hamilton (2013); Reyes (2018).
26.   University Innovation Alliance (2019).
27.   Association of American Universities (2019).
28.   A graded system of funding, based on family income, may be wiser, however. Incentives to enroll Pell Grant students may lead to a bifurcated student population—large enrollments of the lowest-income students on one end and the wealthiest (who can pay out-of-state tuition) on the other. Thus, students who just miss the Pell cutoff can be harmed by focus on the Pell benchmark.
29.   Owen-Smith (2018, 55).
30.   See Fox (2004); Gilens (1995, 1999); Poterba (1997); Weir, Orloff, and Skocpol (1988).
31.   Stevens and Gebre-Medhin (2016).
32.   Black students borrow more than other students for the same degrees (Huelsman 2015). This is, in part, because Black borrowers have, on average, lower family wealth and income (Addo, Houle, and Simon 2016). In contrast, Latinx students, on average, display a reluctance to borrow for higher education (Cunningham and Santiago 2008). It is problematic to view either borrowing "aversion" or high levels of borrowing as the primary issues to fix;

this individualizes the structural inequalities that place Black and Latinx families in difficult positions. Student loan debt contributes to classed and racialized economic disparities that are inherited across generations (Houle and Addo 2019; Seamster and Charron-Chénier 2017).

33. Seamster and Charron-Chénier (2017). Also see Cottom (2017).
34. See Goldrick-Rab and Miller-Adams's (2018) defense of existing "free college" plans, in the face of recent critique.
35. Goldrick-Rab (2016) discusses the non-tuition costs of higher education.
36. See Kraemer (2013). This is, in part, because community colleges are resource starved and serve the most-disadvantaged students. See Rosenbaum, Deil-Amen, and Person (2006).
37. Goldrick-Rab and Miller-Adams (2018) discuss issues with "last dollar" plans.
38. College Board (2013); Goldrick-Rab and Kendall (2014).
39. Mettler (2014).
40. Eno (2019).
41. Also see Owen-Smith (2018).
42. The Education Trust (2015, 2017) documents the wide variation in Black student and Pell Grant recipient graduation rates among organizational peers.
43. Ravitch (2010, 2013) has written extensively on problems with No Child Left Behind.
44. Cottom (2017) describes the "education gospel"—that is, faith in schooling as the primary means of getting ahead in US society.
45. The state can raise or lower the stakes of education. In Sweden, for example, policies to reduce the consequence of class position, equalize income gaps, and reduce the risks associated with prolonged unemployment—including progressive taxation and redistribution through the welfare state—limit the extent to which educational credentials determine citizens' quality of life (see Breen 2010; Erikson and Jonsson 1996; Korpi and Palme 2004).
46. Hout (2012) offers a thorough review of the benefits that flow to individuals through higher education.
47. See Cottom (2017); Horowitz (1987).
48. On the criminalization of youth of color in schools, see Rios (2011) and Shedd (2015).
49. Reich (2016) makes this broader point.

APPENDIX

1. Collins (1990).
2. Armstrong and Hamilton (2013).
3. Hamilton et al. (2019).
4. Soja (1996); Starr (2004).
5. See Lerma, Hamilton, and Nielsen (2019).
6. Conwell (2016).

7.   Robinson ([1983] 2000).
8.   Omi and Winant (2015).
9.   Lewis and Diamond (2015); Tyson (2011).
10.   Du Bois (1898); also see Conwell (2016).
11.   Ray (2019).
12.   Carter (2012); Tyson (2011).
13.   Crow and Dabars (2015).

References

Abbott, Andrew. 1991. "History and Sociology: The Lost Synthesis." *Social Science History* 15:201–38.

Adair, Vivyan C. 2002. "Branded with Infamy: Inscriptions of Poverty and Class in the United States." *Signs* 27:451–71.

Addo, Fenaba R., Jason N. Houle, and Daniel Simon. 2016. "Young, Black, and (Still) in the Red: Parental Wealth, Race, and Student Loan Debt." *Race and Social Problems* 8:64–76.

Adkins, Lisa. 2012. "Out of Work or Out of Time? Rethinking Labor after the Financial Crisis." *South Atlantic Quarterly* 111:621–41.

AFSCME 3299. 2012. "No to UC's Debt Privatization & New Tuition Hikes." Retrieved from https://afscme3299.org/2012/06/14/no-to-ucs-debt-privatization-new-tuition-hikes/#prettyPhoto.

———. 2018. "Pioneering Inequality: Race, Gender, and Income Disparities at the University of California." Retrieved from https://afscme3299.org/documents/reports/Pioneering-Inequality_WhitePaper.pdf.

Aguinis, Herman, Steven A. Culpepper, and Charles A. Pierce. 2016. "Differential Prediction Generalization in College Admissions Testing." *Journal of Educational Psychology* 108:1045–59.

Ahmed, Sara. 2012. *On Being Included: Racism and Diversity in Institutional Life.* Durham, NC: Duke University Press.

Allen, Walter R., and Joseph O. Jewell. 2002. "A Backward Glance Forward: Past, Present and Future Perspectives on Historically Black Colleges and Universities." *Review of Higher Education* 25:241–61.

Alley, Keith E. 2007. "Creating the Infrastructure for Graduate Education and Research at a New Research University." Pp. 61–68 in *From Rangeland to Research University: The Birth of University of California, Merced,* edited by Karen Merritt and Jane F. Lawrence. Hoboken, NJ: Wiley Periodicals.

American Association for the Advancement of Science. 2019. "Federal R&D as Percent of GDP." Retrieved from https://www.aaas.org/sites/default/files/s3fs-public/RDGDP%253B.jpg.

Anderson, Elijah. 2012. "The Iconic Ghetto." *Annals of the American Academy of Political and Social Science* 642:8–24.

Anderson, Elizabeth. 2010. *The Imperative of Integration*. Princeton, NJ: Princeton University Press.

Anderson, Gregory M. 2005. "In the Name of Diversity: Education and the Commodization of Race in the United States." *Urban Review* 37:399–423.

Anderson, Nick. 2015. "UC-Riverside vs. U.S. News: A University Leader Scoffs at the Rankings." *Washington Post*, September 9.

Anzaldúa, Gloria E. 1987. *Borderlands/La Frontera: The New Mestiza*. San Francisco: Aunt Lute Books.

Armbruster-Sandoval, Ralph. 2017. *Starving for Justice: Hunger Strikes, Spectacular Speech, and the Struggle for Dignity*. Tucson: University of Arizona Press.

Armstrong, Elizabeth A., and Laura T. Hamilton. 2013. *Paying for the Party: How College Maintains Inequality*. Cambridge, MA: Harvard University Press.

Arum, Richard, Adam Gamoran, and Yossi Shavit. 2007. "More Inclusion Than Diversification: Expansion, Differentiation, and Market Structure in Higher Education." Pp. 1–38 in *Stratification in Higher Education: A Comparative Study*, edited by Yossi Shavit, Richard Arum, and Adam Gamoran. Stanford, CA: Stanford University Press.

Ashkenas, Jeremy, Haeyoun Park, and Adam Pearce. 2017. "Even with Affirmative Action, Blacks and Hispanics Are More Underrepresented at Top Colleges Than 35 Years Ago." *New York Times*, August 24.

Association of American Universities. 2019. "Membership Policy." Retrieved from https://www.aau.edu/who-we-are/membership-policy.

Baker, David P. 2014. *The Schooled Society: The Educational Transformation of Global Culture*. Stanford, CA: Stanford University Press.

Baker, Dominique J. 2019. "Pathways to Racial Equity in Higher Education: Modeling the Antecedents of State Affirmative Action Bans." *American Educational Research Journal*, https://doi.org/10.3102/0002831219833918.

Baker, Rachel, Sabrina Solanki, and Connie Kang. 2019. "Conceptualizing Racial Segregation in Higher Education: Examining Within- and Between-Sector Trends in California Public Higher Education, 1994–2014." EdWorkingPaper 19–134. Retrieved from Annenberg Institute at Brown University, https://doi.org/10.26300/e5sb-0f03.

Banks, Patricia. 2019. "Diversity Capital and Corporate Cultural Patronage." *Consumers & Consumption American Sociological Association Section*. Retrieved from https://asaconsumers.wordpress.com/2019/01/28/consume-this-diversity-capital-and-corporate-cultural-patronage/.

Baradaran, Mehrsa. 2019. *The Color of Money: Black Banks and the Racial Wealth Gap*. Cambridge, MA: Harvard University Press.

Barley, Stephen R., and Gideon Kunda. 1992. "Design and Devotion: Surges of Rational and Normative Ideologies of Control in Managerial Discourse." *Administrative Quarterly* 37:363–99.

Bastedo, Michael N. 2009. "Convergent Institutional Logics in Public Higher Education: State Policymaking and Governing Board Activism." *Review of Higher Education* 32:209–34.

Bastedo, Michael N., ed. 2012. *The Organization of Higher Education: Managing Colleges for a New Era.* Baltimore: Johns Hopkins University Press.

Bastedo, Michael N., and Nicholas A. Bowman. 2009. "U.S. News & World Report College Rankings: Modeling Institutional Effects on Organizational Reputation." *American Journal of Education* 116:163–83.

Bastedo, Michael N., and Patricia J. Gumport. 2003. "Access to What? Mission Differentiation and Academic Stratification in US Public Higher Education." *Higher Education* 46:341–59.

Beattie, Irenee, and Megan Thiele. 2016. "Connecting in Class? College Class Size and Inequality in Academic Social Capital." *Journal of Higher Education* 87: 332–62.

Becker, Gary S. (1957) 1971. *The Economics of Discrimination.* Chicago: University of Chicago Press.

Bell, Joyce, and Douglas Hartmann. 2008. "Diversity in Everyday Discourse: The Cultural Ambiguities and Consequences of 'Happy Talk.'" *American Sociological Review* 72:895–914.

Benitez, Michael Jr. 2010. "Resituating Culture Centers within a Social Justice Framework: Is There Room for Examining Whiteness?" Pp. 119–34 in *Culture Centers in Higher Education,* edited by L. D. Patton. Sterling, VA: Stylus.

Benneworth, Paul, and Ben W. Jongbloed. 2009. "Who Matters to Universities? A Stakeholder Perspective on Humanities, Arts, and Social Sciences Valorisation." *Higher Education* 5:567–88.

Berg, Martin. 2012. "The Isolated Fortress of USC." *LA Weekly,* May 10.

Berman, Elizabeth P. 2012a. *Creating the Market University: How Academic Science Became an Economic Engine.* Princeton, NJ: Princeton University Press.

———. 2012b. "Explaining the Move toward the Market in US Academic Science: How Institutional Logics Can Change without Institutional Entrepreneurs." *Theory and Society* 41:261–99.

Berman, Elizabeth Popp, and Catherine Paradeise. 2016. "Introduction: The University Under Pressure." *Research in the Sociology of Organizations* 46:1–22.

Bernstein, Daniel I. 2017. "Public-Private Partnerships: It's the Right Time." National Association of College and Business Officers.

Berrey, Ellen. 2015. *The Enigma of Diversity: The Language of Race and the Limits of Racial Justice.* Chicago: University of Chicago Press.

Best, Joel, and Eric Best. 2014. *The Student Loan Mess.* Berkeley: University of California Press.

Bickel, Robert D., and Peter F. Lake. 1999. *The Rights and Responsibilities of the Modern University: Who Assumes the Risks of College Life?* Durham, NC: Carolina Academic Press.

Binder, Amy, Daniel B. Davis, and Nick Bloom. 2016. "Career Funneling: How Elite Students Learn to Define and Desire 'Prestigious' Jobs." *Sociology of Education* 89:20–39.

Birnbaum, Robert. 2001. *Management Fads in Higher Education: Where They Come From, What They Do, Why They Fail*. San Francisco: Jossey-Bass.

Black, Rachel, and Aleta Sprague. 2016. "The Rise and Reign of the Welfare Queen." *New America*, September 22.

Blair, Bruce L., and Adam M. Williams. 2017. "University Housing Development: A PPP Approach." *Journal of Public and Nonprofit Affairs* 3:320–35.

Bleemer, Zachary. 2020. "Affirmative Action, Mismatch, and Economic Mobility After California's Proposition 209." Berkeley Center for Studies in Higher Education Occasional Paper Series: CSHE.10.2020.

Blyth, Mark. 2013. *Austerity: The History of a Dangerous Idea*. Oxford: Oxford University Press.

Boggs, Abigail, Eli Meyerhoff, Nick Mitchell, and Zach Schwartz-Weinstein. 2019. "Abolitionist University Studies: An Invitation." Retrieved from https://abolition.university/invitation/.

Bok, Derek. 2003. *Universities in the Marketplace: The Commercialization of Higher Education*. Princeton, NJ: Princeton University Press.

Bonilla-Silva, Eduardo. 1997. "Rethinking Racism: Toward a Structural Interpretation." *American Sociological Review* 62:465–80.

———. 2010. *Racism Without Racists: Color-Blind Racism and the Persistence of Racial Inequality in America*, 3rd ed. Plymouth, UK: Rowman & Littlefield.

Bound, John, Breno Braga, Gaurav Khanna, and Sarah Turner. 2016. "A Passage to America: University Funding and International Students." NBER Working Paper No. 22981.

Bound, John, and Sarah Turner. 2007. "Cohort Crowding: How Resources Affect Collegiate Attainment." *Journal of Public Economics* 91:877–99.

Bourdieu, Pierre. 2000. *Pascalian Meditations*. Stanford, CA: Stanford University Press.

Bowen, Howard R. 1980. *The Costs of Higher Education*. San Francisco: Jossey-Bass.

Bowen, William G., and Derek Bok. 1998. *The Shape of the River: Long-Term Consequences of Considering Race in College and University Admissions*. Princeton, NJ: Princeton University Press.

Bowen, William G., Matthew M. Chingos, and Michael S. McPherson. 2009. *Crossing the Finish Line: Completing College at America's Public Universities*. Princeton, NJ: Princeton University Press.

Bradley, Steven W., James R. Garven, Wilson W. Law, and James E. West. 2018. "The Impact of Chief Diversity Officers on Diverse Faculty Hiring." NBER Working Paper No. 24969.

Brandenburger, Adam M., and Barry J. Nalebuff. 1996. *Co-opetition*. New York: Currency Doubleday.

Brayboy, Bryan M. J. 2003. "The Implementation of Diversity in Predominately White Colleges and Universities." *Journal of Black Studies* 34:72–86.

Breen, Richard. 2010. "Educational Expansion and Social Mobility in the 20th Century." *Social Forces* 89:365–88.

Brigham, Carl C. 1923. *A Study of American Intelligence*. Princeton, NJ: Princeton University Press.

Brint, Steven. 2018. *Two Cheers for Higher Education: Why American Universities Are Stronger Than Ever—and How to Meet the Challenges They Face*. Princeton, NJ: Princeton University Press.

Brint, Steven, and Jerome Karabel. 1989. *The Diverted Dream: Community Colleges and the Promise of Educational Opportunity in America, 1900–1985*. New York: Oxford University Press.

Brint, Steven, Mark Riddle, and Robert A. Hanneman. 2006. "Reference Sets, Identities, and Aspirations in a Complex Organizational Field: The Case of American Four-Year Colleges and Universities." *Sociology of Education* 79:229–52.

Brint, Steven, Sarah R. K. Yoshikawa, Matthew B. Rotondi, Tiffany Viggiano, and John Maldonado. 2016. "Surviving and Thriving: The Adaptive Responses of U.S. Four-Year Colleges and Universities during the Great Recession." *Journal of Higher Education* 87:859–89.

Brown, Patricia L. 2017. "Creating a Safe Space for California Dreamers." *New York Times*, February 3.

Brown, Phil. 1995. "Race, Class, and Environmental Health: A Review and Systemization of the Literature." *Environmental Research* 69:15–30.

Brown, Wendy. 2015. *Undoing the Demos: Neoliberalism's Stealth Revolution*. New York: Zone Books.

Brunsma, David L., Eric S. Brown, and Peggy Placier. 2012. "Teaching Race at Historically White Colleges and Universities: Identifying and Dismantling the Walls of Whiteness." *Critical Sociology* 39:717–38.

Buchanan, James M. 1970. *Academia in Anarchy: An Economic Diagnosis*. New York: Basic Books.

Buckner, Elizabeth. 2017. "The Worldwide Growth of Private Higher Education: Cross-National Patterns of Higher Education Institution Foundings by Sector." *Sociology of Education* 90:296–314.

Burawoy, Michael. 1979. *Manufacturing Consent: Changes in the Labor Process under Monopoly Capitalism*. Chicago: University of Chicago Press.

Byrd, Carson. 2017. *Poison in the Ivy: Race Relations and the Reproduction of Inequality on Elite College Campuses*. New Brunswick, NJ: Rutgers University Press.

Byrd-Chichester, Janell. 2001. "The Federal Courts and Claims of Racial Discrimination in Higher Education." *Journal of Negro Education* 69:12–26.

California Department of Education. 1960. "A Master Plan for Higher Education in California, 1960–1975." Retrieved from http://www.ucop.edu/acadinit/mast plan/MasterPlan1960.pdf.

———. 2017. "Graduation Rates." Retrieved from https://www.cde.ca.gov/.

California LAO. 2012. "Maximizing State Benefits From Public-Private Partnerships." November 8.

Campaign for College Opportunity. 2015. Retrieved from https://collegecampaign.org /wp-content/uploads/2015/04/2015-State-of-Higher-Education_Latinos.pdf.

Carlson, Jennifer. 2019. "Police Warriors and Police Guardians: Race, Masculinity, and the Construction of Gun Violence." *Social Problems*, doi:10.1093/socpro/spz020.

Carnevale, Anthony P. 2016. "White Flight Is Creating a Separate and Unequal System of Higher Education." *Washington Post*, December 7.

Carnevale, Anthony P., and Jeff Strohl. 2013. "Separate & Unequal: How Higher Education Reinforces the Intergenerational Reproduction of White Racial Privilege." Georgetown Public Policy Institute.

Carter, Prudence L. 2012. *Stubborn Roots: Race, Culture, and Inequality in U.S. and South African Schools*. New York: Oxford University Press.

Center for Collegiate Mental Health. 2017. "Annual Report." Retrieved from https://sites.psu.edu/ccmh/files/2018/02/2017_CCMH_Report-1r4m88x.pdf.

Chen, Rong. 2012. "Institutional Characteristics and College Student Dropout Risks: A Multilevel Event History Analysis." *Research in Higher Education* 53:487–505.

Chen, Ya-Ru, Randall S. Peterson, Damon J. Phillips, Joel M. Podolny, and Cecilia L. Ridgeway. 2012. "Introduction to the Special Issue: Bringing Status to the Table—Attaining, Maintaining, and Experiencing Status in Organizations and Markets." *Organization Science* 23:299–307.

Cherng, Hua-Yu Sebastian. 2017. "If They Think I Can: Teacher Bias and Youth of Color Expectations and Achievement." *Social Science Research* 66:170–86.

Chetty, Raj, John N. Friedman, Emmanuel Saez, Nicholas Turner, and Danny Yagan. 2017. "Mobility Report Cards: The Role of Colleges in Intergenerational Mobility." Working Paper.

Clark, Burton R. 1960. "The 'Cooling-Out' Function in Higher Education." *American Journal of Sociology* 65:569–76.

Clemens, Elisabeth S. 2006. "Sociology as a Historical Science." *American Sociologist* 37:30–40.

Clotfelter, Charles T. 2017. *Unequal Colleges in the Age of Disparity*. Cambridge, MA: Harvard University Press.

Cobham, Afeni B., and Tara L. Parker. 2007. "Resituating Race into the Movement toward Multiculturalism and Social Justice." *New Directions for Student Services* 120:85–93.

Cochrane, John. 2009. "Fiscal Stimulus, Fiscal Inflation, or Fiscal Fallacies." Version 2.5, February 27. Retrieved from http://faculty.chicagobooth.edu/john.cochrane/research/Papers/fiscal2.htm.

Cohen, Michael D., James G. March, and Johan P. Olsen. 1972. "A Garbage Can Model of Organizational Choice." *Administrative Science Quarterly* 17:1–25.

College Board. 2013. "Trends in Student Aid: 2013." College Board Trends in Higher Education Series.

———. 2018. "Trends in Higher Education: Undergraduate Enrollment and Percentage Receiving Pell Grants over Time." College Board Trends in Higher Education Series.

Collins, Patricia Hill. 1990. *Black Feminist Thought: Knowledge, Consciousness, and the Politics of Empowerment*. New York: Routledge.

———. 2004. *Black Sexual Politics: African Americans, Gender, and the New Racism*. New York: Routledge.

Collins, Patricia Hill, and Sirma Bilge. 2016. *Intersectionality*. Cambridge: Polity Press.

Combahee River Collective. (1977) 1983. "The Combahee River Collective Statement." Pp. 272–82 in *Home Girls: A Black Feminist Anthology*, edited by Barbara Smith. New York: Kitchen Table; Women of Color Press.

Connell, Raewyn. 2019. *The Good University: What Universities Actually Do and Why It's Time for Radical Change*. London: Zed Books.

Conrad, Clifton, and Marybeth Gasman. 2015. *Educating a Diverse Nation: Lessons from Minority-Serving Institutions*. Cambridge, MA: Harvard University Press.

Conwell, Jordan A. 2016. "Josephs without Pharaohs: The Du Boisian Framework for the Sociology of Education." *Journal of Negro Education* 85:28–45.

Cooper, Melinda. 2017. *Family Values: Between Neoliberalism and the New Social Conservatism*. New York: Zone.

Cottom, Tressie McMillan. 2017. *Lower Ed: The Troubling Rise of For-Profit Colleges in the New Economy*. New York: New Press.

Courteau, Rose. 2016. "The Problem with How Higher Education Treats Diversity." *The Atlantic*, October 28.

Cramer, Katherine. 2020. "Understanding the Role of Racism in Contemporary US Public Opinion." *Annual Review of Political Science* 23, https://doi.org/10.1146/annurev-polisci-060418-042842.

Crenshaw, Kimberlé W. 1991. "Mapping the Margins: Intersectionality, Identity Politics, and Violence against Women of Color." *Stanford Law Review* 43:1241–99.

———. 2007. "Framing Affirmative Action." *Michigan Law Review First Impressions* 105:123–33.

———. 2016. "Keynote Address: On Intersectionality." Presented at Women of the World Festival, London, March 14. Retrieved from https://www.youtube.com/watch?v=-DW4HLgYPlA, June 18, 2018.

Crow, Michael M., and William B. Dabars. 2015. *Designing the New American University*. Baltimore: Johns Hopkins University Press.

Cunningham, Alisa F., and Deborah H. Santiago. 2008. *Student Aversion to Borrowing: Who Borrows and Who Doesn't*. Institute for Higher Education Policy and Excelencia in Education, Washington, DC.

Curs, Bradley R., and Ozan Jaquette. 2017. "Crowded Out? The Effect of Nonresident Enrollment on Resident Access to Public Research Universities." *Educational Evaluation and Policy Analysis* 39:644–69.

Dahlander, Linus, and Daniel A. McFarland. 2013. "Ties That Last: Tie Formation and Persistence in Research Collaborations over Time." *Administrative Science Quarterly* 58:69–110.

Davies, Scott, and David Zarifa. 2012. "The Stratification of Universities: Structural

Inequality in Canada and the United States." *Research in Social Stratification and Mobility* 30:143–58.

Davis, Daniel, and Amy Binder. 2016. "Selling Students: The Rise of Corporate Partnership Programs in University Career Centers." *Research in the Sociology of Organizations* 46:395–422.

Deil-Amen, Regina. 2015. "The 'Traditional' College Student: A Smaller and Smaller Minority and Its Implications for Diversity and Access Institutions." Pp. 133–68 in *Remaking College: The Changing Ecology of Higher Education*, edited by Michael W. Kirst and Mitchell L. Stevens. Stanford, CA: Stanford University Press.

Deming, David J., and Christopher R. Walters. 2017. "The Impact of Price Caps and Spending Cuts on U.S. Postsecondary Attainment." NBER Working Paper No. 23736.

Desrochers, Lindsay A. 2007. "A Fragile Birth." Pp. 27–40 in *From Rangeland to Research University: The Birth of University of California, Merced*, edited by Karen Merritt and Jane F. Lawrence. Hoboken, NJ: Wiley Periodicals.

Dickson, Lisa. 2010. "Race and Gender Differences in College Major Choice." *ANNALS of the American Academy* 627:108–24.

DiNapoli, Thomas. 2013. "Private Financing of Public Infrastructure: Risks and Options for New York State." Office of the State Comptroller.

Dirks, Nicholas B. 2015. "Rebirth of the Research University." *Chronicle of Higher Education*, April 27.

Douglas, Priscilla H. 2008. "Affinity Groups: Catalyst for Inclusive Organizations." *Employment Relations* 34:11–18.

Douglas, Susan J., and Meredith W. Michaels. 2004. *The Mommy Myth: The Idealization of Motherhood and How It Has Undermined All Women*. New York: Free Press.

Douglass, John Aubrey. 2007. *The Conditions for Admission: Access, Equity, and the Social Contract of Public Universities*. Stanford, CA: Stanford University Press.

———. 2000. *The California Idea and American Higher Education, 1850 to the 1960 Master Plan*. Palo Alto, CA: Stanford University Press.

Dow, Sheila C. 2015. "The Role of Belief in the Case for Austerity Policies." *Economic and Labour Relations Review* 26:29–42.

Du Bois, W. E. B. 1898. "The Study of the Negro Problem." *Annals of the American Academy of Political and Social Science* 11:1–23.

———. (1935) 1999. *Black Reconstruction in America 1860–1880*. New York: Simon and Schuster.

———. 1935. "Does the Negro Need Separate Schools?" *Journal of Negro Education* 4:328–35.

Eagan, Kevin, Ellen Bara Stolzenberg, Abigail K. Bates, Melissa C. Aragon, Maria R. Suchard, and Celilia Rios-Aguilar. 2016. *The American Freshman: National Norms Fall 2015*. UCLA Higher Education Research Institution.

Eason, John M. 2017. *Big House on the Prairie: Rise of the Rural Ghetto and Prison Proliferation*. Chicago: University of Chicago Press.

Eaton, Charlie. 2020a. *Bankers in the Ivory Tower: Finance and the Rise of Inequality in*

U.S. Higher Education and Society. Manuscript under contract with University of Chicago Press.

———. 2020b. "Agile Predators: Private Equity and the Spread of Shareholder Value Strategies to U.S. For-Profit Colleges." *Socio-Economic Review*, https://doi: 10.1093/ser/mwaa005.

Eaton, Charlie, Adam Goldstein, Jacob Habinek, Mukul Kumar, Tamera L. Stover, and Alex Roehrkasse. 2013. "Bankers in the Ivory Tower: The Financialization of Governance at the University of California." IRLE Working Paper No. 151–13.

Eaton, Charlie, Jacob Habinek, Mukul Kumar, Tamera L. Stover, Alex Roehrkasse, and Jeremy Thompson. 2013. "Swapping Our Future: How Students and Taxpayers Are Funding Risky UC Borrowing and Wall Street Profits." *Berkeley Journal of Sociology* 57:178–99.

Eaton, Charlie, Jacob Habinek, Adam Goldstein, Cyrus Dioun, Daniela Godoy, and Robert Osley-Thomas. 2016. "The Financialization of US Higher Education." *Socio-Economic Review* 14:507–35.

Eaton, Charlie, Sheisha Kulkami, Robert Birgeneau, Henry Brady, and Michael Hout. 2019. "The Organizational Ecology of College Affordability: Research Activity, State Grant Aid Policies, and Student Debt at U.S. Public Universities." *Socius* 5:1–19.

Eaton, Charlie, and Margaret Weir. 2015. "The Power of Coalitions: Advancing the Public in California's Public-Private Welfare State." *Politics & Society* 43:3–32.

Education Trust. 2015. "The Pell Partnership: Ensuring a Shared Responsibility for Low-Income Student Success."

———. 2017. "A Look at Black Student Success: Identifying Top- and Bottom-Performing Institutions."

Edwards, Julie, Glenda Crosling, and Ron Edwards. 2010. "Outsourcing University Degrees: Implications for Quality Control." *Journal of Higher Education Policy and Management* 32:303–15.

Elevate. 2015. "The Elevate Employee Resource Group (ERG) Academy Releases the Best Companies for ERGs."

Emirbayer, Mustafa, and Victoria Johnson. 2008. "Bourdieu and Organizational Analysis." *Theory and Society* 37:1–44.

Eno, Jared. 2019. "The Reconstruction of Racialized Classification Schemes in US Higher Education During the 1960s and 70s." Dissertation proposal, University of Michigan-Ann Arbor.

Erickson, David J. 2009. "Housing Policy Revolution: Networks and Neighborhoods." Washington, DC: Urban Institute.

Erikson, Robert, and Jan O. Jonsson. 1996. "The Swedish Context: Educational Reform and Long-Term Change in Educational Inequality." Pp. 65–93 in *Can Education Be Equalized? The Swedish Case in Comparative Perspective*, edited by Robert Erikson and Jan O. Jonsson. Boulder: Westview Press.

Espeland, Wendy, and Michael Sauder. 2016. *Engines of Anxiety*. New York: Russell Sage Publications.

Espenshade, Thomas J., Chang Y. Chung, and Joan L. Walling. 2004. "Admission Preferences for Minority Students, Athletes, and Legacies at Elite Universities." *Social Science Quarterly* 85:1422–46.

Evans, Peter, and William Sewell. 2013. "The Neoliberal Era: Ideology, Policy, and Social Effects." Pp. 35–68 in *Social Resilience in the Neo-Liberal Era*, edited by Peter Hall and Michèle Lamont. Cambridge: Cambridge University Press.

Fabricant, Michael, and Stephen Brier. 2016. *Austerity Blues: Fighting for the Soul of Public Education*. Baltimore: Johns Hopkins Press.

Fain, Paul. 2019. "ASU Looks Overseas with New Spin-Off." *Inside Higher Ed*, August 27.

Fairlie, Robert W., and Alexandra M. Resch. 2002. "Is There 'White Flight' into Private Schools? Evidence from the National Educational Longitudinal Survey." *Review of Economics and Statistics* 84:21–33.

Faller, Mary Beth. 2018. "ASU Breaks Ground on Mirabella Project." Retrieved from https://asunow.asu.edu/20180221-arizona-impact-asu-breaks-ground-mirabella-project.

Fang, Jenn. 2014. "Filipinos Are Underrepresented at Most Selective of UC Campuses." Retrieved from http://reappropriate.co/2014/12/filipinos-are-under represented-at-most-competitive-of-uc-campuses-blockblum-iamnotyour wedge/.

Feagin, Joe R., Hernán Vera, and Nikitah Imani. 1996. *The Agony of Education: Black Students at White Colleges*. New York: Routledge.

Ferguson, Roderick A. 2012. *The Reorder of Things: The University and Its Pedagogies of Minority Difference*. Minneapolis: University of Minnesota Press.

Fligstein, Neil. 1990. *The Transformation of Corporate Control*. Cambridge, MA: Harvard University Press.

———. 2001. *The Architecture of Markets: An Economic Sociology of Twenty-First-Century Capitalist Societies*. Princeton, NJ: Princeton University Press.

Flores, Nelson, and Jonathan Rosa. 2015. "Undoing Appropriateness: Raciolinguistic Ideologies and Language Diversity in Education." *Harvard Educational Review* 85:149–71.

Fourcade, Marion, and Kieran Healy. 2007. "Moral Views of Market Society." *Annual Review of Sociology* 33:285–311.

———. 2013. "Classification Situations: Life-Chances in the Neoliberal Era." *Accounting, Organizations, and Society* 38:559–72.

Fox, Cybelle. 2004. "The Changing Color of Welfare? How Whites' Attitudes toward Latinos Influence Support for Welfare." *American Journal of Sociology* 110:580–625.

Freedle, Roy O. 2003. "Correcting the SAT's Ethnic and Social-Class Bias: A Method for Reestimating SAT Scores." *Harvard Educational Review* 73:1–43.

Friedman, Milton. 1951. "Neoliberalism and Its Prospects." Collected Works of Milton Friedman Project records, Hoover Institution Archives. Retrieved from https://miltonfriedman.hoover.org/objects/57816.

———. (1962) 2009. *Capitalism and Freedom*. Chicago: University of Chicago Press.

Fryar, Alisa H. 2015. "The Comprehensive University: How It Came to Be and What It Is Now." Pp. 19–42 in *The University Next Door: What Is a Comprehensive University, Who Does It Educate, and Can It Survive?*, edited by Mark Schneider and K. C. Deane. New York: Teachers College Press.

Fukuyama, Francis. 1989. "The End of History?" *The National Interest*: 3–18.

Gaddis, S. Michael. 2014. "Discrimination in the Credential Society: An Audit Study of Race and College Selectivity in the Labor Market." *Social Forces* 9:1451–79.

Garcia, Gina Ann. 2019. *Becoming Hispanic Serving Institutions: Opportunities for Colleges & Universities*. Baltimore: Johns Hopkins University Press.

Gardner, Lee. 2019. "The Rise of the Mega-University." *Chronicle of Higher Education*, February 18.

Gastón, Pablo. 2019. *A Caring Class: Labor Contention and the Moral Economy of Care in California Hospitals*. Book manuscript.

Geiger, Roger L. 2004. *Knowledge and Money: Research Universities and the Paradox of the Marketplace*. Stanford, CA: Stanford University Press.

Gelbgiser, Dafna. 2018. "College for All, Degrees for Few: For-Profit Colleges and Socioeconomic Differences in Degree Attainment." *Social Forces* 96:1785–1824.

Gilens, Martin. 1995. "Racial Attitudes and Opposition to Welfare." *Journal of Politics* 57:994–1014.

———. 1999. *Why Americans Hate Welfare*. Chicago: University of Chicago Press.

Gilmore, Ruth W. 2007. *Golden Gulag: Prisons, Surplus, Crisis, and Opposition in Globalizing California*. Berkeley: University of California Press.

Gladieux, Lawrence E., and Thomas R. Wolanin. 1976. *Congress and the Colleges: The National Politics of Higher Education*. Lexington, MA: Lexington Books.

Golash-Boza, Tanya. 2016. *Race and Racisms: Brief Edition*. New York: Oxford University Press.

Golash-Boza, Tanya, and Zulema Valdez. 2018. "Nested Contexts of Reception: Undocumented Students at the University of California, Central." *Sociological Perspectives* 61:535–52.

Goldrick-Rab, Sara. 2016. *Paying the Price: College Costs, Financial Aid, and the Betrayal of the American Dream*. Chicago: University of Chicago Press.

Goldrick-Rab, Sara, and Nancy Kendall. 2014. "Redefining College Affordability: Securing America's Future with a Free Two-Year College Option." Lumina Foundation.

Goldrick-Rab, Sara, and Michelle Miller-Adams. 2018. "Don't Dismiss the Value of Free-College Programs. They Do Help Low-Income Students." *Chronicle of Higher Education*, September 7.

Gomer, Justin, and Christopher Petrella. 2017. "How the Reagan Administration Stoked Fears of Anti-White Racism." *Washington Post*, October 10.

Grawe, Nathan D. 2018. *Demographics and the Demand for Higher Education*. Baltimore: Johns Hopkins University Press.

Grollman, Eric A. 2014. "Multiple Disadvantaged Statuses and Health: The Role of Multiple Forms of Discrimination." *Journal of Health and Social Behavior* 55: 3–19.

Habley, Wesley R. 2004. *The Status of Academic Advising: Findings from the ACT Sixth National Survey*. Manhattan, KS: National Academic Advising Association.

Hacker, Jacob. 2002. *The Divided Welfare State: The Battle over Public and Private Social Benefits in the United States*. New York: Cambridge University Press.

Hall, Peter A., and Michèle Lamont. 2013. *Social Resilience in the Neoliberal Era*. Cambridge: Cambridge University Press.

Hallett, Tim. 2010. "The Myth Incarnate: Recoupling Processes, Turmoil, and Inhabited Institutions in an Urban Elementary School." *American Sociological Review* 75:52–74.

Hallett, Tim, and Marc J. Ventresca. 2006. "Inhabited Institutions: Social Interactions and Organizational Forms in Gouldner's *Patterns of Industrial Bureaucracy*." *Theory and Society* 35:213–36.

Hamilton, Darrick, and William A. Darity Jr. 2017. "The Political Economy of Education, Financial Literacy, and the Racial Wealth Gap." *Federal Reserve Bank of St. Lewis REVIEW*. First Quarter: 59–76.

Hamilton, Laura. 2016. *Parenting to a Degree: How Family Matters for College Women's Success*. Chicago: University of Chicago Press.

Hamilton, Laura T., Elizabeth A. Armstrong, J. Lotus Seeley, and Elizabeth M. Armstrong. 2019. "Hegemonic Femininities and Intersectional Domination." *Sociological Theory* 37:315–41.

Hamilton, Laura T., Josipa Roksa, and Kelly Nielsen. 2018. "Providing a 'Leg Up': Parental Involvement and Opportunity Hoarding in College." *Sociology of Education* 91:111–31.

Hampshire College. 2019. "FAQ about Hampshire's Test Blind Admission Policy." Retrieved from https://www.hampshire.edu/admissions/faq-about-hampshires-test-blind-admission-policy.

Haney López, Ian. 2014. *Dog Whistle Politics: How Coded Racial Appeals Have Reinvented Racism & Wrecked the Middle Class*. New York: Oxford University Press.

Harring, Alex, and Elizabeth Lawrence. 2019. "Coalition of Faculty, Students Launch Campaign to Spread 'U' Resources to Flint and Dearborn Campuses." *The Michigan Daily*, January 31.

Hart, Oliver. 2003. "Incomplete Contracts and Public Ownership: Remarks, and an Application to Public-Private Partnerships." *Economic Journal* 119:69–76.

Hartocollis, Anemona. 2019. "SAT 'Adversity Score' Is Abandoned in Wake of Criticism." *New York Times*, August 27.

Haveman, Heather A., and Gillian Gualtieri. 2017. "Institutional Logics." In *Oxford Research Encyclopedia of Business and Management*, edited by Ray Aldag. New York: Oxford University Press.

Hays, Sharon. 2003. *Flat Broke with Children: Women in the Age of Welfare Reform*. New York: Oxford University Press.

Hearn, James, Darrell R. Lewis, Lincoln Kallsen, Janet M. Holdsworth, and Lisa M. Jones. 2006. "'Incentives for Managed Growth': A Case Study of Incentives-Based Planning and Budgeting in a Large Public Research University." *Journal of Higher Education* 77:286–316.

Hefner, David. 2002. "Black Cultural Centers: Standing on Shaky Ground?" *Black Issues in Higher Education* 18:22–29.

Henriques, Gregg. 2014. "The College Student Mental Health Crisis." *Psychology Today*, February 15.

Hertel, Curtis, and Jon Hoadley. 2019. "University of Michigan Students in Flint and Dearborn Are Shortchanged. That Has to Stop." *Detroit Free Press*, May 15.

Higher Education Act of 1965 (HEA). Pub.L. 89–329.

Hinderaker, Ivan, and Birk Hinderaker. 1998. Oral history and transcript. Retrieved from http://www.ucrhistory.ucr.edu/pdf/hinderakeri.pdf.

Hirschman, Daniel, and Laura Garbes. 2019. "Towards an Economic Sociology of Race." *Socio-Economic Review*, https://doi.org/10.1093/ser/mwz054.

Hirshfield, Laura E., and Tiffany D. Joseph. 2012. "'We Need a Woman, We Need a Black Woman': Gender, Race, and Identity Taxation in the Academy." *Gender and Education* 24:213–27.

HispanicPR. 2012. "PepsiCo's Adelante Named 2011 Employee Resource Group at Latina Style 50 Awards." Retrieved from http://www.hispanicprblog.com/pepsico-adelante/.

Hiss, William C., and Valerie W. Franks. 2014. "Defining Promise: Optional Standardized Testing Policies in American College and University Admissions." Retrieved from https://www.luminafoundation.org/resources/defining-promise.

Holland, Megan, and Karly Ford. 2020. "Legitimating Prestige through Diversity: How Higher Education Institutions Represent Ethno-Racial Diversity Across Levels of Selectivity." *Journal of Higher Education*, https://doi.org/10.1080/00221546.2020.1740532.

Hollinger, David A. 2013. "The Wedge Driving Academe's Two Families Apart." *Chronicle of Higher Education*, October 14.

Hong, Grace Kyungwon. 2015. "Neoliberalism." *Critical Ethnic Studies* 1:56–67.

Hong, Peter Y. 2004. "Last Hurdle Cleared, UC Merced on Track for Debut." *Los Angeles Times*, August 14.

hooks, bell. 1984. *Feminist Theory: From Margin to Center*. Cambridge: South End Press.

Horowitz, Helen Lefkowitz. 1987. *Campus Life: Undergraduate Cultures from the End of the Eighteenth Century to the Present*. Chicago: University of Chicago Press.

HoSang, Daniel M. 2010. *Racial Propositions: Ballot Initiatives and the Making of Postwar California*. Berkeley: University of California Press.

Houle, Jason N. 2013. "Disparities in Debt: Parents' Socioeconomic Resources and Young Adult Student Loan Debt." *Sociology of Education* 87:53–69.

Houle, Jason, and Fenaba Addo. 2019. "Racial Disparities in Student Debt and the Reproduction of the Fragile Black Middle Class." *Sociology of Race and Ethnicity* 5:562–77.

House Committee on Education and the Workforce. 2014. "The Just-In-Time Professor: A Staff Report Summarizing eForum Responses on the Working Conditions of Contingent Faculty in Higher Education." U.S. House of Representatives.

Hout, Michael. 2012. "Social and Economic Returns to College Education in the United States." *Annual Review of Sociology* 38:379–400.

Hoxby, Caroline M., and Sarah Turner. 2019. "Measuring Opportunity in U.S. Higher Education." Stanford University and NBER Working Paper.

Huang, Georgene. 2017. "90% of Fortune 500 Companies Already Have a Solution to Gender Equality But Aren't Utilizing It." *Forbes*, November 13.

Huelsman, Mark. 2015. *The Debt Divide: The Racial and Class Bias Behind the "New Normal" of Student Borrowing*. New York: Demos.

Hunt, Justin, and Daniel Eisenberg. 2010. "Mental Health Problems and Help-Seeking Behavior Among College Students." *Journal of Adolescent Health* 46:3–10.

Hurtado, Aida. 1996. *The Color of Privilege: Three Blasphemies of Race and Feminism.* Ann Arbor: University of Michigan Press.

Inwood, Joshua F. J. 2015. "Neoliberal Racism: The 'Southern Strategy' and the Expanding Geographies of White Supremacy." *Social & Cultural Geography* 16: 407–23.

Irizarry, Yasmiyn. 2015a. "Utilizing Multidimensional Measures of Race in Education Research: The Case of Teacher Perception." *Sociology of Race and Ethnicity* 1:564–83.

———. 2015b. "Selling Students Short: Racial Differences in Teachers' Evaluations of High, Average, and Low Performing Students." *Social Science Research* 52: 522–38.

Jack, Anthony A. 2019. *The Privileged Poor: How Elite Colleges are Failing Disadvantaged Students*. Cambridge, MA: Harvard University Press.

Jackson, John P., and Nadine M. Weidman. 2006. *Race, Racism, and Science: Social Impact and Interactions*. New Brunswick, NJ: Rutgers University Press.

Jacob, Brian, Brian McCall, and Kevin Stange. 2018. "College as Country Club: Do Colleges Cater to Students' Preferences for Consumption?" *Journal of Labor Economics* 36:309–48.

Jaggars, Shanna S. 2011. "Online Learning: Does It Help Low-Income and Underprepared Students?" Working Paper, Community College Research Center, Teachers College, Columbia University.

Jaquette, Ozan, Bradley R. Curs, and Julie R. Posselt. 2016. "Tuition Rich, Mission Poor: Nonresident Enrollment Growth and the Socioeconomic and Racial Composition of Public Research Universities." *Journal of Higher Education* 87: 635–73.

Jaquette, Ozan, Dennis A. Kramer, and Bradley R. Curs. 2018. "Growing the Pie? The Effect of Responsibility Center Management on Tuition Revenue." *Journal of Higher Education* 89:637–76.

Jayakumar, Uma M., and Samuel D. Museus. 2012. "Mapping the Intersection of Campus Cultures and Equitable Outcomes among Racially Diverse Student Populations." Pp. 1–27 in *Creating Campus Cultures: Fostering Success among Racially Diverse Student Populations*, edited by Samuel D. Museus and Uma M. Jayakumar. New York: Routledge.

Jones, Janelle. 2017. "The Racial Wealth Gap: How African-Americans Have Been

Shortchanged out of the Materials to Build Wealth." Economic Policy Institute. Retrieved from https://www.epi.org/blog/the-racial-wealth-gap-how-african-americans-have-been-shortchanged-out-of-the-materials-to-build-wealth/.

Kahlenberg, Richard D. 2015. "How Higher Education Shortchanges Community Colleges." Century Foundation.

Kamenetz, Anya. 2019 "What if Elite Colleges Switched to a Lottery for Admissions?" NPR Education, March 27.

Kao, Grace, and Jennifer S. Thompson. 2003. "Racial and Ethnic Stratification in Educational Achievement and Attainment." *Annual Review of Sociology* 29: 417–42.

Karabel, Jerome. 2005. *The Chosen: The Hidden History of Admission and Exclusion at Harvard, Yale, and Princeton*. New York: Houghton Mifflin.

Kendi, Ibram X. 2019. *How to Be an Antiracist*. Random House: New York.

Kerr, Clark. (1963) 2001. *The Uses of the University*, 5th ed. Cambridge, MA: Harvard University Press.

King, C. Judson. 2018. *The University of California: Creating, Nurturing, and Maintaining Academic Quality in a Public University Setting*. Berkeley: University of California Press.

Kohler-Hausmann, Julilly. 2007. "'The Crime of Survival': Fraud Prosecutions, Community Surveillance, and the Original 'Welfare Queen.'" *Journal of Social History* 41:329–54.

Konings, Martijn. 2018. *Capital and Time: For a New Critique of Neoliberal Reason*. Stanford, CA: Stanford University Press.

Korpi, Walter, and Joakim Palme. 2004. "Robin Hood, St. Matthew, or Simple Egalitarianism? Strategies of Equality in Welfare States." Pp. 153–79 in *A Handbook of Comparative Social Policy*, edited by Patricia Kennet. Cheltenham, UK: Edward Elgar.

Kotsko, Adam. 2018. *Neoliberalism's Demons: On the Political Theology of Late Capital*. Stanford, CA: Stanford University Press.

Kraemer, Jackie. 2013. "Statistic of the Month: Comparing Community College Completion Rates." National Center on Education and the Economy. Retrieved from http://ncee.org/2013/05/statistic-of-the-month-comparing-community-college-completion-rates/.

Krippner, Greta R. 2005. "The Financialization of the American Economy." *Socio-Economic Review* 3:173–208.

———. 2011. *Capitalizing on Crisis: The Political Origins of the Rise of Finance*. Cambridge, MA: Harvard University Press.

Krogstad, Jens M., and Richard Fry. 2014. "More Hispanics, Blacks Enrolling in College, But Lag in Bachelor's Degrees." PEW Research Center, April 14.

Kuang, Chris. 2017. "The Unlikely Couple: The Rise of Public-Private Partnerships in the United States." *Harvard Political Review*, June 14.

Kwak, Young H., YoungYi Chih, and C. William Ibbs. 2009. "Towards a Comprehensive Understanding of Public Private Partnerships for Infrastructure Development." *California Management Review* 51:51–78.

Labaree, David F. 2010. *Someone Has to Fail: The Zero-Sum Game of Public Schooling.* Cambridge, MA: Harvard University Press.

———. 2017. *A Perfect Mess: The Unlikely Ascendancy of American Higher Education.* Chicago: University of Chicago Press.

Lake, Peter. 2013. *The Rights and Responsibilities of the Modern University: The Rise of the Facilitator University*, 2nd ed. Durham, NC: Carolina Academic Press.

Lambert, Matthew T. 2014. *Privatization and the Public Good: Public Universities in the Balance.* Cambridge, MA: Harvard University Press.

Lee, Elizabeth, and Chaise LaDousa, eds. 2015. *College Students' Experiences of Power and Marginality: Sharing Spaces and Negotiating Differences.* New York: Routledge.

Lee, Jennifer, and Min Zhou. 2015. *The Asian American Achievement Paradox.* New York: Russell Sage Foundation.

Lee, Robert, and Tristan Ahtone. 2020. "Land-Grab Universities." *High Country News*, March 30.

Leland, Dorothy, and John Moore. 2007. "Strategic Focusing: Securing Competitive Advantage." *Public Purpose Magazine*, September–October. Association of American Colleges and Universities.

Leong, Nancy. 2013. "Racial Capitalism." *Harvard Law Review* 126(8):2153–25.

Lerma, Veronica, Laura Hamilton, and Kelly Nielsen. 2019. "Racialized Equity Labor, University Appropriation, and Student Resistance." *Social Problems*, https://doi.org/10.1093/socpro/spz011.

Lewis, Amanda. 2003. *Race in the Schoolyard: Negotiating the Color Line in Classrooms and Communities.* Piscataway, NJ: Rutgers University Press.

Lewis, Amanda E., and John B. Diamond. 2015. *Despite the Best Intentions: How Racial Inequality Thrives in Good Schools.* New York: Oxford University Press.

Lewis, James L., Holly Menzies, Edgar I. Nájera, and Reba N. Page. 2009. "Rethinking Trends in Minority Participation in the Sciences." *Science Education* 93: 961–77.

Liddell, Debora. 2018. "JCSD Supplemental Style Guide for Bias-Free Writing." *Journal of College Student Development* 59:1–2.

Link, Bruce G., and J. Phelan. 1995. "Social Conditions as Fundamental Causes of Disease." *Journal of Health and Social Behavior* 35:80–94.

Looney, Adam, and Constantine Yannelis. 2015. "A Crisis in Student Loans?" *Brookings Papers on Economic Activity* 2:1–89.

Loss, Christopher P. 2012. *Between Citizens and the State: The Politics of American Higher Education in the 20th Century.* Princeton, NJ: Princeton University.

Lounsbury, Michael, and Hayagreeva Rao. 2004. "Sources of Durability and Change in Market Classifications: A Study of Produce Categories in the American Mutual Fund Industry." *Social Forces* 82:969–99.

Lowen, Rebecca S. 1997. *Creating the Cold War University: The Transformation of Stanford.* Berkeley: University of California Press.

Lubiano, Wahneema. 1992. "Black Ladies, Welfare Queens, and State Minstrels: Ideological War by Narrative Means" Pp. 323–63 in *Race-ing Justice, En-gendering Power*, edited by Toni Morrison. New York: Pantheon.

MacLean, Nancy. 2017. *Democracy in Chains: The Deep History of the Radical Right's Stealth Plan for America*. New York: Penguin.

Malkiel, Nancy W. 2016. *"Keep the Damned Women Out": The Struggle for Coeducation*. Princeton, NJ: Princeton University Press.

Malter, Daniel. 2014. "On the Causality and Cause Returns to Organizational Status: Evidence from the Grans Crus Classés of the Médoc." *Administrative Science Quarterly* 59:271–300.

Marcus, Jon. 2017. "Graduate Programs Have Become a Cash Cow for Struggling Colleges. What Does that Mean for Students?" *PBS News Hour*, September 18.

Marginson, Simon. 2016. *The Dream Is Over: The Crisis of Clark Kerr's California Idea of Higher Education*. Berkeley: University of California Press.

Martin, Isaac, Jerome Karabel, and Sean W. Jaquez. 2005. "High School Segregation and Access to the University of California." *Educational Policy* 19:308–30.

Massey, Douglas S., and Nancy Denton. 1993. *American Apartheid: Segregation and the Making of the Underclass*. Cambridge, MA: Harvard University Press.

Matthew, Dayna B. 2015. *Just Medicine: A Cure for Racial Inequality in American Health Care*. New York: New York University Press.

Matthew, Patricia A. 2016. *Written/Unwritten: Diversity and the Hidden Truths of Tenure*. Chapel Hill: University of North Carolina Press.

McCabe, Janice. 2009. "Racial and Gender Microaggressions on a Predominantly-White Campus: Experiences of Black, Latina/o and White Undergraduates." *Race, Gender & Class* 16:133–51.

McMurtrie, Beth. 2017. "In California, Tensions over Growth Divide a Campus." *Chronicle of Higher Education*, January 19.

Mehta, Seema, and Melanie Mason. 2017. "After Dividing California Democrats in 2014, Affirmative Action Resurfaces in the Race for Governor." *Los Angeles Times*, August 13.

Melamed, Jodi. 2006. "The Spirit of Neoliberalism: From Racial Liberalism to Neoliberal Multiculturalism." *Social Text* 89:1–24.

Merritt, Karen, and Jane F. Lawrence, eds. 2007. *From Rangeland to Research University: The Birth of University of California, Merced*. Hoboken, NJ: Wiley Periodicals.

Mettler, Suzanne. 2011. *The Submerged State: How Invisible Government Policies Undermine American Democracy*. Chicago: University of Chicago Press.

———. 2014. *Degrees of Inequality: How the Politics of Higher Education Sabotaged the American Dream*. New York: Basic Books.

Miraftab, Faranak. 2004. "Public-Private Partnerships: The Trojan Horse of Neoliberal Development?" *Journal of Planning Education and Research* 24:89–101.

Mirowski, Philip. 2014. *Never Let a Serious Crisis Go to Waste: How Neoliberalism Survived the Financial Meltdown*. London: Verso.

Mitchell, Michael, Michael Leachman, and Kathleen Masterson. 2017. "A Lost Decade in Higher Education Funding. State Cuts Have Driven Up Tuition and Reduced Quality." *Center on Budget and Policy Priorities*, August 23.

Mohr, John W., and Helene K. Lee. 2000. "From Affirmative Action to Outreach: Discourse Shifts at the University of California." *Poetics* 28:47–71.

Molesworth, Mike, Richard Scullion, and Elizabeth Nixon, eds. 2011. *The Marketisation of Higher Education and the Student as Consumer*. New York: Routledge.

Moore, Mignon R. 2017. "Women of Color in the Academy: Navigating Multiple Intersections and Multiple Hierarchies." *Social Problems* 64:200–205.

Moore, Wendy L. 2008. *Reproducing Racism: White Space, Elite Law Schools, and Racial Inequality*. Lanham, MD: Rowman & Littlefield.

———. 2018. "Maintaining Supremacy by Blocking Affirmative Action." *Contexts* 17:54–59.

Moretti, Enrico. 2013. *The New Geography of Jobs*. New York: Houghton Mifflin Harcourt Publishing Company.

Morgan, Kimberly, and Andrea Campbell. 2011. *The Delegated Welfare State: Medicare, Markets, and the Governance of Social Policy*. New York: Oxford University Press.

Morphew, Christopher C., and Peter D. Eckel, eds. 2009. *Privatizing the Public University: Perspectives from Across the Academy*. Baltimore: Johns Hopkins University Press.

Mudge, Stephanie L. 2008. "What Is Neo-Liberalism?" *Socio-Economic Review* 6: 703–31.

———. 2018. *Leftism Reinvented: Western Parties from Socialism to Neoliberalism*. Cambridge, MA: Harvard University Press.

Murphy, Katy. 2016. "University of California Debt Soars to $17 Billion; Regents Consider New Borrowing Policy." *Mercury News*, September 14.

Nenga, Sandi Kawecka, Guillermo A. Alvarado, and Claire S. Blyth. 2015. "'I Kind of Found My People': Latino/a College Students' Search for Social Integration on Campus." Pp. 29–45 in *College Students' Experiences of Power and Marginality: Sharing Spaces and Negotiating Differences*, edited by E. M. Lee and C. LaDousa. New York: Routledge.

Newfield, Christopher. 2008. *Unmaking the Public University: The Forty-Year Assault on the Middle Class*. Cambridge, MA: Harvard University Press.

———. 2016. *The Great Mistake: How We Wrecked Public Universities and How We Can Fix Them*. Baltimore: Johns Hopkins Press.

Nichols, Andrew H., and Denzel Evans-Bell. 2017. "A Look at Black Student Success: Identifying Top- and Bottom-Performing Institutions." Washington, DC: Education Trust.

Nielsen, Kelly. 2015. "'Fake It 'til You Make It': Why Community College Students' Aspirations 'Hold Steady.'" *Sociology of Education* 88:265–83.

Ochoa, Gilda L. 2013. *Academic Profiling: Latinos, Asian Americans, and the Achievement Gap*. Minneapolis: University of Minnesota Press.

Olivares, Abraham, Lionel Onsurez, Michal Allen, Jeff Wheeler, Andrew Pianka, Katie Hatfield, Luannie Colina, Emily Wentworth, Gregg Herken, and Justine Issavi. 2009. *The Fairy Shrimp Chronicles: An Informal History of the Founding of UC Merced*. Merced: University of California, Merced.

Olsen, Gary. 2010. "Why Universities Reorganize." *Chronicle of Higher Education*, August 15.

Olzak, Susan, Suzanne Shanahan, and E. West. 1994. "School Desegregation, Interracial Exposure, and Antibusing Activity in Contemporary Urban America." *American Journal of Sociology* 100:196–241.

Omi, Michael, and Howard Winant. 2015. *Racial Formation in the United States*, 3rd ed. New York: Routledge.

Ortved, John. 2013. "Ratchet: The Rap Insult That Became a Compliment." *The Cut*, April 11.

Owen-Smith, Jason. 2018. *Research Universities and the Public Good: Discovery for an Uncertain Future*. Stanford, CA: Stanford University Press.

Owens, Ann. 2017. "Racial Residential Segregation of School-Age Children and Adults and the Role of Schooling as a Segregating Force." *RSF: The Russell Sage Foundation Journal of the Social Sciences* 3:63–80.

P3 Higher Education Summit. 2018. Retrieved from https://www.p3highereduca tion.com/, July 16.

Pager, Devah. 2007. *Marked: Race, Crime, and Finding Work in an Era of Mass Incarceration*. Chicago: University of Chicago Press.

Panzar, Javier. 2015. "It's Official: Latinos Now Outnumber Whites in California." *Los Angeles Times*, July 8.

Patel, Leigh. 2019. "The SAT's New 'Adversity Score' Is a Poor Fix for a Problematic Test." *The Conversation*. Retrieved from https://theconversation.com/the-sats -new-adversity-score-is-a-poor-fix-for-a-problematic-test-117363.

Patton, Lori D. 2006. "The Voice of Reason: A Qualitative Examination of Black Student Perceptions of Black Culture Centers." *Journal of College Student Development* 47:628–46.

Patton, Lori, ed. 2010. *Culture Centers in Higher Education: Perspectives on Identity, Theory, and Practice*. 2010. Sterling, VA: Stylus Publishing.

Pettit, Becky, and Bruce Western. 2004. "Mass Imprisonment and the Life Course: Race and Class Inequality in U.S. Incarceration." *American Sociological Review* 69: 151–69.

Policano, Andrew J. 2016. *From Ivory Tower to Glass House: Strategies for Academic Leaders During Turbulent Times*. Irvine, CA: Zepoli.

Postsecondary National Policy Institute. 2015. "Hispanic-Serving Institutions [HSIs]: A Background Primer." Retrieved from https://www.newamerica .org/post-secondary-national-policy-institute/our-blog/hispanic-serving -institutions-hsis/.

Poterba, James M. 1997. "Demographic Structure and the Political Economy of Public Education." *Journal of Policy Analysis and Management* 16:48–66.

Prasad, Monica. 2006. *The Politics of Free Markets: The Rise of Neoliberal Economic Policies in Britain, France, Germany, and the United States*. Chicago: University of Chicago Press.

Preer, Jean L. 1982. *Lawyers v. Educators: Black Colleges and Desegregation in Public Higher Education*. Westport, CT: Greenwood Press.

Price, Asher. 2019. "A Secret 1950s Strategy to Keep Out Black Students." *The Atlantic*. Retrieved from https://www.theatlantic.com/ideas/archive/2019/09/how -ut-used-standardized-testing-to-slow-integration/597814/.

Princes, Carolyn D. 2005. "The Precarious Question of Black Cultural Centers versus Multicultural Centers." Pp. 135–46 in *Black Culture Centers: Politics of Survival and Identity*, edited by Fred. L. Hord. Chicago: Third World Press.

Pyne, Jaymes, and Eric Grodsky. 2019. "Inequality and Opportunity in a Perfect Storm of Graduate Student Debt." *Sociology of Education* 93:20–39.

Quadagno, Jill. 1994. *The Color of Welfare: How Racism Undermined the War on Poverty.* New York: Oxford University Press.

Queiroz, Regina. 2016. "Neoliberal TINA: An Ideological and Political Subversion of Liberalism." *Critical Policy Studies* 12:227–46.

Rai, Kul B., and John W. Critzer. 2000. *Affirmative Action and the University: Race, Ethnicity, and Gender in Higher Education Employment.* Lincoln: University of Nebraska Press.

Ramirez, Marcella L. 2018. "Schoolhouse of Resistance: Critical Counterstories of Grassroots Organizers and Campus Change Agents in California Cultural Centers." Unpublished dissertation.

Ravitch, Diane. 2010. *The Death and Life of the Great American School System: How Testing and Choice Are Undermining Education.* New York: Basic Books.

———. 2013. *Reign of Error: The Hoax of the Privatization Movement and the Danger to America's Public Schools.* New York: Vintage Books.

Ray, Rashawn, and Bryant Best. 2015. "Diversity Does Not Mean Equality: De Facto Rules That Maintain Status Inequality among Black and White Fraternity Men." Pp. 152–68 in *College Students' Experiences of Power and Marginality*, edited by Lee and LaDousa.

Ray, Victor. 2019. "A Theory of Racialized Organizations." *American Sociological Review*, https://doi.org/10.1177/0003122418822335.

Ray, Victor, and Louise Seamster. 2016. "Rethinking Racial Progress: A Response to Wimmer." *Ethnic and Racial Studies* 39:1361–69.

Reardon, Sean. 2016. "School Segregation and Racial Academic Achievement Gaps." *RSF: The Russell Sage Foundation Journal of the Social Sciences* 2:34–57.

Redford, Patrick. 2017. "Cal Is Fucked Because of Its Stupid Stadium Deal." *Deadspin*, June 7.

Regents of the University of California. 2015. "Minutes from the Committee on Health Services Meeting on Jan. 22." Retrieved from http://regents.universityof california.edu/minutes/2015/h1.pdf.

Reich, Robert B. 2016. *Saving Capitalism: For the Many, Not the Few.* New York: First Vintage Books.

Reid, Roddey. 2013. "The Crisis of the Humanities and the Public Research Universities: University of California, San Diego, as a Case Study." *Occasion: Interdisciplinary Studies in the Humanities* 6:1–15.

Reinhold, Robert. 1992. "California Forced to Turn to I.O.U.'s." *New York Times*, July 2.

Renzulli, Linda A., and Lorraine Evans. 2005. "School Choice, Charter Schools, and White Flight." *Social Problems* 52:398–418.

Reuben, Julie A. 2001. "Merit, Mission, and Minority Students: The History of

Debate over Special Admissions Programs." In *A Faithful Mirror: Reflections on the College Board and Education in America*, edited by Michael C. Johanek. New York: College Board.

Reyes, Daisy. 2018. *Learning to Be Latino: How College Shape Identity Politics*. New Brunswick, NJ: Rutgers University Press.

Rhoads, Robert A. 1998. *Freedom's Web: Student Activism in an Age of Cultural Diversity*. Baltimore: Johns Hopkins Press.

Riegle-Crumb, Catherine, Barbara King, and Yasmiyn Irizarry. 2019. "Does STEM Stand Out? Examining Racial/Ethnic Gaps in Persistence Across Postsecondary Fields." *Educational Researcher*, https://doi.org/10.3102/0013189X19831006.

Ringquist, Evan J. 2005. "Assessing Evidence of Environmental Inequities: A Meta-Analysis." *Journal of Policy Analysis and Management* 24:223–47.

Rios, Victor. 2011. *Punished: Policing the Lives of Black and Latino Boys*. New York: New York University Press.

Rivard, Ry. 2014. "Public to Private MBA at UCLA." *Inside Higher Ed*, June 30.

Rivera, Lauren. 2015. *Pedigree: How Elite Students Get Elite Jobs*. Princeton, NJ: Princeton University Press.

Robbins, Rich. 2013. "Advisor Load." National Academic Advising Association. Retrieved from http://www.nacada.ksu.edu/Resources/Clearinghouse/View -Articles/Advisor-Load.aspx.

Robinson, Cedric J. (1983) 2000. *Black Marxism: The Making of the Black Radical Tradition*. Chapel Hill: University of North Carolina Press.

Rogers, Ibram H. 2012. *The Black Campus Movement: Black Students and the Racial Reconstitution of Higher Education, 1965–1972*. New York: Palgrave Macmillan.

Roksa, Josipa, and Richard Arum. 2015. "The State of Undergraduate Learning." Pp. 756–62 in *The Structure of Schooling*, edited by Richard Arum, Irenee R. Beattie, and Karly Ford. Thousand Oaks, CA: Sage Publications.

Roksa, Josipa, Eric Grodsky, Richard Arum, and Adam Gamoran. 2007. "Changes in Higher Education and Social Stratification in the United States." Pp. 165–91 in *Stratification in Higher Education: A Comparative Study*, edited by Yossi Shavit, Richard Arum, and Adam Gamoran. Stanford, CA: Stanford University Press.

Rosenbaum, James E., Regina Deil-Amen, and Ann E. Person. 2006. *After Admission: From College Access to College Success*. New York: Russell Sage Foundation.

Rosenberg, Alec. 2016. "UC Steps Up Efforts to Address Student Mental Health." *University of California News*, March 24.

Rosenberg, Tina. 2012. "Beyond SATs, Finding Success in Numbers." *New York Times*, February 15.

Rosenfield, Sarah. 2012. "Triple Jeopardy? Mental Health at the Intersection of Gender, Race, and Class." *Social Science & Medicine* 74:1791–1801.

Rust, Betsy. 2016. "Nursing Homes Fade Even as Baby Boomers Age." *STAT News*, June 23.

Ryan, James E. 2010. *Five Miles Away A World Apart: One City, Two Schools, and the Story of Educational Opportunity in Modern America*. New York: Oxford University Press.

Ryman, Anne. 2018. "Why Is Arizona State So Large, and Why Does It Keep Growing?" *AZCentral*, February 16.

Sagalyn, Lynne B. 2011. "Public-Private Partnerships and Urban Governance: Coordinates and Policy Issues." Pp. 191–211 in *Global Urbanization*, edited by Eugenie L. Birch and Susan M. Wachter. Philadelphia: University of Pennsylvania Press.

Samuels, Albert L. 2004. *Is Separate Unequal? Black Colleges and the Challenge to Desegregation*. Lawrence: University Press of Kansas.

Santelices, Maria V., and Mark Wilson. 2010. "Unfair Treatment? The Case of Freedle, the SAT, and the Standardization Approach to Differential Item Functioning." *Harvard Education Review* 80:106–33.

Seamster, Louise. 2019. "Black Debt, White Debt." *Contexts* 18:30–35.

Seamster, Louise, and Raphaël Charron-Chénier. 2017. "Predatory Inclusion and Education Debt: Rethinking the Racial Wealth Gap." *Social Currents* 4:199–207.

Seeley, Lotus. 2016. "Repairing Computers and (Re)producing Hierarchy: An Ethnography of Support Work and Status." Dissertation prepared for Women's Studies and Sociology at the University of Michigan.

Seltzer, Rick. 2016. "Farewell to Departments." *Inside Higher Education*, June 21.

———. 2017. "Proliferating Partnerships." *Inside Higher Education*, July 14.

Sewell, William H. 1992. "A Theory of Structure: Duality, Agency, and Transformation." *American Journal of Sociology* 98:1–29.

Shedd, Carla. 2015. *Unequal City: Race, Schools, and Perceptions of Injustice*. New York: Russell Sage Foundation.

Sheffrin, Steven M. 2004. "State Budget Deficit Dynamics and the California Debacle." *Journal of Economic Perspectives* 18:205–26.

Sherkat, Mojan. 2016. "UC Riverside Recognized for Graduation Rate Success by Association of Public and Land-Grant Universities." *UCR Today*, July 27.

Shields, James W. 2017. "Creating Campus Value through Developer-Led Student Housing." Retrieved from http://ideas.hga.com/creating-campus-value -through-developer-led-student-housing.

Shotton, Heather J., Star Yellowfish, and Rosa Cintrón. 2010. "Island of Sanctuary: The Role of an American Indian Culture Center." Pp. 49–62 in *Culture Centers in Higher Education: Perspectives on Identity, Theory, and Practice*, edited by Lori Patton. Sterling, VA: Stylus Publishing.

Skrentny, John D. 2002. *The Minority Rights Revolution*. Cambridge, MA: Harvard University Press.

Slaughter, Shelia, and Gary Rhoades. 2004. *Academic Capitalism and the New Economy: Markets, State and Higher Education*. Baltimore: Johns Hopkins University Press.

Slobodian, Quinn. 2018. *Globalists: The End of Empire and the Birth of Neoliberalism*. Cambridge, MA: Harvard University Press.

———. 2019. "Anti-'68ers and the Racist-Libertarian Alliance: How a Schism among Austrian School Neoliberals Helped Spawn the Alt Right." *Cultural Politics* 15:372–86.

Small, Mario L. 2002. "Culture, Cohorts, and Social Organization Theory: Understanding Local Participation in a Latino Housing Project." *American Journal of Sociology* 108:1–54.

Smith, William A., Walter R. Allen, and Lynette L. Danley. 2007. "'Assume the Position … You Fit the Description': Psychosocial Experiences and Racial Battle Fatigue among African American Male College Students." *American Behavioral Scientist* 51:551–78.

Soares, Joseph A. 2012. "For Tests That Are Predictively Powerful and Without Social Prejudice." *Research & Practice in Assessment* 7:5–11.

Soederberg, Susan. 2014. *Debtfare States and the Poverty Industry: Money Discipline and the Surplus Population*. New York: Routledge.

Soja, Edward W. 1987. "Economic Restructuring and the Internalization of the Los Angeles Region." Pp. 178–97 in *The Capitalist City: Global Restructuring and Community Politics*, edited by Michael P. Smith and Joe Feagin. New York: Blackwell.

———. 1996. "Los Angeles, 1965–1992: From Crisis-Generated Restructuring to Restructuring-Generated Crisis." Pp. 426–40 in *The City: Los Angeles and Urban Theory at the End of the Twentieth Century*, edited by Allen J. Scott and Edward W. Soja. Berkeley: University of California Press.

Stancil, Will. 2018. "The Scandal That Reveals the Fiction of America's Educational Meritocracy." *The Atlantic*, December 19.

Starr, Kevin. 2004. *Coast of Dreams*. New York: Knopf.

State of Arizona. 2010. House Bill 2281.

Stevens, Mitchell L. 2007. *Creating a Class: College Admissions and the Education of Elites*. Cambridge, MA: Harvard University Press.

Stevens, Mitchell L., and Ben Gebre-Medhin. 2016. "Association, Service, Market: Higher Education in American Political Development." *Annual Review of Sociology* 42:121–42.

Stevens, Mitchell L., Cynthia Miller-Idriss, and Seteney Shami. 2018. *Seeing the World: How US Universities Make Knowledge in a Global Era*. Princeton, NJ: Princeton University Press.

Strauss, Valerie. 2017. "Federal Judge Tells Arizona It Can't Ban Mexican American Studies." *Washington Post*, December 28.

Strayhorn, Terrell L., ed. 2013. *Social Identities and Black Collegians*. Charlotte, NC: Information Age Publishing.

Stripling, Jack. 2015. "The Making of a Higher-Ed Agitator." *Chronicle of Higher Education*, April 24.

Taylor, Keeanga-Yamahtta. 2019. *Race for Profit: How Banks and the Real Estate Industry Undermined Black Homeownership*. Durham: University of North Carolina Press.

Taylor, Paul, Rakesh Kochhar, Richard Fry, Gabriel Velasco, and Seth Motel. 2011. "Wealth Gaps Rise to Record Highs between Whites, Blacks and Hispanics." Washington, DC: Pew Research Center.

Thomas, James M. 2018. "Diversity Regimes and Racial Inequality: A Case Study of Diversity University." *Social Currents* 5:140–56.

———. 2020. *Diversity Regimes: Why Talk Is Not Enough to Fix Racial Inequality at Universities.* New Brunswick, NJ: Rutgers University Press.

Tilly, Charles. 1998. *Durable Inequality.* Berkeley: University of California Press.

Tooze, Adam. 2018. "Neoliberalism's World Order." *Dissent Magazine.* Retrieved from https://www.dissentmagazine.org/article/neoliberalism-world-order-review-quinn-slobodian-globalists.

Townsend, Tony, John Pisapia, and Jamila Razzaq. 2013. "Fostering Interdisciplinary Research in Universities: A Case Study of Leadership, Alignment, and Support." *Studies in Higher Education* 40:658–75.

Traub, James. 1999. "The Class of Prop 209." *New York Times,* May 2.

Trow, Martin. 2005. "Reflections on the Transition from Elite to Mass to Universal Access: Forms and Phases of Higher Education in Modern Societies since WWII." Institute of Governmental Studies, University of California–Berkeley.

Turner, Erika. 2020. *Suddenly Diverse: How School Districts Manage Race and Inequality.* Chicago: University of Chicago Press.

Tyson, Karolyn. 2011. *Integration Interrupted: Tracking, Black Students, & Acting White After Brown.* New York: Oxford University Press.

UC Board of Regents. 2007. "Regents Policy 4400: Policy on University of California Diversity Statement." Retrieved from http://regents.universityofcalifornia.edu/governance/policies/4400.html.

———. 2017. "Regents Policy 2109: Policy on Nonresident Student Enrollment." Retrieved from http://regents.universityofcalifornia.edu/governance/policies/2109.html.

UC Office of the General Council. 2015. "Guidelines for Addressing Race and Gender Equity in Academic Programs in Compliance with Proposition 209." Retrieved from http://www.ucop.edu/general-counsel/_files/guidelines-equity.pdf.

UC Office of the President. 2003. "Undergraduate Access to the University of California after the Elimination of Race-Conscious Policies." Retrieved from https://web.archive.org/web/20070808175053/http://www.ucop.edu/sas/publish/aa_final2.pdf.

———. 2016. "Budget for Current Operations 2016–17: Summary & Detail." Retrieved from https://www.ucop.edu/operating-budget/_files/rbudget/2016-17budgetforcurrentoperations.pdf.

———. 2017a. "Global Food Initiative: Food and Housing Security at the University of California." Retrieved from http://www.ucop.edu/global-food-initiative.

———. 2017b. "Major Features of the California Master Plan for Higher Education." Retrieved from http://www.ucop.edu/institutional-research-academic-planning/_files/California-master-pan-topic-brief.pdf.

UC-Riverside. 1954. "UC Riverside Dedication 1954." Retrieved from https://www.youtube.com/watch?v=ol9KYd_9CwM&feature=channel_page.

———. 2010. "UCR 2020: The Path to Preeminence." Retrieved from https://strategicplan.ucr.edu/documents/UCR%202020%20-%20Final.pdf.

———. 2018. "Optimizing Resource Allocation for Teaching: An Experiment in

Activity-Based Costing in Higher Education." Retrieved from https://www
.ucop.edu/institutional-research-academic-planning/_files/UCRiverside-ABC
-whitepaper.pdf.

University Innovation Alliance. 2019. "Who We Are." Retrieved from http://www
.theuia.org/#home, September 14, 2019.

University of California. 2018. "Annual Report on University Private Support:
2017–2018." Retrieved from: https://www.ucop.edu/institutional-advancement
/_files/annual-reports/2018.pdf.

———. 2019a. "Student Faculty Ratio." University of California Info Center. Retrieved from https://www.universityofcalifornia.edu/infocenter/student
-faculty-ratio.

———. 2019b. UC Alumni Graduate Degree Outcomes. Infocenter. Retrieved from
https://www.universityofcalifornia.edu/infocenter/alumni-grad-outcomes.

Urban Universities for Health. 2015. "Faculty Cluster Hiring for Diversity and Institutional Change."

Urciuoli, Bonnie. 2018. "The Irony of Diversity Numbers." *Signs and Society* 6:
88–110.

U.S. Department of Education. 2014a. "Distribution of Federal Pell Grant Recipients by Expected Family Contribution and Family Income, Award Year 2012–
2013." Retrieved from https://www2.ed.gov/finaid/prof/resources/data/pell
-2012-13/pell-eoy-2012-13.html.

———. 2014b. "Percentage of Full-Time and Part-Time Undergraduates Receiving
Federal Aid, by Aid Program and Control and Level of Institution: 2007–08 and
2011–2012." Retrieved from https://nces.ed.gov/programs/digest/d13/tables
/dt13_331.90.asp.

U.S. News & World Report. 2014. "How U.S. News Calculated the 2015 Best Colleges
Rankings." Retrieved from http://www.usnews.com/education/best-colleges
/articles/2014/09/08/how-us-news-calculated-the-2015-best-colleges-rankings
?page=3.

Valdez, Zulema, and Tanya Golash-Boza. 2018. "Master Status or Intersectional
Identity? Undocumented Students' Sense of Belonging on a College Campus."
Identities: Global Studies in Culture and Power, https://doi.org/10.1080/1070289X
.2018.1534452.

Valdivia, Walter D. 2013. "University Start-Ups: Critical for Improving Technology
Transfer." Center for Technology Innovation at Brookings, November.

Van der Zwan, Natascha. 2014. "Making Sense of Financialization." *Socio-Economic
Review* 12:99–129.

Van Doom, Bas W. 2015. "Pre- and Post-Welfare Reform Media Portrayals of Poverty
in the United States: The Continuing Importance of Race and Ethnicity." *Politics
& Policy* 43:142–62.

Van Dyke, Nella. 1998. "Hotbeds of Activism: Locations of Student Protest." *Social
Problems* 45:205–20.

Vargas, Nicholas, and Julio Villa-Palomino. 2018. "Racing to Serve or Race-ing for Money? Hispanic-Serving Institutions and the Colorblind Allocation of Racialized Federal Funding." *Sociology of Race and Ethnicity*, doi:10.1177/23326492 18769409.

Verger, Antoni. 2012. "Framing and Selling Global Education Policy: The Promotion of Public-Private Partnerships for Education in Low-Income Contexts." *Journal Education Policy* 27:109–30.

Vidal-Ortiz, Salvador. 2017. "Latinxs in Academe." *Inside Higher Ed*, September 22.

Vincent, Roger. 2018. "Arizona State to Expand into Downtown L.A. at Historic Herald Examiner Building." *Los Angeles Times*, August 21.

Wacquant, Loïc. 2001. "Deadly Symbiosis: When Ghetto and Prison Meet and Mesh." *Punishment & Society* 3:95–133.

Walters, Dan. 2002. "UC Merced Boondoggle." *San Mateo County Times*, May 12.

Warikoo, Natasha K. 2016. *The Diversity Bargain: And Other Dilemmas of Race, Admissions, and Meritocracy at Elite Universities*. Chicago: University of Chicago Press.

Washington, Marvin, and Edward J. Zajac. 2005. "Status Evolution and Competition: Theory and Evidence." *Management and Organizations* 48:282–96.

Washington Monthly Editors. 2014. "Introduction: A Different Kind of College Ranking." *Washington Monthly*, September/October.

Watanabe, Teresa. 2017. "African American Students Thrive with High Graduation Rates at UC Riverside." *Los Angeles Times*, June 14.

Watkins, Nicole L., Theressa L. LaBarrie, and Lauren M. Appio. 2010. "Black Undergraduates' Experiences with Perceived Racial Microaggressions in Predominately White Colleges and Universities." Pp. 25–49 in *Microaggressions and Marginality: Manifestation, Dynamics, and Impact*, edited by Derald W. Sue. Hoboken, NJ: John Wiley & Sons, Inc.

Weare, Christopher. 2003. "The California Electricity Crisis: Causes and Policy Options." Public Policy Institute of California.

Webber, Douglas A. 2017. "State Divestment and Tuition at Public Institutions." *Economics of Education Review* 60:1–4.

Weir, Margaret, Ann Shola Orloff, and Theda Skocpol. 1988 "Introduction: Understanding American Social Politics." Pp. 3–36 in *The Politics of Social Policy in the United States*, edited by Margaret Weir, Ann S. Orloff, and Theda Skocpol. Princeton, NJ: Princeton University Press.

Wekullo, Caroline Sabina. 2017. "Outsourcing in Higher Education: The Known and Unknown about the Practice." *Journal of Higher Education Policy and Management* 39:453–68.

Welbourne, Theresa M., and Lacey L. McLaughlin. 2013. "Making the Business Case for Employee Resource Groups." *Employment Relations Today* 40:35–44.

Western, Bruce. 2006. *Punishment and Inequality in America*. New York: Russell Sage Foundation.

Wilkins, Amy C. 2014. "Race, Age and Identity Recovery in the Transition to College for Black and First-Generation White Men." *Sociology of Education* 87:171–87.

Williams, Damon A., Joseph B. Berger, and Shederick A. McClendon. 2005. "Toward a Model of Inclusive Excellence and Change in Postsecondary Institutions." In

Making Excellence Inclusive: Preparing Students and Campuses for an Era of Greater Expectations. Association of American Colleges and Universities.

Winerman, Lea. 2017. "By the Numbers: Stress on Campus." *Monitor on Psychology* 48:88.

Wingfield, Adia H. 2009. "Racializing the Glass Escalator: Reconsidering Men's Experiences with Women's Work." *Gender & Society* 23:5–26.

Wingfield, Adia H., and Renee Alston. 2013. "Maintaining Hierarchies in Predominately White Organizations: A Theory of Racial Tasks." *American Behavioral Scientists* 58:274–87.

Winston, Gordon C. 1999. "Subsidies, Hierarchy and Peers: The Awkward Economics of Higher Education." *Journal of Economic Perspectives* 13:13–36.

Wisconsin Hope Lab. 2015. "Costs and Productivity in Public Higher Education: Convening Summary." Retrieved from https://hope4college.com/wp-content/uploads/2018/09/Costs-and-Productivity-in-Higher-Education-Workshop-Summary.pdf.

Wooten, Melissa E. 2015. *In the Face of Inequality: How Black Colleges Adapt*. Albany: State University of New York.

Zambrana, Ruth E. 2018. *Toxic Ivory Towers: The Consequences of Work Stress on Underrepresented Minority Faculty*. New Brunswick, NJ: Rutgers University Press.

Zelizer, Viviana A. 2011. *Economic Lives: How Culture Shapes the Economy*. Princeton, NJ: Princeton University Press.

Zemsky, Robert, Gregory R. Wagner, and William F. Massy. 2005. *Remaking the American University: Market-Smart and Mission-Centered*. New Brunswick, NJ: Rutgers University Press.

Index

academic advising: interactional styles and, 124–26; UC-Merced caseload, 122–30; at public universities, 122–23

acceptance rates: determination of selectivity and, 37–38, 240nn39–40; at UC-Merced, 56–59

activity-based costing (ABC), at UC-Riverside, 106–9, 118

Adelante student group (UC-Riverside), 184

adjunct faculty: hiring of, 37–38, 112; at UC-Merced, 140

administrative austerity culture: cultural centers and, 136–39; decision-making complexity and, 238n10; impact on leadership of, 116–18; managerial discourse and, 238n12; at public universities, 97–101, 191; tolerable suboptimization policies and, 119–22

Advance Placement (AP) classes, racial barriers in, 22

adversity narratives, diversity marketing and, 185–87

adversity score (SAT), 196

affirmative action: attacks on, 11–14; higher education and, 10–11; individualist logic in, 229n26; limits of, 195

African Student Programs (ASP) (UC-Riverside), 34–35, 61–72; Employee Resource Groups and, 183–84; growth of, 16; multiculturalism as threat to, 170–72

Afrikan Unity Day, 168

AFRO Hall (Afrikans for Recruitment and Outreach Hall) (UC-Merced), 157–61

Ahmed, Sara, 160, 194

alumni contributions, public university reliance on, 85–86, 236n43, 237n47

American Apartheid: Segregation and the Making of the Underclass (Massey & Denton), 56

American Federation of State, County, and Municipal Employees (AFSCME), 65–66, 82, 233n41

anti-affirmative action initiatives: growth of, 11–14; university cultural centers and, 171–72, 195

Arizona State University (ASU): corporate partnerships at, 114, 237n5; cost-cutting strategies at, 108; enrollment growth at, 102–3; global outposts of, 114; interdisciplinary research clusters at, 108–9; international student recruitment at, 114; monetization of infrastructure at, 110; new university status of, 5–6, 95–96; rankings for, 46, 49

Armstrong, Elizabeth A., 211

Asian American and Native American Pacific Islander Serving Institution (AANAPISI), 5; UC-Merced status as, 57

Asian Pacific Student Program, 162

Asian students: changing population of UC-Riverside and, 31; predominance of UC-Merced students from, 55–59; representation in focal universities, 16; representation in schools within universities, 113–114; sampling and, 19, 214; selective inclusion and, 37; subgroups considered historically underrepresented, 4

Association of American Colleges & Universities (AACU), inclusive excellence model, 40–41

Association of American Universities (AAU), 45–46, 198; universities aspiration for membership in, 102

austerity: administrative culture under, 97–101, 115–18, 191; Barrett Honors College, 103; cost cutting as response to, 105–9; enrollment increases as strategy under, 101–5; in higher education, 10; impact on new universities of, 25; international student recruitment as strategy under, 114–18; market-smart strategies under, 109–14; neoliberal ideology of, 8–9; at new universities, 95–97; postsecondary racial neoliberalism and, 20–24; public university strategies under, 101–18; threat to cultural centers under, 170–72

Austerity: The History of a Dangerous Idea (Blyth), 118

backdoor borrowing, public-private partnerships as, 62, 236n33

Bakke, Allan, 11

banking, racial neoliberal cycle in, 192

Baradaran, Mehrsa, 192

Barclays Capital, UC system retention of, 81–83

Becker, Gary, 7–8, 238n16

Becker, Howard, 98

Berrey, Ellen, 36–37, 184

big science model, interdisciplinary research clusters and, 108–9

bilingualism, racialization of, 221n1

Binder, Amy, 173

biology, race theory and, 8

Black Enterprise magazine, 183

Black fraternities and sororities, 162

Black Graduation (UC-Riverside), 164, 167

Black House (UC-Riverside), 162

Black Lives Matter: Black Student Task Force formation and (UC-Riverside), 168–69; method and relationship to, 215; town hall (UC-Riverside), 164; university support for, 136

Black Marxism: The Making of the Black Radical Tradition (Robinson), 218

Black Queens Week, 166

Black students: academic advising resources for, 128–30; borrowing rates for, 247n32; campus activism by, 145–46; college enrollment increase for, 14–15; corporate-university partnerships and hiring of, 177–81; counseling services accessibility for, 132–34; cultural centers for, 134–35, 137, 166–69; diversity regimes and, 149; enrollment patterns for, 22–23; graduation gaps for, 43–44; insufficient organizational support for, 155–59; new university enrollment of, 16; overrepresentation in social sciences and humanities of, 112–14; student racism targeting, 156–59; test scores as admission barrier for, 21–22; at UC-Riverside, 34–35, 162–66; in UC system, 78–80, 235n21

Black Student Task Force (UC-Riverside), 168–69, 171

Black Student Union (UC-Merced), 158–59

Black Student Union (UC-Riverside), 169

Blue and Gold Opportunity Plan, 235n14
Blyth, Mark, 118
Bourdieu, Pierre, 242n3, 242n9
Brown, Jerry, 42, 54
Brown v. Board of Education, 5, 8
Buchanan, James, 8, 223n36
Building Common Ground (UC-Riverside), 151–52
Burawoy, Michael, 242n3
Burton, John, 54
business model at public universities, 111–12
Butler, Jonathan, 169

Cal Grant program, 235n14
Calhoun, John C., 223nn36–37
California Master Plan for Higher Education, 52–55, 76, 234n8, 234n12
California State University-Fullerton, 182
California State University system, 80–83; financing for, 236n37
Carnegie Classification for Research, 102; research university ranking and, 5, 79, 235n23
Carnegie Commission on Higher Education, 79
Carter, Prudence, 219
Center for Educational Partnership (CEP) (UC-Merced), 60, 232n22
Center for Equal Opportunity, 12
Chavez, Cesar, 163
Chetty, Raj, 44
Chicano/Latino Youth Conference (UC-Riverside), 164
Chicano Link Peer Mentor program, 167–69
Chicano movement, 163
Chicano Student Programs (CSP) (UC-Riverside), 34–35, 161–72; growth of, 16; multiculturalism as threat to, 170–72
Chicano Studies (UC-Riverside), 166
chief diversity officers (CDOs), 152–54, 244n23

Cintana Education corporation, 237n7
class dynamics: corporate-university partnerships and, 179–81; post-secondary racial neoliberalism and, 20–24; at UC-Merced, 57–59; at UC-Riverside, 30–36, 45–47
cohort theory, 239n31
Cold War University: federal and state funding for, 10, 97, 201; UC-Riverside as, 30, 228n1
Cole, Jonathon, 239n30
College Board, 196
college testing regime, 195–97
Collins, Patricia Hill, 210
colorblind racism: challenges to, 194–95; diversity regimes and, 147–54, 191; diversity rhetoric and, 24; market approach and, 113–14; neoliberal ideology of, 9; postsecondary racial neoliberalism and, 20–24; US law enforcement and, 243n20
community colleges: academic advising resources at, 122–23; gatekeeper role of, 246n1; racially marginalized student enrollment in, 4; transfer to UC system universities from, 163, 234n12
conditional hospitality of universities, marginalized students and, 229n30
Congressional Hispanic Caucus, 117
Connell, Raewyn, 191–92
Connerly, Ward, 12
Conwell, Jordan, 218
co-opetition for UC system resources, 86–91
Córdova, France, 229n17
core universities, for corporate partnerships, 176–77
corporate-university partnerships: diversity marketing and, 174–75, 181–85, 245n9; Employee Resource Groups, 181–85; at new universities, 111–12, 237n5, 237n7; race and, 175–76
Cortes, Carlos, 163

cost-cutting measures, as austerity strategy, 105–9

Cottom, Tressie McMillan, 188

Council of UC Faculty Associations, 82

Counseling and Psychological Services (CAPS) (UCM), 131, 133–34

counseling services, increase in post-secondary education of, 130–31

Crow, Michael, 5–6, 95, 99, 102, 108, 114, 237n5, 239n30

cultural centers at universities: admin-istration appropriation of, 159–61; challenges to diversity logics and, 194–95; collective action by, 161–72; diversity regimes and, 148–54; equity-oriented centers, 162–66; housing community coordination with, 166–69; importance for ra-cially marginalized students, 3, 26; marketing of inclusive excellence and, 38–40; multiculturalism as threat to, 170–72; threats to, 170–72; tolerable suboptimization cost-cutting and, 134–39; UC-Riverside and impact of, 16–17, 34–35, 162–66

cultural logics of race: diversity re-gimes and, 147–54; racialized equity labor and, 154–61

cultural resources: austerity culture and, 97–100; cohort effects and, 239n31; diversity work and, 234n6; Employee Resource Groups and, 183–84; organizational wealth linked to, 30–31

Davis, Daniel, 173

Deferred Action for Childhood Arrivals (DACA), 185

Denton, Nancy, 56

Design-Bid-Build (DBB) contracts, uni-versity construction and, 233n38

Designing the New American University (Crow), 5–6, 95

Development, Relief, and Education for Alien Minors (DREAM) Act, 185, 241n82

Diamond, John, 20

Diversity Inc. magazine, 183

diversity regimes: challenges to, 194–95; colorblind ideology and, 147–54, 191; commodification of social inequality in, 187–89; corporate-university partnerships and, 179–81; cultural centers as part of, 134–39; elite vs. public universities use of, 230n31; inclusive excellence model and, 41–42; inclusivity problem in, 154–55; institutional diversity in UC system and, 75–80, 235n19; insuf-ficient organizational support for, 155–59; marketing of, 185–87, 245n3; people of color as face of, 234n6; public university hierarchies and, 24, 228n147, 234n5; racialized equity labor and, 146–47, 154–61; racially marginalized students and, 25–26, 146–47; threat to cultural centers under, 170–72; university appropri-ation of racialized equity labor and, 159–61

diversity transactions, 174–75

Du Bois, W. E. B., 6, 20, 218

Early Academic Outreach Program (UC-Riverside), 163

Eaton, Charlie, 54–55

Education Trust, 43

Elevate program, 182–83

elite universities: corporate-university partnerships and, 179; endowment assets at, 104, 236n43, 237n47; enrollment stability at, 104, 240nn39–40; financialization strategies for, 54–55; organizational wealth of, 14; racially marginalized students at, 2–3; selective inclusion at, 36–37; social mobility and grad-uation from, 231n55, 241n72; *U.S. News* rankings for, 47–50; *Washing-*

ton Monthly rankings for, 48. *See also* flagship public universities; private universities

Employee Resource Groups (ERGs), 181–85

employment: corporate-university partnerships as path to, 176–81

endowment assets, of private and flagship public universities, 54–55, 237nn46–47

"End of History?, The" (Fukuyama), 98–99

engineering and science programs: academic advising resources for, 126–30; organizational support for, 112–14

Enigma of Diversity, The: The Language of Race and the Limits of Social Justice (Berrey), 184

enrollment in public universities: Black student enrollment, 14–16, 22–23, 78; increase in, as austerity strategy, 61, 101–5, 239nn36–37; in-state enrollment, 76, 88–89, 234n11, 234n13; international student enrollment, 14–16; Latinx student enrollment, 15–16, 22–23; out-of-state enrollment, 14–16, 78; stigma of enrollment growth at, 104–5; Tidal Wave II (UCR) enrollment initiative, 16–17, 34–36

equity, organizational culture for, 163–66

equity advisors (UC-Merced), 153–54

equity-oriented logics, 194–95

ethnic studies, funding cuts in Arizona, 172

ethnographic research methodology, overview of, 18–20, 209–20, 226n118, 227n119

Eugenics Society, 22

faculty hiring, business-based criteria for, 112

faculty resources: racially marginalized faculty, 156–59; ranking of institutions based on, 37–38; tolerable suboptimization policies and, 119–22

federal funding: decline in research grants from, 236nn41–42; UC system reliance on, 85–86, 200

Feitelberg, Dan, 61, 63–64, 67

financial crisis of 2007–2008, public university defunding and, 13–14

financialization strategies, UC-Merced development and, 54–55

"Finish-in-Four" campaign (UC-Riverside), 43

flagship public universities: affirmative action bans at, 12; corporate-university partnerships and, 179; financialization strategies for, 54–55; international and out-of-state enrollment at, 14–16; lack of racially marginalized students at, 1–3; market approach at, 114; organizational hierarchies in, 23–24; organizational wealth at, 14–15; predominantly white enrollment at, 5, 12; privatization of, 90–91; selective inclusion at, 36–37; state funding for, 199–200; in University of California system, 15–16

Fordist family wage, 8–9

for-profit universities: commodification of inequality at, 188; federal student aid at, 202; market ideology at, 62; racially marginalized student enrollment in, 4, 14

Free Application for Federal Student Aid (FAFSA), 202

free market ideology: affirmative action attacks based on, 11–12; racism and, 7–9. *See also* market economy

free tuition plans, 76–77, 201–3

Friedman, Milton, 7–8, 238n16

Fukuyama, Francis, 98–99

"Future of Higher Education, The: Creating Opportunity, Assessing Value," 90–91

Gastón, Pablo, 242n3

Gawande, Atul, 240n39

gender: counseling services accessibility and, 132–34; race scholarship and, 210–11; student disparities across academic fields and, 114

Georgia State University, 46

global higher education, racial neoliberal cycle in, 191–92

Graduate Cultural Resource Center (GCRC) (UC-Merced), 139

graduate degrees: self-funding for, 110–11; UC-Merced undergraduates moving to, 140

graduation rates: social mobility and, 44–45; at UC-Riverside, 42–44

Graduation Rate Task Force (UC-Riverside), 42–43

grant funding: faculty hiring linked to, 112; UC-Riverside as recipient of, 44

Great American University, The (Cole), 239n30

Great Mistake, The: How We Wrecked Public Universities and How We Can Fix Them (Newfield), 100

Green New Deal, 201

group-based graduations, cultural center sponsorship of, 167

habitus, Bourdieu's concept of, 242n9

Hampshire College, 197

Hayek, Friedrich, 7

Heller, Walter, 238n16

higher education: reassertion of public interest in, 203–4. See also postsecondary education

Higher Education Act 1965 (HEA), 10, 202

Higher Education Act 1972, 12–13, 202

Higher Education Act 1992, 13, 202

Highlander Empowerment Student Services Referendum (HESSR), 171–72

Hinderaker, Ivan, 16, 30–31, 98

Hispanic Serving Institution (HSI),
5; student demographics at, 221n6; Title V programming at, 244n9; UC-Merced status as, 57, 60; UC-Riverside status as, 17

Historically Black College and Universities (HBCUs), 5, 224n68, 226n100

housing patterns, racial neoliberal cycle in, 192

housing policies at new universities: Black students and, 159–60; cultural center coordination with, 166–69; tolerable suboptimization cost-cutting and, 139–40

human capital theory, educational investment and, 238n16

identity, diversity marketing and, 185–87, 245n3

immigrant communities: public university enrollment and increase of, 34–35; UC-Merced development and role of, 53–55

imperialism, neoliberalism in aftermath of, 7–9

inclusive excellence: at UC-Merced, 60; UC-Riverside marketing of, 38–42; U.S. News and World Report rankings and, 42–47

inclusivity: Black students and problems with, 157–59; diversity regimes and problem of, 154–55

Indigenous land, public universities and dispossession of, 222n17

indirect cost recovery (IDR), UC system reliance on, 84–86

infrastructure development at UC campuses: austerity culture impact on, 97–101; equity-oriented development, 194–95; monetization of, 109–14; public-private partnerships for, 62, 68

inhabited institutions ideology, higher education organizations and, 226n115

in-state student enrollment: cost of,

234n13; UC system commitment to, 76, 88–89, 234n11, 237n51
institutional diversity, in UC system, 75–80, 235n19, 237n51
institutional whiteness in research, 146
instruction cost-cutting, strategies for, 106–9
Intercultural Hub (UC-Merced), 139, 154–55; digital protest activities by, 159–61
interdisciplinary research clusters, 108–9
International Association of Counseling Services, 130
international students: increased enrollment in public universities of, 14; recruitment of, as austerity strategy, 114–18

Jack, Anthony, 22
Jayakumar, Uma, 163
J. P. Morgan, 82

Kendi, Ibram X., 195–96
Kerr, Clark, 95, 116, 241n81

land grant universities: creation of, 222n15; predominantly white enrollment in, 5
Latinx students: academic advising resources at UC-Merced for, 124–30; borrowing rates for, 247n32; California population demographics and rise of, 34–36, 232n17; corporate-university partnerships and hiring of, 177–81; counseling services accessibility for, 132–34; cultural centers for, 134–35, 137, 166–69; diversity regimes and, 149–51; Employee Resource Groups and, 184; enrollment patterns for, 22–23; new university enrollment of, 15–16; overrepresentation in social sciences and humanities of, 112–14; predominance of UC-Merced students from, 51–59; at

UC-Riverside, 163–66; in UC system, 78–80
laundering of privilege, racism and, 22
Legislative Analyst Office, 82
Lehman Brothers, UC system retention of, 81–83
Leland, Dorothy, 51, 60–61, 99–100, 116–17
Lerma, Veronica, 145–72, 214–15
Lewis, Amanda, 20
Lewis, Randall, 16
LGBTQ+ students: counseling services accessibility for, 132–34; cultural centers for, 162
LGBT Resource Center (UC-Riverside), 162
"Living the Promise" fund-raising campaign (UC-Riverside), 43
logics, of austerity culture, 97–101
lottery admissions systems, 196–97
low-income students: funding in UC system for, 235n14; out-of-state tuition as subsidy for, 236n38; at UC-Merced, 55–59

market economy: austerity culture and, 99; commodification of social inequality in, 187–89; diversity marketing in, 173–75, 185–87; inclusive excellence and, 38–42; market-smart austerity strategies and, 109–14; public university tuition and, 12–13; research universities' embrace of, 173; resource collaboration in, 199–200; student commodification in, 173–75
Markey, Ed, 201
Marx, Karl, 218
Massey, Douglas, 56
Medicare and Medicaid, 62
mental health support services, tolerable suboptimization cost-cutting impact on, 130–34
mentor programs, cultural centers as resource for, 167–69

Merced Student Council, 145
Merced 2020 Project: awards for, 233n42; budget planning and financing issues, 66–67; future funding constraints in, 68; initiation of, 50–52, 55, 61; mismatched interests in, 68–69; state funding for, 61, 74
merit, racialized construction of, 14–15, 197; penalization of UC-Riverside status based on, 36–38; postsecondary racial neoliberalism and, 21–24
Mexican American Studies (UC-Riverside), 163
Middle Eastern Student Center (UC-Riverside), 43, 162
Minority Serving Institution (MSI) designation: cultural centers and, 135; UC-Merced and, 55
Mirabella Senior Living Project, 110
Mitchell, Ted, 43, 50
Mohammad, Faisal, 133
Monday morning group, lobbying for UC-Riverside by, 35–36
monetization of assets, as austerity strategy, 109–14
Moody's credit rating, UC system and, 82
Moore, Wendy, 148
Morrill Acts of 1862 and 1890, 222n15, 222n17
Movimiento Estudiantil Chicano de Aztlán (MEChA), 163
Multicultural Center (UC-Merced), 159
multicultural initiatives: diversity regimes and, 149–50; inclusivity problems and, 154–55; insufficient organizational support for, 155–59; neoliberal framework for, 244n18; threat to cultural centers from, 170–72
Museus, Samuel, 163

naming rights for infrastructure, as monetization strategy, 109–10
Napolitano, Janet, 51

National Employee Resource Group Summit, 182
National Pan Hellenic organizations, Black fraternities and sororities in, 162
Native American scholars and activists, as UC-Riverside, 34–35
Native American student programs, 162
neoliberalism: austerity culture and, 99–101; diversity regimes and colorblindness of, 149; educational policies and, 7–9; higher education policies and, 6; multiculturalism and, 244n18; origins of, 7; race studies and, 217–20. See also postsecondary racial neoliberalism
Newfield, Christopher, 100
news media: diversity marketing and, 183, 185–87; public university coverage in, 44–45; UC-Merced coverage in, 59–60; UC-Riverside coverage in, 43–44
new universities: Arizona State University as, 5–6, 95–96; characteristics of, 4–6; commodification of social inequality in, 187–89; corporate partnerships with, 111–12; cultural centers at, 135; diversity regimes at, 146–47; Employee Resource Groups (ERGs) and, 181–85; global outposts for, 114–18; growth of, 3; impact of austerity in, 25; inclusion in UIA of, 45–47; international student recruitment in, 114–18; marginalized populations served by, 190–92; national outreach by, 115; origins of, 10–15; overview of research on, 18–20; penalization of racial inclusion and status of, 37–38; postsecondary racial neoliberalism and, 20–24; public-private partnerships at, 25–26; racialized neoliberal cycle in, 190–93; racially marginalized students at, 146; research mission at, 4–5; social change and role of, 26; student commodification in, 173–75;

survival strategies and organizational practices of, 15–17; UC-Merced status as, 55–59; UC-Riverside conversion to, 30–36; underrepresented racially marginalized student concentration in, 3–6, 11–15

New York Excelsior Program, 201

New York Times: Black student enrollment in UC system in, 78; coverage of UC-Merced in, 185–87; coverage of UC-Riverside in, 33, 44; diversity marketing and, 185–87; undocumented students in UC system in, 59, 185–87

No Child Left Behind Act, 203

non-tenure-track labor, as cost-cutting measure, 107–9

Nuestra Cosa (UC-Riverside student newspaper), 163

Ocasio-Cortez, Alexandria, 201

Omi, Michael, 218

One University Campaign (University of Michigan), 73–74

online courses, as cost-cutting strategy, 107–9

open-access schools, racially marginalized student enrollment in, 4

opportunity hoarding strategies, higher education inequalities and, 10–11

Orbach, Ray, 17, 31–36, 38–40, 60, 97–98, 103, 116, 230n41, 238n20

Oregon University System, disbanding of, 90–91

Organisation for Economic Cooperation and Development (OECD), 62

organizational hierarchies: challenges to, 197–99; in college rankings, 23, 29, 190–91; in public universities, 23–24

organizational identity, at UC-Merced, 59–60

organizational wealth: at elite private universities, 14; inequality in higher education of, 2–3, 11

out-of-state students: competition for, in UC system schools, 88–89, 234n11; increased enrollment in public universities of, 14; new universities' recruitment of, 115–18

Owen-Smith, Jason, 200

Pan-African Theme Hall (PATH), 166–69

"Pathway to Preeminence" Strategic Plan for 2020 (UC-Riverside), 40

Paying for the Party: How College Maintains Inequality (Armstrong & Hamilton), 210

Pedigree: How Elite Students Get Elite Jobs (Rivera), 176

Pell Grant recipients: criteria for, 221n10; graded funding systems and, 247n28; graduation rates for, 46–47; public university rankings linked to, 46; revenue from, 202; at UC-Merced, 17, 55–59; in University of California system, 74–75, 76–77

PepsiCo, Inc.: diversity initiatives at, 246n18; Employee Resource Groups at, 181–85; UC-Riverside partnership with, 111, 174–81

per-student endowment rates, inequalities in, 2–3

philanthropic contributions: naming rights for infrastructure and, 109–10; public university reliance on, 85–86

Plenary Properties Merced, 51–52, 66, 233n40

politics of resentment, racism and, 9

population demographics: at UC-Merced, 55–59; UC-Riverside conversion to new university status and, 34–36

postsecondary education: affirmative action and, 10–11; austerity in, 10; counseling center usage and, 130–31; growth strategies in, 102–3; human capital theory and, 238n16; infrastructure development and

postsecondary education (*continued*)
revision, 68; neoliberal defunding
of, 8–9; organizational wealth and
resource inequalities in, 2–3, 23–24;
political-economic context in, 6–9;
postsecondary racial neoliberalism
and, 20–24; public perceptions of,
44; public-private partnerships in,
63–64, 70–72; race and social segregation in, 3, 5–6; racial neoliberal
cycle in, 190–93; reduced public
commitment to, 6; reinvestment in,
200–203. *See also* private universities; public universities

postsecondary racial neoliberalism:
competition for UC system resources and, 90–91; defined, 20–24;
penalization of racial inclusion and,
37–38

pre-collegiate education, University
of California system programs for,
229n10

predominantly white universities
(PWU): corporate partnerships and
preferential hiring at, 176; cultural
centers at, 134; flagship universities as, 5, 12; racially marginalized
students at, 146; racial privilege
leverage at, 173–75; UC-Riverside as,
29–31; *U.S. News* rankings for, 48–50

preferential hiring practices, race and
corporate-university partnerships
and, 175–76

prestige rankings, penalization of racially inclusive new universities and,
36–38, 190–91

primary school funding, 203

Prison Alley, UC-Merced location in,
17, 134

private revenue sources: austerity logics and, 99; naming rights for infrastructure and, 109–10; re-benching
in UC system of, 89–91, 199–200,
237n53; UC system reliance on, 83–
86, 236n43

private universities: academic advising

caseloads at, 122–23; corporate-
university partnerships and, 179;
endowment assets at, 104, 236n43,
237n47; enrollment stability at, 104;
federal funding of, 202; financialization strategies for, 54–55; organizational wealth of, 14; racially marginalized students at, 2–3; selective
inclusion at, 36–37; social mobility
and graduation from, 241n72; *U.S.
News* rankings for, 47–50; *Washington Monthly* rankings for, 48. *See also*
elite universities

privileged poor disadvantaged students, admission to elite schools for,
22–23

producerism ideology, 224n52

Proposition 209 referendum, 12, 33–
34, 235n19; diversity regimes and,
149–50; repeal efforts for, 195; UC-
Riverside growth and, 17; university
cultural centers and, 171

public infrastructure: austerity culture
of administration in, 97–101; public-
private partnerships for, 62, 68

public-private partnerships (P3s):
budget planning and financing
issues, 66–67; characteristics of,
61–62, 191; criticism of, 62–63; for
disadvantaged populations, 69–72;
diversity marketing and, 174–75;
faulty assumptions in, 66; future
funding constraints and, 68; impact
on university leadership focus of,
116; information vacuum in, 66–69;
lack of change accommodation in,
68; lack of control and flexibility
in, 67–68; mismatched interests in,
68–69; new universities and, 25–26;
at UC-Merced, 63–69; UC-Merced
experience with, 50–52; workforce
diversity and, 111–12

public universities: academic advising
resources at, 122–23; affirmative
action bans in, 12; austerity logics
and, 100–101; austerity practices

at, 101–18; collaborative systems in, 199–200; defunding of, 12–15; disbanding of state university systems, 90–91; enrollment increase as austerity strategy in, 101–5; financialization strategies for, 54–55; new university growth and, 3; organizational hierarchies in, 23–24; predominantly white enrollment in flagship schools, 5, 12; private revenue sources, reliance on, 85–86, 236n43; public-private partnerships at, 52, 70–72; racial neoliberal cycle in, 190–93; racially marginalized students at, 1–3; redistribution of resources by, 199–200; reinvestment in, 200–203; tuition increases at, 12–13; *Washington Monthly* rankings for, 48. *See also* flagship public universities

race and racism: corporate partnerships and, 175–76; cultural centers and, 138–39; diversity regimes and, 147–54; enrollment growth as austerity strategy and, 104–5; higher education's role in reduction of, 192–93; inclusivity problems and, 154–55; neoliberalism and, 6–9, 222n35; racialized equity labor and, 146–47; student commodification and, 173–75; at UC-Riverside, 36–38; UC-Riverside collective action on, 165–66; university programming on, 151–54

race-based think tanks, diversity regimes and, 183–84

race scholarship: on diversity regimes, 147; institutional diversity work and, 75–80; methodology in, 18–20, 209–20, 226n118, 227n119

racialized equity labor: by Black students, 156–59; diversity regimes and, 154–61; Employee Resource Groups and, 183; inclusivity problems and, 154–55; at public universities, 146;

student labor as, 166–69; terminology and definition, 243n5; university appropriation of, 159–61

racial justice, neoliberalism and, 7–9

racial matching, corporate-university partnerships hiring practices and, 178–81

Rally against Racism (UC-Riverside), 38–39

"Rapping with the Chancellor" (UC-Riverside), 39

Ray, Victor, 30–31, 193, 218

Reagan, Ronald, 8–9, 11–12, 225n88

re-benching of resources, in UC system, 89–91, 199–200, 237n53

recruiting practices: corporate-university partnerships and, 177–81; Employee Resource Groups, 181–85

Regents of the University of California v. Bakke, 11

Reich, Robert, 43

reinvestment in public higher education, 200–203

research funding: business model for, 101–5, 239nn36–37; student enrollment and, 101–5, 199–200, 239nn36–37; UC system reliance on, 84–86, 199–200

research universities: Carnegie Classification categories, 5; R1 status and funding at, 102; R2 classification for UC-Merced, 79; racially marginalized student enrollment in, 4–6; ranking of, 4–5; tuition as funding for, 102; UC-Riverside as, 16–17, 235n23

resource gaps, at public universities, 2–3

Responsibility Management Center (RMC) (UC-Riverside), 107–9

Rivera, Lauren, 176

Rivera, Tomás, 17, 34–35, 229n18

Robinson, Cedric, 218

Rothbard, Murray, 8, 223n37

San Joaquin Valley, UC-Merced and, 52–53, 60, 231n3

SAT test: as admission barrier, 21–22; elimination of, 195–97

Schraer, Rosemary, 229n17

Schultz, Theodore, 98, 238n16

Scull, Andrew, 87

Seamster, Louise, 192

secondary school funding, 203

segregation, higher education and, 5, 8, 15–17, 224n66

selective inclusion, at elite universities, 36–37

self-funded graduate degrees, as austerity strategy, 110–11

Servicemen's Readjustment Act of 1944 (GI Bill), 10

Shanghai Academic Ranking of World Universities, 114

silo-ing, diversity regimes and, 149

Slobodian, Quinn, 7

smog crisis of 1970s, impact on UC-Riverside of, 31–33

social inequality, commodification of, 187–89

social mobility: college selectivity and, 231n55, 241n72; postsecondary education and, 44–45

Social Mobility Index (SMI), 46

social sciences and humanities programs: academic advising resources at UC-Merced for, 123–30; organizational support inequalities for, 112–14

socioeconomics, UC-Merced student demographics and, 57–59

Southeast Asian students: enrollment in UCR and UCM of, 16, 226n108; at UC-Riverside, 229n5

Spectrum Knowledge, 182–83

"Speed Diversity Dialogue" (UC-Merced), 151–52

Sproul, Robert Gordon, 36

staffing policies: racially marginalized staff, 156–59; tolerable suboptimization and, 119–20; workforce planning at UC-Merced and, 120–22

Starbucks College Achievement Plan, 237n5

State Assembly Bill 94, 82–83

state funding of public universities: in Cold War era, 97; decline in, 12–15; graded system for, 247n28; international comparisons, 248n45; restructuring of, 106–9, 199–200

state legislature, UC system institutional diversity commitment from, 75–76

state university systems, disbanding of, 90–91

Stevens, Mitchell, 22

student aid: privatization of, 13–15; public university funding linked to, 12–13; reinvestment in, 201–3; tolerable optimization cost-cutting and, 139–40

student debt: privatization of student loans and, 13–15; self-funded degrees and, 110–11

student labor: at cultural centers, 155–59; reduction and configuration of, 166–69; at UC-Merced, 145–47; at UC-Riverside, 147

student loans: privatization of, 13–15; racial borrowing patterns, 247n32

student services: academic advising resources at UC-Merced for, 124–30; cultural centers, 134–39; mental health support services, 130–34

student-to-tenure-track faculty ratio, 140

Study of American Intelligence, A, 22

Supplemental Education Opportunity Grants, 202

target universities, for corporate partnerships, 176

taxation, neoliberal opposition to, 8–9

Taylor, Keeanga-Yamahtta, 192

teaching technology, as cost-cutting measure, 107–9

test scores: as admission barrier, 21–22, 228n131; determination of selectivity and, 37–38; elimination of, 195–97

Thatcher, Margaret, 8, 99

TheDemands.Org student activism
website, 145

Tidal Wave II, UCR enrollment initiative, 16–17, 34

Title V grants, 17

tolerable suboptimization cost-
cutting, 105; academic advising
resources and, 122–30; cultural
programming, 134–39; impact
at UC-Merced of, 140–41; mental
health support services and, 130–34;
racialized equity labor and, 242n3;
student aid and, 139–40; UC-Merced
case study in, 119–41; workforce
planning at UC-Merced and, 120–22

Trump, Donald, 132, 187

tuition: free tuition plans, 76–77, 201–
3; out-of-state tuition, UC system
reliance on, 84–86, 236n38; public
university increases in, 12–13

Tyson, Karolyn, 219

UC Academic Council, 87–88

UC Board of Regents, 89

UC Office of the President (UCOP),
82–83, 89

UCR 2020 Path to Preeminence
plan, 42

underrepresented racially marginalized students (URS): academic
advising resources at UC-Merced for,
124–30; admission patterns for, 22–
24; adversity narratives of, 186–87;
campus activism of, 145–72; college
enrollment increase for, 14–15; college experience for, 2–3; corporate-
university partnerships and hiring
of, 177–81; counseling services accessibility for, 132–34; cultural centers for, 134–39; disparities across
academic fields of, 112–14; diversity
marketing of, 173–75; diversity regimes and, 148–54; equity-oriented
cultural centers and, 162–66;
funding inequalities for, 199–203;

inclusivity problems for, 154–55;
market strategies' targeting of,
110–14; neoliberal policies and, 7–9,
190–93; new university enrollment
of, 3–6, 11–15, 190–93; penalization
of UC-Riverside status based on,
36–38; public-private partnership
impact on, 69–72; public universities' support for, 74; racialized equity
labor for, 154–61; social mobility
and graduation rates for, 47–50; as
student labor, 166–69; terminology for, 221n8; at UC-Merced, 52,
55–59; UC-Riverside enrollment of,
32–36; undocumented students, 117,
226n117; university appropriation of
racialized equity labor by, 159–61;
workforce diversity and hiring of,
111–12

Undocumented Student Programs
(UC-Riverside), 162, 166, 171

undocumented students, 117, 162, 166,
226n117, 241n82

Únete a Mundo (Mundo), 166–69

unified system model, UC-Riverside
and, 35

United Nations Children's Fund
(UNICEF), 62

University Innovation Alliance (UIA),
45–47, 115, 197–99

University of California-Berkeley:
Black student enrollment at, 78;
as Cold War university, 97–98; endowment assets at, 86; out-of-state
student enrollment at, 76; undocumented students at, 187

University of California-Davis School
of Medicine, admissions criteria
at, 10

University of California-Los Angeles,
out-of-state student enrollment
at, 76

University of California-Merced
(UCM): academic advising caseloads
at, 122–30; acceptance rates at, 56–
59; affordable housing initiative at,

University of California-Merced (UCM) (*continued*)
69; appropriation of racialized equity labor at, 159–61; Black students' lack of support at, 155–59; Carnegie R2 classification for, 79; commodification of social inequality and, 188–89; co-opetition for UC system resources by, 86–91; cost-cutting measures at, 105–9; cultural centers at, 135–39, 150–51; decline of white students at, 55–59; Design-Bid-Build (DBB) contracts at, 233n38; diversity marketing at, 185–87; diversity regime at, 148, 149–54; endowment assets at, 85–86; enrollment increases at, 61, 103–4; financialization strategies at, 54–55; history of, 17; housing services at, 139–40; in-state student enrollment in, 76; interdisciplinary research clusters at, 108–9; mental health support services at, 130–34; naming rights for infrastructure at, 109–10; non-resident student enrollment at, 115–16; organizational identity of, 59–60; organizational vulnerabilities at, 25; planning and development of, 52–55; pressures on leadership at, 116–17; public-private partnership at, 50–52, 63–69; racial and class composition at, 113; racialized equity labor at, 154–61; racially marginalized student enrollment at, 15–16, 51–59, 77–78; recruiting efforts at, 56–59; research funding linked to faculty hiring at, 112–13; resource gaps at, 2–3; self-funded graduate degrees at, 110–11; state funding for, 53–55, 61, 79–80; student aid program at, 139; student labor at, 145–72; student protests at, 51–52; student-to-tenure-track-faculty ratio at, 140; tolerable suboptimization at, 105–9, 119–41; UC system financing and, 83; UC system institutional diversity and role of, 76–80; workforce planning at, 120–22

University of California-Riverside (UCR): accessibility issues for, 230n45; budget and cost-cutting strategies at, 106–9; business school at, 241n77; commodification of social inequality and, 188–89; conversion from predominantly white university to racially marginalized students in, 29–36; conversion to new university status by, 30–36; co-opetition for UC system resources by, 86–91; cost-cutting at, 105–9; cultural centers at, 150–51, 161–72, 194–95; demographic and structural factors in conversion of, 34–36, 228n3; diversity regime at, 149–54; Employee Resource Groups and, 181–85; endowment assets at, 85–86; enrollment growth at, 101–5; equity commitment in cultural centers at, 162–66; graduation rates at, 42–47; history of, 16–17, 30–31; inclusive excellence marketing at, 38–42, 44–47; in-state student enrollment in, 76; interdisciplinary research clusters at, 108–9; leadership of, 30–36, 38–40, 116, 229n17; multiculturalism initiatives at, 170–72; national outreach initiatives at, 115; organizational hierarchy at, 197–99; PepsiCo, Inc. partnership with, 111, 174–81; pressures on leadership at, 116–17; public-private partnership proposal at, 70; racial and class composition at, 30–36, 45–47, 77–78, 112; racially marginalized student enrollment at, 15–16, 25, 30–36; racial status and penalty at, 36–38; referral pool process and, 102–3, 198; research designation for, 16–17, 235n23; School of Natural Sciences at, 44; state funding for, 31, 35–36,

79–80, 231n5; student labor at, 166–69; UC system financing and, 83; UC system institutional diversity and role of, 76–80; *U.S. News and World Report* ranking of, 42–47

University of California-San Diego, 48; Employee Resource Group collaboration at, 182; out-of-state student enrollment at, 76

University of California-San Francisco, 232n11

University of California system: contestation of resources within, 86–91; counseling services in, 130; debt burden of, 82; Diversity Statement, 147–48; endowment assets at, 85–86, 237n46; expansion and leadership status of, 15–17, 224n65; financial strategies adopted by, 81–83, 236n33, 238nn19–20; free tuition plan in, 76–77, 201; funding campaigns in, 85–86, 236n33; funding for UC-Riverside and UC-Merced from, 79–80; funding restructuring and decrease, 80–83; institutional diversity work in, 75–80; intrasystem resource distribution in, 74–75; market resource competition in, 115; new universities in, 4; out-of-state students in, 76, 84–86; outreach programs in, 229n10; per-student expenditure statistics for, 81–83; private revenue sources for, 83–86, 236n43; racial representation by campus, 77–78, 234n4; ranking of institutions in, 15–16; referral pool process in, 102–3; research investment patterns in, 231n4; resource collaboration in, 199–200; resource inequalities in, 25; social mobility and role of, 74–75, 234n3; state funding policies and, 106–9; threats to unification in, 75; tuition policies at, 84–86, 236n38; UC-Merced public-private partnership and, 65–66

University of Central Florida, 46

University of Michigan-Ann Arbor, 75; One University Campaign at, 73–74

University of Virginia, neoliberal research at, 8

University of Wisconsin-Milwaukee, public-private partnership proposal at, 70–72

US law enforcement, as race-making institution, 243n20

U.S. News and World Report college rankings, 4–5; ASU in, 114; diversity index in, 230n36; penalization of racial inclusion in, 37–38; pressures on universities for shifts in, 47–50; racialized hierarchies in, 23, 29, 190–91, 198; UC-Riverside in, 29–30, 42–47

US Student Association, 82

Volcker, Paul, 8

Volcker Shock, 9

Warren, Elizabeth, 100

Washington Monthly magazine, 46; elite university rankings in, 48

wealth racialization, 201–3

welfare queen stereotype, 9, 11, 223n49

welfare state: demonization of, 224n54; neoliberal opposition to, 7–9

Western Region Public Finance Group (J. P. Morgan), 82

White, Timothy, 40

white flight, UC-Merced student demographics and role of, 56–59

whiteness: challenging perceptions of, 194; methodology in study of, 209–20; organizational wealth linked to, 30–31; postsecondary racial neoliberalism and, 20–24, 227n122

white students: decline at UC-Merced of, 55–59; diversity ideology for, 24, 228n147; diversity regimes and, 148–54; dominance at flagship uni-

white students (*continued*)
versities of, 5, 12; overrepresentation
in engineering of, 112–14; postsecondary racial neoliberalism and,
20–24
Wilcox, Kim, 42–47, 99–100, 106,
116–17
Williams, Steven, 246n18
Winant, Howard, 218
Winston, Gordon, 109

Women's Resource Center (UC-
Riverside), 162
workforce planning, tolerable suboptimization policies and, 120–22
work-study funding, 202
World Bank, 62
World Trade Organization (WTO), 7

Yiannopoulos, Milo, 187
Yudof, Mark, 111–12

Made in the USA
Coppell, TX
16 January 2024

27778563R00167